GOD'S REMEDY

GOD'S REMEDY

*Exposition of Bible Doctrines,
Taking the Epistle to the Romans as a
Point of Departure*

Volume III

Romans 3:21-4:25

by

DONALD GREY BARNHOUSE
Editor of *Eternity* Magazine

*Wm. B. Eerdmans Publishing Company
Grand Rapids, Michigan*

Third printing, March 1966

By the Same Author

Teaching the Word of Truth

Exposition of Bible Doctrines:—

Contents

Preface

It is with some astonishment, and even more gratitude to God, that we issue this second edition. Readers evidently consider the work to be of lasting value. It has been a joy to me, while traveling over the world, to find that it has been a means of blessing to so many. In many countries, missionaries and national pastors are adapting these studies to their preaching. For all this we thank the Lord who thus proves Himself, once more, to be the God of all grace.

The reissuance of this volume, with the help of a valued editorial secretary, Miss Antha E. Card, makes it possible to correct typographical errors, and to soften one or two unloving judgments written in days when the Lord had not whittled me down as much as He has done in the interim since I began to present these studies.

There is still so much whittling to be done, that I crave from each reader who is in any wise blessed by the reading of this book, that he will daily remember me in prayer, that the Lord may continue His grace to me.

D.G.B.

Τῷ ἀγαπῶντι ἡμᾶς καὶ λύσαντι
ἡμᾶς ἐκ τῶν ἀμαρτιῶν ἡμῶν
ἐν τῷ αἵματι αὐτοῦ.

Rev. 1:5

CHAPTER I

But Now

"But now the righteousness of God without the law is manifested, being witnessed by the law and the prophets" (Rom. 3:21).

THE TRUE understanding of the Bible consists in a true understanding of the meaning of its main words. No one can claim to know anything about the Bible if he is not thoroughly conversant with the meaning of such words as "sin," "salvation," "justification," "santification," "redemption," "imputation," "the new birth," and similar terms that are the links in the chain that holds the whole Scripture together. But in addition to these great words there are some shorter words that might seem insignificant to the casual reader, but which take on tremendous importance as we go deeper into the meaning of the revelation which God has given us.

In our study of the Epistle to the Romans we have arrived at a point where two little words separate all that has gone before from all that comes after.

A mountain climber in the high Alps sometimes comes to the top of a ridge almost razor sharp, dividing two slopes. Such is the division which is to be found in the beginning of the twenty-first verse of the third chapter. Had I been the one to divide the Bible into chapters, I would have made the division here. Certainly this is the dividing line which separates the first two and a half chapters, which have been on the subject of man's complete ruin in sin, from the next section, which is occupied with God's perfect remedy in Christ.

The two little words are BUT NOW . . .

A careful study of the epistles of Paul shows that in his mind all time was divided into *then* and *now*. *Then,* was everything that had happened before Christ died. *Now,* is everything that is contingent upon the death of the Saviour. *Then* we were dead in sins; *now* we are alive forevermore. *Then* we were under the law, slain; *now* we are under grace, raised from the dead by the gospel.

THEN — NOW

God has given to us a wonderful symbol of this complete change by ordering our lives so that most of us pass through the stages of meeting someone, falling in love, wooing or being wooed, marrying and establishing a home. People who are happily married will understand me perfectly when I say that life quickly takes on a new pattern with marriage, and the married ones little by little forget the things that happened in life in the single days. Those days recede into the years until people who have been married for four or five years may say, "I can hardly remember when I wasn't married. Life took on a new pattern and the old pattern simply faded away. Then, life was in preparation, but now life is mature and complete." Then and now. Life has such changing and transforming episodes. And when we understand this, we can understand a little more of the meaning of the Bible teaching that marriage is a symbol of the union of the believer with the Lord Jesus Christ, and that a divorce is not only a misfortune and a sin, but is, in a spiritual sense, a blasphemy.

So, for Paul, all time was divided into *then* and *now*; first, for himself in his own personal experience, and, second, theologically, into the period *before* Christ had made the joy of salvation possible and after the cross of Calvary had brought all of the plan of God into present focus.

For himself, of course, it was the Damascus Road that made him see all of life in a new light. There the scales dropped from his spiritual eyes, and he saw clearly the truth of the person and the work of the Lord Jesus. There the light of Heaven came through to his heart, his mind, and his conscience, so that the old prejudices dropped away, and he saw the truth of God in its eternal and universal aspects. Like the blind man who was healed by Jesus in the temple, he could cry, "One thing I know, that whereas once I was blind, now I see."

A NEW DISPENSATION

But here in our text Paul speaks of the change not so much in the sense in which it affected him personally as in the sense in which such a transformation was made possible for all men.

Christ had died, and a new dispensation had been brought in. Now that I have used the word dispensation, let me digress for a moment to bring some teaching that is greatly needed in our day. The word dispensation is in the Bible as the translation of the Greek word *oikonomia* from which our English word "economy" is derived. It is a word that is made up of the Greek words for house and law. In the ears of the Greeks, the word must have sounded somewhat as the word "houselaw" would sound in our ears. It had to do with the method of governing and administering the affairs of a household. In the New Testament, the word is used for God's methods of administering His plans, for governing those who are of the household of faith, and its usage shows that God has administered His plans differently at one time and another.

In late years, the word has been seized upon by those who would nullify certain truths that are in the Scriptures. Some of these maintain that in this age there is not to be water baptism of any kind because such things were for another dispensation, or age. Some even claim that there is to be no communion service for this age. Such error has rightly been branded as heretical, and we are the first to join with those who attack such dispensationalism. But we must not abandon the truth, that there have been different dispensations of God's dealing with His household, simply because some people have taken the word and twisted it in an attempt to cancel out certain truths.

In one sense every Christian is a dispensationalist. If you do not have a lamb killed for the remission of your sins, as did Moses and David, you are, of course, recognizing that the dispensation of God's dealings changed when the New Testament was brought in. If you keep the first day of the week, the Lord's day, the day of the resurrection of Christ, instead of the seventh day, the Jewish Sabbath, the day of death, when the body of our Lord was in the tomb, you are recognizing that God changed His methods of dealing with His people. If you recognize that the gospel of Jesus Christ is open and available to all men instead of merely to the members of one race, then you are recognizing the principle that there was a drastic change made at the time when our Lord Jesus Christ died on the cross and rose again from the dead.

But, in recognizing these changes, we must never fall into the error of believing that man was ever saved in any other way than that which is set forth through Christ. Moses was saved by looking forward to Christ just as we are saved in looking backward to Christ. We are quite in accord with those who condemn the idea that there is any method of salvation apart from faith in the finished work of the Lord Jesus Christ. The men of the Old Testament were saved by believing God's Word about the substitutionary sacrifice which was slain on the altar. It was a picture of the death of Christ the Savior, and God counted their faith, no matter how uninformed it might have been, for the righteousness which they did not have in themselves. On down into the future, to the end of time, God will save men still on the basis of faith in the grace manifested when Christ gave His life for us on the cross.

LAW — GRACE

So we reach the ridge which divides the two valleys, and Paul says, "But now. . ." In understanding this change, we comprehend the nature of the law and the nature of the gospel. Newell has an excellent paragraph on this subject. After showing that it is more difficult to dislodge legalists from the law than it is the heathen from their ceremonies, he writes: "In just the same way Christendom has become fixed in its defense of its 'religious' convictions. Scripture names, doctrines, and ordinances—falsely explained—have seized hold upon the convictions of men, so that it is more difficult to dislodge them from their position than the heathen themselves. We know from Scripture, for example, that 'days, seasons, months, and years,' do not belong to the Christian position in the least degree, but are Jewish or pagan in origin. Christmas, Lent, Easter, the whole 'church calendar,' forms, ritual, the confessional, the mass, clergy,—where are these found in the epistles of the New Testament? They are not found! Yet try once to dislodge them from those in whose hearts they have been planted! For their heart-hopes are bound up with these false traditions.

"None but those taught of God, and they with extreme difficulty and constant watchfulness, escape legal hope. For the question ever before the conscience is, If keeping God's law avails nothing

for righteousness in His sight, why did He give it? WHY DID HE
GIVE IT?

"And this difficulty becomes all the greater, the more the
excellency of the law is discovered! For our judgment sees these
things of the law to be 'holy, righteous, and good.' And we know
(if we are honest) that 'God spake all these words'—of the law.

"Therefore, the heart's only relief is to hear God's own Word
concerning seven questions: to all of which the coming chapters
of Romans will give answer: (1) To what nation did He give the
law; (2) Why did He give the law; (3) What the law's ministry
was; (4) How it was set aside or 'annulled,' for another principle
entirely; (5) What is meant by the words 'under grace'; (6) How
does the walk 'in the Spirit' take the place of walking by external
enactments; and, (7) How that only in those not under the law
is 'the righteous state' (*dikaioma*) of the law fulfilled!

"Now it is apparent that to bring men off from their false
hopes in their law-obedience, three things must become evident
to them: (1) That law having been broken, can only condemn;
(2) That even were men enabled now to begin keeping perfectly
the law of God, that could not make up for the past disobedience,
or remove present guilt; and, (3) That keeping law is NOT
God's way of salvation, or of blessing."

It will take the study of more than five chapters of Romans
to bring out all these truths to the full, but we have announced
them here, as a lawyer outlines his case before he begins to marshall
the evidence that shall prove the points he is seting forth.

RIGHTEOUSNESS PROVIDED

Coming to the section beginning with "But now," we find the
righteousness of God manifested in Christ. What could not be
produced *by* man is here seen as provided *for* man. What could
not come by law is presented as coming by grace. What could
not arise from Moses can flow freely from Christ.

A number of years ago I published some pages from one of
my Bibles showing a system of markings. I had begun to mark
my Bible when I was in my teens and had studied diligently for
several years, marking passages in a way that could bring forth

their relationship to other passages. Over the paragraphs which we are now about to study, I had drawn a heart; and in my notes I said that this passage was not only the heart of Romans, but the heart of the New Testament and the heart of the whole Bible.

I am convinced today, after these many years of Bible study, that these verses are the most important in the whole Bible. Understand them and you will understand the whole Bible. Fail to comprehend their true meaning, and you will be in darkness concerning most of Scripture. For here is the revelation of the being of God and the nature of His being; here is the revelation of sin and of the depths of sin; here is the revelation of God's righteousness and the infinite demands and provisions of that righteousness; here is one of the keys of human history and the explanation of much that happened before the time of Christ, as well as the revelation of the principles that were to prevail in God's dealings with men since Christ; here the mouths of those that would slander God because of His free pardon of sinners are closed forever; here is the vindication of the nature and character of God, righteous in all that He does.

It might be well before looking at the details of our text to put down together a collection of the passages that use the word "now" to show the changes that have come with the death of the Lord Jesus Christ. In the fifth chapter, Paul will write, "Being now justified by his blood" (v. 9), and, "we have now received the atonement" (v. 11). Later, "But now being made free from sin" (6:22), "ye became the servants of righteousness" (6:18); and again, "Now we are delivered from the law" (7:6). The great eighth chapter will begin, "There is therefore now no condemnation to them which are in Christ Jesus" (8:1). In the eleventh chapter, Paul will remind the Gentiles that in time past they had not believed God "yet ye have now obtained mercy" (11:30). And the epistle will close with the declaration that the great secret of righteousness apart from the law is to be freely known to the Gentiles, and almost the last line of the epistle will say, "But now this is made manifest" (16:26).

It may be well to remind all who read these words that in the Corinthian epistle the Holy Spirit has declared, "Now is the accepted time; behold, now is the day of salvation" (II Cor. 6:2).

And to the Ephesians, He has pronounced that we, who are by nature the uncircumcised dogs of Gentiles, are now in the place of blessing: "But now ye who once were afar off are made nigh by the blood of Jesus Christ" (Eph. 2:13). In this same epistle, it is pointed out that much truth which was hidden from the patriarchs and the prophets is *now* revealed (Eph. 3:10). And in one of his last epistles, written to young Timothy, Paul sums it all up by saying, that Christ "hath saved us, and called us with an holy calling, not according to our works, but according to his own purpose and grace, which was given us in Christ Jesus before the world began, but is *now* made manifest by the appearing of our Savior Jesus Christ, who hath abolished death, and hath brought life and immortality to light through the gospel" (II Tim. 1:9, 10).

RIGHTEOUSNESS DISCLOSED

But returning to our text in Romans we read, "But now God's righteousness hath been disclosed apart from law." In the first chapter we studied at some length the revelation of the righteousness of God that the gospel was setting forth. That which was announced there is declared here. Why is it called "the righteousness of God?" There might be several answers to this question, and since all of them are true, they are probably all parts of the complete answer which we will only know fully when we have been made like Him. The righteousness of God is specifically His because of the nature of His being. He is the One who is righteousness in Himself. But also because it is His righteousness, He must demand it of us. The righteousness which He is must be the righteousness with which He surrounds Himself. Therefore He must demand of us a righteousness equal to His own. However, since none of us can produce this righteousness, it is proper to call it the righteousness of God because it is also the righteousness which He provides freely for us.

After I had written the above paragraph, I read it over very carefully and the temptation came to me to alter it, to water it down, to simplify it in some way because it might be over the heads of some people. But I could not change it because of the importance

of its truth. The theme of the Epistle to the Romans is the righteousness of God. It is God as the center of righteousness, it is God as
the source of righteousness, it is God as the stream of righteousness
outflowing. God is righteousness, God demands righteousness,
and God provides righteousness. If those three statements are
understood, then the whole gospel will be understood. If those three
statements are not understood, then the gospel can never be understood. Wherever there is heresy, men have departed from the
idea that God is righteousness, and that therefore He must demand
that righteousness of all His creatures; and, that since none can
have it apart from Him, because His nature is also love, He provides
His righteousness in His way.

I believe that it would be possible to group all heresies under
three headings, listing them for their departure from one of those
three truths. A departure from the first—that God is all righteousness—includes those men who believe that because God is love
His righteousness will take a second place and that, therefore,
there can be no eternal punishment, no final dealing with sin.
Under this head also are all the distortions of the idea of God
that are to be found in the midst of the heathen world. A departure
from the second—that God must demand righteousness of all His
creation—includes all those men who believe that surely God will
let men get by His judgment on some lower scale, such as human
good works. All the heresies that proclaim men can reach Heaven
without the sacrifice of Christ must be grouped here. The heresies
of salvation by character, the heresies of salvation through rites and
ceremonies, through church membership, ordinances or sacraments
—all these are departures from the idea that God must demand
a righteousness equal to His own. A departure from the third—
that God provides righteousness to every man through Jesus Christ
—includes those men who believe that Jesus is merely a man, and
therefore incapable of providing a substitutionary atonement for
all sinners. Others have also departed from this truth in another
direction by believing that, although Christ is God, salvation and
righteousness are provided partly by the Saviour and partly by the
cooperation of the individual.

But true Christianity is the unswerving avoidance of any of
these pitfalls. The Word of God leads us in a straight road and

will keep us from any of these side paths which lead into the swamps of false thinking and, ultimately, to judgment and the lake of fire. God is righteous; He is indeed all-righteousness. God must demand righteousness because the very nature of His being requires Him to require of all that which He is in Himself. Since no individual can ever provide that which God demands, God in His love has provided it equally for all.

RIGHTEOUSNESS MANIFESTED

Finally, our text states that this righteousness of God is manifested. What does the word "manifest" mean? Some of these great words of the New Testament are hidden from many because of the distance in time from the giving forth of the Word and because of the development of language through the centuries that have passed. Time has dimmed the sense of Latin meanings, and many of our words have lost much of their original meaning because of this departure from the roots. It is evident—what is the meaning of "evident"? Some have tried to create a word for television that would be akin to the word "radio" and have gone back to the Latin to get "video" from whose root comes "evident." And when we realize that the word "manifest" comes from two Latin words, *manus*, "hand," and *fendo*, "strike," we can comprehend that a thing is manifest when it is as plain as a hand that seeks to strike you.

Today, it is the hand of God that holds out the righteousness of God for you to see. And if you say that you do not see anything in His hand, I ask you to look at the hand itself. For you will see that the hand has the print of a nail, that the hand was pierced, and that you may, by faith, put out your hand and touch that wound. And when you do, you will know that there is evidence, the manifestation of the righteousness of God. "Evidence" you can see it; "manifestation"—God makes it as plain as a striking hand. Today is the day of grace; the hand will not strike you in judgment because it was, itself, struck in judgment for you. "He was wounded for our transgressions, he was bruised for our iniquities: the chastisement of our peace was upon him; and by his stripes we are healed" (Isa. 53:5).

Reach out by faith in this hour and say to your Creator: "Oh,

God, as best I know, in all the weakness and sinfulness of my fallen nature, I reach out to that hand that was wounded for me, and—as best I know—I stop trusting in anything which has its source or its spring in me, but build my hope in the Lord Jesus Christ, and in Him alone." If you will do that in this hour, He will come and manifest His love within your heart, and you will know, on His own evidence, His righteousness has been put to your account.

CHAPTER II

Righteousness Without the Law

"But now the righteousness of God without the law is manifested, being witnessed by the law and the prophets" (Rom. 3:21).

RIGHTEOUSNESS apart from Law. This is the theme of the Epistle to the Romans, and in reality it is the theme of the New Testament and of the whole Bible. We have it in our text. Now, if a man were to come over the roof of the world from Tibet and were to ask me what the Christian religious Book talked about, I would tell him in a sentence: the Bible was the setting forth of the divine plan whereby God could take sinful men, clean them up, and bring them into His own perfect Heaven without fouling up Heaven and without losing His own righteousness by touching sinners. Righteousness apart from law. Righteousness apart from human doing. Righteousness apart from a man's own deserving. Righteousness given freely to those who do not deserve it. Righteousness streaming forth from the heart of God because of the nature of His being. This is the theme of the Word of God.

COUNTERFEITS

There are counterfeits, but the counterfeits are always easy to detect when you know the real thing. The inspectors of the Treasury Department will tell you that every counterfeit piece of currency that has ever been made has some distinguishing mark that reveals its false origin. It may also be said that every religion has the mark of the counterfeit, for every religion in the world is a counterfeit of true, revealed Christianity. And the mark in all counterfeit religions is the same. Every religion, except that which was brought down by God himself in His planning for Jesus Christ and in the coming of Jesus Christ, is marked by something that man is supposed to do for God. But the grace of God that brings salvation has appeared to all men, and has shown us that God has done everything for man. That is the great difference between the faith that has been revealed from Heaven and the faiths that originate with men.

Look into your own heart and see whether you are trusting, even in a small fraction, in something that you are doing for yourself or that you are doing for God, instead of finding in your heart that you have ceased from your works as God did from His and that you are resting on the work that was accomplished on the cross of Calvary. This is the secret of reality: Righteousness apart from law. Righteousness apart from human doing. Christianity is the faith that believes God's Word about the work that is fully done, completely done. It is finished.

It was the Scotch divine, Thomas Chalmers, who wrote, "The foundation of your trust before God, must be either your own righteousness out and out, or the righteousness of Christ, out and out. . . If you are to lean upon your own merit, lean upon it wholly—if you are to lean upon Christ, lean upon Him wholly. The two will not amalgamate together; and it is the attempt to make them do so, which keeps many a weary and heavy-laden inquirer at a distance from rest, and at a distance from the truth of the gospel. Maintain a clear and consistent posture. Stand not before God with one foot upon a rock and the other upon a treacherous quicksand. . . We call upon you to lean not so much as the weight of one grain or scruple of your confidence upon your own doings— to leave this ground entirely, and to come over entirely to the ground of a Redeemer's blood and a Redeemer's righteousness."

NOT NEW WITH PAUL

Righteousness without law. Righteousness apart from human character. Righteousness without even a consideration of the nature of the being that is made righteous. Righteousness that comes from God upon an ungodly man. Righteousness that will save a thief on the cross. Righteousness that is prepared for you. Righteousness that you must choose by abandoning any hope of salvation from anything that is in yourself or that could be produced by yourself. God's own righteousness. And underline this—it is the only righteousness that can produce practical righteousness in you.

Our text now states that this principle of divine righteousness was not new with Paul. One of the greatest lies that theologians have ever perpetrated was the lie that Paul distorted the kind and gentle religion of Christ into an idea of salvation by the blood of the substitute. This idea, our text now sets forth, was not Paul's idea, but was a salvation provided by God and witnessed by the law and the prophets. Every minister should read the great book that was written by the late, distinguished Professor Gresham Machen, under the title, *The Origin of Paul's Religion*. There he assembles the evidence that Paul was merely the channel for setting the truth before the world, but that the roots of all that Paul taught are to be found in the Old Testament and in Christ Himself. It is as foolish to think that Paul started anything in religion as it is to think that an oak tree begins with the soil line and that it does not have a root system.

A remarkable scholar, C. S. Lewis, of Cambridge, has written a series of books that sneak up on the skeptic on his blind side— that could be any side of a skeptic, for the skeptic is in darkness— and presents great truths by logical argument, apart from any declaration of Scriptures. When *Time* published Mr. Lewis' picture on its cover, the editors wrote a long study of his life and his work, and concluded that he was a great evangelical force. Only in his latest books, however, has Mr. Lewis been leaning more and more on the Word of God as he sets forth the truths of Christianity.

Now, in his preface to a new translation of the Pauline epistles, Mr. Lewis writes, "A most astonishing misconception has long dominated the modern mind on the subject of St. Paul. It is to this effect: that Jesus preached a kindly and simple religion (found in the Gospels) and that St. Paul afterward corrupted it into a cruel and complicated religion (found in the epistles). This is really quite untenable. All the most terrifying texts came from the mouth of our Lord; all the texts on which we can base such warrant as we have for hoping that all men will be saved come from St. Paul." Mr. Lewis is overhopeful in this expression, for there can be no doubt that Paul, as well as Christ shows that not all men will be saved. It would have been better had Mr. Lewis confined himself to saying that all the texts on which we can base such warrant as we have for knowing that a great many members of Adam's sinful race will be in God's righteous Heaven come from St. Paul.

Mr. Lewis then continues, "If it could be proved that St. Paul

altered the teaching of his Master in any way, he altered it in exactly
the opposite way to that which is popularly supposed. But there
is no real evidence for a pre-Pauline doctrine different from St.
Paul's. The epistles are, for the most part, the earliest Christian
documents we possess. The Gospels came later. They are not 'the
gospel,' the statement of Christian belief. They were written for
those who had already been converted, who had already accepted
'the gospel.' They [the four Gospels] leave out many of the 'complications' (that is, the theology) because they are intended for
readers who have already been instructed in it. In that sense the
epistles are more primitive and more central than the Gospels—
though not, of course, than the great events which the Gospels recount. God's act (the Incarnation, the crucifixion, and the Resurrection) comes first: the earliest theological analysis of it comes in the
epistles: then, when the generation who had known the Lord was
dying out, the Gospels were composed to provide for believers a
record of the great Act and some of the Lord's sayings.' The
ordinary popular conception has put everything upside down. Nor
is the cause far to seek. In the earlier history of every rebellion
there is a stage at which you do not yet attack the King in person.
You say, 'The King is all right. It is his Ministers who are wrong.
They misrepresent him and corrupt all his plans—which, I'm sure,
are good plans if only the Ministers would let them take effect.'
And the first victory consists in beheading a few Ministers; only at
a later stage do you go on and behead the King himself. In the same
way, the nineteenth-century attack on St. Paul was really only a
stage in the revolt against Christ. Men were not ready in large
numbers to attack Christ Himself. They made the normal first move
—that of attacking one of His principal ministers. Everything they
disliked in Christianity was therefore attributed to St. Paul. It
was unfortunate that their case could not impress anyone who had
really read the Gospels and the epistles with attention; but apparently few people had, and so the first victory was won. St.
Paul was impeached and banished and the world went on to the
next step—the attack on the King Himself."

PAUL AND MOSES

We can be certain that the attack upon the Old Testament

has come from the same mutinous group. The attack upon Moses was an attack upon Christ. Now our text links Paul in the New Testament and Moses in the Old Testament, and the Holy Spirit tells us that the truth of God as expressed by Paul has a witness in Moses, and that the law is a witness for the prosecution. In the course of writing this study, when I came to the previous sentence, I at first thought and wrote that the law was a joint witness for the defence. But our side is not the side of the defence. We are not defending the truth of the Word of God. The truth of God needs no defence. Our side is the side of the prosecution. As we declare the truth, every mouth is stopped and all the world is brought guilty before God.

Someone, on the defence, may cry out against our argument and say, "But how can you call the law into the witness box to testify against itself? Does not the law proclaim that men must keep it? And how, then, can the law be made to witness to the fact that there is no righteousness to be achieved by the law, but that righteousness must come apart from the law, that righteousness may come by grace alone, through the Lord Jesus Christ?" But the law answers: "I never pretended to bring righteousness. I am like an engineer who is helping to plan the route on a highway. I can take a pencil and draw the line upon the map and show which way the road should go. But when I draw the line upon the map, my pencil does not plow away the side of a hill and bring the road into existence. All that my pencil can do is to show the way. If I press on the pencil too firmly, the point will break. And if I ever take my pencil out into the field where the road is to pass through and start pushing against a granite boulder, I shall merely reveal the weakness of my own folly."

THE LAMB OF GOD

How, then, does the law itself witness to the righteousness of God apart from law? The answer is that when the law was given the lamb was also given. At the same time God gave the provisions of the law which expressed the righteousness of God, God provided an altar and a substitute where the blood could flow and men could see that salvation was not in the attempted keeping of the law's demands, but in reliance upon the provision of the substitute which God had Himself ordained and provided. One of the most wonderful things about Old Testament study is to see all the analogies of Christ. We turn to the first pages of the Bible and see the first Adam in a deep sleep while God takes Eve from his side, for his wife. In this we see the Lord Jesus Christ, dying on the cross, and God taking the true believers from the wounded side of the Saviour, as the bride for Christ. We turn the page and find God promising that the Seed of the woman shall bruise the serpent's head. In this we see the Lord Jesus on the cross, crushing the power of Satan, and providing the judicial groundwork for the enemy's ultimate destruction.

We come to the law itself, and we see that beside Moses God raises up his brother Aaron, and in Aaron we see the Lord Jesus who is to come under a greater priesthood, being Himself, both priest and offering. We go to the door of the tabernacle and see men bringing their offerings, and we know that God in Christ has provided a sacrifice. Each one of these lambs that died on the altars of Israel was a testimony to the truth of our verse. Righteousness comes apart from the law. Righteousness is imputed to you on the basis of the shedding of the blood.

Now we know that it was not the blood of bulls and of goats which could take away sins (Heb. 10:4). The New Testament tells us that God did not desire the death of sacrificial animals. In the Psalms we read, "Sacrifice and offerings thou didst not desire . . . burnt-offering and sin-offering hast thou not required" (Ps. 40:6). Now if God did not desire nor require, why did He command them throughout the Old Testament period? And why did He cut off those who refused to bring the sacrifices? The answer is in the nature and purpose of the sacrifices themselves.

It can be best illustrated by a modern discovery in the field of physical reactions. Early in the century there was a Russian physician, Pavlov, who studied certain phenomena and gave to the scientific world the phrase "conditioned reflex." Pavlov first took a small puppy from its mother just when it was born, and began to feed it under very special conditions. Every time the dog was given food a certain bell was rung. Never did the dog have food, month after month, except when the bell was rung. Now we know that when a dog is in the presence of his food his mouth salivates, preparing to receive the food. Its glands excrete the saliva in large quantities to help digest the food. A dog does not salivate unless the food is before him. But Pavlov, after conditioning this dog for months with the bell and food, prepared a test. While students watched the dog with close scrutiny, the bell was rung—the bell without whose sound the dog had never tasted food in his life. Immediately the glands of the dog's mouth began to flow and the saliva poured forth, though there was no food in sight whatsoever. Thus Pavlov demonstrated that it is possible for outside influences to have a definite physical effect on the life of an individual.

That this is true in human life is shown, for instance, by the fact that a certain woman fainted every time she heard a fire siren. These fainting spells had been occurring for about five years. When a psychiatrist attempted to find out the reason why, he discovered that, one day as she sat by the telephone and had just heard of the serious injury to her son, a fire engine roared by the front door with siren wailing and she fainted. Some time later she heard a fire siren wailing and she fainted once more. After that, every time she heard the siren, she fainted. It was when the psychiatrist pointed out to her the connection between the siren and the son's accident, that she was able to comprehend the relationship between the two. Her son had recovered, and so, when next the siren wailed, she was able to relax, thankful that her son had been spared.

Now the Lord God Almighty wished to establish a conditioned reflex before all of His people in order to teach them and us that righteousness could not come by the law. He arranged the law and its offerings in such a way that every time a man sinned there came to his memory that he had to bring a sacrifice. He brought the lamb to the priest and placed his hand upon the head of the beast, confessing the fact that he was a sinner. It was as though his sin flowed down his arm, and through his hand, and that thus the guilt passed into the animal. Then the priest took the animal over to the altar, and killed the lamb in the presence of the sinner.

Just as Pavlov created in the dog the pattern of thought—bell means dinner, bell means dinner—and just as the woman had the wires of her mind fused into a pattern—siren means my son is in danger, my son is in danger,—so the Lord God Almighty created the pattern in the minds of His people,—sin means death, sin means death, sin means death.

Your sin means your death or the death of a substitute. You have sinned, and the soul that sinneth, it shall die. (Ezek. 18:4). You shall die because of your sin, because God is holy. There is a way out, however. The Lord your God has furnished a substitute. The lamb will die in your stead. This is the picture of the fact that God shall come to earth in the Lord Jesus Christ and shall be wounded for your transgressions and bruised for your iniquity. He shall die for you. Sin means death. Sin means death. Sin means your death or the death of the Saviour.

But now that Christ has died, that object lesson, meant to teach the infant race of the vicarious, substitutionary atonement provided by the Saviour, is manifested as revealing the righteousness of God apart from law. Christ has died; therefore there is righteousness without works; righteousness without law; righteousness without character; righteousness without effort; righteousness imputed and imparted solely on the basis of the essential grace of God, and what He is in Christ. Our earthly righteousness and character will grow out of this.

SAVED BY HIS DEATH

We are not even to cloud the issue by seeking to show that, what the law demanded, Christ fulfilled, and that the perfect fulfillment of the law by Christ is put to our account. That is not true. To think such a thing is to rob the Saviour of some of His glory. Yes, Christ did keep the law. He did, indeed, fulfill its every provision. But it was not Christ's law-keeping which saves us. The merit, if any, which is to be found in the fact that Christ kept the law, is not placed to our account. That keeping of the law merely rendered Christ eligible to die. The animal of the sacrifice had to be without spot or blemish. So Christ had to be perfect. He was perfect. We are not saved by the perfection of His life. We are saved by the nature of His Death. It was His life that made Him eligible to die. It was His death which satisfied

God the Father and provided the basis of righteousness without works to be imputed and imparted to us who trust in that work which the Lord Jesus performed in dying upon the cross. Righteousness without law, but righteousness witnessed by the law. The testimony of the law is perfect, showing that men are saved by the work of the Saviour.

The heart of the Old Testament ritual was the veil in the temple that separated the Holy place from the Holy of Holies. Man was kept away from the presence of God by the fact that he was a sinner. Never could anyone approach God without the sacrifice of the altar. The High Priest could not go into the Holy of Holies except once a year, and then only after two sacrifices, one for himself and one for the sins of the people. After this second sacrifice, he could walk through the Holy place and take hold of the veil, pulling it aside for a moment to allow him to reach in with the censer until the plumes of its smoke had clouded the inner room. Then only could the High Priest come inside for the moment of placing the blood from the second sacrifice on the mercy seat of the ark of the covenant.

But when the Lord Jesus died, the veil in the temple was torn in two from top to bottom and the way was open for anyone, Jew and Gentile alike, to come into the innermost presence of God by virtue of the death of the Lord Jesus Christ. The tearing away of the veil was the tearing away of the law. The righteousness of God was now to be possessed apart from law, but the law even in its destruction, was yielding one more witness to the fact that of itself it was powerless to furnish righteousness, but that the Saviour's righteousness was now available for all. Thus the believer may come into the very presence of God, unhesitant, unafraid.

We do not come in any righteousness of our own. We do not come in any righteousness that was of the law. We do not come in a righteousness that was lived by Jesus Christ during His earthly life when He was keeping the law. We come only in the righteousness of God which He provided through the death of the Lord Jesus Christ on the cross. This is the righteousness that is ours apart from the law, but witnessed by the law.

CHAPTER III

The Witness of the Prophets

"But now the righteouness of God without the law is manifested, being witnessed by the law and the prophets" (Rom. 3:21).

THE LAW of God always demanded two witnesses to any fact. If there was an accusation, it had to be attested by at least two witnesses. "At the mouth of two witnesses" is a phrase that occurs on several occasions throughout the Word of God (Deut. 17:6; 19:15; Matt. 18:16; II Cor. 13:1; I Tim. 5:19; Heb. 10:28).

The Lord Jesus Christ, when called upon to be a judge by the men who wished to accuse Him, availed Himself of this fact in order to manifest His grace. When the leaders brought the woman taken in adultery and asked the Lord Jesus whether He would uphold the law of Moses and have her stoned or whether she should go free, He stooped and wrote on the ground, and then told the accusers that the one who was without sin was first to cast a stone at the woman. When they had all slunk out, the Lord Jesus looked up from the ground and asked the woman where her accusers were. There were none and so the case was dismissed, even under the most rigorous demands of the law. There were no witnesses; therefore, there was no case. He then could apply the grace of the gospel and save her through His own righteousness.

TWO WITNESSES

In the passage which we are studying in Romans 3, we saw in our last chapter that the righteousness of God is declared apart from law. We are saved not by anything we are or by anything that we could do, but by the righteousness of the Lord Jesus Christ provided for us on Calvary where He was made unto us wisdom, righteousness, sanctification, and redemption (I Cor. 1:30). But that righteousness which is provided at the cross has two witnesses, as in the case of all of God's doings for us. The witnesses are the law itself and the prophets of God. In our last study we saw that the law in every part witnessed to the fact that it had no power to provide righteousness. The law could slay, but the law could not make alive. The law could condemn, but it could not justify. The law could witness to its own powerlessness, but it could furnish no power. What the law could not do, in that it was weak through the flesh, God could do by sending His Son to die for us (Rom. 8:3).

But in addition to the witness of the law there is the witness of the prophets. In this present study we shall call to the witness box the prophets of God; and, even though they were the mighty voices for God under the law of Moses and throughout the history of the Old Testament regime, they were constant witnesses that there was no righteousness in the system they preached, but that righteousness had to come entirely by the grace of God.

THE PROMISE TO ABRAHAM

The law of Moses illustrated the righteousness of God in all of the sacrifices provided. The prophets of God witnessed the righteousness of God by announcing that it would come. The first time that righteousness is ever mentioned in the Bible is in connection with the faith of Abraham: he believed God and it was counted unto him for righteousness (Gen. 15:6). Here was the announcement of a righteousness that was apart from man. The promise was thus given to Abraham, and God tells us in the Epistle to the Galatians that the law, which came four hundred and thirty years after Abraham, could not disannul that it should make the promise of none effect (Gal. 3:17). The law could witness to the truth of righteousness apart from itself, but it could not bring righteousness nor cancel out the promise.

Now the prophet's witness is seen in Abraham, for in this connection he must be looked upon as the first of the prophets, since the doctrine is first set forth in him. David, in the Psalms, must also be considered as a prophet. We have New Testament authority for this, because, on the day of Pentecost, Peter, quoting a Psalm of David concerning freedom from death and Hell, says that David was not speaking of himself, but being a prophet, and knowing that God had announced that of his seed the Messiah should come, spake of Him, the Lord Jesus, that His soul was not left in Hell and that His body would not see corruption (Acts 2.31).

We may turn to the Psalms and find many passages that testify to the fact that righteousness could not come by human works or by demands of the law, but that it was entirely by the grace of God. Everywhere David shows that he recognizes the principle of righteousness on the basis of the blood sacrifice. In the fourth Psalm, for instance, he says, "Offer the sacrifice of righteousness, and put your trust in the Lord" (4:5).

DAVID'S WITNESS

The fifty-first Psalm has always been considered by devout commentators as the Psalm of repentance when David had committed adultery and then ordered murder to protect himself from the consequences. Yet in this Psalm, time and again, there is set forth the whole idea of righteousness from God on the basis of His grace and apart from any character in the person who is being declared righteous. Certainly we do not have to look any further for a picture of a sinner. Here is David, a man who stands before God with filthy hands and an impure heart. On his hands is the blood of Uriah and in his heart is the lust for Bathsheba. He stands convicted. But God brings him to gracious repentance and sets before him the whole glorious story of salvation through God's own provision. Thus David abandons any thought of righteousness in himself and comes to God's altar to receive righteousness on the basis of the shedding of the blood.

In analyzing this Psalm, we see, first, that David prays for grace on the basis of God's loving-kindness and tender mercies. He then asks to be washed from his iniquity and cleansed from his sin. For David completely acknowledges the fact of sin. He admits that he belongs to the race of Adam and that he was born of sin. He knows that there is nothing in himself that could ever commend him to the love of God. He confesses that the chief part of his sin is that it is sin against God. Even though he had sinned against the woman in violating her honor; even though he had sinned against the man in taking his wife and then taking his life; even though he had sinned aginst the nation in bringing judgment upon it because of his sin; even though he had caused the death of many soldiers in battle—he sees that none of this is even to be brought into comparison with the fact that the really serious aspect of sin is that it is sin against God. "Against thee, thee only have I sinned, and done this evil in thy sight." Let us remember this when we think that it is possible to commit sin without being seen.

"PURGE ME WITH HYSSOP"

But then comes the approach to the altar of God. David prays, "Purge me with hyssop and I shall be clean; wash me and I shall be whiter than snow." To understand this we must understand one detail in connection with some of the sacrifices as they were performed by the priests of Israel. Whenever the priest had to sprinkle the blood of the sacrifice in the midst of the ritual of cleansing, he used what we would call a brush. Our brushes, today, of course, are machinemade, and all of the bristles are even. But the brush that was used in the ritual of the Jewish tabernacle was handmade by the priest and consisted of three parts. The handle was a piece of cedar wood, the brush portion was a wisp of the hyssop plant, and the hyssop was tied to the handle by a piece of scarlet cord. The cedar was the highest tree, the hyssop was the lowliest shrub. It was as though the heavenly nature and the earthly nature of the Lord Jesus were combined in one, and the scarlet cord showed forth the salvation provided by His blood.

The cedar wood had a fragrant odor and, of course, reminds us that "Christ also hath loved us, and hath given himself for us an offering and a sacrifice to God for a sweet-smelling savour" (Eph. 5:2).

The hyssop is a plant that grows in crevices in the stone walls of Palestine. If you have seen a picture of the Wailing Wall of Jerusalem, the hyssop is the plant that you see over the heads of those who stand at the foot of the wall in bitter lamentation. The hyssop is remarkable in the fact that its root is not over a quarter or half inch long, but the plant that grows from such a tiny root is sometimes fifteen or twenty feet long. It is a great illustration of all that may grow out of the clinging property of a tiny faith, that is firmly fastened to the rock.

When the priests had taken a wisp of the hyssop plant and tied it to the cedar by the scarlet cord, they had a practical little brush which they dipped into the blood on some occasions, or into water on other occasions, for the ceremonial cleansings required by the law of God.

Thus, in the Psalm of repentance which David sings, "Purge me with hyssop," it is a poetical way of saying, "Cleanse me by thy blood." (See Exod. 12:22; Lev. 14:4, 6, 49, 51, 52; Num. 19:6, 18; Heb. 9:19.) Thus when David says that the Lord rewarded him and recompensed him according to his righteousness, he is setting forth his faith in a righteousness that was not his own, but that was given to him on the basis of the sacrifice (Ps. 18:20, 24).

And this is the eternal righteousness which shall be preached when the nation of Israel is saved, for we read that the generation that shall come (that is, the generation of Israel living when the Lord returns) shall declare His righteousness unto a people—the Gentiles—that shall be born (Ps. 22:31). And David closes the Psalm of repentance with the phrase, "Then shalt thou be pleased with the sacrifices of righteousness, with burnt-offering and whole burnt-offering" (Ps. 51:19).

RIGHTEOUSNESS APART FROM THE LAW

Time and again, David sings in terms of the Lord's righteousness as being a righteousness apart from the law, or human doings. Thus we have such expressions as these; "In thee, O Lord, do I put my trust; let me never be ashamed: deliver me in thy righteousness" (Ps. 31:1). "Judge me, O Lord my God, according to thy righteousness" (35:24). "Continue . . . thy righteousness to the upright in heart" (36:10). "I have not hid thy righteousness within my heart" (40:10). "The heavens shall declare his righteousness, for God is judge himself" (50:6). "Deliver me from bloodguiltiness . . . and my tongue shall sing aloud of thy righteousness" (51:14). "In thy righteousness shall [Thy people] be exalted" (89:16). "Quicken me in thy righteousness" (119:40).

There is another famous passage in one of the Psalms which is a true witness to righteousness apart from the law. Looking down to the end of the age when wars shall be made to cease by the coming of the Lord and when righteousness shall be spread out over the earth by the fact of the coming of His government from Heaven, David sings: "I will hear what God the Lord will speak: for he will speak peace unto his people [Israel], and to his saints [the church]: but let them not turn again to folly. Surely his salvation is nigh them that fear him; that glory may dwell in our land. Mercy and truth are met together; righteousness and peace have kissed each other. Truth shall spring out of the earth; and righteousness shall look down from heaven" (Ps. 85:8-11).

In this beautiful passage we have a declaration of the righteousness of God apart from human doings. It is the consummation of His righteousness that shall come because He shall return with righteousness from Heaven. Christ provided it on the cross for individual believers, and He will bring it from Heaven for the nations at the end of the age. Only thus can righteousness and peace kiss each other. The cross of Christ is righteousness and the future kingdom of Christ is peace. When men seek to have peace on earth apart from the Lord Jesus Christ, it is the equivalent of seeking peace in the heart without receiving Christ as personal Saviour. If individual righteousness were to come by the law, Paul writes to the Galatians, Christ was dead in vain (Gal. 2:21). We might well put it that if national peace and righteousness were to come by the United Nations or by any other contrivance of man, Christ would be dead in vain. But when we look at the whole of the work of our Saviour God, then righteousness and peace have kissed each other.

The last quotation that I will bring from the Psalms as a witness to the doctrine of righteousness apart from law of any kind, is that of the ninety-eighth Psalm. "O sing unto the Lord a new song," cries the king, "for he hath done marvelous things. His right hand, and his holy arm, hath gotten him the victory. The Lord hath made known his salvation: his righteousness hath he openly showed in the sight of the nations" (98:1, 2 marg.). I am almost inclined to add this verse of the Psalms to the list of verses that are quoted in the New Testament from the Old. It is not thus listed in the commoner reference Bibles, nor do I find references to it in the better known studies on quotations from the Old Testament. But surely our text in Romans, which declares that now the righteousness of God apart from law is manifested, is nothing more than the text in the Psalms which states that He has openly shown His righteousness in the sight of the nations. Could there be a plainer reference to the cross of Christ? For where else is the righteousness of God to be seen in the sight of the nations?

THE LAW AND THE PROPHETS

We have brought forth a score of witnesses from the Psalms. Let us now turn to the writers who are called the prophets. It should be realized, in passing, that when our text speaks of the witness of the law and the prophets, it is not speaking, in the narrow sense, of the law as meaning the books of Moses, and the prophets as meaning the books that are usually called the major and minor prophets. The phrase, "law and prophets," was the term in Christ's day that was used for all of the Bible that was then existing and was a comprehensive term that covered everything. If I have divided the phrase to speak, in our last study, of the witness of the law and its sacrifices, and, in this study, of the witness of the prophetic writings, it is because there is such a double witness: the law showing forth the righteousness of God in the pageant of the sacrifices and the ritual, and the prophets showing forth the righteousness of God by great declarations that we might call theological statements. All of them combine to demonstrate the great Biblical truth that God has provided righteousness for men who do not have any of their own, and that Christ manifested this righteousness by His dying on the cross—not by His faithfully fulfilling the law. Righteousness comes out of the righteous heart of God as a gift of His sovereign grace and is totally apart from law, even apart from Christ's perfect keeping of the law.

One of the key words of the Book of Isaiah is the word "righteousness." It is found in the English 51 times, but even more in the Hebrew. And the righteousness that is set forth is the righteousness of God. It is a witness to the fact that the Lord Jesus Christ will come and provide the reconciliation between God and man. Thus we read, "Surely one shall say, in the Lord have I righteousness and strength" (Isa. 45:24). And the fact that righteousness shall ultimately come upon this earth, not through the works of man, but through the intervention of the Lord, is fully set forth: "Hearken unto me, ye hard hearted, ye that are enemies of righteousness [thus it is in the Hebrew]: I bring near my righteousness; it shall not be far off, and my salvation shall not tarry; and I will place salvation in Zion for Israel, my glory" (Isa. 46:12, 13). The poet surely had this verse in mind when he wrote that stanza of the great hymn:

> Bring near Thy great salvation,
> Thou Lamb for sinners slain;
> Fill up the roll of Thine elect,
> Then take Thy power and reign;
> Appear Desire of Nations—
> Thine exiles long for home;
> Show in the Heaven Thy promised sign;
> Thou Prince and Saviour, come.

And it is not astonishing that a hundred years ago Henry Alford, meditating on this passage as he wrote that hymn, included in an earlier stanza the phrase,

> O day for which creation
> And all its tribes were made.

For God will bring His righteousness to triumph through the Lord Jesus Christ. That which He began at Calvary He shall complete from the Mount of Olives.

TWO CONCLUSIONS

There are two conclusions which we must draw from this doctrine found in every part of the Word of God, manifested at the cross, and witnessed by the law and the prophets. The one conclusion is for the individual and the other is for society in general and the nations of the earth. I will mention the latter first, so that I may finish on the note of your own personal relationship to this manifested righteousness.

The only hope of the world, whether in the government of nations or in the various phases of society and civilization, is the return of the Lord Jesus Christ to bring His righteousness and establish it upon the earth. The efforts of man have been proven bankrupt throughout the ages; and, as time goes on, the efforts of man will be shown more and more to be hopeless for the solution of the problems that face society. In fact, the great purpose of history is to demonstrate that there is no good in man that can satisfy God, and that righteousness can come only from God by the Lord Jesus Christ. Thus any attempt to ameliorate the conditions of society or to solve its problems is really the attempt to drain a sewer with a one-inch pipe when there is a six-inch inflow pipe, continuously bringing in more pollution. Men will continue their pumping at the one-inch pipe of human effort, and they will continue to be engulfed in the rising horror from the six-inch inflow pipe of the product of man's own heart.

The other conclusion is similar, but it is on the level of the individual life. You have problems that you cannot solve. You have pangs of conscience that will not be stilled. You are aware of the passage of time, the approaching end of life, the necessity of meeting your Creator, and the sense of the inadequacy of your own righteousness to stand before that penetrating light of the eternal holiness of God. There is no answer within yourself and within the field of your efforts. Everything that has its source in you has been condemned by God and has been revealed as worthless to do the task that must be done. Three centuries ago, John Donne, the English poet, using the mythological story of the labors of Hercules, the strong man of the ancient world confronted with the task of cleaning out the Augean stables, says that though Hercules was able to perform his task, man cannot clean the much greater filth of the human heart. He writes,

> Lord, I confess that Thou alone art able
> To purify this Augean stable.
> Be the seas water, and the land all soap
> Yet if Thy blood not wash me—there's no hope.

You must face these facts and come to your definite decision on the matter of your own position before God. Will you stand in your own righteousness and be lost forever, or will you stand in the righteousness of God apart from anything in yourself, a righteousness which will be given to you when you turn away from yourself in order to build your hope on Christ alone?

JUDGMENT TO COME

Out in the world the unregenerate writers and thinkers are telling us that the civilization of the world is sick. They are telling us that it is much later on the clock of time than men think. The unsaved see the handwriting on the wall. Where, a few years ago, it was the preachers who were warning men of the wrath to come, today the unsaved are the men who are the prophets of doom. The other day a man remarked that the first World War had been fought with guns, the second with bombs, the third would be fought with atomic bombs and the fourth with bows and arrows. It was the world's way of saying that it sees its own doom approaching.

But the Word of God gives us the accurate picture and tells us that the judgment of God will come in His way and His own time. And that judgment will come to you individually. This is more important to you than that judgment shall come to the nations. The outcome of that judgment rests on your choice of the alternatives that God has placed before you. You have the gospel in front of you. In your heart is complete responsibility and God will hold you eternally accountable for your decision. You can cling to something that you have and are and you can ride it into the lake of fire; or you can abandon the whole thing now and receive the righteousness of God in Christ and be carried by it into the presence of God forever. Behold, now is the accepted time; behold, now is the day of salvation.

CHAPTER IV

"Unto All"

"Even the righteousness of God which is by faith of Jesus Christ unto all and upon all them that believe: for there is no difference" (Rom. 3:22).

AFTER a great storm, there is frequently a calm. After a clap of thunder, there is an intensity of silence. In our studies in the Book of Romans we have passed through the great storm of the first chapters which brought us all the reverberations of the thunders of Mount Sinai, blasting within our ears and penetrating our very hearts. We stood before the mountain that could not be touched, and that burned with fire, and the blackness and darkness and tempest. We heard the sound of a trumpet and the voice of words; and, like those that stood there in Moses' day, we entreated that the word should not be spoken unto us any more (Heb. 12:18, 19). Even as Moses himself said at that time, "I exceedingly fear and quake," so we speak and then stand dumb in the intensity of the silence of our conviction and guilt.

GUILT

Bishop Moule has expressed it: "The law has driven in upon the soul of man, from many sides, that one fact—guilt; the eternity of the claim of righteousness, the absoluteness of the holy will of God, and, in contrast, the failure of man, of the race, to meet that claim and do that will. It has told man, in effect, that he is 'depraved' (*depravatus;* twisted, wrenched from the straight line), that is to say, morally distorted. He is 'totally depraved,' that is, the distortion has affected his whole being, so that he can supply on his own part no adequate recovering power which shall restore him to harmony with God. And the law has nothing more to say to him, except that this condition is not only deplorable, but guilty, accountable, condemnable; and that his own conscience is the concurrent witness that it is so. Man is

30

a sinner. To be a sinner is before all things to be a transgressor
of the law. It is other things besides. It is to be morally diseased,
and in need of surgery and medicine. It is to be morally unhappy,
and an object of compassion. But first of all it is to be morally
guilty, and in urgent need of justification, of a reversal of sentence,
of satisfactory settlement with the offended—and eternal—law of
God."

At the point we have reached in our studies, the law has
spoken. The unchangeable conditions have been set forth. The
law has announced the just sentence of death and having spoken
stands silent before the sinner who is now silenced forever. The
law has no warrant to do anything for the sinner. The law cannot
relieve his fears. The law cannot allay his grief. The law cannot pay his debts. The law has its horrible business to attend to.
The law can do nothing but thunder: "Thou shalt not sin," and,
"The wages of sin is death." The law lays hold on conscience
which had become unconscious and rouses it to attention. And
then the law speaks into the quivering ear of conscience far more
than it had ever realized before of the horror and doom of sin. When
this has happened the conscience within us, like a sentinel aroused
by the approach of the enemy, or like a lone watcher aroused
by the outbreak of fire, goes crying along the corridors of our
whole being that we are in mortal danger. Conscience must beat
on every door within our hearts. Conscience must cry out until
its voice penetrates the stupor of our sin-drugged sleep. Conscience must take hold of us and shake us from our lethargy.
Conscience must dash us with the icy waters of reality that we
may arise and flee from the doom of our own condition.

A LIVING RECORD

And again Bishop Moule says, "Is this merely an abstract
picture? Or do our hearts, the writer's and the reader's, bear any
witness to its living truthfulness? God knoweth these things are
no curiosities of the past. We are not studying an interesting
phase of early Christian thought. We are reading a living record
of the experiences of innumerable lives which are lived on earth
this day.

"There is such a thing indeed in our time, at this hour, as

conviction of sin. There is such a thing now as a human soul, struck dumb amidst its apologies, its doubts, its denials, by the voice and then the silence of the law of God. There is such a thing at this hour as a real man, strong and sound in thought, healthy in every faculty, used to look facts of daily life in the face, yet broken down in the indescribable conviction that he is a poor, guilty, lost sinner, and that his overflowing need at this moment is not a solution of the problems of being, but the assurance that his sin is forgiven. He must be justified, or he dies. The God of the law must somehow say that He has no quarrel with him, or he dies a death which he sees, as by intuition peculiar to conviction of sin, to be in its proper nature a death without hope, without end.

"Is this 'somehow' possible?

"Listen, guilty and silent soul, to a sound which is audible now. In the turmoil of either secular indifference or blind self-justification you could not hear it; at best you heard a meaningless murmur. But listen now; it is articulate, and it speaks to you. The earthquake, the wind, the fire, have passed; and you are indeed awake. Now comes 'the sound of stillness' in its turn."

God now speaks, and we read in Romans 3:21, 22, "But now, apart from law, God's righteousness stands displayed, attested by the law and the prophets; but it is God's righteousness, through faith in Jesus Christ, prepared for all, and bestowed upon all who believe in him."

At this point I must digress from the exposition in order to record the fact that the commentators have been greatly divided as to the question of the phrase "upon all." Newell spends pages trying to argue that the phrase does not belong in the Bible, that it was not in the best manuscripts, that its inclusion is an error, and that we must proceed as though it were not there. But after having read with great care all that he has to say, as well as all that the best known and most important commentators have to say, I accept the phrase as Biblical and proceed to explain it. I believe that we can reach Newell's conclusions without omitting the phrase, nor will it be necessary for us to adopt a Roman Catholic position because of the presence of these words. We shall see that they can be expounded with blessing.

A SMALL DISTINCTION

Two things are now said about the righteousness of God. In the King James Version we read that this righteousness is "unto all and upon all them that believe." Whenever in the Bible we have a phrase like this, with a difference that seems very slight, it is well to stop and study the matter closely. Some of God's greatest blessings are to be found in these small distinctions. Here in this passage we are told that the righteousness of God is "unto all and upon all them that believe."

First of all, we must realize that this verse follows closely on a long passage in which it has been set forth that the law was originally given to Israel. There was no salvation before the time of Christ for anyone outside of Israel. The Book of Ephesians points out that before Christ died the Gentiles were godless, hopeless, and Christless (Eph. 2:11, 12). There was only one way for a Gentile to be saved under the law and that was by changing his nationality, so that he might be adopted into one of the tribes and have a priest of Israel offer a sacrifice for his sins on the altar of the tabernacle, or, later, upon the altar of the temple.

But now all things are changed. Now, since Christ has died, the righteousness of God is manifested as being "unto all." Now the gospel is to be preached to every creature under Heaven. No longer is there any distinction because of race and background. There are no more *goyim*, dogs of Gentiles, who may not approach the altars of God. We who were sometimes afar off are made nigh by the blood of Jesus Christ (Eph. 2:12-15). We who were aliens from the commonwealth of Israel and strangers from the covenants of God are now brought near through the promises of God. We who were strangers and foreigners are able to become fellow citizens with the saints and members of the household of God (Eph. 2:19).

The gospel is now "unto all." It is now possible for the church to sing:

> From Greenland's icy mountains,
> From India's coral strand,
> Where Afric's sunny fountains
> Roll down their golden sand,

From many an ancient river,
From many a palmy plain,
They call us to deliver
Their land from error's chain.

And as we sing such a hymn we can pray the prayer:

Saviour, quicken many nations,
Fruitful let Thy sorrows be;
By Thy pains and consolations
Draw the Gentiles unto Thee:
Of Thy cross the wondrous story
Be to all the nations told;
Let them see Thee in Thy glory
And Thy mercy manifold.

There is no child of Adam's race who may not come freely
and boldly unto the Lord Jesus Christ and find the miracle of
new life in Him. Throughout the world there are those who come
and who find transformation and salvation in His death for sinners,
and who know that the righteousness of God is manifest, and that
its direction is universal. The righteousness of God is unto all.

IN FAR PLACES

I have had the wonderful privilege, beyond that given to
most men, to travel over the face of the earth into far places
beyond strange shores. I can recall multitudes of men and women
whose tongue was strange to me, but who have known the glory
of the gospel coming into their lives. I remember an incident
that took place when I was in Japan. I was told about one of the
leaders of the Japanese church who had had a wonderful con-
version from the stark paganism of his parents. I sought him out
and heard the story from his own lips. He told of traveling from
a small village in Japan to a larger town on the day of a great
market-festival. While he was wandering along the street, he
came to a place where a Christian colporteur was selling the
Scriptures and preaching Christ to those who would stop to
listen. The young man had never before heard the gospel; he
had never before heard even the name of Christ. He stood for
more than an hour listening to the testimony of the colporteur
and watching the sale of Scripture portions to those who became

interested. Finally, he bought a New Testament and went on his way. He returned to his own village and began to read the Scriptures. He became so interested in what he found that he made a return journey to the town where he had bought the Testament, but searched in vain for the colporteur. He learned that the colporteur had evidently come from a yet more distant city, and that his visits had been very rare. The young man returned to his village and kept on reading the New Testament. Finally there came one evening when he knew that the Lord Jesus Christ had died for him, and there, alone in his room, he believed God's Word about the death of the eternal Son, and passed out of death into life.

As he read and studied the Word month after month, he saw that there was the ceremony of baptism, and wondered how he should be baptized. He made a trip to the city once more, looking in vain for the colporteur, and finally returned home, somewhat saddened that he could not find another Christian in the world in order that he might be baptized. Then one evening when he was reading in his room, he prayed to the Lord about the matter, because he saw from the Scriptures that they who gladly received the Word were baptized. He rose from his desk and walked to his window which opened wide on the roof of the floor below. He stepped out into the night and there was a gentle rain falling. He told me how he had lifted his face to Heaven and had prayed as the rain fell on his face. How he had cried out to the Lord that since there was no other Christian who could baptize him, that he would accept the water falling from Heaven as the water of his baptism, and he prayed, "I receive this baptism from Heaven, in the name of the Father, and of the Son, and of the Holy Spirit. Amen." The power of the Lord came upon him, and it was not long before he had led a group of his fellow-villagers to the knowledge of the Lord Jesus as the Saviour, God the Son.

When, much later, he was discovered by Baptist missionaries, he told his story and the story of the little church that had been founded by him and that was meeting in his house. He studied formally and was ordained to the ministry, and was in the ministry at the time I was in Japan, but he had never lost the power of that strange and beautiful moment he had had alone with God on the rooftop in the rain, when he had learned that the righteousness of God was unto all, even to the village boy in far Japan.

MEN IN EVERY CLIME

It would be possible for me to tell story after story that would proclaim the freedom of God's grace to lost men in every clime. I have held in my hands the hands of many men who know the Lord Jesus Christ, Japanese and Chinese, Indian and Malayan, Persian and Arab, Europeans of every nation, Africans of many a tribe, and I know that the gospel is unto all, for I have seen men of every nation who have come to the knowledge of God. Among these men whom I have met, there have been men of low degree and men of high degree, but the gospel of Christ is unto all. I have taken the hand of Emperor Haile Selassie who testified to his faith in the finished work of Christ; and the hand of a pastor who in his early days had been a cannibal, eating human flesh; and I have seen the power of God to them and to men of every rank. I have talked with men who were eminent in wisdom beyond most of the men of earth, and with simple people who were unable to read and write, but I have seen that the righteousness of God is unto all.

One of the grandest privileges which is ours who are ministers of the gospel of Christ is to proclaim that the gospel of Jesus Christ is for any man who will receive it. Whosoever will may come unto Christ and receive fully and freely the salvation that was bought by the Saviour, and become the object of the love that was manifested on Calvary.

> Give the winds a mighty voice;
> Jesus saves! Jesus saves!
> Let the nations now rejoice;
> Jesus saves! Jesus saves!
> Shout salvation full and free
> Highest hills and deepest caves;
> This our song of victory;
> Jesus saves! Jesus saves!

TO GENTILES

The righteousness of God is unto all. How wonderful this text is to us who are Gentiles. How wonderful it is to me. If I had been living in the time of Moses, or in the time of David, or at any time before the manifestation of the righteousness of God in Christ, there would have been no hope for me. If we had come over the top of a hill, looking down upon the encampment where the children of Israel were in their tents, we could not have gone freely to the altar where the lamb was to be killed for the remission of sin. We might have wandered down through the camp, but when we reached a certain spot we would have been turned back. We were Gentiles and the middle wall of partition was there to bar us from the free access that we would have needed to come to the altar of redemption and forgiveness.

Even if I had been a Jew, I could not have gone all the way. A Jewish woman could have gone farther than a Gentile would have been permitted to go, but she would have been stopped at the end of the court of the women. A Jewish man who was not of the tribe of Levi could have gone farther than his wife, but he would have been stopped at the rail where the lambs were taken by the priests to be offered upon the altar. The priest could have taken the lamb and killed it, and could have gone on with the incense of prayer within the temple as far as the second altar, but there he would have been stopped. The access into the holiest of all was barred to him. Only once a year, on the day of atonement—*yom kippur*— could the high priest have gone beyond the second curtain into the Holy of Holies where the Ark of the covenant, the Ark of the presence of God was kept. And even he, the high priest, could never go within the veil until he had first offered a sacrifice for his own sins, and then a sacrifice for the sins of the people.

But there came that day when the Lord Jesus Christ died on the cross outside the city gate. The sun grew dark with mystery; the voice of God the Father was silent; the Son of God was nailed to the cross, and hung there dying for me. When I look to Him I can know that God hates sin and that He wants the way opened so that I may come boldly into His presence.

FREE ACCESS

As He dies there is a great earthquake. The inner veil in the temple is torn in two from top to bottom so that all may look within and see what had been the holy precincts. Outside, the middle wall of partition that kept the Gentiles from coming with free access to the emplacement of the altar was broken down also. Now the righteousness of God apart from the law is manifested. Now the righteousness is seen to be unto all. Now I, dog of a Gentile, can walk down through the camp and come with holy boldness. There is no more court of the Gentiles with a wall to bar my progress. Now I can come through with confidence in the love of God in the work of His Son. Now a woman is no longer stopped because she is a woman. She, too, finds her glorious liberty in the death of the Son of God. Now she can approach with boldness, even as I. Now the Jew who is not of the tribe of Levi can come within the gate. The altar is bare, for no other lamb shall die for sin after the Lamb of God has suffered to take away the sin of the world. He can walk to the holy precinct and find that the veil has been torn away. The priest who was once stopped there can come along with the rest of us, Gentiles and women and men who are not of Aaron. The very high priest can no longer be barred on a day that is not a festival day. Together we may all come, every son of Adam's race, and be sure that we shall be received when we come, because now, apart from the law, the righteousness of God is manifested, and that righteousness is unto all.

It makes no difference, then, whether your flesh be black or white or brown, the dying Saviour wore for all a thorny crown. It makes no difference, then, whether you be male or female. It makes no difference, then, whether you be of high or low estate. The Lord Jesus Christ died for all, and so the righteousness of God is unto all.

RIGHTEOUSNESS FOR ALL

One of the greatest glories of Christianity is the universality of the gospel call. It is not like a religion that says that God will take anyone into Heaven without any consideration of His own righteousness. We are not offering a cheap universalism that would make Heaven a dirty place filled with dirty people, unchanged. We are offering a rich, full gospel of the righteousness of God unto all. It is a righteousness which comes to men wherever they are, but does not leave them as they are. It is a righteousness which does not disregard the righteous demands of the Father's holy

nature, but it is a righteousness thàt offers itself to all men so
that they may leave the unrighteousness which is theirs by nature
in order to enter into the righteousness which is provided for them
in the Saviour. It is a righteousness that is extended unto you
today, just as you are and just where you are. You may read these
words while sitting alone by your desk, or upon your bed. You
may read these words while you are free and able to move where
you will, or you may be confined in prison, but the offer is still
the same. The righteousness of God is unto all. And that simplicity
is the glory of God's grace.

CHAPTER V

"Upon All"

"Even the righteousness of God which is by faith of Jesus Christ unto all and upon all them that believe: for there is no difference" (Rom. 3:22).

THE GOSPEL of Jesus Christ is the power of God unto salvation to every one that believes. It is to the Jew first, and also to the Gentile. Whosoever will may come and take of the water of life freely. The righteousness of God is unto all.

But there is something more than the free offer of grace. The righteousness of God is not only unto all, it is also upon all them that believe. Actually there are two aspects of the righteousness of God: We have the righteousness of God put upon us, but we also become the very righteousness of God in Christ.

When we speak of the righteousness of God as being "upon all them that believe," we must understand first of all what it does not mean. We are not to think of the righteousness of God simply as something outside of us that is merely laid upon us and as being added to us. Some have fallen into the error of thinking that the righteousness of God was placed about us, sinners that we are, as a beautiful robe might be placed about a filthy person, hiding his filth and his rags. There is no intention in the teaching of the epistles to convey the thought that God covers up our sins with a cloak of righteousness, or that He merely adds divine righteousness to sinful people.

At least to one commentator, Newell, there is a contradiction in terms between "unto" and "upon" all, and he spends several pages trying to point out that we are made the righteousness of God and that, therefore, there is nothing put upon us. But he is missing the point. The ideas are no more contradictory than those which say we become sons of God by the new birth, and that we are declared sons of God by adoption. The ideas are not contradictory but complementary.

RIGHTEOUSNESS AS A GARMENT

The righteousness of God is *upon all them that believe*. It is righteousness placed upon believers as a garment. In the third chapter of Genesis, we have the story of the fall, and we are presented there with man clothed in three different sets of garments. Before the fall man is clothed in the light of the righteousness which had been given him in the creation. When sin entered that light disappeared and man discovered that he was naked. It is not bareness of skin that is being talked about but the absence of the light of righteousness. Immediately, therefore, man proceeds to make a substitute of fig leaves. Man clothed himself with that which he had made himself. It is the symbol of good works proceeding from self-effort and from a heart that is estranged from God. God will have nothing to do with it, and so God gives to the man and woman the promise of a Redeemer; and, *when they believed,* however dimly, in the truth of God's Word, God provided them with a new covering by shedding the blood of animals and clothing the man and the woman with the skins of this sacrifice. It is the picture of that which is to be found throughout the Bible. Righteousness is seen as a garment.

The image is used in many ways. The righteousness of the unregenerate is presented as filthy rags (Isa. 64:6). Job says, "I put on righteousness and it clothed me; my justice was as a robe and a diadem" (Job 29:14, Heb.). The Psalmist sings: "Let thy priests be clothed in righteousness; and let thy saints shout for joy" (Ps. 132:9). The prophet speaks of the coming of the Saviour Messiah, and says, "Righteousness shall be the girdle of his loins, and faithfulness the girdle of his reins" (Isa. 11:5). And elsewhere righteousness is said to be the breastplate of the Messiah in His coming judgments (Isa. 59:17). Isaiah rejoices for himself that he has been dressed in the righteousness of the Lord, and he breaks forth in what might be called a Psalm, singing, "I will greatly rejoice in the Lord, my soul shall be joyful in my God; for he hath clothed me with the garments of salvation, he hath covered me with the robe of righteousness, as a bridegroom decketh himself with ornaments, and as a bride adorneth herself with her jewels" (Isa. 61:10).

THE BRIDE'S CLOTHING

In the light of all of these wonderful promises, it is not astonishing that the writer of the Epistle to the Romans should speak of righteousness upon all them that believe. And that this is a New Testament truth is abundantly proved by the announcement in the last book of the Bible that the Church, clothed as a bride for the coming of the heavenly Bridegroom, is to meet the Lord decked in the garments of righteousness. "Let us be glad and rejoice, and give honor to him: for the marriage of the Lamb is come, and his wife hath made herself ready. And to her was granted that she should be arrayed in fine linen, clean and white: for the fine linen is the righteousness of the saints" (Rev. 19:7, 8).

The poets of the church have not been slow to seize upon this great and glorious truth, and as a result we have some of the most beautiful hymns of our worship.

> Jesus, Thy blood and righteousness
> My beauty are, my glorious dress.
> 'Mid flaming worlds in these arrayed,
> With joy shall I lift up my head.

Thus sang Zinzendorf, while Edward Mote wrote:

> When He shall come with trumpet sound,
> O may I then in Him be found,
> Dressed in His righteousness, alone,
> Faultless to stand before the throne.

In this light, also, is to be understood the parable of the guest who came to the wedding without the wedding garment. The story is told by the Lord Jesus and recorded by Matthew as follows: "And when the king came in to see the guests, he saw there a man which had not on a wedding garment: And he said unto him, Friend, how camest thou in hither not having a wedding garment? And he was speechless. Then said the king to the servants, Bind him hand and foot, and take him away, and cast him into outer darkness; there shall be weeping and gnashing of teeth" (Matt. 22:11-13).

The explanation of the parable is to be found in the oriental custom whereby the king provided the garments for all those who came to a royal wedding. The man who came in to the wedding without this garment might easily have spent everything he had in providing a garment which could have outshone the garment which the king provided for the guests. But it was not the garment of the king's providing. Thus it is with the King of kings and the marriage supper which God has prepared for all those who come to Him through Christ. He provides His own righteousness as a garment and commands that we appear before Him dressed in this righteousness alone. Woe be unto the man who dares appear before Him in some garment of his own providing. As seen today with the eyes of men the righteousness of man may appear to be glorious in comparison with the righteousness of God. For men today see through a glass, darkly, and cannot discern the differences between the righteousness of men and the righteousness of God.

INVISIBLE TO MEN

The righteousness of God is invisible to the eyes of the world. Even as the Lord said that the Holy Spirit would never be received by the world because the world could not see Him (John 14:17), so the world cannot see the righteousness of God as being different from the best in human righteousness. But the day shall come when all things shall be seen in another light and then shall the righteousness of God shine forth. There is an illustration of this that is to be found in the great museum of science in Philadelphia which has been named in honor of Benjamin Franklin. In the museum there is a display of rocks of various kinds that is housed in a special room which must be entered by a corridor which is in absolute darkness. The reason for this darkness is to accustom the eyes to see with a different light which is diffused in the special exhibit room. The light which is turned on in that room is an indirect fluorescent light of rays that are ordinarily invisible to the human eye. But here in that darkness this light shines upon rocks that would usually appear to the eye in tones of gray and dun brown. In the new light they glow with a brilliance and a beauty which is almost incredible. In fact, I believe that the colors which come back to the eye from these dull rocks under this special lighting are the most beautiful colors that my eyes have ever seen.

I can remember many brilliant and beautiful scenes both in nature and in art. I can remember the brilliance of tropical sunsets, and the sheen of exotic fish. I know the colors of flaming floral displays, and the warmth of the blues and the greens in the waters of tropical beaches. But I have never seen colors as beautiful as those reflected from the dull gray and brown rocks under the rays of invisible light in a dark room. I have seen the most beautiful pastel shades that men have ever been able to mix upon their palettes, and the translucence of the most stately stained glass windows that art has contrived and the ingenuity of man has developed, but I have never seen colors to equal those of dull gray rocks under the invisible rays of light in the dark room of a scientific museum.

So it is with the righteousness of God as seen through the eyes of the world and as seen through the eyes of the Spirit. The world looks upon the righteousness of God as a drab thing, even imagining that it robs men of the happiness that the world promises so freely and gives so poorly. The unsaved, the Word of God tells us, think it strange that the believer runs not with them to the same excess of riot (I Pet. 4:4).

The world, therefore, adorns itself in its own garments and refuses the righteousness of God in Christ. But the day is coming when the King shall look upon all the guests and shall cast into outer darkness those who have dared to approach Him in a righteousness which is of their own providing. Those who are willing to accept by simple faith the truths which God sets forth concerning Himself, His holiness, His righteousness, His choice of the method of salvation through the Lord Jesus Christ, shall know the miracle of regeneration. Around the shoulders of the poorest sinner shall be draped the robe of the divine righteousness, unto all and upon all who believe.

IN CHRIST

But there is something even more wonderful than the expressed fact that the righteousness of God has been put upon us as a robe and that His own holiness is ours for a glory and a covering. The whole of our passage in the third of Romans is teaching us that the righteousness of God more than covers us, more than penetrates us. We are looked upon as being in Christ and are become the very righteousness of God. In Corinthians we will read, "God made Christ to be sin for us, who knew no sin, that we might be made the righteousness of God in him" (II Cor. 5:21). And again we read, "But of him are ye in Christ Jesus, who of God is made unto us wisdom, and righteousness, and sanctification, and redemption: that, according as it is written, He that glorieth, let him glory in the Lord" (I Cor. 1:30, 31).

A NEW CREATION

We were formerly looked upon in ourselves as being alien to God and as being in Adam condemned sinners. By the death of the Lord Jesus Christ we are taken out of Adam and placed in Christ. We are made partakers of the divine nature. "If any man be in Christ, he is a new creation: old things are passed away; behold, all things are become new" (II Cor. 5:17, marg.). This verse bothered me for many years because I was filled with the old idea of righteousness being placed upon me as something outside; and, while I believed in the Lord and was aware of the fact that I was a new creation in Christ Jesus, I knew very well that all things, *all things*, had not become new. I could not resolve the seeming contradiction between such a verse describing the new creation and the one in Romans seven which speaks of the continuing presence of the old Adamic being. But when we comprehend the real nature of the work which God performs within the life and being of the one who is born from above, the difficulties are all resolved and the problems disappear.

For when God justifies us, it is not merely the throwing of a robe of righteousness around the nakedness of our fallen being. When God justifies us He reckons us as being as perfect as the Lord Jesus Christ Himself. When you look through rose-colored glasses everything is seen in a rosy hue. When you look through yellow glasses, the surrounding panorama takes on the yellow hue. And the glorious truth of the gospel is that when the Lord God Almighty looks at the one who has trusted completely in the work of the Lord Jesus Christ on the cross of Calvary, He sees us in all the white holiness of Christ. God looks at me through Christ the moment I am in Christ and He sees me as He sees Christ. It is the glorious truth that is expressed in the English hymn:

Near, so near am I to God,
Nearer I cannot be;
For in the Person of His Son
I'm just as near as He.

Dear, so dear am I to God
Dearer I cannot be;
The love wherewith He loved His Son,
Such is His love to me.

This is what is meant by being in Christ. This is what is meant by being justified. God looks down from Heaven and sees the man who believes in the Lord Jesus and says, in effect: "I declare that this man is righteous. Even though he may be outwardly the child of sinful Adam, yet I declare this man to be righteous because I have looked upon him through Christ. I, God, operate a bookkeeping record with reference to members of the human race, and it has pleased Me to write this man down in My books as being righteous. It is not because there is any righteousness within the man of his own doings, for there is nothing that I could accept as righteousness. But because the Lord Jesus Christ has died, and because I have looked upon this ungodly man as being in My Son, I count this man as righteous and write him down in My books as righteous. He is accepted in the Beloved. I the Lord say this."

We must not be led aside from the truth that is expressed both in our text in Romans and that in Corinthians, by the presence of our old Adamic nature. There is always the tendency to look upon spiritual things through the eyes of the flesh. It is hard to understand what we really are in our position in Christ because of what we see in our condition in ourselves.

One of the best stories which I ever heard to illustrate this truth concerned a young scion of a noble house of England. The story goes that the younger son in a certain family of the ruling classes disgraced his name and family by outrageous conduct. The family told him that if he would leave the country, he would receive a check each quarter that would permit him to live in some comfort, but that he would be refused all income if he remained in England. He emigrated to Canada and received his check every three months and immediately spent it within a few days, living the rest of the time the precarious existence of a semi-

bum. He drifted down into the United States, making arrange-
ments for the Canadian bank to send him his money at a certain
time and place. In the meantime his father died suddenly and
his older brother was killed in an automobile accident, all within
a matter of hours. He thus, by British law, was the heir of the
title and estates. That was his position. But he had dropped
from sight in the United States and could not be traced. His
wife left England and arrived in New York and undertook the
search for her husband. He had just drawn a remittance and
supposedly would not be heard from for another three months.
The best detectives were employed to locate him and within a few
days he was traced to a small town not far from Chicago where
he was eking out a precarious existence, employed as an elevator
operator in a cheap hotel at a few dollars a week. His position
was that of a noble earl of England with access to the House of
Lords. His condition was that of an underpaid starvling in a run-
down hotel in a Midwestern town. His wife flew to meet him and
took him back to New York. It was then that the newspapers
discovered the story and printed the details. The man was in
New York, and was now in the process of acquiring a new ward-
robe, and awaiting his passage on the steamship that was to take
him back to his ancestral castle, his estates, and his new life.

SONS AND HEIRS

The unregenerate men and women of this world are estranged
from God, alienated from His life, and are dead in trespasses
and sins. Those who have become true believers in the Lord
Jesus Christ have passed from death into life, and are immediately the possessors of their titles in Christ. They are sons
of God, heirs of God and joint heirs with Christ. They have an
inheritance that is incorruptible and undefiled, and that fadeth
not away, and that is reserved in Heaven for them. They may
be living far beneath their rank and privileges, but nothing can
change what they have become by grace through the Lord Jesus
Christ. Their position before God in Christ is that of absolute
perfection. There is not an item in the inventory of all that they
possess in Christ that is theirs because of prayer or Christian

living, but all is theirs because they have been accepted in the beloved. It is on the basis and grounds of their high position that Christians are called upon to live lives of holiness.

It is the new birth that gives us our position of justification before God. The matter of our sanctification is quite another question. We will not be drawn aside into futile arguments based on experience rather than upon the Scriptures as to what we are to think in cases where people fail to live up to their profession, and kindred difficulties that arise when men look to circumstances instead of looking to the Word of God for their evidence. These things we brush aside as irrelevant at the present time. We are not dismissing them permanently, for they will come up for treatment when we come to those sections of the epistle which deal with the outworking of the Christian life.

At present we are concerned with obstetrics and not with pediatrics. We are occupied with the question of the birth of the child and not with the question of the growth of the child. Here in this section of Romans we are seeing that the righteousness of God is unto all and upon all them that believe. We are finding out that God covers the sins of man with the work of the Saviour and henceforth looks upon the redeemed sinner as being one with Christ.

RIGHTEOUS IN CHRIST

The wise Christian will learn the great lesson that he is in Christ, and that for his own peace and joy, and for his own strength and walk he must never consider himself for even an instant apart from his oneness with Christ. If we look at ourselves, in ourselves and apart from Christ, we are seeing ourselves in the place of defeat and death. If we look at ourselves as God sees us in Christ, we are faced with the stunning truth that we are seen to be perfect in Christ, joined to Him, and are one with Him and in Him forever. We who have no intrinsic righteousness are seen to be what we are not of ourselves nor ever could be: we are righteous in Christ.

The believer is justified and accounted as righteous even at a moment when he is ungodly, and this accounting is done by God because of Christ. The day will come, of course, when the believer shall be presented faultless before the presence of God. But the believer is declared righteous at the moment of his regeneration, even while he is yet ungodly. If God changed him before declaring him righteous, it would not be the declaration of an ungodly man as being accepted in Christ but the acceptance of a man that has been made godly. But thanks be to God, we are accepted in Christ even when we are unrighteous, ungodly, lost, dead, alienated; and from that moment that we are seen in Christ, we are seen to be complete, perfect, accepted. The love of Christ constrains us, and the long slow progress of the outgrowth of the life begins to make itself manifest.

The acorn is a tiny one, but it takes root. As in the case when an acorn falls into the brush, the annual growth of grass may hide it for several years, but eventually it will be seen for what it is — an oak tree that will dominate the countryside and resist all the winds that blow, giving shelter to many weary travelers. But in the beginning the whole oak is in the acorn, hidden for long months before manifesting the life that is within. Even so are we in Christ and Christ is in us. And in Him we are all the righteousness of God.

CHAPTER VI

Implanted Righteousness

"Even the righteousness of God which is by faith of Jesus Christ unto all and upon all them that believe: for there is no difference" (Rom. 3:22).

THE TEACHER who would follow the whole counsel of God is faced, at times, with some of the paradoxes of faith. There is no doubt that there are passages in the Bible which present truths which seem to alter or contradict other truths. Only when we are looking upon all truth from the point of view of Heaven itself will we understand and harmonize all truth. If we could understand God, we would be God.

Therefore, when we come to a text that presents one side of the truth, it is our duty to present that side with all the force at our command; and when we come to the presentation of the corresponding truth, we present it, also, with all the wisdom and strength with which we may avail ourselves by the power and blessing of God.

We have spoken of the fact that the righteousness of God is unto all and upon all, and that this work is God's work, done entirely by Him, without respect to the person who is the object of the work of His sovereign grace. We now concentrate upon the phrase which sets forth that all of this work is done by God for those who believe. We turn aside from the argument concerning which comes first, true faith or true life, and present to the unbeliever in this hour the fact that God calls upon him to believe. The righteousness of God is unto all and upon all who believe. It follows, necessarily, that you can never be seen in the righteousness of God if you do not believe God's Word about the work of our Lord Jesus Christ. Therefore, God calls you to believe in His Word about His Son.

50

MAN'S RESPONSIBILITY

Everywhere throughout the Bible the doctrine of man's responsibility is taught. From the very first pages of the Bible, we have set forth the fact that man is placed in a position of choice and is called upon to work in the center of God's will and to choose for God and righteousness. To all who read these lines comes the direct command of God that they should lay hold upon His promises and believe His Word about the sinfulness of their position and about the death of His Son.

First of all, we must point out that there is no magic in mere faith. It is not enough to say that you believe. The Word sets forth that you must believe the right things and that you must believe them in the right way. We find in the Word of God that there is a type of faith that is totally vain. The Holy Spirit speaks through James, saying, "Thou believest that there is one God; thou doest well: the demons also believe and tremble. But wilt thou know, O vain man, that faith without works is dead?" (Jas. 2:19, 20, marg.)

There is no contradiction between this statement of James and that which we have been seeing in the writings of Paul. James is presenting the truth from the human point of view; Paul is presenting the matter from the divine point of view. Do you comprehend that salvation is by faith alone? That is what God teaches us, for He can see the nature and quality of the faith. Wherever there is true faith that faith is seen by God, as the fruit of life planted within the believer. We do not have the attributes of God that would permit us to look within the hearts of our fellow creatures to find whether the faith that is professed is of the right essence. How can we know if the faith is indeed true faith, saving faith? The answer is that true faith will prove itself to men around us by the nature of the fruit that it bears.

FOUNDATIONS

We understand this in ordinary life. We recognize that faith is worthless unless it has foundations. A man may drive a car over a bridge because he believes that the bridge will support the car; but, if a freshet has recently washed away the underpinning, the faith will not keep the car from being wrecked.

Faith must have a foundation. And it is not enough to believe this or that religious theory. The truth is in Christ, and there is not any truth outside of Christ. It was He who said, "I am the way, the truth, and the life; no man cometh unto the Father but by me" (John 14:6).

If it be objected that certainly there is some truth to be found in religions outside of Christ, I answer that it is not so, for a lie, in its very essence, is the intent to deceive; and, when a fact that is truth in itself in one interpretation is used in order to deceive, it becomes a lie and is no more truth. For example, it is a fact that God is love, and that truth can be one of the most precious in all of the revelation of the nature and being of God when it is held in proper balance with all of the rest of truth. But when someone seeks to tell you that God is love and that therefore He will not punish sin, the very truth becomes a lie and can take one to eternal judgment if it is trusted. For the whole of the truth is necessary to salvation, and the love of God must be balanced by the justice of God and the holiness of God.

In fact, a false religion with a high percentage of what is called truth may be the most cunning artifice of Satan because of the incorporation of that amount of truth with the essential lie. A counterfeit silver dollar that is made of wood will deceive almost no sane person. If the counterfeit is made of lead, it will deceive an unwary child. If it has a small percentage of silver, it will deceive not a few adults; while if it has a larger percentage of silver, it will deceive still more. The more true silver in the counterfeit, the more people it will deceive. In like manner, when we consider the matter of religious faith we must not look at the fact that there is this or that phase of truth in the religion which we are studying, but whether there is the one mark of authenticity upon it, lacking which we must be bold to call it counterfeit.

In the matter of money the question of reality is in the ownership of the mint by the government and the issuance of the coinage by the authority of that government. In the matter of religious truth the question of reality is in the source of the truth in the Lord Jesus Christ, guaranteed by His resurrection from the dead, and the authenticity of the revelation which He has given through the Word which conveys all truth to us. The authority cannot be in a man or in a group of men, nor in an organization of men. It cannot, therefore, be in a church, whatever its nature or pretentions. The authority must be in the Word of Christ's revelation, and in that alone. It is this that must be believed.

THE RIGHT FOUNDATION

Not only must we point out that there is no magic in faith, but, secondly, that faith must be on the right foundation. We then comprehend that each man is entirely responsible to God whether he will or will not admit the fact of his responsibility.

We recognize the fact of responsibility in many other phases of life. A child is responsible in the home. He must obey the parents if there is not to be disorder and confusion. A soldier is responsible to all his superiors. The law of the land picks him up through the draft and sets him down in a camp, puts a uniform upon him and regulates every part of his outward existence. It tells him when he must arise and when he must turn out his lights. It gives him his food and orders his work. It may transfer him to any spot on the globe that it wishes. The soldier is absolutely responsible. If he wishes to argue that responsibility, he will find himself in the guard house.

The creature is also responsible to the Creator. There is no use arguing about it; you yourself are absolutely responsible to God, and you will one day answer for that responsibility. You cannot see God as a soldier sees the authority of the army, but the authority of God is no less real. In fact, the authority of God is even more real. It is conceivable that a soldier might desert and remain undiscovered. It is conceivable that a soldier might arrange a pretty easy life for himself within the army and get away with it for some length of time, but with God there will be no hiding nor evasion.

I heard a story about a soldier on a work detail where it was the custom to have men with picks work for fifteen minutes and rest for fifteen minutes while men with shovels took their turn. After that the men with picks would work again. One particular soldier carried both pick and shovel and rested with the pick men, pick in hand, when it was their turn to rest, and rested with the shovel men, shovel in hand, when it was their turn to rest. When his ruse was discovered, it was decided that he would make a good sergeant. But duties cannot be avoided with God even though it may appear to be the fact that men live for years without any accountability. You may think you are getting away with something, but you are not.

We must distinguish very sharply between accountability and responsibility. You are at present responsible, and you are also accountable. The accountability will become evident at the judgment of God, and you will see then that you have been responsible all along, even if you did not like to admit it.

PERFECTION REQUIRED

The next point to be considered, then, is for what are you responsible and accountable? The answer is that you are responsible and accountable to God to be absolutely perfect, without ever having had a single thought in your mind or heart that was not a thought of God and His glory. "Thou shalt love the Lord thy God with all thine heart, with all thy soul, with all thy mind and with all thy strength. And thou shalt love thy neighbor as thyself." Now it is obvious that you have not done any such thing. You are therefore declared to be guilty and accountable in judgment unless you will accept a certain set of formulas with your mind and believe them absolutely. God says that if you will accept this set of formulas, He will perform a work of bookkeeping and write off all your sin and incompleteness to the account of Christ and will count you as justified in Christ. It is entirely His work and it will be totally apart from anything in you, but will proceed wholly from God's own heart and desire. He says He will do it that way because He pleases to do it that way and that you are to take it or leave it.

Now whether we like it or not that is the essential nature of Christianity. We know that the carnal mind of man hates to be put squarely before a set of facts and told that he may take them or leave them but that he may not argue them in any way. Thus we are told that the carnal mind is enmity against God, and is not subject to the law of God (Rom. 8:7). There is nothing more

calculated to bring out hatred in human nature than a blunt statement that there is one thing to do and that nothing can be done
about it otherwise. Yet that is exactly what God has done.

God comes to the race today and tells men that if they will
believe a set of formulas, He will work a miracle within them
and put a new life to their account that will enable them to live
on an entirely new plane. This new life will be pleasing to Him
because it no longer proceeds from the roots of the old nature of
Adam that lingers on in us, but will come from an entirely different root, namely, the Lord Jesus Christ.

What are these formulas, then, which God demands that we
accept and for which He will hold us accountable? The first is
that we must admit without any reservation that we are less
perfect than God, and that, therefore, we should be cursed from
God and separated from Him forever. God simply will not tolerate
that anyone shall come to Him with any kind of human righteousness or human achievement and present it to Him as a down payment or a part payment for a place in His Heaven. The greatest
insult that can be offered to Deity is the insult of presenting Him
with something which we have done or something that we are
supposed to be in ourselves. According to the whole tenor of the
Bible, both the Old and the New Testament, the most abominable
thing in the sight of God is the offer of anything that is of human
manufacture or human devising as a substitute for the divine
perfection which alone can satisfy the demands of His nature.

GOD'S VERDICT

So, first of all, God says to you: "I want you to admit the
truth about yourself. I do not want it to be a truth that is colored
by your own viewpoint. I want it to be an admission that is totally
objective. The only being in the universe who is capable of being
totally objective is I, the Lord God. Therefore I want you to bow
before My verdict about yourself and admit that there is nothing
that you could ever produce which would satisfy Me."

The whole of Scripture and the whole of life are calculated
to prove the truth of that divine assertion. It is the summing up
of a hundred verses and more which declare that man is un-

righteous in the sight of God and that he can do nothing which would ever satisfy the demands of divine holiness. Since the admission of this fact is one of the bitterest pills, if not the bitterest, that the nature of man must swallow, I have sought for many illustrations to show to men the truth of the verdict.

There is one example which I have used most frequently and which has brought help to many people. I ask if you would be willing to take a drink of the finest spring water, the purest water that could be obtained by any chemical standards of analysis. You will answer, of course, that you would most certainly be willing to drink such water; and then I tell you that I have not said a word about the glass into which the water is to be poured in order to bring it to your lips. That should give you pause, for the glass in which that pure spring water is conveyed to you has just been emptied of diphtheria culture in a medical laboratory and has spread multitudes of deadly germs throughout the water. Now will you take a drink? You refuse, of course. It is even so with God. You may argue or boast about the works which you have produced, and you may even think that by your standards of analysis your works should be acceptable to God. But the Word of God comes bluntly to tell you that your good works are contained in the glass of your sinful, Adamic heart and that they have infected every part of your being so that they are an offense to God because they have touched you.

Therefore the primary demand of God is that you bow before Him and admit that nothing which has ever touched you can henceforward be acceptable to God. You are less perfect than He is; you are contaminated by sin; you are therefore declared to be a sinner, and hence you are declared to be lost. First of all, you must admit this formula and accept it without question.

SINNERS SAVED BY GRACE

When you have thus taken your place as a guilty sinner, you are then in a position to be told of the work which God has done on your behalf. This is why Christians are so happy to admit their sinfulness and sing about it most joyfully in some of our grandest hymns.

> Guilty, vile and helpless we,
> Spotless Lamb of God was He.
> Full atonement — can it be?
> Hallelujah! What a Saviour.

It is not because of a complex that wishes self-degradation that we are willing to sing of ourselves in terms that describe us as the lowest of sinners. A hundred of our hymnwriters have ransacked the vocabulary of loathesomeness to present us before God as what we really are. Charles Wesley sang of us as being vile offenders, restless wanderers, poor, maimed, halt, blind, guilty, condemned, lost sinners, thankless creatures, a weary and burdened and reprobate race, lepers, helpless, hopeless, worthless, defenseless. Faber added to the list other names for us: frightened sheep, foolish hearts; and other poets have gone through the dictionary seeking all the words of baseness, ingratitude and foul sinfulness to sing of what we were by nature before we were touched by the Lord in salvation.

What is the answer to this? Can we pass it over as some complex that has arisen in the minds of a great many people who are some sort of religious fanatics, seeing darkness where none exists?

The answer comes from the heart of multitudes. We sing:

> And from my stricken heart with tears
> Two wonders I confess —
> The wonders of redeeming love,
> And my own worthlessness.

It is the wonder of our own sinfulness which makes us comprehend the greater wonder of His love for us. And that is the second of the two formulas which God demands that we accept. We are to admit that when we were in the wretched state of sin which we have acknowledged, the Lord moved toward us in great grace and loved us when we were in that condition. He commends His love toward us in that while we were yet sinners Christ died for the ungodly (Rom. 5). He demands that we look away from anything in ourselves and look alone to that which He has done for us, accepting His statement that He accounts us righteous in Christ. There is not another thing that we can do to prepare ourselves for Heaven. It is when we admit that we would foul up God's Heaven if we were taken there as we are by nature, that

God intervenes and declares that we are righteous, even with His own righteousness, and all this on the basis of a fathomless love that is exercised toward us in sheer grace because it pleased Him to look upon us in our sin and do something about it.

BELIEVE AND LIVE

If you want it in the simplest terms, it is this: God wants you to believe His Word that He is satisfied with the death of Jesus Christ instead of your death. The most important thing that ever could be said about the death of Jesus Christ is that God the Father is satisfied with it. If He, the righteous judge, is pleased to remit all penalties against us by virtue of what the Saviour did in dying on the cross, then there is no case against us forevermore. That is the amazing thing about the faith that is set forth for us to believe. It is complete; it is eternal. It is merely a question of believing God's Word about a set of facts: the fact of our sin and the fact of the divine provision through the Lord Jesus Christ.

Now our text in Romans declares explicitly that the Lord God counts divine righteousness unto all and upon all that believe. And the context of our passage, as well as all of Scripture, abundantly testifies that the things which God demands that we believe are the two great parts of the divine revelation: that man was completely ruined in sin but that a perfect remedy has been provided in Christ.

Even when we read that God commands men to repent (Acts 17:30), we must understand it in connection with what we have seen here. Repentance is the equivalent of the military command to do an about face. You have been facing unbelief, you are commanded to turn around and face the simplicity of faith. You have been believing lies, now you must turn around and believe truth. You have been walking in darkness, you must now turn into the light of faith.

Perhaps you will say that you cannot believe. Even such a statement is a symptom of your lost condition. If you do not believe, it is because you will not believe. The Lord Jesus Christ spoke to men who had been reading the Scriptures and said to them, "Ye search the Scriptures, for in them ye think ye have eternal life, and they are they which testify of me; and ye will not come unto me that ye might have life" (John 5:39, 40). Your hard heart says that you cannot believe but the core of that hard heart is a will that is determined not to believe.

Several years ago I was preaching in Boston, and I had a young instructor at Harvard come to talk with me in my hotel room by an appointment which had been made through a friend who was interested in his salvation. We went over the gospel together, and he was not willing to submit himself to it. I took him to John 3:19 where he read, "And this is the condemnation, that light is come into the world, and men loved darkness rather than light, because their deeds were evil." He flared out in anger against the verdict, crying: "That's the trouble with you Christians. You are always calling people evil. There is nothing evil that is keeping me from accepting your propositions." I answered: "Your difficulty is that you do not understand what constitutes evil. I am not accusing you of theft, or of running off with a neighbor's wife. I believe that your evil may be intellectual pride, the evil of sitting in the stacks of the Widener Library filled with pride because you in your research have discovered a fact of history that no other person in the world knows." He settled back in his seat, somewhat mollified that I had removed him from the category of vileness which he considered to be sin, and had placed him in a category of moral pride which he did not consider to be sin. But he, even as all who read these words, is totally responsible for believing the formulas which the Word of God places before you all in the gospel.

If you do not believe these things, you will be condemned to outer darkness. If you do believe them, God will plant within you the life of Christ; will record you in Heaven as being accepted in Christ; and will begin to work within you the marvelous transformation that proceeds in all believers throughout all the Christian life, step by step, revealing His Son in us and making us, day by day, more like unto Him. And then there will come that day when death will release us from the binding of the old nature, or the coming of the Lord will complete the transformation, and we shall be like Christ forever. And all this because the righteousness of God is unto all and upon all that believe these things.

CHAPTER VII

"No Difference"

"Even the righteousness of God which is by faith of Jesus Christ unto all and upon all them that believe: for there is no difference" (Rom. 3:22).

"THERE is no difference." One of the best known texts in the Bible now comes before us in the orderly course of our exposition. "There is no difference." And at the outset we make bold to say that many of the expositors and commentators who have come to this verse have failed to see the meaning that is set forth in this great declaration by God. "There is no difference"—and most writers have explained the text as meaning that there is no difference between men in the facts of their essential humanity, no difference between men in the nature of their original sin, no difference between men in their basic need, no difference between men in their standing before God, no difference between men in the fact that they were all the objects of His love and grace in Calvary, no difference between men in the way that they must take for salvation.

Now all of these things are true, and there is no difference between men in any of these liabilities or assets that are in the accounting, but these things may not be deduced from our text. If you wish to find the basis for such thinking, turn rather to the second chapter of Romans and read that with God there is no respect of persons.

THE BIBLE AND THE CHURCH

In the sermons that have been printed on our present text, there have been great truths set forth, magnificently expressed, but they belong, in reality, to other texts in the Scripture. Some who read these words may immediately cry out that we are buttressing their position that man is incapable of interpreting the Bible, that there must therefore be a church to interpret it infallibly, and that man must salute superior orders and not be concerned with anything except what he is told he must believe by some church authority. Nothing could be farther from the truth. The Bible is infinite, and we may take that word *infinite* in the fullness of its mathematical meaning. It can never be fully comprehended by the finite. If it were possible for any man or group of men to understand the Bible perfectly, they would cease to be men and would be Deity itself. The Trinity would be enlarged to include many other persons, and the Godhead would no more consist of three persons. We must ever keep in mind that God has given us His Word in our hands and that this gift has been balanced by the Holy Spirit in our hearts. The Holy Spirit is the true vicar of Christ, and no man can be called by that name without dethroning the Holy Spirit. The Scriptures are not a gift *from* the church, but were written *to* the church. It is very important to note that the first verse of almost every one of the epistles contains the flat statement that it is written *to* the church. Then let the church be submitted to the Bible, and let us have an end of talking about the Bible being submitted to the church.

We must not forget that the Holy Spirit has told us that there must be divisions, sects, denominations, in order that the truth might be made manifest. If all men hold the same religious idea, a nation quickly sinks to a low level of civilization. It is only where there is free study with the minds of men unshackled that the truth will ultimately triumph in individual minds. For those who follow the Bible there can be no index of expurgated writings, there can be no prohibitions against logic, there can be no barriers across highways of the mind. God has made man with a freedom for which he is totally responsible and absolutely accountable. The day will come when every man will be judged solely on the basis of what is written in this book, the Bible. In that day, if any man dare to whimper that he thought that he had to follow what a church taught him, he will be most solemnly judged. The truth is in the Book, and no man may shirk accountability to the Book. The Holy Spirit stands at the side of the man who will take up the Word in simplicity and ask the Lord to teach him. Christ Himself said, "If any man will determine to do God's will he shall know of the doctrine whether it is of God or whether it is from man" (John 7:17).

MEN DO NOT DIFFER

Before going to our text to find out some of that which is meant by the great declaration that "there is no difference," let us stop for a moment with one of the great expositors of the last century, with one who has been called the prince of expositors, Alexander Maclaren of Birmingham. In his chapter on our text, he has presented truth in a beautiful way; if his paragraphs had been set forth under other texts, they would have been of even greater value.

His opening words, however, deserve to be quoted here, even though they introduce a study that is alien to our text. "The things in which all men are alike," he writes, "are far more important than those in which they differ. The diversities are superficial, the identities are deep as life. Physical processes and wants are the same for everybody. All men, be they kings or beggars, civilized or savage, rich or poor, wise or foolish, cultured or illiterate, breathe the same breath, hunger and thirst, eat and drink, sleep, are smitten by the same diseases, and die at last the same death. We have all of us one human heart. Tears and grief, gladness and smiles, move us all. Hope, fear, love, play the same music upon all heart-strings. The same great law of duty over-arches every man, and the same Heaven of God bends above him.

"Religion has to do with the deep-seated identities and not with the superficial differences. And though there have been many aristocratic religions in the world, it is the great glory of Christianity that it goes straight to the central similarities, and brushes aside, as of altogether secondary importance, all the subordinate diversities, grappling with the great facts which are common to humanity, and with the large hopes which all may inherit."

All of this is indeed gloriously true, and it is possible to go on from there and see that in the deepest and most important things there is no difference, and thus the gospel is a gospel for the whole world, because it deals with all men on the same level. We believe, however, that we have covered this facet of the truth by showing that the gospel is universal. We have abundantly covered the fact of the universality of man's sin as we have come down the terrible road of the first chapters, leading through the swamps of men's sins and causing us to know the stench of all that is decayed, and decaying along the highway of humanity. Likewise, we have shown that the righteousness of God is unto all. The gospel of Jesus Christ is the power of God unto everyone that believeth, regardless of racial or religious background.

Our text at this point is not, then, a repetition of that which has gone before, nor is it a summary of the truths which have been expressed. It is the announcement of all that follows, and refers rather to God than to man. It would be merely trite at this point in the epistle to declare that there is no difference between man and man.

A DIVINE DECREE

The simple meaning of our text at this point is that there is no difference between the method that God uses to declare men lost sinners and the method He uses to declare that they are as righteous as Himself. The text applies to God and not to man. In spite of all that man may argue, there is a divine decree which has gone forth declaring that all have sinned and come short of God's glory. And in exactly the same way there has gone forth a divine decree that God will justify the sinner who believes in Christ by a declaration that it is so, and not by any intrinsic righteousness that is in the man.

What makes right and wrong? Anthropologists who have abandoned the Bible will tell you that the standards of morality differ under a hundred skies and that what is right in one civilization is taboo in another civilization. The natives of a tropical island, who have been separated from their fellow men for several years, have developed systems of living that are intricate and which flow from the rigidity of their circumstances. For example, in a society where some disease wiped out a large segment of the feminine population there has arisen a pagan civilization of polyandry and the minority of women that remain have several husbands apiece. In other tribes the opposite situation has developed, and there is to be found a polygamy which grants to men the use of several wives. In some lands the number is limited, in other places it is unlimited.

When we come to the lands of the Bible, we are faced with

a flat statement that one man is to have one wife and that while either lives there is to be no divergence from this rule whatsoever. The reason for our position is the flat statement of the Word of God. God has spoken and that is the end of all argument. At this point our Roman Catholic friends may argue that Protestants who claim to follow the Bible are most lax in their application of the Biblical principles. We are first to agree and to say that here the followers of Rome are correct because in this instance their doctrine is in accordance with the Bible. We go so far as to claim that many Protestants take a lax view of marriage in spite of the Bible and not because of it, and that frequently they have built up for themselves a rationalization to protect their own thinking —thinking which the Bible would call adulterous and which the Bible announces will be brought under the scrutiny of God at the judgment that will surely come.

THE ONLY ARBITER

Inherent in our text, then, is the idea that the Word of God is the only arbiter of right and wrong. God makes a decree and that decree will stand forever, or until He brings in some new principle that will make the first decree void. Thus the statement of any man that is contrary to the Word of God is condemned in advance by the divine Word.

A Hollywood actress goes to Italy and has an affair with an Italian director. When the illegitimate child is born, the nation's outstanding radio commentator pleads with the public for tolerance and for understanding. After all, he argues, true love is a rare and wonderful thing, and how noble for a woman to follow after and be willing to risk all for love. This should cause our profound admiration. But the Word of God says simply, as we shall see when we come to the seventh chapter of this epistle, "The woman that hath an husband is bound by the law to that husband so long as he liveth . . . so then if, while her husband liveth, she be married to another man, she shall be called an adulteress" (Rom. 7:2, 3). There is no room for what men might call interpretation; the fact is absolute and there is no honest room for departure from the flat statement of the Word of God.

Thomas Carlyle translated Luther's great hymn:

> God's Word, for all their craft and force,
>   One moment will not linger;
> But in spite of Hell, shall have its course:
>   'Tis written by His finger.
> And though they take our life,
> Goods, honor, children, wife,
> Yet is their profit small:
> These things shall vanish all;
> The Word of God remaineth.

While our text, then, carries with it the implications of the finality of the revealed will of God as being the only test for right and wrong, the primary meaning of the text concerns the oneness of the method of the two operations of God concerning the declaration of guilt and the declaration of righteousness. If we may paraphrase our text it will read as follows: "God's method of imparting righteousness is a divine method. It is witnessed by the law and the prophets. It is a method of offering righteousness to every member of the human race and of making the righteousness operative and effective in all of those who believe God's simple Word. There is no difference between this method of offering righteousness by the *fiat* of God and the declaration of man's sinfulness by the *fiat* of God. I, God, declared that all men in the world of time and space have sinned and have come short of My glory, and it is so because I say it is so. In exactly the same way I now declare to be perfect in My sight, and absolutely perfect, all those who believe in My Word about the Lord Jesus Christ, and they are perfect because I say they are perfect, and it is so because I say it is so."

RIGHTEOUS IN CHRIST

Now at this point—in our exposition into the Epistle to the Romans—there is no further need of laboring the argument that God has declared that all men have sinned. But we shall now be spending many a chapter, the Lord willing, in showing that the righteousness of God is declared upon us and within us who believe, and that we are declared to be righteous in Christ totally apart from what we are or what we do.

God flatly says that He looks upon all believers as being perfect as the Lord Jesus Christ is perfect. He says that He sees us in Christ and that we are thus joined to Christ and to be found in Him. If believers can lay hold upon the glory of this truth and realize that they are to be seen by God as being in Christ, then a thousand theological questions are settled, and a thousand practical questions are settled also. We need never have another doubt as to our eternal acceptance before God in Christ, and we can know that our salvation is an eternal fact. We may be like the old Scotch lady who said that she often trembled on the rock, but that she had learned that the rock never trembled under her. We may even go beyond this and come to the place where we are so attached to the rock that our own trembling ceases.

If we come to that place, where we are aware of our position in Christ, we will be like the other Scotch lady whose answer to her young minister showed such clear faith and realization of the truth of her position in Christ. The story goes that a young minister came to visit in the home of an aged woman who was dying. He was recently out of theological seminary and had more theology than Bible in his head, and had not known much of the experimental joys of long and close living with the Saviour in the knowledge and power of the divine love. He was somewhat appalled at the apparent joy and certainty of the patient and began to counsel her to give diligence to make her calling and election sure. But the dear old saint had been walking with the Lord for many a year and was long past the stage of learning the ABC's of the gospel. She gave a testimony so clear that the young man was frightened and pressed her to go back and be less presumptuous with God. She answered, "Young man, if I should nae be in Heaven the guid Lord would lose more than I cauld ever lose." This amazed him more than her first attitude, and he broke out at once, asking for an explanation. The old lady answered, "If I should nae be in Heaven all that I could lose would be my own soul, for that is all I have to lose. But if I should nae be in Heaven the guid Lord would lose His name and honor, for He has promised to save them to the uttermost that come to Him by Christ, and that is the way which I have come." And of course, she was perfectly right.

SAFETY AND CERTAINTY

That is the point of the great declaration that is here set before us. God is saying to us: "You have accepted My verdict about your lost position and your sinfulness in my sight? Then accept with the same certainty My verdict that I have declared you to be righteous in and through the Lord Jesus Christ. It is a finished work." There is no difference between the two declarations.

God declares that when the Lord Jesus Christ died, I died with Him. God declares that when Jesus Christ was buried my sins were buried with Him. God declares that when the Lord Jesus Christ was raised from the dead I was raised with Him. God declares that when the Lord Jesus Christ ascended to Heaven I was taken up to Heaven with Him. God says that when Jesus Christ took His seat on the throne of the Father in Heaven I was seated with Him in the Heavenly places. Therefore, says God, you are to look upon yourself as being in Christ in every phase of His being. And since He is at present seated on the throne of Heaven, then that is where the true believer is in the sight of God.

The safety of the believer in Christ depends upon the fact that there is no difference between the method which God adopted in declaring him once lost and the method He has adopted in declaring him now forever righteous in Christ. Here is the basis and ground of our confidence and trust. This should be the theme of our song: We are forever righteous in Christ—God has declared us righteous.

And yet I find no hymns which sing the truth thus. I have beside me an English hymn book with over a thousand of the greatest hymns of the church. I turn to it frequently for expression of truth in the great poetry of our hymnody. But when I began to turn through the book to find a hymn that would illustrate the truths I have just been setting forth, I found none. The book is divided in an orderly fashion. After hymns of adoration and worship, there are hymns concerning God the Father, with subdivisions for His being, His work in creation and providence, and His love in redemption. Then there are almost two hundred hymns about Christ—His glory, name, and grace; His incarnation; His life, teaching, and example; His sufferings and death; His resurrection and ascension; His priesthood and sympathy; His kingdom, present and future. Following this there are hymns on the Holy Spirit; hymns on the Scriptures, hymns on the gospel call; and then three hundred hymns on the Christian life. I searched through these three hundred hymns diligently to find some verse that might describe the truth I am setting forth here, and I could not find one. Then I sat back and thought of hymns that I had heard that were not in the book. Finally, I remembered a verse from a hymn by Paul Rader. It was not in any of our great hymnals, but I believe that he had seized this same truth, for he wrote:

> Buried with Christ, and raised with Him, too,
> What is there left for me to do?
> Simply to cease from struggle and strife,
> Simply to walk in newness of life.

And even that is only a part of it, for we are to understand that God has declared it so, and that therefore it stands more eternally true than the mountains. Perhaps the verse I need is

> How firm a foundation, ye saints of the Lord,
> Is laid for your faith in His excellent Word.
> What more can He say than to you He hath said,
> To you, who for refuge to Jesus have fled?

If it be understood that this refers to the declaration that He has made us righteous in Christ and counts us thus righteous forever, then this can be the song of praise that wells from our hearts. What more can He say than to you He hath said? There is nothing more that can be said.

GOD SPEAKS

The declaration of our righteousness stands upon a foundation as sure as that on which stands the declaration of our guilt. It was the declaration of our guilt that caused us to bow before the wrath of God. It is the declaration of our righteousness in Christ that can cause us to stand boldly before Him in that day and even today. For there is no difference: both are by declaration. It was the declaration of our guilt that caused our conscience to be stricken. It is the declaration of our righteousness in Christ that stills our conscience forever. For there is no difference: it is God who declares it. It was the declaration of God that declared me to be dead in trespasses and sin. It is the declaration of God that declares me to be alive forevermore in Christ. For there is no difference in the *modus* of the two declarations. You were condemned, God thunders from Mount Sinai. I tremble and die before the word. You are free and righteous, God sings from Calvary. I arise and live. For there is no difference between the sources of the verdicts. In both cases it is God who speaks. In both cases He is talking about me. Then if I fall before His speech at one declaration, I must rise by His speech because of the other declaration. There is no difference.

When first I began to come to the knowledge of the meaning of this verse, I hesitated to set it forth as I have done because such an explanation is not to be found in any of the commentaries. For hundreds of years men have been reading this passage, and have been saying that there was no difference between men in their place of sin before God. High and low, rich and poor. One man illustrates it by saying that in a prison there are men there for life sentences for great crimes and men that are there for a year or two for lesser crimes, but that in the sight of the law there are no innocent men; there is no difference. And while, as we have said, all of that is true, and we admit that it is true, yet there is something more glorious here.

From my prison position, I who was condemned by the Word of God, now stand forth as justified. I will not even say any more that I am a pardoned sinner. I claim a far higher place. The Judge who once declared me guilty has not now declared me free, but has declared me righteous. The Word of Him who placed me under death has now placed me in life. The declaration that once announced that I was of the first man, of Adam's brood and condemned in Adam, now takes me from the side of Christ and declares me to be the bride of the second Man, who is the Lord from Heaven. If the one declaration was true because it was God who said it, then the second declaration is true because it is the same God who says it. There is no difference. We are now declared righteous, and this by God Himself. I will not yield my position: it is true—in Christ I am the righteousness of God. Saved and safe. Saved, safe, and righteous. God said it.

CHAPTER VIII

Falling Short

". . . There is no difference: for all have sinned, and come short of the glory of God" (Rom. 3:22, 23).

THERE is no difference between the way, on the one hand, in which God has declared men to be sinners, and therefore condemned, and the way, on the other hand, in which God declares men to be righteous, without respect to their antecedents or their characters, or their good works.

The first of the declarations is now summarized for the last time. The whole section of the Epistle to the Romans from the point at 1:16, following the introduction, down to the present text has been the setting forth of man's complete ruin in sin. Now the whole doctrine is crystallized in one phrase. All have sinned and are falling short of the glory of God.

SIN UNIVERSAL

The statement presents to us God's verdict as to the universality of sin, the nature of man's shortcoming, and the goal which he has failed to reach.

It will not be necessary for us to labor the first of these points at length. The ground has been largely covered in the previous expositions. At this point, however, God is declaring all men to be sinners in a different way from that which He has employed in the previous statements presenting this doctrine. In the first chapter man was declared to be a sinner, and examples of his depravity were brought forth to prove it. In the second chapter the entire race was declared to be sinful, and one by one the hiding places of these who sought to deny the truth in one way or another were laid bare and the nakedness of their false position was made obvious. In the third chapter the doctrine was presented yet again, and the whole of the nature and being of man was dissected by the divine scalpel and the sinfulness of every member made manifest.

Now the declaration is of a different nature. The key, as we have seen in our last study, lies in the true meaning of the phrase, "There is no difference." God announces: "I, the Lord God Almighty, say what is good and what is bad; I am the One who announces what is holy and what is unholy. It is My Word which decides who is sinful and who is righteous. I am the Lord who searches the hearts and tries the thoughts; therefore, I the Lord shall be the only one to say what is righteous and what is sinful. There is no difference between the method by which I announce men are sinners and the method by which I declare men righteous. And in this text I declare that all have sinned. I would not have to bring a single proof if I did not wish to do so. It would be enough that I say that men displease Me. Who is there to argue the case? To what court would they appeal for a hearing? To what law would they resort to bolster their case? I am the Lord, and beside Me there is no other. Therefore, hear the Word of the Lord: All have sinned."

This is the flat declaration of the Creator of the universe and the Author of the supernatural Word. All have sinned. It makes no difference what your thought is about the matter: all have sinned. It makes no difference what your religious ideas: all have sinned. It makes no difference if you declare that sin is an error of mortal mind: all have sinned. You may attempt to do away with the idea of sin by philosophical speculation. It makes no difference: all have sinned. When the Communists came to power in Russia they published a new dictionary. Under the Russian word for "sin" was the definition: "archaic and bourgeois word denoting the transgression of a mythical divine law." Such definitions make no difference: all have sinned.

COMPLETE LACK

In the second place, our text declares that all have fallen short of the glory of God. We cited this verse in a previous study to show one of the various characteristics of sin, and pointed out that the word used here is a term which was used in ancient times for a "complete lack," for "want" in the sense of being devoid of something. For example, we know of people who sometimes get financially involved to the point where they have many debts and no cash. When the liabilities exceed the assets, there are times when the individual sees no way out other than to go before the court for a reorganization of his affairs, and to be declared a bankrupt. It is conceivable that, in ancient times, the Greek word that is in our text might have been used to describe a man in such a condition. In that case our text would read: For all have sinned and are bankrupt of the glory of God.

The papyri discoveries in Egypt show the word was used in the very days of Christ for an illiterate—in which case we would translate our text: All have sinned and are illiterate of the knowledge of God. And again, even while our Lord was alive on earth, the word was used to express the idea of missing the season, when a farmer failed to get his seed in the ground on time, and thus failed to get a crop. Thus we might read the text: for all have sinned and have missed the season of the glory of God.

A REQUIRED STANDARD

That is enough of dictionary definitions for the term. Let me now give you an example from modern life that will, perhaps, help some better to understand the meaning of this great text. After World War I, there were many tens of thousands of American soldiers left in France whose supreme desire was to get home as rapidly as possible. Discipline was greatly relaxed from the tension of the actual wartime, and the men were securing as much leave as possible in order to see the sights of Europe. In a certain village about a hundred miles from Paris, there was a group of American soldiers, consisting of a lieutenant and about forty men, whose duty was to guard an ammunition dump. Thousands of cases of shells were stored in a field and guards walked their rounds to protect the explosives. There was little to do outside of the brief periods of guard duty, and the men amused themselves as best they could and waited for the day when they would receive orders to embark for home.

There came a time when the lieutenant received permission to go on leave for two weeks, and he left the group in charge of the master sergeant. A few days afterwards, there came a motor-

cycle messenger from General Pershing's headquarters bringing
an order that greatly excited the soldiers. The order stated that
2,700 men were to be chosen to march in the peace parades of
London, Paris, Brussels and Rome. When the corporal and sergeant
read the order they looked at each other and said, "Boy, that
would be something to go around Europe at the expense of the
Government!" But as they read on, they discovered that there
were two conditions imposed as standards for selection. The first
brought them no difficulty, for it stated that every candidate had
to have a clean record—no man would be chosen who had been
court-martialed. But the second condition gave them pause. The
order stated that every man applying had to be at least one meter
and eighty-six centimeters tall.

The corporal looked at the sergeant and the sergeant looked
at the corporal, and then one of them asked how much one meter
and eighty-six centimeters was. Neither knew the answer. Then
the corporal said the most natural thing under the circumstances:
"At any rate, Sarge, I am taller than you."

MAN-MADE STANDARDS

When mess time came and the news spread around the group,
it was the same thing over again. No one knew the metric
system. The men got into an argument as to their relative heights,
and soon they were standing up, back to back, to see who was the
tallest man in the company. Finally, they knew their comparative
heights, all the way from Slim down to Shorty. Slim was very
proud and told them that he would send them a post card from
Rome and would take a look at the English girls for the rest of
them. Poor Shorty received the good-natured banter of his fellows.

Under the circumstances, I repeat, they did the normal, natural
thing. They were in ignorance of the required standard. The
appointment was greatly desired. This led them to set up artificial
standards of their own and measure themselves by themselves.
There was some pride developed in the men who were taller, for
were they not the most probable candidates?

But there soon came the day when the lieutenant returned.
The news was communicated to him, and he asked if there were
any candidates. The sergeant replied, "The trouble is, sir, that we

do not know what one meter and eighty-six centimeters is." The lieutenant knew enough French to go out into the village and bring back a meter measure. Soon a mark was made on the wall of the required height. Now the men were no longer measuring themselves with themselves. They had to go up against a mark on the wall that was unchanged and unchangeable according to the orders from headquarters. One or two men backed up to the mark and their companions told them that they were an inch or so short of the requirement. Some men merely looked at the mark and knew that there was no hope. Finally, a call was made for Slim and he came to be measured. He puffed himself up to his greatest possible height and stood there, rigid and swollen as they measured him. When the ordeal was ended, it was discovered that even he was too short, though by no more than a quarter of an inch. Thus, not one of that group qualified by General Pershing's standard.

AN ABSOLUTE REQUIREMENT

Of course, General Pershing got his 2,700 men. I saw them when they came under the Arch of Triumph on Bastille Day, the fourteenth of July, in what must have been one of the greatest parades of all history. These men, all in new uniforms, and with American Beauty roses tied to their bayonets, made a stirring sight as they marched down the Champs Elysees, each one of them at least one meter and eighty-six centimeters tall, that is, more than 6 feet one and a fifth inches.

Now, the point of my story, however, lies in the fact that Pershing did not secure any of his marching men from the group I have described. He was not asking that they be *about* so tall, but that they fill an absolute requirement. His was no demand of an approximation, but a rigid, inflexible demand. And the heart of my story lies in the fact that tall Slim did not march in the parade any more than did short Shorty.

The spiritually minded will readily see the application that I make of this simple story. Only those whose hearts are blinded can fail to see its truth. God is in His Heaven and is telling men on what basis they may enter in to abide with Him. He has the right to make His own rules, even as we human beings make the rules for entry into our houses. You do not go to a man's house in the middle of the night and seek to enter silently and surreptitiously by a ladder through a second story window. If you attempted to do such a thing and received a charge of buckshot in the head, any reasonable jury would acquit the householder of the shooting without a moment's hesitation. If you wish entry into a man's house, you go to his front door and ring the bell, or knock on the door, or make some other noise signifying your presence. Now the Lord God has as much right, yes, far more right to make the rules for entry into His home, Heaven, than any man has for the entry into an earthy home.

The rule which God has made for entry into Heaven is that men shall measure up to His glory and be as perfect as He is. This rigorous standard is to be found throughout the Bible. The Old Testament was built around the command of God, "Ye shall be holy, for I am holy" (Lev. 11:44). It is exemplified in the Man, Christ Jesus.

ABSOLUTE PERFECTION

If you wish to understand what I have called the doctrinal plot of the Bible, you must realize that God has demanded absolute perfection as the prerequisite for entry into Heaven. It is quite reasonable, for if He should demand anything less, it would mean that Heaven would slowly become filled with men who were imperfect. Thus Heaven would never more be Heaven, but merely earth moved to Heaven. Stop and think of your own case. If you were taken into Heaven exactly as you are at this present moment, without any change whatsoever, you would befoul Heaven; and it would be no longer pure and holy, as it must be in order to be a fit dwelling place for the holy God.

But, when the law was given to men, they, like the soldiers in my story, did not understand the meaning of the terms. "Be ye holy" meant no more to them than one meter eighty-six centimeters meant to the soldiers in the village. So men did the most natural thing in the world. They began measuring themselves among themselves. Little by little the human race adopted various standards which classify human beings, not according to their physical stature from Shorty down to Slim, but according to various other classifications, from the height of pride down to the dwarfed outcast. Some men are even so foolish as to measure by the pigmentation of their skins. They have thought that intrinsic worth had something to do with whether a man was white or dark-skinned. Any sensible man knows, immediately, that there are going to be white men in Hell as well as in Heaven, and there are going to be Negroes in Heaven as well as in Hell.

> It makes no difference whether the flesh
> Be black, or white or brown.
> The dying Saviour wore for all
> The thorny crown.

There have been others who have measured themselves on the basis of a human culture, or educational attainment, or the performance of certain rites or ceremonies. All of this is as futile as the measuring of the soldiers in the French mess hall. How unjust God would be if He made salvation on the basis of something in man. For if He had made such a standard, it would mean that some would be totally incapable of fulfilling the requirements and others would have a natural advantage that would give them a head start.

Suppose that God had made entrance into Heaven on the basis of money. If the requirements were the possession of a hundred million dollars, then ninety-nine and a fraction per cent of all men would be condemned to Hell at the start without any possible hope of meeting the requirements. If God had made salvation on the basis of human intelligence, then Heaven would be peopled with a few Einsteins, Newtons and similar minds, and the morons and the ordinary people would be in Hell. Such standards would be totally unjust, because men are born without the possibilities of fulfilling either the standard of money or the standard of brains. In the same way, if God had made salvation on the basis of human character, He would have been unjust. A man or woman fortunate enough to have been born in a home where godly parents kept a good strap and applied it properly to give the children the lessons in character training that were necessary, would have an inestimable advantage over a poor unfortunate born to a dissolute woman and a perverted father. Such an one, permitted from infancy to run his own way in the warrens of our city slums, for example, would speedily develop a life of sin that would mark him before he even came to the age of accountability as one who was destined, first, for skid row, and then for Hell.

But God Almighty does not work on any such unjust basis. He puts up His perfect standard, measures you by it, declares that you are short and can never do anything to meet His requirements, and then proceeds, by the same method, to declare righteous the ungodly who believe in the Lord Jesus Christ.

In the case of the soldiers, Pershing found tall men in other camps. But with God there were none who could fulfill His standards. All have sinned and are falling short of the glory of God. He put up His standard of measurement and the whole race is declared to fall short of that which He demands. You may look at that standard of measurement in the document of the law of God, or you may see it embodied in the Saviour, the Lord Jesus Christ. But either way you look at it, you and all other men have fallen short of the glory of God. If you measure yourself by the written law, you are short; you have sinned. If you seek to stand beside the Lord Jesus Christ, you are immediately seen to be pitifully dwarfed in comparison.

FAR SHORT

Nor should any man ever think that he gets anywhere near the standard that has been set by God. In our story of the soldiers, Slim missed the mark by only a quarter of an inch. But the Lord Jesus Christ says that men have fallen short of God's mark by much more than this. In the Sermon on the Mount, there is an application of the principle we are setting forth. The Lord looked out over the people and said, "Except your righteousness shall exceed the righteousness of the scribes and Pharisees, ye shall in no case enter into the kingdom of Heaven" (Matt. 5:20). These men had whittled down the law and had put spiritual wedges in their shoes and had said, "We pass. We pass." The Lord says to the multitude: "It is not so. They do not pass." And our Lord adds: "Which one of you by taking thought can add one cubit unto his stature?" (Matt. 6:27). A cubit is eighteen inches. The

Lord, briefly, is telling men that they are not merely a fraction of an inch short, but that they are short in a proportion that makes it impossible for a man to provide the difference which is lacking. No man can grow to the stature that will meet God's moral requirements. And any man who attempts to make stilts for himself and to pass the day of measurement will discover that the judgment of God is according to truth, and he will surely be cut down. There is no escape. All have sinned and are falling short of the glory of God.

I have been citing this verse as it reads in the Greek, for in the original there is a very interesting change of tense. Literally it reads, "All sinned and are falling short of the glory of God." I am inclined to believe that God designed this difference in tense for a definite purpose. "All have sinned" does not refer so much to the fact that we have committed overt acts of sin through the determination of our own choice, but that when Adam sinned we sinned also. The whole genetic pattern of the human race was affected, and the disease of sin became a part of the racial burden. Sin is not acquired, it is congenital. God is looking upon the race in this verse as a part of Adam, and is declaring that in His sight the defection took place when Adam sinned. We will not go into the matter further at this point because the argument will occupy a large place in our exposition of the fifth chapter. Here it is enough to say that God tells us that in consequence of the sin of our original parents every member of the human race is constantly falling short of the glory of God. The falling short is a continuous process.

OUR CASE HOPELESS

The Greek verb which, in our text, is translated "come short" is found in many places in the New Testament and is translated by nine different English words. These are "come behind, come short, be destitute, fail, lack, suffer need, want, to be in want, and to be the worse." Truly our case is hopeless apart from the intervening grace of God. No matter what your efforts, you are falling short of the glory of God. If I take you out into a field and tell you to jump to the moon, some of you would not get more than six inches or a foot off the ground. The world's champion high jumper would be able to get about six feet off the ground. With the use of a pole, the champion pole vaulter could swing himself twenty-odd feet off the ground. But that is all. No man could reach the moon by his unaided efforts. And the man who gets twenty feet off the ground is not much nearer the moon than the decrepit old lady who might be able to jump but six inches, or the invalid who cannot move at all. All sinned and are falling short of the glory of God.

No man has ever made a gesture toward God that has reached God. That is why the Lord summarizes the commandments with the slaying word, "Thou shalt love the Lord thy God with all thy heart, and with all thy soul, and with all thy mind . . . Thou shalt love thy neighbor as thyself" (Matt. 22:37, 39). What condemnation is here! What death! What a revelation of the failure of man! Have you ever had an emotion of the heart that was not for God? Then you are falling short of His glory. Have you ever had a rising of the soul that was not for God? Then you are falling short of His glory. Have you ever had a thought of the mind that was not toward God? Then you are falling short of His glory. Have you ever loved yourself more than your neighbor? Then you are falling short of His glory.

Stop your efforts then, and rest in the work which He has done and which is all sufficient, and which alone satisfies God. If you will completely stop trusting yourself and if you will utterly trust Christ, God will count you righteous in His Son.

CHAPTER IX

The Glory of God

"For all have sinned, and come short of the glory of God" (Rom. 3:23).

THERE are some phrases which we use so often that their meaning is no longer known to us. I have learned to test myself on all phrases that I read in the Bible, for it is possible to hear them from childhood and think that they are understood when in reality they are mere words that have no clear meaning for us. The present is an example for though it contained a phrase that I have used, perhaps, ten thousand times, I found that I did not know what it meant until I had spent a good many hours in plunging into some of its depths.

That phrase is "the glory of God." "For all sinned, and are falling short of the glory of God." What is the glory of God?

GLORY

First of all, we have to find out the meaning of the word *glory*. That may seem an easy matter but it is not so simple as it seems. I tested several people to find out their concept of the word. Giving a piece of paper and a pen to an individual, I would say: "Write down in two minutes your idea of the meaning of the word *glory;* then write down the meaning of the phrase *the glory of God."* They were not allowed to consult a dictionary or to talk with anyone else about the matter. What would you say if you had only a few minutes to express your understanding of the meaning of the word *glory* and the phrase *the glory of God?*

As I tell you the definitions that were written down by the persons I interviewed, you must not take their definitions as correct; some phrases are right and some are wrong. I am merely stating what I found before proceeding to give you the result of deeper study of the subject. A business man wrote that glory is "complete and uninterrupted satisfaction and perfection"; and he added that

the glory of God is "the daily defeat of Satan and the ultimate vindication of God's righteousness." Another person, with many years
of university education and graduate degrees in English literature,
could find no other word for glory than the single word "luminosity."
A high school graduate who is a student in one of the Bible in-
stitutes wrote that glory is "something splendid and brilliant; a
blast of breathtaking beauty and splendor"; while the glory of
God is something that is "breath-taking and inexplainable." Another
similar student wrote "all honor and beauty, all dominion, beauty
and perfection." Another wrote, "beauty, praise and power."
A professor of philosophy wrote down first the German word,
Herrlichkeit, and followed this with "that which belongs to a
lord"; while for the definition of the glory of God he wrote, "the
effulgence of the inexpressible; the manifestation of the luminous;
the exaltation of the majestic; the incarnation of the divine."

It can readily be seen that there are widespread variations
in the concept, yet through all of the minds that I questioned there
runs the general idea of something that is dazzlingly brilliant,
and that is beyond human capacity to comprehend. This at least
has a nearness to a part of the truth. But now let us go to the
dictionaries for a moment to see what the lexicographers have
set down through the centuries. It is interesting that the group
of people whom I questioned failed, with one exception, to define
the term glory, as apart from the glory of God, in any way that
accorded with the primary dictionary definitions. The high school
graduate won over the university trained people in setting down
the word "praise" as her definition. For the Oxford English Dictionary, which has the glory of being the greatest dictionary in
the world in any language, defines the term thus: "Exalted, and
in modern use, merited praise, honor, or admiration accorded by
common consent to a person or thing; honorable fame; renown."

EARTH'S GLORY

It is in this sense that Sophocles wrote: "It is the brave man's
part to live with glory, or with glory die." And Cicero was thinking in the same way when he declaimed: "There is a sufficient glory
in the very consciousness of a noble deed." Another classical

writer, Publilius Syrus, before the time of Christ, said: "How hard it is to maintain inherited glory."

This glory and fame of man has been sought by many who have ended up with nothing more than vainglory. When men have sought nothing more than the praise of men, they have spent much for little, and their plight is best expressed by Michel de Montaigne, who wrote: "Who is there that does not voluntarily exchange health, repose and life itself for reputation and glory, the most useless, frivolous, and false coin that passes current amongst us?" Shakespeare realized how futile human glory could be, and wrote: "Like madness is the glory of this life," and in another place:

> Glory is like a circle in the water,
> Which never ceaseth to enlarge itself
> Till, by broad spreading it disperse to naught.

The Bible gives us many illustrations of the swift passing of earth's glory, and the uselessness of its pursuit. All of the Scripture teaching was well summed up by Thomas à Kempis, in his *Imitation of Christ,* when he wrote in a phrase that has become a modern proverb: *O quam cito transit gloria mundi!* "How quickly passes away the glory of this world!" For men will seek renown and praise and honor (which three things may sum up human glory) in things that are foolish. How often they seek glory merely because the human ego wishes to be recognized. Shakespeare, in one of his sonnets, speaks of the trivial things that men spend themselves on:

> Some glory in their birth, some in their skill,
> Some in their wealth, some in their bodies' force,
> Some in their garments, though newfangled ill;
> Some in their hawks and hounds, some in their horse.

Frederick the Great understood that the praise, fame and honor given by the multitude was, in reality, worthless, and wrote in a letter to Voltaire: "When we examine what glory is, we discover that it is nearly nothing. To be judged by the ignorant and esteemed by imbeciles, to hear one's name spoken by a rabble who approve, reject, love or hate without reason — that is nothing to be proud of."

As long as men are men some will have praise and honor and esteem of others. Some will seek it when they do not fully deserve it. Some will seek the deeds that bring it and care little for the honor that comes, living for the doing of the deeds and not for the approbation.

GOD'S GLORY

It is against the background of all this, that our text comes with striking impact, "All have sinned, and are falling short of the glory of God." For if the glory of man is honor, esteem, praise, reputation and an estimate of genuine and merited worth, the glory of God is the honor, esteem, praise, reputation and estimate of the genuine and merited worth of God. It is for this reason that the shades of meanings between some of these words are so difficult to distinguish. In our own language, the shades of difference are very slight between such words as honor, esteem, glory, praise, magnify and still others whose definitions shade off toward other meanings. This same overlapping is to be found in the Greek words of the New Testament and in the Hebrew of the Old Testament. The proof is in the fact that the English word *honor* is used to translate two different Greek words, which between them are translated by a total of nine different English words. Three different Greek words are translated by the English word *glory*; and these same three Greek words are also rendered by ten other English words.

The commonest of the Greek words translated *glory* is *doxa*. It has come down to us in our word *doxology*. How it got to mean glory, praise and honor is an interesting study. Hundreds of years before Christ, there was a word commonly used in Greece which means "to seem, to appear." The noun of the words came to mean "an opinion," which is the way a matter appears or seems to one person. This word for opinion has given to us such words as *paradox, orthodox,* and *heterodox* for "strange opinion," "straight opinion," and "other opinion," respectively. Little by little the word began to be used for an opinion *of a person,* whether a good opinion or a bad opinion, and, finally, in the Bible, it began to be used for a good opinion only. From there on, it comes to mean praise, honor and glory resulting from the good opinion.

Now it is evident that the word *glory*, both in our language and in the Biblical languages, means something much more than mere praise and honor. By putting together what we have seen about the original word and the growth of the idea, we are able to comprehend some of the meaning of the glory of God. Men who had the right opinion of God were able to form a correct estimate of His greatness and majesty. Hence, they began to consider more and more of the attributes of God which He has revealed: His power; His majesty; His love; His greatness; His lovingkindness; His tender mercies; His goodness; His perfections without end. Therefore, little by little, the word for "opinion," which became the opinion about God, came to include praise of God for all that He is and for all that He thinks and does. I would say that in the word *glory* dwells all the fulness of the Godhead philologically. The friends who submitted to my test and wrote down their definitions of the word *glory* are all correct in a sense, for there is nothing that can be said of the praise of God that does not redound to His glory. When the philosophy professor gave me the German word *Herrlichheit* as a definition, it was indeed true, for if that word be broken into pieces we find that it begins with the German word for the Lord Jehovah, *der Herr*. And the whole word means "lordliness." Therefore "glory" would mean anything that becomes the Lord Jehovah.

WORSHIP

We have a word in English which has come down to us from the Anglo-Saxon and which might have been the ordinary word used for glory except that the French word *gloire* was the one that was adopted in practical use. The Anglo-Saxon word which competed with the word "glory" for a time is our word "worth." When we think of the worth of God we are thinking of the glory of God. And when we praise Him, we are acknowledging His worth and are therefore engaged in the contemplation of His worthship. Now as "worth-ship" was hard to pronounce, the difficult letters were dropped in the course of time and our noun "worship" is the result. There is no difference in meaning between the worship of God, the praise and adoration of God and the glory

of God. One of our great hymns of true worship expresses the
difficulty of containing all of these thoughts in human language:

> O could I speak the matchless worth!
> O could I sound the glories forth
> Which in my Saviour shine!
> I'd soar and touch the heavenly strings,
> And vie with Gabriel while he sings
> In notes almost divine.
>
> I'd sing the precious blood He spilt,
> My ransom from the dreadful guilt
> Of sin and wrath divine.
> I'd sing His glorious righteousness
> In which all perfect Heavenly dress,
> My soul shall ever shine.
>
> I'd sing the character He bears,
> And all the forms of love He wears,
> Exalted on His throne;
> In loftiest songs of sweetest praise,
> I would to everlasting days,
> Make all His glories known.

On several occasions in the New Testament men were told
to give glory to God. How and why this was to be done is apparent
in the context of the verses. In one case, Luke 17:18, glory was
given to God by declaring one's gratitude to God for blessings
received. In another case, Romans 4:20, Abraham is said to have
given glory to God by not distrusting the promises of God. In
other instances, there is said to be "glory due" to God, and this
is expressed by celebrating His praises. The man born blind who
received his sight through the Lord Jesus was told by the Pharisees
to give the glory to God (John 9:24). This shows that they
realized that it was glorifying to God for man to acknowledge
that any gift or work of power and majesty could come from God
alone. This was, of course, true, but they did not realize that
there stood among them the Lord Jesus Christ, whom they knew
not. Thus the blind man properly gave the glory to the Lord
Jesus Christ because He is God. It was the failure of King Herod
to do this very thing that caused his death. In the Book of Acts
it is recorded that when Herod made an oration the people cried
that it was the voice of a god and not the voice of a man. And

because Herod did not give the glory to God, the account states that the angel of the Lord smote him dead (Acts 12:23).

MAN'S CHIEF END

The glory of God is the wonderful being of God: His names of love and justice; His acts of kindness and judgment; His praise and His perfections. It is also the splendor that surrounds Him, the burning bliss that causes the seraphim to veil their faces. No wonder, therefore, that the Westminster fathers who wrote the famous catechism used for so long in Scotland and in the church that derives from that Scriptural heritage, begins with the question: "What is the chief end of man?" and answers the question with the great statement: "Man's chief end is to glorify God and enjoy Him for ever."

This inner glory of God has an outward manifestation. Now the original Greek word *doxa* was used to translate a Hebrew word *shekinah* which has given to the word *glory* a second meaning that is far different from the one we have been considering. This Hebrew word means "splendor" and "brightness." It was this meaning that prompted one of my helpers to write as her definition for "glory" the word *luminosity*. The word, frequently used in this sense in the Talmud but not in the Bible, adds much to the meaning of the text in Romans, which states that man sinned and is falling short of the glory of God.

It was this splendor of God that Stephen saw when he was about to die. "He, being full of the Holy Spirit, looked up stedfastly into heaven, and saw the glory of God, and Jesus standing on the right hand of God" (Acts. 7:55). This is the glory by which heavenly beings are surrounded when they come to the earth, as in the case of Moses and Elijah in the transfiguration (Luke 9:31). This is the glory with which Moses' face shone so that the people could not look upon him when he came down from the mount (II Cor. 3:7).

This is the glory that was symbolized by a cloud throughout the Scriptures. For, of course, when it speaks of the cloud of glory it is not talking of a rain cloud. It has nothing to do with what we know as a cloud. This cloud, the cloud of glory, first appeared as the children of Israel were about to come out of

Egypt. It was darkness toward the Egyptians and light toward the people of God. This glory that went before them was fire by night and cloud by day. This is the glory which stood above the house until the time when their sin had become so great that the Lord removed the glory to Heaven, and it was said that the glory of the Lord had departed from Israel. This was the glory which appeared in the Heavens when the Lord Jesus was born and the shepherds were in the field. This is the cloud of glory into which Jesus ascended when He left earth for Heaven: He ascended into Heaven and a cloud of glory received Him out of their sight. This is the cloud that is announced for the return of the Lord when we read, "Behold, he cometh with clouds; and every eye shall see him" (Rev. 1:7). This is the glory with which we shall one day be clothed when we shall see Him and be like Him, seeing Him as He is.

FALLING SHORT

The commentators are quite divided on the meaning of the phrase "falling short of the glory of God." Calvin takes it to mean merely "the approbation of God," and quotes the verse from John's Gospel where it is explained that many people believed on the Lord Jesus but they did not confess Him for fear of the Pharisees, "for they loved the praise of men more than the praise of God" (John 12:43). The word "praise" is the word that is translated "glory" in our text, but I am convinced that Calvin fell far short of the true meaning of this text. It would be a weak thought, indeed, if there were no more here than a statement that all sinned and are falling short of the approval of God. That is, of course, true, but somewhat inadequate. The word is so much more vast than this that we must seek a deeper meaning.

Other commentators give still other meanings. Beza, for instance, thinks that this is a statement that man never reaches the happiness which God bestows, and that this cannot be attained by human labor but by the rest of faith. Other commentators think that the verse teaches that man comes short of rendering the praise that is truly due to God.

I would make the text to mean all of this and something more. Since, in the mind of Paul, the original word *doxa* included all that we have seen above, plus the old Hebrew word for brilliance and splendor, we may consider that man has come short of all of the inner and outer glory of the Lord. We have long held that man in the Garden of Eden was clothed before the fall with light; and, that when sin came, Adam and Eve realized that the light was gone and that they were naked. The nakedness was not the nudity of the skin, but the absence of the glorious brilliance and splendor of righteousness. When man sinned, man lost this brightness and rushed to cover himself with fig leaves. This covering was, of course, no substitute, and it was not until the blood was shed and the skins of the animals given to our first parents that they were symbolically covered, having been relieved of the filthy rags of their own fig-leaf righteousness.

All of the efforts of the human race since that time have never availed to give even one individual the righteousness of God which was lost in the fall. All sinned (the aorist and not the perfect is used) and are falling short (present tense) of the glory of God. No man is attaining to the perfections of God which must be his if he is to fellowship with God in His Heaven. Once more we quote Binney's famous hymn:

> Eternal Light! Eternal Light!
> How pure the soul must be,
> When placed within Thy searching sight
> It shrinks not, but with undisturbed delight
> Can live, and look on Thee.
>
> The spirits that surround Thy throne,
> May bear the burning bliss,
> But that is surely theirs alone,
> Since they have never, never known
> A fallen world like this.
>
> O how shall I, whose native sphere
> Is dark, whose mind is dim,
> Before th' ineffable appear
> And on my unprotected spirit bear
> That uncreated beam.

"Little Binney," as his contemporaries called him, had seized the heart of the truth. It is the fact that God dwells in a brightness that no man can approach. Here is hidden all that the Bible teaches concerning the fact that no man can see God and live.

THE TABERNACLE

This truth becomes all the more evident when we consider the verses which follow our text. Paul was a Hebrew and had been raised with the teaching of the Old Testament, and his whole training was in the line of the worship prescribed in the Levitical code. He knew the tabernacle and everything that it stood for. He realized that the pillar of cloud and fire had hung over the Holy of Holies, and that this represented the dwelling place of God among men. He knew that men had to approach God but that they could not see Him face to face because of the brightness of His glory. In the next verses Paul will begin to talk about the mercy seat and the propitiatory sacrifices made by the shedding of the blood.

Paul is thinking of the tabernacle as he writes this verse. Men are afar off from God. They have fallen short. The cloud of glory hangs over the Holy place, and man could not approach it. He was kept away because of His own sins. Unless a way could be found for him to enter into the Holiest of all, he could never see God. That way is now about to be declared. Paul, who has already seen the glory on the road to Damascus, realizes that it must be entirely by the grace of God. He brings man therefore to the barrier and halts him there. Beyond the barrier lies the altar where the Lamb is to be slain. Unless the Lamb dies no man can come into the glory of God. In this verse he leaves us there, outside the barrier. But already we can look over into the verses which follow and we can see, by faith, that the Lamb will die, the laver will become a sea of crystal, the veil in the temple will be rent in twain, and the glory of the Lord shall be put to our account through the Lord Jesus Christ who cried out to God in His Gethsemane prayer: "The glory thou gavest me I have given them" (John 17:22). It is toward the altar and the sacrifice and the glory that we will now proceed to move.

> There is a way for man to rise
> To that sublime abode:
> An offering and a sacrifice,
> A Holy Spirit's tender energies,
> *An advocate with God.*

These, these prepare us for the sight
Of holiness above;
The sons of ignorance and night
May ever dwell in the eternal light,
Through the eternal Love.

CHAPTER X

Justification Without a Cause

"Being justified freely by his grace through the redemption that is in Christ Jesus" (Rom. 3:24).

THOUGH all sinned and are falling short of the glory of God, the Bible tells us that the Lord Jesus Christ brought us back to glory. The glory which man lost in Adam, and which he could never regain by his own efforts, the Lord Jesus Christ secured and brought to us by His redemptive death. "For it became him, for whom are all things, and by whom are all things, in bringing many sons into glory, to make the author of their salvation perfect through sufferings" (Heb. 2:10, marg.).

How were we brought back to the glory which had been lost to us forever so far as any worth in ourselves was concerned? Our text in the third of Romans now sets it forth: "Being justified freely by his grace through the redemption that is in Christ Jesus" (Rom. 3:24).

When man first sinned, God had no way of testing him other than His own perfect glory. Man, of course, had come short of that glory, and there was nothing to do but declare him dead in trespasses and sins and to evict him from the presence of God. But in the same way that God declared man to be a sinner, falling short of His glory, so God declares a man righteous, justifying him freely by His grace through the redemption that is in Christ Jesus.

DEFINITIONS

We have now come to the point in our study where we must set forth the true meaning of the term *justify,* and the cognate words *justification, just,* and *justifier.* I turn to the dictionary and am not at all satisfied with the definition that is given there. Even the Oxford English Dictionary falls short of the Biblical meaning when it defines the verb "justify" in the following terms:

91

"To absolve, acquit, exculpate; especially in theology, to declare free from the penalty of sin on the ground of Christ's righteousness, or to make inherently righteous by the infusion of grace." There is an approach to the truth but there is far more involved in the idea. Perhaps we can come to a truer meaning if we proceed, as a doctor would in making a diagnosis, by a process of elimination. Let us find some of the things that the term does not mean, and then we will be able to establish better what is the true meaning.

First of all, the verb *justify* is not a mere synonym for forgiveness. It includes forgiveness but it also includes so much more that to speak of justification in terms of forgiveness only is to lose the true sense of the word. Take, for example, a convict who has committed a great crime. The man against whom the crime was committed might freely forgive the criminal for the wrong that had been done, but that would not change his status before the law. He would still be a criminal, guilty in every way. Forgiveness does not take away guilt. Nor does the word mean nothing more than pardon. The law itself might pardon the criminal, but thenceforward he is nothing more than a pardoned criminal. But justification is far more than this.

When we consider God's justifying the ungodly, it is necessary that we think clearly in order not to fall into similar errors. We must not look upon justification as a making up of the deficit that is owed by man. For example, if we should say, arbitrarily, that each man owed to God one hundred per cent, and that one man had performed fifty per cent and another thirty and another twenty, we must never think of God making up the lack and giving the first man fifty, the second man seventy and the third man eighty in order to total, in each case, the one hundred per cent that was demanded by God. God rejects with a curse all that man has done and gives him a new and different one hundred per cent in each case.

NO TIME ELEMENT

Nor must we think of justification in terms of the life span of the individual. There have been those who wrongly thought that God applies forgiveness to an individual from the time of his birth up to the time of his salvation. If, for example, a young man is twenty when he trusts in Christ, there are those who believe that his sin from birth to the age of twenty is removed. If such were the case, it would constitute one of the strongest arguments for delaying salvation. The man who was able "to call his shots well" could postpone accepting Christ till the latest possible moment in his life, and thus have the grace of God for the longest period of his sinful existence. There have been some foolish enough to claim that such a principle is true.

The Bible teaches, of course, that, whatever justification is, it happens to a man instantaneously, and that it covers his whole being in the totality of his existence. When a man is justified, he is accepted in his person and being in all of his life, past, present, and future.

CLEANSING

Perhaps I can make the matter clearer by a simple story. When I was still in my teens in California, I was invited to speak on a certain occasion at a county Christian Endeavor convention some distance from my home. The home where I was to be entertained was in a new subdivision; and, though the sidewalk had been laid, the street was not yet paved. As I walked toward the house, I noticed in front a large puddle of water that covered a good portion of the street. It had evidently been there for days for there were indications that small boys had been playing around its edges, perhaps wading in it, and there was the wreck of a small wooden boat lying near it.

My hostess had a small boy, four or five years of age, dressed in clean clothes, who was pleading with his mother to allow him to go outside to play. She finally was persuaded by him and gave him permission to go out on the front steps only, with strict warning that he was not to go down the front walk to the gate or street. As I sat by the window reading, I noticed the conduct of the boy. First he went to the bottom step and began to play. After a while he left the step and went two or three paces down the walk. Then he came back to the step and played for a few minutes, leaving again to go down the walk five or ten steps. He then returned once more to play on the steps. A moment later, he went all the way down to the gate and climbed up on its lower bar. He then returned to the steps to play for a brief period. Once more he went down to the gate, and this time he opened it and swung on it. He then returned to the steps and seemed to give up the idea of any further excursion. He played so long on the steps that I became engrossed in my reading and did not look out the window to watch his movements. Suddenly there was an outcry from the boy. He had fallen from the sidewalk into the mud puddle. Covered with mud and water, he came crying toward the gate. His mother, who had heard him as soon as I, met him at the gate. She took him by the hand and led him firmly around toward the back of the house. He was whimpering: "Don't whip me; don't whip me, mama." As they passed the window, I heard his mother say: "Stop your crying. I forgive you." When his mother told him that he was forgiven, his crying stopped. Forgiveness for him meant but one thing: remission of penalty. He would not receive the thrashing he deserved. But forgiveness meant much more to the mother. She stripped the dirty clothes from him, and I heard unmistakable sounds of a boy being scrubbed. She put fresh clothes on him, and in a few minutes brought him into the room where I was reading, sat him firmly down on a chair and said, "Now you sit there and talk to Mr. Barnhouse."

The application is simple. We are all sinners. By virtue of the grace of Christ, God first pronounces that we are forgiven. To us that may mean remission of penalty: we shall not go to the lake of fire which we deserve by virtue of our sin. But to God, because His nature is grace, it means much more. The blood of Jesus Christ cleanses us so that we stand before Him in Christ dressed in Christ's righteousness. But even that is not all.

DECLARED RIGHTEOUS

We have seen that man is not merely a forgiven criminal still suffering for his crime; and we have seen that man is not merely a pardoned criminal, forgiven of the guilt and of the penalty. There is more. Our text declares that the sinner is justified: that is, he is forgiven, pardoned, and declared to be essentially righteous. This is far more than being declared innocent. God does not proclaim that the sinner is innocent. It would have been wonderful if fallen men had been restored to the position of Adam before the fall, yet how precarious would have been that state, for the first parents were not able to maintain it. But when we are justified we are lifted much higher than Adam. We are made higher than the angels through Christ who was made lower than the angels (Heb. 2:7). We are made higher than the seraphs and the cherubs. We are made higher than Lucifer was before he became Satan. We are counted as one in Christ, and are given the position of sons with the Father, and are destined to share the government of the universe with the Creator. Righteousness now belongs to the justified one even as it belongs to God, for we have been made partakers of the divine nature (II Pet. 1:4), and are a new creation (II Cor. 5:17). This does not mean that we are sinless, but it does mean that we have been declared righteous.

This means that the sinner can look away from himself and look to the cross of the Lord Jesus Christ. We are not for a moment teaching that a man can believe and then do as he pleases, for though we believe in eternal security, we do not believe in eternal presumption. But we *are* insisting that there is only one meaning to justification in the sight of the living God and in the light of His revealed Word. Therefore, let no man consider his *feelings*, but let him *trust* in the Word of God about the cross of the Lord Jesus Christ.

FREELY

All of this change takes place, as the text says, "freely," and "by his grace." The word translated *freely* carries with it a rich connotation. It is found nine times in the New Testament and is revealed to man "without price, without return, without cause." It is the word that is twice used in the well known verse, "Freely ye have received, freely give" (Matt. 10:8). It is the word that is twice used at the end of the Bible to tell all men that they may take of the water of life freely (Rev. 21:6; 22:17).

But the richest meaning is to be found in a verse that speaks of the manner in which men hated Christ when He was here on earth. In the upper room when the Lord Jesus talked about the hatred which the world would bear to the believer, because the world already bore the same hatred to Him, He concludes the passage with the word: "This cometh to pass, that the word might be fulfilled which was written in their law, They hated me without a cause" (John 15:25). The translators have used three English words—*without a cause*—to translate the one Greek word. What was the manner of the hatred of men toward Christ? The answer is: "without a cause." That is the meaning of our word here. "Freely ye have received, freely give," could be translated, "Ye have received without any remuneration; give without any remuneration." Our text would then read: "Being justified without a cause in you."

When we understand this, we can see the true basis of our salvation. There was absolutely nothing within man that could recommend him to God. God did not sit in Heaven and look down upon this earth until He had found something in some men that recommended them to Him. He gave salvation to men who deserved Hell. There will not be one person in Heaven who deserved Heaven except the Lord Jesus Christ. He is the only one who merited Heaven. But an innumerable company who merited Hell are going to be in Heaven simply because the grace of God decided that they should be there.

NOT A REWARD

We must even move away from the heresy that thinks that salvation is a reward for faith. It is false to conceive of God as looking over the population of earth with a sort of frustrated longing, saying, "O, where in humanity is another man in whom I can find a bit of faith which I can reward with salvation?" Such is not the Biblical picture of God. Rather do we see God proceeding in the majesty of His eternal Being, on the plane of deity, and counting as righteous those that believe in Christ because it pleases Him to declare them righteous. There is no difference between the method wherein He declares them to be sinners and the method wherein He declares them righteous.

One evening I was speaking in Washington, D. C., and at the close of the meeting a group of about a dozen men crowded around me to ask questions. One of them was fighting all that

I had been teaching. He insisted that justification could not be *entirely* God's work. It stood to reason, he said, that God would not justify a man without finding in him something on which to base the justification. Patiently, I took him through many of the verses which show that there is nothing in man upon which God bases His choice. He argued that he had been preaching to some men in a particular school, that some of them had accepted Christ, and that surely when the decision had been reached it was because of something that was in them. I asked him to tell me what it would be, and he looked at me triumphantly and said, "Their faith!" And then he started to quote Ephesians 2:8, 9, "For by grace are ye saved through faith . . ." Suddenly his voice trailed off to silence, and I could see the working of his mind as he began to comprehend what was the very next clause in the verse. I would not let him stop but insisted that he go on. "And where did the faith come from?" I pressed him. And he was man enough to finish the quotation: "And that not of yourselves: it is the gift of God: not of works, lest any man should boast."

ALL A GIFT

He left that and started on a different track. He presented another verse that had to do with seeking. I pointed out to him that an earlier verse in the third of Romans states that there is "none that seeketh after God," that these invitations to seek were given to those who were already believers, and not to the Gentiles round about. After about five starts, each of which was effectively blocked by plain statements from the Word of God, he said, "But . . . but . . . that would mean that God does it all!" There was almost wonderment in his voice, and I let the Word of God sink in and do its work. Then, suddenly, there burst upon him the full realization that we are justified freely, or, as the Greek could have it, justified without a cause.

That is the glorious truth which our hearts must feed upon. Our justification does not have its roots in us: if it were otherwise we would always be in constant doubt as to whether we had properly fulfilled the requirements. But when we know that we are justified without a cause in ourselves, then we know that it is all based upon the loving nature of God's being, and we can rest quietly, assured that the life that He gives is because of the love that He is.

> Awake, my soul, in joyful lays,
> And sing my great Redeemer's praise;
> He justly claims a song from me,
> His loving kindness, oh, how free.
>
> He saw me ruined in the fall,
> And loved me, notwithstanding all.
> He saved me from my lost estate,
> His loving kindness, oh, how great.

Justified by His grace, without a cause in us. How shall we define such grace? In my ministry I have found it easier to illustrate grace than it is to define it, and there comes to my mind a story that I used in my earliest ministry. It had slipped my mind for many years but comes back today, strong and fresh. When I was in my teens I was invited to speak for a week in a little church in Southern California. There was such blessing that I was invited to continue for a second week, but I was in a quandry for I had no more sermons. I went in to Los Angeles to get some books; and, while I was browsing at the shelves of a store, I ran across a little book (which I did not buy) whose name I do not remember and which I have never seen since. I remember one story out of it which I frequently used in those days, and which comes back to me only today.

A BETTER PITCHER

In the days of Moody, there was a minister named Harry Morehouse who often helped Moody in his campaigns. One morning he was walking along the street in a poor part of one of our great cities and witnessed a minor tragedy. A small boy, who could not have been more than five or six years of age, came out of a store with a pitcher of milk in his hands. The little fellow was making his way carefully along the street when he slipped and fell, the pitcher breaking, and the milk running all over the sidewalk. He let out a wail, and Harry Morehouse rushed to see if he were hurt. There was no physical damage but he would not be consoled, crying out over and over, "My mama'll whip me! My mama'll whip me."

Mr. Morehouse said to him, "Maybe the pitcher is not broken in too many pieces; let us see if we can put it together again." The boy stopped crying at once, as he had no doubt seen bits of crockery glued together to remake a broken plate or cup. He watched as Mr. Morehouse placed the base of the pitcher on the sidewalk and started building up the pieces. There were one or two failures and the pieces fell apart. At each failure the boy started crying again, but was silenced by the big preacher who was helping him so much. Finally, the entire pitcher was reconstructed from the pieces, and it stood there in perfect shape on the sidewalk. The little fellow was given the handle, and he poked it toward the place where it belonged, and, of course, knocked the whole thing apart once more. This time there was no stopping his tears, and it was then that Mr. Morehouse gathered the boy in his arms and walked down the street with him to a nearby crockery store. He entered with the lad and bought a new pitcher. Then he went back to the milk store, had the pitcher washed and filled with milk. Carrying the boy on one arm and the pitcher of milk in the other hand, he followed the boy's instructions until they arrived at his home. Very gently he deposited the lad on his front steps, carefully put the pitcher in his hands and then said to him, "Now will your mama whip you?" A smile broke on the boy's streaked face, and he answered, "Aw, no sir! 'cause it's a lot better pitcher 'an we had before."

GOD'S GRACE

The story may be very simple, but it represents faintly what the Lord Jesus Christ did for me and for you. Whether you will accept the fact or not, you had dropped the pitcher of your life and its milk was spilled beyond regathering. You may have spent much time in trying to patch the pieces together again, but God assures you that you are broken beyond repair. It was when we were thus, broken and hopeless, in the despair of our lost soul and our crashed hopes that the Lord Jesus intervened to save us. He may have watched our efforts at patching for a while, until we could come to the place where we believed beyond question that it is impossible for us to repair our lives in a way that would ever satisfy the holiness of the Heavenly Father. It was then that He carried us in His arms and purchased for us an entirely new nature, a new life, which He imparted to us on the basis of His loving kindness and tender mercies. It was not because there was good in us, but because there was grace in Him. It was not because there was righteousness in our hearts, but because there was grace in His heart.

No one had to plead with Him to save us; He did not come because of any promptings of His earthly mother, for example; but He came from Heaven because He, the Lord Jesus Christ, was full of all grace, and that grace was abounding to us through the redemption which He provided in dying for us. It was not our works that saved us but His grace. It was not our character that recommended us to Him, but His grace. If He had not been all grace, we would have forever lain in the misery of our broken hopes. But His very name is love. He is gracious. And that is why I know in this hour that I have new life. He justified me freely, without any cause in me, and all by His grace. And thus I am saved by grace.

CHAPTER XI

Redemption

"Being justified freely [without any cause in us] by his grace through the redemption that is in Christ Jesus" (Rom. 3:24).

THE GREATEST paragraph in the Bible continues to unfold before us. We have seen that our salvation, our justification, is from God, and that He originated this salvation without reference to anything in man that could recommend us to Him. It was entirely through grace.

We now proceed to see that it is on this basis of the redemption that is in Christ Jesus, whom God hath set forth to be a propitiation, a mercy seat, through faith in His blood, that God justifies us.

GUILT REMOVED

Let us be quite clear, once more, as to the meaning of the word "justify" before we proceed to the basis and method of its communication to us. Thomas, in his devotional commentary on *Romans,* says: "To justify means to declare, or pronounce righteous . . . It must be clearly distinguished from to make righteous, which is to sanctify, and although the two ideas are inseparable in Christian experience, they must always be distinguished in our thought of these things. To justify is to regard as righteous, to restore to the status of one who is righteous (and, I may add, this occurs when the sinner is still in the ungodly state). It does not mean merely to forgive and to remove the condemnation of sin, but also, and still more, to regard as right, as though the sinner had never sinned. It includes the removal of his guilt as well as of his condemnation. This is the great difference between a human tribunal and the divine judgment. A king of his royal clemency can pardon, but he cannot reinstate the criminal in the position of one who has not broken the law. God does both, and this is the meaning of justification. Pardon concerns the past only, and cannot possibly deal with a man's future relation to the law; but God deals with both, and the two are justification."

The manner by which God justifies us is freely, gratis, without any cause in us. The basis of our justification is redemption.

REDEEM

The English word *redeem*, outside of its Biblical usage, is found today commonly in the language of the pawn shop. The prefix *re* means "again, "as in a re-copy, re-wash, re-write, and so on. The main part of the word is from a basic root that means "to purchase, to buy." So an article that is left in pawn can be redeemed by paying the money that was borrowed, plus the interest charges. The word is also used in finance for the redemption of bond issues, where a company finds it possible to call some of its bonds representing indebtedness, pay the borrower, and cancel the obligation.

In the Bible, the word also covers the idea of deliverance by the payment of a price. Our English word *redeem* translates three different Greek words, each of which has a rich meaning in connection with our salvation. The word that is used here in Romans 3:24, *apolutro*, contains the basic idea of "loosing, untying, delivering." The modern French form of the word *deliver*, which is *délier*, is the exact Latin counterpart of the Germanic *unbind*. The idea is to be found in the first chapter of Revelation where a Psalm is sung "unto him who loved us, and loosed us from our sins through his own blood" (Rev. 1:5, Gk.).

In his famed Greek Lexicon, Thayer says of this verb: "Everywhere in the New Testament this word is used to denote deliverance effected through the death of Christ from the retributive wrath of a holy God and the merited penalty of sin."

It might be well at this point to discuss the two other Greek words, though they are not found here, that are used in the Scriptures and translated by our word *redemption*. The first is *agorazo* and is the common Greek word for marketing. A few years ago the Rockefeller Foundation made a grant to the American archaeological school in Athens for excavations in the ancient market place, or *agora*, that lies to the west of the Acropolis, just below

Mars' Hill. The place had been covered over with cheap houses. These were purchased, the buildings razed, and the ancient *agora* exposed to sight. In English, we have the noun *market* for a place where buying and selling of goods is carried on—the market place, and we have a verb *to market,* which usually means the selling side of a transaction, as when a farmer markets his crops. In ancient Greek they had the noun *agora* for the market place and the verb *agorazo* for the buying. In the New Testament the word is applied to the purchase of souls. This would be readily understood in the ancient world since there was a slave market that operated almost every day, and the traffic in slaves was very great. In fact almost half of the population in the Greek and Roman worlds were slaves to the other half, and this, of course, without regard to color or race. The ancients would have understood the term very easily. That Christ should have walked into the slave market and purchased or redeemed men who were slaves of sin, would be an idea that would be completely understandable.

THE PRICE

This idea is further clarified by the fact that the Scripture speaks of the price of our redemption. "Forasmuch as ye know that ye were not redeemed with corruptible things, as silver and gold, from your vain manner of life [Gk.] received by tradition from your fathers; but with the precious blood of Christ, as of a lamb without blemish and without spot" (I Pet. 1:18, 19). Thus the believer sings:

> Nor silver, nor gold hath obtained my redemption,
> No riches of earth could have saved my poor soul;
> The blood of the cross is my only foundation,
> The death of my Saviour now maketh me whole.
>
> I am redeemed, but not with silver,
> I am bought, but not with gold;
> Bought with a price, the blood of Jesus,
> Precious price of love untold.

Now in another phrase of the New Testament there is another very beautiful side light on this truth of our redemption by purchase in the market place. In Peter's epistle we are called "a peculiar people." The English word *peculiar* has degenerated in its meaning until today it indicates that there is something queer, strange or erratic about a person who is called peculiar. But to one familiar with etymology the word is indeed very precious. The word *peculiar* derives from the old Latin root word for cattle. In those days there was no such thing as money as we know it in coin or paper. Almost everything was priced in a value of cows, even as in much of Africa today many articles are priced in terms of goats. In Nigeria, for example, the price of a wife runs around eight goats. If a thing in the Latin world had a high value, it was worth a lot of cows—the word is *pecus*—and, therefore, it had a cow value, a pecuniary value. And an article which was rare and valuable was peculiar, worth a great price. Only much later, by extension, did the idea of what we might call a slang meaning of the word become attached to it so that something that was eccentric or queer was called peculiar.

When the Bible tells us that we are a peculiar people, it is referring to the idea that we are a people redeemed at a great price, and that our redemption cost the death of the Lord Jesus Christ, and the shedding of His blood. Thus, the very same Greek words translated "peculiar people" in Peter's epistle are translated "purchased possession" in Ephesians (1:14), where we, the believers, are described as the object of the redemptive work of Christ, and as the center of His work even in the future when the work shall be completed and we shall be one with Him forever. Thus the idea of redemption is bound up with the thought of the Saviour going into the slave market and purchasing the life of a slave with the price of His own life.

OUT OF THE MARKET

There is still another Greek word, much like the one we have been considering, which gives an additional light to the thought of redemption. It is, in fact, exactly the same Greek word with the prefix *ex* in front of it. The word is *exagorazo*, and carries the idea of buying something *out* of the market. In other words, there is a difference between a purchase that is for resale and a purchase that is made in order to take the article out of commerce. For example, the famous Philadelphia dealer in rare books and fabulous works of art, Rosenbach, frequently purchased an item at a London or New York sale, and held it for resale to one of his customers. Some pictures, books, manuscripts and other art objects are bought and sold again and again. But, quite differently when some great work of art is bought by a museum, it is taken out of circulation permanently. An example of this is a Shakespeare folio which was bought and sold in several sales until it came to rest in the Folger Shakespeare Library in Washington, D. C., and, under the terms of the trust, it is to remain there permanently, and can never be put into the market again.

The Greek word *exagorazo* carries this connotation. When the Lord Jesus Christ stepped into the slave market and paid the ransom for guilty sinners, it was a purchase made once for all. It can never be repeated. On the cross He cried out, "It is finished" (John 19:30). It is a ransom that can never be required again, even by the just and holy Father, the Lord God Almighty. The Lord bought us in order that He might take us out of the market. It is possible, then, for each of us to say, "I am persuaded that neither death, nor life, nor angels, nor principalities, nor powers, nor things present, nor things to come, nor height, nor depth, nor any other creation [Gk.] shall be able to separate us from the love of God, which is in Christ Jesus our Lord" (Rom. 8:38, 39).

HOSEA A TYPE

One of the most beautiful illustrations in all of Scripture perfectly sets forth this truth. We remember that Hosea the preacher was married to a harlot, and he loved her more and more as she sank to the utmost degradation, continuing to provide for her on her frightful course into iniquity. It is the perfect picture of the Lord furnishing man the strength to run away from Him. But there came the day when Hosea's wife was reduced to slavery, was brought to the auction block to be sold to the highest bidder. The story is in the third chapter of Hosea: "Then said the Lord unto me, Go yet, love a woman beloved of her friend, yet an adulteress, according to the love of the Lord toward the children of Israel, who look to other gods, and love flagons of wine." To my mind that verse contains the greatest line in the whole Bible. Very often we have been told that John 3:16 is the greatest verse in the Bible, with its familiar, "God so loved the world . . ." But when I ask you the meaning of the word "so" in that "God so loved the world . . ." you can best answer me by taking me to the auction block where Hosea is commanded to purchase his wife, a harlot, who is being sold, naked, in the sight of all Jerusalem. Then hear God telling the preacher to buy this woman, in terms of love: "Love her according to the love of the Lord toward the children of Israel." Now I know how God loves when I see Christ dying. Now I can comprehend the love of God when I see Him coming into the slave market and laying down the price of His blood to purchase me and take me out of the market forever.

The next verse tells the story. "So I bought her to me for fifteen pieces of silver, and for a bushel and a half of barley." Now the husband has become her owner. Before this moment if Hosea had harmed his wife, he would have been accountable with his life. But now that he has bought and paid for her, she is his as a chattel to do with as he wishes. So what does he do? Listen to the thrilling words of love as he puts her veil back on her face and shields her from the gaze of Jerusalem. We read, "And I said unto her, Thou shalt abide for me many days; thou shalt not play the harlot, and thou shalt not be for another man." The husband bought her in order that she might be faithful to him. And then the climax of it all, as the husband says to his wife whom he has purchased in the market in order to take her *out* of the market and to his own love, "So will I also be for thee."

Surely there is no greater love than this. The Lord Jesus redeemed us. We are His purchased possession. He paid Himself for us that He might have us to dwell in, to fill our hearts; that Christ might be formed within us, and revealed through us, so that men might glorify and praise Him for His love and grace and mercy.

Thus when we put all three of the words for redemption together, we discover that our Lord went down into the slave market where we were exposed to the gaze of the universe as slaves of sin, lost, dead and under the curse of God, that He bought us with the price of His own life in order that He might take us out of the market place forever, and this in order that we might be to the praise of the glory of His grace, exhibits of His eternal love, and that we might be forever delivered from sin and sins.

CHRIST JESUS

Further, in this connection, it is important that we note the order of the names of our Lord and Saviour as they are presented here in this verse. We believe that our God has given us this revelation of Himself in the precise terms in which He wishes us to have the truth. There is not a word or a phrase in the Bible that has been given for the sake of mere literary effect. There is nothing that is set forth that is extraneous. All shows the marks of the hand of the divine Author, and thus we look deeply at every shade of meaning. When, therefore, we read that we are "justified freely by His grace, through the redemption that is in Christ Jesus," we even stop to ask why He is called Christ Jesus instead of Jesus Christ.

We have pointed out elsewhere that the word *Lord* is of Germanic origin, the word *Jesus* is Hebrew, being the translation of *Ioshue,* and the word *Christ* is Greek for the Anointed One, the Messiah. The meaning of the name Joshua, or Jesus, is Saviour. Therefore, when we are told that we are justified through the redemption that is in Christ Jesus, we are being told that we are declared righteous through the redemption that is in the Messiah Saviour. It is a way of saying that the Old Testament, the book of the Messiah, and the New Testament, the book of the Saviour, are all bound up in the person of our Lord and in the basis of our redemption. We Christians readily admit that if Jesus is not the Messiah, then we have no Saviour and are of all men the most miserable. In the future, when the Messiah comes to earth, we believe that He will be none other than the Lord Jesus come back a second time.

In passing, let me quote one of the most thrilling paragraphs that I have read in recent times. There is a journal published in New York City under the title *Commentary.* In a recent issue they carried an article entitled "A Religious Bridge Between Jew and Christian." The article was written by Professor Hans Joachim Schoeps, who is himself a Jew, and professor in the University of Marburg, Germany. Professor Schoeps says: "The Church of Jesus

Christ has preserved no portrait of its Lord and Saviour. If Jesus were to come again tomorrow, no Christian would know His face. But it might well be that He who is coming at the end of days, He who is awaited by the Synagogue as by the Church, is One, with one and the same face."

I have long been convinced that that thought, expressed by this noted Jewish leader, is true. But, in addition, the one who is coming as the Messiah has already come as our Saviour. When He was born it was said, "Thou shalt call his name Jesus: for he shall save his people from their sins" (Matt. 1:21). In the light of what we have seen about the meaning of the word *redemption,* it can readily be seen that *Jesus* is especially the name of the Redeemer. For as redemption means to buy in the market place, take out of the market place and loose from one's sins, so the name *Jesus* was given in connection with our being saved from our sins.

SET FREE FROM SINS

It must ever be pointed out that God does not save His people in their sins, but from their sins. It is true that it was when we were sinners Christ died for the ungodly. It is true that we were declared righteous when we were still in our sin, but the purpose of all of this is our holiness. There can be no true comprehension of redemption apart from the fact that He bought us to set us free from sins in order that we might become the servants of righteousness. The deliverance includes freedom from the guilt or penalty of sin, from the mastery or power of sin in our daily lives, and, ultimately, our deliverance from even the presence of sin.

And we must tie all of this up with the thought back in verse 21, where we are told that "now the righteousness of God, apart from the law, is manifested." I will come back to the word "righteousness" again in the next two verses, but though the word itself is not in our text the thought is here. It is the thread that is holding all the passage together.

Thomas has a paragraph on this that is very illuminating: "The need of righteousness must first of all be understood. It means 'righteous,' that is, the state of being right. Sometimes the word refers to God's character, as in 3:5, when it means either His righteousness as vindicating Himself, or His character as inflicting righteous retribution on sin (2:5). In other cases the term 'righteousness' applies to man, and has reference to his rightness, or state of being right with God. It means conformity in every respect to the divine law. When thus understood it is a very inclusive term, covering remission of sins, reinstatement in a true position and relation to God, renewal of inward character, and reestablishment in outward conduct. This wide meaning is demanded by the fact that sin is at once, a disease, and a departure."

Sin is a debt to the justice of God, a disease which is incurable in man by himself, and a departure from God and His righteousness. The debt requires to be paid, and this may be called justification. The disease requires to be healed, and this may be called sanctification. The departure requires to be corrected, and this may be called consecration. These varied aspects are not all and always included in every passage where the word occurs. Sometimes the emphasis is on justification (as in 3:21–5:21); sometimes on sanctification (as in chapters 6 to 8); and sometimes on consecration (as in chapters 12 to 16).

HOLINESS OF LIVING

Many souls have found their rest in the passage that we are discussing, and among these, Dr. Dale, in his *Christian Doctrine,* has bequeathed a paragraph concerning his own personal thinking, rich in the compelling, constraining movement to holiness of personal living, that is the result of redemption through Christ. Dale writes: "When I discover that I am forgiven I shall condemn my sin—condemn it, perhaps, more sternly than ever. I see that it was inexcusable; I abhor it as I may never have abhorred it before; I may feel as I had never felt, that it justly provoked the divine indignation and wrath; but when I approach God through Christ as the propitiation for my sin, the guilt of it crushes me no longer; God is at peace with me; I have perfect rest in His love. It is not merely at the commencement of the Christian life that the death of Christ has this wonderful power. Its power endures. Day after day, year after year, when we are troubled by the consciousness of moral failure and of ill desert, we find in the death of Christ for our sin, power to trust in the divine mercy, and to implore the divine forgiveness with an absolute confidence that we shall receive it."

Thus our discussion is not an academic, theological essay, but a warm, pulsing, living communication of life from God through the Word.

Newell, closing his thought on the passage, says: "Before you leave verse 24 apply it to yourself, if you are a believer. Say of yourself, 'God has declared me righteous without any cause in me, by His grace, through the redemption from sin's penalty that is in Christ Jesus.' It is the bold, believing use for ourselves of the Scripture we learn, that God desires; and not merely the knowledge of Scripture." May God help each one who reads these words to make that application to self.

CHAPTER XII

The Mercy Seat

"Whom God hath set forth to be a propitiation through faith in his blood, to declare his righteousness for the remission of sins that are past, through the forbearance of God" (Rom. 3:25).

A N ENGLISH farmer, plowing his field, came upon a treasure in Roman coins that had lain hidden there for two thousand years. The London *Times* in a reminiscent mood wrote of the feet that had walked that field and of the treasure that had lain there so long. I plow another field, the Word of God, and frequently I find rich treasures for myself, but I also find great joy in knowing the history of other treasures that have been found in the field. I could wish that someone would bring together in one volume the hundreds of stories of men who have been saved through the reading of certain verses in the Scripture. In the thirteenth chapter of Romans we shall come to Augustine's verse. In the first chapter we have already seen Luther's verse. But here, in this third chapter and twenty-fifth verse, we also have a text that God has used for more than one man.

PADRE PAOLO SARPI

Moule tells of one. Padre Paolo Sarpi (1552-1623), "Councillor, and Theologian" to the Venetian Republic, and historian of the Council of Trent, was one of the many eminent men of his day who never broke with the Roman Church, yet had genuine spiritual sympathies with the Reformation. The record of his last hours is affecting and instructive, and shows him reposing his hope with great simplicity on the divine message of this chapter, though the report makes him quote it inexactly. "Night being come, and want of spirits increasing upon him, he caused another reading of the Passion written by St. John. He spake of his own misery, and of the trust and confidence which he had in the blood of Christ. He repeated very often those words, *Quem proposuit*

Deus Mediatorem per fidem in sanguine suo, 'Whom God hath set forth to be a Meditator through faith in His blood' in which he seemed to receive an extreme consolation. He repeated (though with much faintness) divers places of St. Paul. He protested that of his part he had nothing to present God with but miseries and sins, yet nevertheless he desired to be drowned in the abyss of the divine mercy; with so much submission on one side, and yet so much cheerfulness on the other side, that he drew tears from all that were present."

WILLIAM COWPER

In the *Memoir of the Early Life of William Cowper,* the poet writes of his own experience in coming to Christ through the text that we are about to study. He says: "The happy period which was to afford me a clear opening of the free mercy of God in Christ Jesus was now arrived. I flung myself into a chair near the window, and seeing a Bible there, ventured once more to apply to it for comfort and instruction. The first verse I saw was the 25th of the 3rd of Romans; 'Whom God hath set forth to be a propitiation through faith in his blood, to declare his righteousness for the remission of sins that are past, through the forbearance of God.'

"Immediately I received strength to believe it, and the full beams of the Sun of Righteousness shone upon me. I saw the sufficiency of the atonement He had made, my pardon sealed in His blood, and all the fulness and completeness of His justification. In an instant I believed and received the peace of the Gospel. Unless the Almighty arm had been under me, I think I should have died with gratitude and joy. My eyes filled with tears; transports choked my utterance. I could only look up to Heaven in silent fear, overwhelmed with love and wonder. But the work of the Holy Ghost is best described in His own words: it is 'joy unspeakable and full of glory.'" Is it any wonder that Cowper later wrote:

> There is a fountain filled with blood,
> Drawn from Immanuel's veins;
> And sinners plunged beneath that flood,
> Lose all their guilty stains.

The dying thief rejoiced to see
That fountain in his day;
And there may I, though vile as he,
Wash all my sins away.

Dear dying Lamb, Thy precious blood,
Shall never lose its power;
Till all the ransomed church of God
Be saved to sin no more.

E'er since by faith I saw the stream
Thy flowing wounds supply,
Redeeming love has been my theme,
And shall be till I die.

PEACE OF SPIRIT

There is indeed comfort and strength in our text; and, if we are willing to take it to ourselves and apply its every part to our own need, we too can have that peace of spirit with which God must begin in the life of the individual and without which there can be no peace of mind or peace of soul. The Liebmanns may write of peace of mind and the Sheens may write of peace of soul, but they are setting up an impossible goal for a human being. It is like telling an embryo in the mother's womb that he should learn to walk. You have to be born before you can learn to walk. You have to be born again before you can have life which makes peace possible in the mind, the heart, and the soul.

We know that we have sin: this fact is written on the conscience of the human race. Every weary pilgrimage, every demon shrine, every practice of fear in the wild religions of the world, every blow of the flagellants upon their bodies, every act of penance, every effort to establish good works, every haunted movement of the human soul, all of these rise to tell us that there is a universal consciousness of sin. The anguished cries of Lady Macbeth and Lady Dedlock reveal the torturings of the human conscience; the precipitous flight of innumerable criminals across the pages of literature and the face of the world illustrates the vain effort to escape from that which man must inevitably carry with him unless he leaves it at the one place that God has provided for the burden of sin to be removed. The great tales of the greatest writers all center around the drama of sin and its effects in the hearts and lives of men. Dostoevsky, in *Crime and Punishment,* explored the dark places of the human spirit and "abstracted mind and will and passion from their background of names and clothes and addresses, and exhibited them in pure disembodied states of being." One reason detective stories and crime news in general have such a hold upon the mind of man is that the human conscience senses the universal oneness of man in the midst of his sin, and is passionately, and occasionally compassionately, joined to the heart of the man who is in trouble because of sin.

But the Christian who knows the Lord Jesus Christ as his personal Saviour has a "peace that passeth all understanding." It garrisons the heart; it quiets the soul; it stills the conscience; it satisfies the mind and brings the calm of God into the remotest fastness of the personality.

A PROPITIATION

We now come to one of the most beautiful illustrations of the work of Christ that is to be found in all the Bible. In order to understand it, we must go back to the Old Testament and explain a part of the worship of the tabernacle of Moses and Aaron that was well-known to Israel at the time the Holy Spirit gave this epistle to the Church. Just as a Frenchman would understand a reference to the destruction of the Bastile, and as an Englishman would understand a reference to Runnymede, where the barons forced King John to confirm Magna Carta, and as an American would understand a reference to Paul Revere and the Battle of Lexington, so the ancient people would have understood this reference to what is called in our translation "a propitiation," but what was known in the original languages as "the mercy seat."

When the Lord God gave the law to Moses, He told him to build a tabernacle that was to house the Ark of the Covenant. The Jews did not have great temples like those in Egypt, Greece and Rome. The demon gods could be satisfied with magnificent piles of stone, magnificent from the human point of view, but the God who created the sun, the moon and the stars could not think of a building made with the hands of men as a place where He could manifest Himself to them. Solomon understood this at the dedication of the temple which he built, and in his prayer of dedication said, "But will God indeed dwell on the earth? behold the heaven, and the heaven of heavens cannot contain thee; how much less this house that I have builded?" (I Kings 8:27).

We must never forget that there is an infinite distance between the true God and any thought that man could have concerning Him. The majesty of Baal, Jupiter and other demon gods of the earth is vileness in the sight of the living God, even as the foolishness of God is wiser than the wisdom of men.

For this reason God chose to have His worship in a simple house that was little more than a covering for the central element in the worship. The tabernacle was what we would call today a prefabricated structure. It was taken down, carried through the wilderness on the shoulders of men, and set up at the next site designated for it by God. In front of the procession went the Ark of the Covenant, and on the top of that Ark was the mercy seat which is mentioned in our text.

THE TABERNACLE

God gave to Moses the detailed description of the Ark of the Covenant. We read in Exodus: "And they shall make an ark of acacia wood; two cubits and a half shall be the length thereof, and a cubit and a half the breadth thereof, and a cubit and a half the height thereof. And thou shalt overlay it with pure gold, within and without shalt thou overlay it, and shalt make upon it a crown of gold round about . . . And thou shalt make a mercy seat of pure gold, two cubits and a half shall be the length thereof, and a cubit and a half the breadth thereof . . . And thou shalt put the mercy seat above upon the ark; and in the ark thou shalt put the testimony that I shall give thee" (Exod. 25:10, 11, 17, 21).

Ever since the New Testament was written the significance of every part of the temple worship has been understood to reveal the work of the Messiah Saviour whom God had sent forth to bear the sins of men. The Old Testament was the preparation for the New Testament. By itself it is a truncated pyramid. With the New Testament it is a complete edifice. It would be possible for us to spend a hundred studies the length of this one in presenting the details of the analogy between the Old Testament worship and Christ. The Epistle to the Hebrews sets forth the fact that Israel was to turn away from the law and turn to Christ. Instead of the lamb, there is Christ. Instead of the priesthood, there is Christ. Instead of the altar, there is Christ. Instead of the tabernacle, there is Christ. Every part of it speaks of our Lord Jesus, and nothing more definitely than the center of all the worship, the Ark and its cover, the mercy seat.

The tabernacle of Israel was in two parts, the first room was oblong and just twice the size of the second room. The first room was called the Holy place, but the second room was the Holy of Holies, or the Holiest of all. In it was but one object, the Ark of the Covenant, with its mercy seat. The Ark was a box, and within that box were several articles which God had commanded to be placed there. First and most important of all, there were the tables of stone on which had been written by the finger of God the ten commandments. You will remember that God had given to Moses the first set of tables; and, as Moses went down the mountain and he saw the sin of the people in their idolatrous worship of the golden calf, he being filled with righteous wrath cast the tables down and the stones were broken (Exod. 32:19). But God commanded Moses to bring two new tables and once more wrote the commandments upon them. These were the tables which God comamnded Moses to lay within the Ark of the testimony.

These unbroken tables speak to us of the Lord Jesus Christ. Man had broken the law of God, but the Lord Jesus Christ came and kept the law perfectly. No other member of the human race was ever perfect. When He was born the Lord Jesus said, "I come to do thy will, O God" (Heb. 10:9). "I was not rebellious, neither turned away back" (Isa. 50:5). He was the Lamb without spot and without blemish (I Pet. 1:19). He was "obedient unto death, even the death of the cross" (Phil. 2:8). Moses, in himself, can give us nothing more than broken tables which show us the state of our own heart. The Lord Jesus Christ is the perfect manifestation of the demands of God, for no other being ever loved the Lord God with all his heart, soul, mind and strength and his neighbor as himself. "Christ is the end of the law for righteousness to every one that believeth" (Rom. 10:4).

THE COVER OF THE ARK

If there had been no cover upon that box, it would have been the testimony of death against the people. No man could have approached it for an instant. For above it, rising up to the sky, stood a pillar of fire by night and a pillar of cloud by day. The holiness of God and the righteousness of God and the wrath of God were all centered in that fire and in that glory. How terrible is that Ark of the Covenant when it is thought of without cover. The box is open and the uncovered law bears its silent witness against each one of us. The open Ark would have been a seat of justice that could have done nothing but condemn. Only because God put a cover on that box could there be a seat of mercy instead of a seat of wrath and justice.

Therefore God, in His love said, "Thou shalt make a mercy seat of pure gold" (Exod. 25:17). This mercy seat was the cover of the Ark and stood between the glory, righteousness and holiness of God and the sinners that were on the earth. The outraged justice within cried out to the fire that hovered above for judgment upon the sinners who had broken the law. The mercy seat came in between and protected the sinner from the wrath of God. Thus it was the perfect picture of the Lord Jesus Christ, and thus it is applied to Him in our text.

In the mythology of the pagans the first woman, Pandora, had a box which, when opened, freed all of the evils and distempers that have since afflicted the human race. Hope alone remained at the bottom of the box to assuage the lot of man. But there is no hope in a box which has contained all miseries, and the legend is but one more illustration of the sub-conscious guilt that lies heavy on all the human race. God alone can bring hope to man by first bringing mercy to man. It is true that the box of the Ark is a good symbol of the guilt of man, and the broken law cries out from the throat of the box for man to be judged. But, blessed be God, the box is covered forever for those who have trusted in the mercy of the Lord which was provided there at Calvary.

THE CHERUBS

On the top of the cover there were two statues of the highest order of angelic beings, the cherubs. These statues were made of gold, and the wings of the cherubs stretched out for a distance of fifteen feet, if we take the measurements of those made for Solomon's temple as the standard (I Kings 6:24-27). The statues were on each end of the cover, the mercy seat, facing inward toward each other, and overshadowing the central portion of the mercy seat. The importance of this will be seen in a moment.

Several years ago when I made a place in my notebooks for supposed contradictions or discrepancies in the Bible, I wrote down an observation concerning a seeming contradiction in the attitude of God in one of the ten commandments and His seemingly changed attitude in His subsequent instructions concerning the building of the tabernacle and its appurtenances. Like all of the other supposed difficulties, the answer soon came, and it was seen, far from being a difficulty, to be rich in teaching spiritual truth. The second of the ten commandments states: "Thou shalt not make unto thee any graven image, or any likeness of any thing that is in heaven above, or that is in the earth beneath, or that is in the water under the earth" (Exod. 20:4). Here was one of the most solemn words of God, spoken to Moses on Mt. Sinai, written into tables of the law. Yet, before the giving of the law was completed, God Himself gave a command to make a statue of two cherubs to put on either end of the mercy seat. When I first contemplated this order from God countermanding what He had just set forth, I began to search for the explanation. It was not enough that I knew that God was greater than His commandments and that He had a right to make an exception to something that He had commanded. I wanted some explanation that would reveal the reason for such a command and reversal. I began to study the matter; and, taking my Hebrew concordance, I read all the passages in the Bible that had anything to do with cherubs. I began to find the answer to the riddle in the very first usage of the word.

"TO KEEP THE WAY"

I soon came to the conclusion that the images on the top of the Ark were an artistic reproduction of a scene which God had caused to be enacted at the door of the Garden of Eden. After Adam and Eve had sinned they were driven out of the garden and we read in Genesis: "So he drove out the man; and he placed at the east of the garden of Eden Cherubims, and a flaming sword which turned every way, to keep the way of the tree of life" (Gen. 3:24).

As a boy I had gathered the impression from a Sunday-school lesson, and from a drawing by some artist supposedly illustrating the scene, that the cherubs were placed at the gate of the garden as the defenders of the way of the tree of life against Adam and Eve. They were out and God meant them to stay out, I thought. He would have cherubs there to act as policemen; and, if they attempted to crawl back in, he would have a sword to prick them and teach them obedience. But, as a man, when I entered into the depth of the study, I soon discovered that the cherubs were not there as the enemies of man but as his protectors. They were the gift of the grace of God.

An altar had been set up at the gate of the garden, probably the altar on which the Lord Himself had slain the animals which furnished the coats of skins with which He had clothed the first pair when He removed their fig-leaf garments from them and gave them the garments of skin. The fig leaves were the symbols of the good works of man; the coats of skins were the symbols of righteousness provided as a gift from God on the basis of the shedding of the blood. Satan was the enemy of man, and God had placed enmity between the Devil and mankind (Gen. 3:15). That hatred would most certainly manifest itself in the effort to destroy the way whereby man might have communion with the holy God and access to His presence for forgiveness and justification. We would understand the passage better if it read that the cherubs were placed by the gate to protect the way or to keep it open and available.

I have found this exact usage of the verb "keep" in the works of the late President Roosevelt. In the interval between the beginning of the second world war in Europe and our entry into it, there were many maneuvers on our part to help Britain with "all aid short of war." First we landed on Iceland in order to protect the sea lanes, and finally the President announced that we would attack any enemy submarines which ventured west of a certain line of longitude. "For," said the President, "we are determined to keep the way to Iceland." In other words it was to be kept free for our ships; it was to be protected against the attacks of the enemy.

Thus, when the Lord exiled the man and the woman from the Garden of Eden they were not deprived of His grace. He was ready to save them and bless them, providing they would come with the offering of the blood sacrifice. It was this which righteous Abel learned and obeyed, and we read that it was through faith that Abel offered a more excellent sacrifice (Heb. 11:4). The way was open and God has always kept it open. When Moses received the pattern for the tabernacle, which is stated to be the pattern of things in the Heavens, it was necessary, therefore, that the statues of the cherubs should be arched over the mercy seat where the blood was to be placed.

The cherubs are the highest of all the orders of angelic beings. These orders, like the ascending ranks of an army which run from private, corporal and sergeant, through lieutenant, captain, major, colonel and the varying ranks of generals, include the lowly and relatively impotent demons very possibly, as Pember has pointed out, the disembodied spirits of the first inhabitants of this earth, and then the angels, the archangel, the principalities and powers, the seraphs and the cherubs. It was from this highest order that Lucifer fell. He was the anointed cherub that governed (Ezek. 28:14), and it was these cherubs that were nearest the throne of God. They seem to be the beings that sustain the majesty and holiness of God. While one of their number did fall away when he allowed sin to originate in his heart, the others are still the protectors of the sovereign way of God, and, therefore, when we approach the Lord God through the Lord Jesus Christ, it is they who keep the Devil and his angels from attacking us. This would seem to be the symbolism of the cover of the Ark.

The great high priest, on the day of atonement—the *yom kippur* which the Jews still celebrate today—entered into the holiest of all bearing the blood of the atonement. This was placed on the Ark, between the two cherubims, in the spot that was called the mercy seat. Between the law which man had violated and the pillar of cloud and fire above, stood the sacrifice of the Lord Jesus Christ. The wrath of God was stilled and man might rest in peace without fear of the falling of that wrath. God had showed Himself to be a God of mercy, grace and love. Jesus Christ has been set forth as the mercy seat through faith in His blood, and there is your confidence and hope.

CHAPTER XIII

The Blood of Christ

"Whom God hath set forth to be a propitiation through faith in his blood, to declare his righteousness for the remission of sins that are past, through the forbearance of God" (Rom. 3:25).

GOD HATH set forth Jesus Christ to be the mercy seat, through faith in His blood. The heart of the ancient worship which God had commanded and prescribed in detail in the Old Testament was an object lesson which taught His people that He must be approached in His own way. Men should talk less about approaching God, every man in his own way, and talk more about every man approaching God in God's own way. For there is a way to approach God and every other way is an offense to God. That is why the heart of the New Testament teaching is built around the declaration of the Saviour Himself: "I am the way, the truth, and the life: no man cometh unto the Father, but by me" (John 14:6). And this is the explanation of the preaching of the disciples who said: "Neither is there salvation in any other: for there is none other name under heaven given among men, whereby we must be saved" (Acts 4:12).

The way to God today is the same way that the Jews approached God in the Old Testament times. Moses did not go to Heaven because he kept the law, but because his brother Aaron shed the blood of a lamb which God had provided as a substitute for sinners. The high priest, once a year, entered into the holiest of all and placed the blood of the sacrifice on the mercy seat between the outstretched wings of the cherubim.

THE PLACE OF THE BLOOD

The mercy seat was the place of the blood. Take that ancient tabernacle and all its worship and tip it on end so that the altar is beneath and then the laver, the Holy place and the Holy of

Holies; you then have a pageant of our approach to our God who is the highest of the Heavens, far above the principalities and the powers (Eph. 1:21). Every step of the way speaks of some portion of the work of Christ for those who put their trust in Him. The altar is the cross of Christ; the laver is the cleansing of the sinner from his daily sins. The seven-branched lampstand represents Christ as the light of the world. The table of shewbread (in Hebrew, the bread that is set forth, or the bread that is arranged in order) stands for Christ the bread of life. The second altar, the altar of incense, sets forth the Lord Jesus Christ as the means of our worship, for no man comes unto the Father except through Christ, who has said that all worship must be in Spirit and in truth. Behind this altar there was the great veil, the veil that was torn in two from top to bottom at the moment the Lord Jesus cried out that His work on the cross was finished. His body was torn for the sins of the believing world, and henceforward man can approach God without fear. The veil of His flesh has been parted, and now the Ark, the mercy seat, and the glory are all visible to the eyes of those who put their trust in Him.

Finally, there was the Holy of Holies into which we enter by the new and living way. We are invited to come boldly where the ancient high priest came with hesitancy and dread. We are invited to come freely, as often as we will, where the Levitical priest could come only on the day of atonement. There stood the mercy seat, covering the box in which were the tables of the law, broken by men but perfectly observed by the Lord Jesus. This speaks to us of the mercy seat where the offering of the blood of the Lord Jesus Christ is presented to us, by which we stand in the presence of God unafraid. It is not a seat of justice—justice was wrought outside on the cross. This is now the seat of mercy.

> From every stormy wind that blows,
> From every swelling tide of woes,
> There is a calm a sure retreat;
> 'Tis found beneath the mercy seat.
>
> There is a place where Jesus sheds
> The oil of gladness on our heads—
> A place than all beside more sweet;
> It is the blood-stained mercy seat.

> There, there on eagle-wing we soar,
> And time and sense seem all no more;
> And Heaven comes down our souls to greet,
> And glory crowns the mercy seat.

MERCY

Mercy is a wonderful word. In English it has come to mean the forbearance and compassion shown by one person to another who is in his power and who has no claim to receive kindness; it is kind and compassionate treatment where severity is merited or expected. And especially, when it is used of the mercy of God, it refers to His forbearance toward sinners and His forgiveness of their offenses.

Now our text specifically states that the kindness and love of God toward us in Christ is through faith in His blood. As this is the first time in the Epistle to the Romans that the blood of the Lord Jesus Christ is mentioned, it is proper that we study the matter in some detail.

Throughout the New Testament the salvation that is presented to us through Jesus Christ is explained in terms of the shedding of His blood. In this connection a German writer, Paul Fiebig, raises an interesting question: "Another remarkable thing is this: Why is precisely the 'blood' of Jesus so often spoken of? Why is the redemption and the forgiveness of sins so often connected with the 'blood' of Jesus? This is remarkable, for the death on the cross was not so very bloody that it should be precisely the blood of Jesus which so impressed the eye-witnesses and the first Christians. The evangelists moreover (except John 19:34) say nothing about it. This special emphasis on the blood cannot be explained therefore from the kind of death Jesus died."

EXPIATORY SACRIFICE

The answer is to be found throughout the pages of the New Testament. For if a death which was not particularly bloody is always mentioned in terms of its blood, there must be a reason and the answer is not far to find. The death of Jesus Christ was mentioned in terms of blood because the New Testament writers all thought of the death of Jesus Christ in terms of a sacrifice—

an expiatory sacrifice. They all understood the death of the Lord
Jesus Christ over against the background of the Jewish sacrifices
for sin, in the sight of which they had been raised, and the
nature of which they had always known in the Jewish practices
in the tabernacle and temple.

Warfield writes: "An interesting proof that they were so understood is supplied by a remarkable fact emphasized in a striking
passage by Adolf Harnack. Wherever the Christian religion went,
there blood sacrifice ceased to be offered—just as the tapers go out
when the sun rises. Christ's death was recognized everywhere
it became known as the reality of which they were the shadows.
He offered His own body once for all and by this one offering
perfected forever them that are sanctified, and it was well understood that there remained no more offering for sin. 'The death
of Christ,' says Harnack—'of this there can be no doubt—made an
end to blood sacrifices in the history of religion.' 'The instinct
which led to them found its satisfaction and therefore its end in the
death of Christ.' 'His death had the value of a sacrificial death;
for otherwise it would not have had the power to penetrate into
that inner world out of which the blood sacrifices proceeded,'—
and, penetrating into it, to meet, and to satisfy all the needs which
blood sacrifices had been invented to meet and satisfy."

There are, of course, blood sacrifices in religions outside the
pale of Christian penetration, but wherever the gospel comes there
is a tendency for the sacrifices to cease.

I would not be in agreement, of course, that primitive man
had devised or invented this idea of blood sacrifices. I believe that
the evidence from the Bible shows plainly that God Himself commanded the sacrifices in the beginning. In the opening pages of
the Word, we find that the first time blood was ever shed in the
history of the human race, it was shed by God Himself in order
to provide the covering of skins for the man and woman who had
just believed His unsupported promise concerning the deliverance
that should come through the seed of the woman (Gen. 3:15, 21).
The first moment that Adam had the opportunity of speaking after
the giving of the promise, he accepted that promise and called
his wife's name "Eve," which is a title and not a name. Thus he

called her "mother'" when there was no motherhood as yet. It was then that the Lord God took coats and skins and clothed them.

That this sacrifice for Adam and Eve was continued at the door of the garden of Eden, we have shown previously by our description of the meaning of the cherubim on the cover of the Ark, the mercy seat. And that God commanded this sacrifice still to be offered is evidenced by the fact that Abel obeyed and continued bringing the sacrifice. When we read in the Epistle to the Hebrews, "By faith Abel offered a more excellent sacrifice than Cain . . ." we are really saying, "By obedience Abel brought a better sacrifice." And thus logically if the sacrifice was brought by obedience it was brought by virtue of a commandment. And thus we find Himself instituting the sacrifice, and thereby giving meaning to all its subsequent use. It was to be a sacrifice for sin.

WHY BLOOD?

Why did the Lord God require a lamb instead of a sheaf of wheat? Is God more favorably disposed to one part of His creation than to another as a gift from His creatures? The answer must be found in the nature of the blood itself.

I was one time preaching in a certain city and made the acquaintance of the outstanding minister of that community. Circumstances put us together at a luncheon table, and he began to speak about the difference between his ministry and mine. He said, "I'm just as evangelical as you, Barnhouse, but I don't have quite the same approach. Now I believe in Christ and all that, but I don't use the word blood in every sermon I preach, and therefore some people think that I am not as conservative as I might be." I had been told that the man was the type of preacher who never says anything against the Bible and its great truths but who never says anything very strongly for the essential truths: his trumpet gave an uncertain sound.

As I answered him, I discovered that he was immensely pleased with the first part of my answer; but, as I proceeded, he became intensely displeased with the second half of the answer. For first of all, I agreed with him that I did not look upon the blood of Christ, when I taught concerning the doctrine and when I used the phrase, as to be primarily a matter of biochemistry. When

I teach the doctrine that God set forth Christ to be a mercy seat through faith in His blood, I do not think of the Scripture as speaking in terms of the liquid that circulates in the arteries and veins of man by which the tissues are constantly nourished and renewed. I am not talking about a blood primarily as so many white corpuscles and as containing a certain hemoglobin count. If that point of view should be taken, there would be ground for sinking into the idolatry of certain forms of paganism that have been baptized with Christian names.

SUPERSTITION AND IDOLATRY

In Bruges, Belgium, I have witnessed the great celebration of what is called the "Feast of the Holy Blood" where on a certain day a rag with a few red stains is taken out and paraded around the city. As it passes, the populace prostrates itself to the ground, rubbing the forehead in the dust, and then goes around the rest of the day to the side shows of the kermis with the mark of the dust still visible. I saw this with my own eyes, and it was a horrible and repugnant bit of paganism dragged into a form of Christendom.

Nor could I follow the strange idea of the acolyte in Jerusalem in the Holy Sepulchre, that strange church building with a half a dozen different sects possessing competitive altars under the same roof, each pretending to be on the exact spot where the cross of Christ had stood. First of all, the church was *within* the city wall, and I knew that the Bible spoke most plainly of Christ's death *outside* the city wall. Therefore, I entered the place as a tourist and in no sense as a worshiper, except that within the temple of my heart the Holy Spirit was present to adore the merciful God who had kept me from the follies of superstition and idolatry. The acolyte showed me a hole near the altar, which was fitted with a glass cover, and he offered to take away the cover and let me plunge my hand into the orifice, explaining that this was the very hole in which the cross of Christ had stood. As I peered at the spot, I thought I saw a dim light beneath, and I noted that there was a jagged rent in the rock. I asked the acolyte about it, and he said that the light came from the tomb of Adam. To my incredulous wonder, he explained to me that the rocks had been rent when

Jesus died and that this allowed the blood to drip down through the hole in the rocks to the cave below where the blood had fallen into the grave of Adam, thus cleansing the race of the original sin of Adam. I could hardly believe my ears, but that is what I saw and heard.

Now, I do not believe for one moment that there was any cleansing value in the actual chemical elements of the blood that flowed from the veins of Christ. The supposed relics of that blood are, of course, a horrible hoax perpetrated upon poor unfortunate people by those who hold them in their power.

If someone should ask me what happened to the literal blood of Jesus Christ that flowed from His veins, I would answer that I never go beyond that which is written in the Word of God; and, since the Bible is silent on the subject, we must be silent on it also. To me it is a matter that is unimportant.

IN THE HEAVENS

Now that was the first half of my answer to the preacher and with this he agreed. But I am not so sure he agreed with the second half, for then I spoke of one verse in the New Testament that speaks of the blood of Christ in such a way that it might be thought to suggest what happened to it. In the Epistle to the Hebrews, after telling us that almost all things were by the law purged with blood, and that without the shedding of blood there is no remission (Heb. 9:21, 22), the passage continues to inform us that the Lord Jesus Christ entered into the Heaven of Heavens now to appear in the presence of God for us, even as the high priest had entered into the Holy of Holies to offer the blood upon the mercy seat. If anyone is going to insist upon a Biblical statement as to the disposal of the actual blood of Christ, then it must be concluded from this verse that the blood was taken to Heaven, and that therefore there is none of it spotting rags or staining steps the Lord is supposed to have walked on.

I am inclined to believe that the actual blood of Christ went to the dust of the earth like any other chemical element, and that it returned to that earth as a part of the earth. It would be the consonant answer to the statement of God to Cain that the voice of his brother's blood cried from the ground demanding justice. The actual blood of Christ could have gone back to the dust of the ground, announcing symbolically (not in the superstition of the acolyte of Jerusalem) that the righteous basis for all judgment has now been established by virtue of which God will take vengeance upon the ungodly and announcing also that one day even the earth itself shall be ransomed from the thralldom of sin's curse and the very desert and waste place shall blossom like the rose.

To me the important thing in the shedding of the blood of Jesus Christ is the fact that it was the pouring out of the life of Christ. In the Old Testament the idea was set forth in the Levitical account: "The life of the flesh is in the blood: for I have given it to you upon the altar to make an atonement for your souls: for it is the blood that maketh an atonement for the soul" (Lev. 17:11). In that which was flowing through the veins of the Lord Jesus Christ there was His very life. Of this life He had Himself said, "No man taketh it from me, but I lay it down of myself. I have power to lay it down, and I have power to take it again" (John 10:18).

LIFE OUT OF DEATH

We must be careful to note that it was not the life which Jesus lived that saves any man, but the life which He poured out in the shedding of His blood which redeems us from our sins. The lamb scampering around the house of the Israelite at the time of the passover could not save the older son from the judgment of the avenging angel. It was the lamb slain and the blood applied to the door which brought safety to the heir of the house. And it is the poured out life of the Lord Jesus Christ that gives peace to the guilty conscience and makes expiation for the sins of those who put their trust in Him, for He gave His life as a ransom for their souls, dying in their stead. My dear old professor of theology, Dr. B. B. Warfield of Princeton, has left a wonderful paragraph on this in one of his lectures. He wrote at length of the way in which some professors were attempting to whittle down the true meaning of the word "Redeemer." And he continued: "I think that you will agree with me that it is a sad thing to see words like these die like this. And I hope you will determine that, God willing, you will not let them die thus, if any care on your part can preserve them in life and vigor. But the dying of the words is not the saddest thing which we see here. The saddest thing is the dying out in the hearts of men of the things for which the words stand. As ministers of Christ it will be your function to keep the things alive. If you can do that, the words which express the things will take care of themselves. Either they will abide in vigor; or other good words and true will press in to take the place left vacant by them. The real thing for you to settle in your minds, therefore, is whether Christ is truly a Redeemer to you, and whether you find an actual redemption in Him,—or are you ready to deny the Master that bought you, and to count His blood an unholy thing? Do you realize that Christ is your Ransomer and has actually shed His blood for you as your ransom? Do you realize that your salvation has been bought, bought at a tremendous price, at the price of nothing less precious than blood, and that the blood of Christ, the Holy One of God? Or, go a step further: do you realize that this Christ who has thus shed His blood for you is Himself your God? So the Scriptures teach." And in a footnote he quotes Acts 20:28, which reads: "Feed the church of God, which he hath purchased with his own blood." He then quotes F. J. A. Hort who says that the reading "God" is "assuredly genuine," and the emphasis upon the blood being the blood of God is very strong.

And the great Warfield, so prosaic in his classes, so profoundly holy in his mind toward Christ, bursts into poetry himself at the thought of the Lord God coming and shedding His blood for our redemption.

> The blood of God outpoured upon the tree!
>   So reads the Book. O mind, receive the thought,
>   Nor helpless murmur thou hast vainly sought,
> Thought-room within thee for such mystery.
> Thou foolish mindling: Dost thou hope to see
>   Undazed, untottering, all that God hath wrought?
>   Before His mighty "shall," thy little "ought"
> Be shamed to silence and humility.

Come mindling, I will show thee what 'twere meet
  That thou shouldst shrink from marveling, and flee
  As unbelievable,—nay, wonderingly,
With dazed but still with faithful praises, greet:
Draw near and listen to this sweetest sweet,—
  Thy God, O mindling, shed His blood for *thee!*

RECONCILIATION

In the Old Testament, when the tabernacle of God had been set up, the sinners of the tribes of Israel could come with burnt offerings, whether lambs or bullocks, and could stand before the gate outside the sacred area. They turned the animals over to the priest who was to immolate them, and then they put their hands upon the heads of the beasts, as though the sin of their hearts and beings was flowing down their arms and out through the palms of their hands upon the animals that were about to be killed in their behalf. Then when the sin had gone from them into the lambs, as it were, the priest put the lambs to death. When the sinner saw the blood of those lambs flow, he knew that God was now reconciled to him and he could go away with the certainty that his transgressions had been forgiven and his sins covered. For those slain lambs spoke of Christ.

We sing in one of our great hymns which deserves to be heard more often in our churches:

Not all the blood of beasts, on Jewish altars slain,
Could give the guilty conscience peace, or wash away the stain.

But Christ the Heavenly Lamb, takes all our sins away;
A sacrifice of nobler name and richer blood than they.

My faith would lay her hand on that dear head of Thine,
While like a penitent I stand, and *there* confess my sin.

And thus I have stood with my hand upon the head of Christ as my Saviour. I have seen Him standing in my place. I have confessed the righteousness of God in condemning me and have accepted the love of God that took the stroke that was my due. I have come to that cross and there realized that He was wounded for my transgressions; that He was bruised for my iniquities; that the chastisement of my peace was upon Him; and that by His stripes I am healed of all my sin.

Can you stand with me there today? The blood of Christ has flowed and salvation is provided and paid for. God is reconciled and now turns toward the sinner. There are not three places in the universe where sin may be; there are only two. Your sin is either upon yourself and will be judged even to the lake of fire; or your sin is on the Saviour and has been judged in the shedding of His blood—in the pouring out of His life. I know that my sin is on the Saviour and that His life poured out has given me life forever. I know that I stand cleansed in His ransom, with all my sins forever paid for by the shedding of this precious blood. Will you in this moment turn away from every alluring voice that would keep you from your salvation and come to the Saviour that His blood might avail for you and cleanse you from all your sin?

Behold now is the accepted time; behold, now is the day of salvation. The day of the flowing fountain of His blood is still here. Today, beware lest the judgment of the cross take the place of the mercy of the cross. For the day of the end of mercy will come and the day of full judgment will succeed it. Woe to the man who is not hidden in the refuge of the riven side of the Lord Jesus Christ. There in that cleft rock from which the blood flowed we shall be forever safe.

CHAPTER XIV

God's Name Vindicated

"To declare, I say, at this time his righteousness: that he might be just, and the justifier of him which believeth in Jesus" (Rom. 3:26).

THINGS are not always what they seem to be. The earth and its objects on the one hand, and our eyes on the other, are so constructed that the impressions vary with the perspective we have of the things we look at. There are optical illusions everywhere, not merely in lines that are drawn in strange patterns in Ripley's *Believe It Or Not*, but in all of nature. We have become so accustomed to these illusions that we often live with them without giving any thought to the deception that lies within our eyes. I can remember, as a small boy, crossing some railroad tracks with my father. As we stood on the tracks I asked that we might walk down to the place where the rails touched, and my father had a difficult time explaining to me the matter of perspective. But as I grew older I accommodated myself, as do all normal members of the human race, to the shifting aspects of objects as they are seen from different angles or from different distances.

PERSPECTIVES

In his famed *Notebooks* Leonardo da Vinci wrote: "Perspective is the bridle and rudder of painting." And in no small sense perspective is the bridle and rudder of theology. It is possible for us to gaze at life from the normal point of view of fallen Adam. In him our true senses died; and, since the fall, no man has been able to behold even himself as he should be seen. Paul had learned this when he told men they were to "judge nothing before the time, until the Lord come, who both will bring to light the hidden things of darkness, and will manifest the counsels of the hearts" (I Cor. 4:5). He went so far as to say that he would not even consider his own opinion about himself (v. 3).

133

When we look away from material things, we find the same distortion in ideas. In 1613 Drummond of Hawthornden wrote, "All, that we can set our eyes on in these intricate mazes of life, is but vain perspective and deceiving shadows, appearing far otherwise afar off, than when gazed upon from a near distance."

Man, by himself, can look upon his outward world or upon his inward world of ideas only from the point of view of his own experience. The Christian can come to the Word of God and see all things from the perspective of God, and can thus measure the illusions of earth and learn to walk in the light instead of in the darkness.

In our study of the third chapter of Romans we come to a passage that is of the highest importance in revealing to us what the Lord God Almighty had in mind when He planned the cross of Jesus Christ. There have been thousands of sermons preached on the death of the cross and by far the vast majority of them have been on the subject of the cross as related to the sins of man. It would also be possible to present studies from the Word of God concerning the cross as it is related to the judgment and downfall of Satan; or as it is related to the ultimate transformation of the animal world so that the lion may one day lie down with the lamb; or as it is related to the very dirt of the ground, so that the desert and the waste places might blossom like the rose; or as it is related to the nation of Israel, which shall some day rule the world because of the triumph of the Lord Jesus Christ. But all of these and all other aspects of the cross are as nothing when they are placed beside the text which we consider here. When the sun rises, the stars grow dim and fade from view. And when we consider the cross of Jesus Christ as it relates to the glory of God, then nothing else can be of comparative importance.

SEEMING COMPROMISE

Our text declares that the purpose of the death of Jesus Christ was to manifest the righteousness of God which, in the centuries which had preceded the incarnation, had seemingly been compromised by His attitude toward sinners. For apart from the death of Jesus Christ there is a stain on the name of God.

A few years ago a society for the spread of atheism issued a leaflet that abundantly demonstrates what our text sets forth and answers. The tract contained a half dozen portrait sketches of old men, and gave to those pictures the names of well known Old Testament characters. The sketches were ugly, in fact they were positively villainous looking, yet they carried the names of such men as Abraham, Jacob, Moses and David.

Below the portraits there were a few lines of printing relating to the lives of these men and certain Bible statements concerning them. Under the face that is supposed to represent Abraham, we read that he was a coward who was willing to sacrifice the honor of his wife, Sarah, in order to save his own skin. The Bible reference is given. Then the atheists point out that elsewhere in the Bible Abraham was called "the friend of God." Finally, they ask what kind of a God is the God of the Bible who had such friends as this dishonorable man. They are perfectly right in thinking that a holy God could not remain holy and yet fellowship with sin.

Their portrait of Jacob represents a man who is described as a cheat and a liar, with the proper Bible references in support. We are told that God wrestled with Jacob and then changed his name to Israel, prince of God. The authors then inquire about the character of a God who would have such a prince, or who would allow Himself to be called "the God of Jacob." And they are perfectly right in making such an inquiry. If it can be shown that God chose such men as these without punishing their sin, then it will go ill with the character of God. What would men think of an earthly judge who imposed a heavy sentence on one law breaker and then, seemingly for no good reason, let a similar criminal go free, appointing him later to be his own assistant? The world would be quick to deplore the existence of such judges on the bench. Justice has but one function. It must search out crime and give it a proper and fitting punishment.

The atheists then present Moses, and point out that he was a murderer and a fugitive from justice when the Lord Jehovah appeared to him and sent him back to Egypt as His own representative, calling him His servant, and setting him up as a leader of a great people, and putting into his bloody hands the tables of the law containing the commandment, "Thou shalt not kill." For a murderer to preach "Thou shalt not kill" is hypocrisy. What kind of a God would use a murderer for such a message? According to the standards of the atheists instead of blessing Moses, God should have punished him. And unless we can find that God did punish Moses' sin, the atheists are right in their thought about such a God.

Another of the characters in the atheists' leaflet is David. He is particularly repulsive in the drawing. We read of his adultery and of his murder in order to protect his adultery. We read of his "sore that ran in the night" in the most horrible language, and then we read that David was "a man after God's own heart." The atheists rightly ask what kind of a God was this God of the Bible who had a heart that could find anything to praise in David.

Now the remarkable thing about all this blasphemy is that it is positively true. God says so Himself. For hundreds of years there was a stain on the name of God. If we had no New Testament, we would not know the answer. God knew that it was not righteous or just to forgive guilty sinners, yet He went right on doing it throughout all of the period of the Old Testament.

THE SOLUTION

Now, in our text in the third of Romans, God condescends to explain to us that He was able to pardon men at that time because He knew that He was going to justify Himself even in the sight of the atheists some day. For the day will come when even the atheists will be forced to admit that God has solved this problem that seems to them unsolvable.

The atheists claim that it is not moral to forgive sinners without punishing their sin. God makes the same claim. He will by no means clear the guilty. Every sin that has ever been committed must be punished by God. The atheists think that the men of the Old Testament, Abraham, Jacob, Moses, David, and the rest of them, deserved a quite different fate than that which they received. If God is holy and these men were sinners, then they should be separated from God forever. Would not a holy God sully Himself in holding such sinners to His bosom in love?

A God, such as the Bible represents Him to be, must be both love and hate. God is love of the sinner and God must be hate of the sin. The atheists are right in reminding us that we must not forget that God is hate of the sinner's sin. That teaching is more needed today, perhaps, than any other! God is hate. God hates sin. When the atheists found mention of a God who seemingly did not punish sin, they exclaimed that they had found proof that there could be no such God. A good God must punish sin.

The atheists are right. All of these men, Abraham, Moses and all the rest deserved to go to Hell. So do I. So do you. Instead, we find that they went to Heaven. How could this be possible? It was because our good Heavenly Father, the God and Father of our Lord Jesus Christ, found a way whereby their sin, your sin, and my sin, could be punished and yet they themselves, you yourself, and I myself, might go free.

That way was found in the Lord Jesus Christ when God set Him forth as a mercy seat through faith in His blood. There at the cross God took sin away from the sinner, put it upon His Son, and punished Him to the full for that sin. Thus it was proved that God is just and holy and loving, and without compromise. That lesson can never be learned except at the cross of the Lord Jesus Christ. The atheists stopped with the Old Testament and so missed the point.

GOD JUSTIFIED

Thousands of books have been written to tell sinners that the death of the Lord Jesus Christ took away their sin, but too little has been said to show that the death of Jesus Christ the Saviour removed a scandal from the name of God. The heart of the whole Bible is to be found here in our text which explains this great fact. Men are "justified freely by his grace through the redemption that is in Christ Jesus: whom God hath set forth to be a [mercy seat] through faith in his blood, to declare his righteousness for the remission of sins that are past, through the forbearance of God" (3:24, 25).

Put that in common words. The Lord declares that all men are sinners, and therefore lost. But because of what our God is, in His heart of love and mercy, He came to die for us on the Cross. If Christ had not died for sinners, God would not have any right to take any sinner into a clean Heaven. Yet He had been saving sinners for centuries before Christ came. Before the incarnation, before Christ died, before any penalty had been paid for sin, God had taken Abraham, Jacob, Moses, David and all the sinful line of saved men to Himself. There was therefore a stain upon the name of God. Seemingly He had done that which was not just. Seemingly He had been guilty of just that unrighteousness of which the atheists accuse Him.

But our text clearly tells us that the death of Christ removes that charge from the name of God forever. By the death of Christ, God has declared His own righteousness, for the remission of sins that are past.

One writer once commented on this text with the thought that the "sins that are past" are those which are committed in our lives before we accept Christ as Saviour. Though it is gloriously true that these past sins as well as all the sins of all our life's span are removed from us and placed on the Son of God, whose blood cleanses us from all sin and all sins, it is not that of which our text speaks. When God tells us that the death of Christ declares His righteousness for the remission of sins that are past, He is declaring that it is now proved that He was just and righteous and holy at the moment when the great list of Old Testament sinners-become-saints found their place in His mercy. The sins of the men of the Old Testament were only "covered over" at the time when they committed them. The Hebrew word for "atonement" is *kaphar,* and has given the word for "cover" to a dozen languages.

When the Lord Jesus Christ died, the sins which had been covered were uncovered, placed upon the Heavenly Lamb, and dealt with by the righteous Judge. God loved us so much that He went to this extreme to show it. Thus the death of Christ shows us that the heart of God had always been a heart of love, and also that He had always acted in holiness.

JUST AND THE JUSTIFIER

It is remarkable that the Holy Spirit repeats the announcement concerning the righteousness of God. For after we read the first statement that the death of Christ is the declaration of God's righteousness for the remission of sins that are past, the Word continues, "To declare, I say, at this time—(that is, since the cross has become a fact in history)—to declare at this time His righteous-

ness that He might be just and the justifier of him which believeth
in Jesus."

Sinner, today, wherever you are, the same message holds good
for you. If you believe that God is righteous, you condemn yourself to eternal separation from Him unless you also believe that
His love and mercy also brought Him to the cross. When you
acknowledge that a righteous God cannot overlook sin, you remove your own defense and are found guilty before God. If you
refuse the Saviour who was punished by the Father for your sin,
you must take the eternal punishment for that sin yourself. There
are not three places in the universe where sin may be—there are
only two. Your sin is either upon yourself or it is on the Saviour.
There is no other place where the guilt may be placed. Your sin
is on yourself or on the Saviour. There are only two places in the
universe where sin may be.

You may have been as dishonorable as Abraham, yet God
can and will save you if you come to the cross of the Saviour and
put your trust in Him. You may have been as tricky and as dis-
honest as Jacob, yet God will delight to call Himself your God,
if you will come through the blood of the cross of Christ. You
may have been as murderous as Moses, yet God will make you
His servant, and use you for Himself if you will come through
the blood of the Lord Jesus Christ. You may have been as vile
as David, yet God will sing sweet Psalms through your heart and
life if you will come through the blood of the cross of the Lord
Jesus Christ.

It is at the cross of the Saviour that a holy God finds it possible to remain holy, even though He is pardoning sinners. You
can become the friend of God, the child of God, a man after
God's own heart, providing that you will submit to His verdict
about the sinfulness of your sin and submit to His verdict that
the death of Jesus Christ perfectly satisfies all that is in His holy
Being. That death is not only the punishment for your sin, but
a perfect proof to all creation, forever, that God is just when He
saves sinners. The atheists and you are right when you say that
God must be holy. The atheists and you are wrong when you
refuse the way of salvation which satisfies all the conditions of
God's holiness and your need.

SALVATION PLANNED

God's dealings with men long before Christ came show the eternal nature of the plan of salvation. God had planned the death of Christ. This is one of the most important facts concerning Calvary. It is relatively unimportant that the Jews delivered Christ to be crucified; it is relatively unimportant that Gentiles did the actual nailing of His body to the cross. The important fact concerning the death of Christ is that God thought of it and planned it. "It pleased the Lord to bruise him; he hath put him to grief" (Isa. 53:10) is the great prophecy of the death of Christ which reveals that God planned that death and brought about its execution. And the New Testament confirmation of this prophecy is found in the statement of Peter on the day of Pentecost, that Christ was "delivered by the determinate counsel and foreknowledge of God" (Acts 2:23). God never acted apart from the eternal purpose which He purposed in Christ (Eph. 1:11). Therefore all of His actions were always righteous.

It should be noticed, also, that all this was done apart from any man, or the faith of any man. Christ's death shows the righteousness of God even if no individual had ever believed it. Newell has a rich paragraph on this: "The essence of the truth concerning what men call the atonement is that God's wrath fell upon Christ bearing our sins. Man's unbelief has sought in every way to avoid or mitigate this awful truth. But if divine wrath fell not upon Christ, *it must fall upon us*; for God cannot let sin pass . . . It has ever been the first step to heresy—the denial that divine wrath for sin fell on Christ. It was, indeed, certainly not anger at Christ's person—He was obediently drinking a cup His Father had given Him. Nor was it anger at the sinner; 'God so loved that He gave.' But it was wrath against sin—the going forth of the infinitely holy nature of God against sin. Alas, how little we feel its awfulness. How poor our knowledge of it; how weak our hatred of sin. But wrath against sin fell upon Christ. We beseech you, hold this fast. God 'spared not His own Son, but delivered Him up for us all' (Rom. 8:32). True, we are also guilty; the penalty of sin is upon us. And that means judgment, and the infliction of wrath. But behind this, and deeper than even our guilt, is the

abhorrence of a holy God against our sin itself. It is the abominable thing His holy Being hates. We must be banished under
wrath from His sight unless Christ die for us. Let all those who
think to stand in the day of judgment before God think on this.
The atonement arises out of a necessity in the nature of God
Himself."

NO ESCAPE

Finally, let me ask you to consider this fact. If the death of
the Son of God meant so much to God the Father, how can you
hope to escape His wrath if you give it no consideration? We
read in the Epistle to the Hebrews: The man who showed contempt for Moses' law died without hope of appeal on the evidence
of two or three of his fellows. How much more dreadful a punishment will he be thought to deserve who has poured scorn upon
the Son of God, treated like dirt the blood of the covenant which
was once made applicable to him, and insulted the very Spirit
of grace. For we know the One who said: Vengeance belongeth
unto Me, I will recompense. And again: The Lord shall judge
His people. Truly it is a terrible thing for a man who has done
this to fall into the hands of the living God (Heb. 10:28-31).

And again we read in that same epistle: We ought therefore,
to pay the greatest attention to the truth that we have heard and
not allow ourselves to drift away from it. For if the message
given [to Moses on Mt. Sinai] through angels proved authentic,
so that defiance of it and disobedience to it received retribution,
how shall we escape if we refuse to pay proper attention to the
salvation that is offered to us today? (Heb. 2:1, 2).

The whole problem of salvation is bound up with the nature
of God. He cannot act in any way that is contrary to His nature.
He had to hate sin because He is holy and sin is hateful. He had
to love sinners, not because they are lovable but because He is
love. The laws of the nature of God are unchanged and unchangeable. With Him is no variation, no change. He is the
immutable one. It is for this reason that the death of Christ had
to be exactly what it is. The love of God was paying a fine to
the justice of God. The love of the Saviour was taking in Him-

self the stroke of the wrath that had to pour forth against sin. Because Christ died God is proved just. Because His death made it possible for ungodly men to be declared righteous, it is proved that God is love.

There is not a thing that you have to do to merit all this grace. You cannot give anything to God; you have nothing to give. But you can believe His Word and His heart will be satisfied to draw you to Himself, strip you of your sin, clothe you with His righteousness, and set you upon the throne with Him where you can be His companion and associate in the government of the universe forever. Believe Him today.

CHAPTER XV

Just and the Justifier

"To declare, I say, at this time his righteousness: that he might be just, and the justifier of him which believeth in Jesus" *(Rom. 3:26).*

THAT HE might be just and the justifier. This is the problem which confronted the Lord God Almighty; this the dilemma within the nature of the Deity. The problem and dilemma were, of course, apparent only to the mind of the creature, to men and angels, for God knew from all eternity how He would resolve them to the credit of His own glory.

NO PROBLEMS WITH GOD

There are no problems with God, and there are no dilemmas with God. He is concerned with teaching us that there is no good apart from Him. He can do that only by showing us that there is no good in ourselves. He is concerned with revealing to us His might and His power. This is most ably demonstrated by the way in which, as it were, He gets Himself into positions which seemingly are impossible from the human point of view, and then resolves the problem so neatly that we are left in awe and worship at the wonder of His wisdom, the splendor of His glory, and the infinite majesty of His power.

It is when we feed upon the truth that rises out of these difficulties and problems that our faith grows and our hearts are satisfied. One of the best illustrations that I ever heard was that of the old Negro mammy who had such confidence and trust in the Lord that someone said to her, "Mammy, you have so much faith that if the Lord told you to jump through a stone wall you would start jumping." The old lady replied, "If de Lawd tole me to jump through a stone wall, it would be mah business to jump, and His business to make a hole in the wall."

That is the situation that is placed before us in our text in the third of Romans. God faces a world of sinners who are desperate in their rebellion and miserable in their sin. The problem is how He can reach down and take hold of sinners without getting His hands dirty. No man could accomplish it. We understand the coal-miner's warning to the girl in the sightseeing party who insisted on wearing white shoes down into a coal mine, when he said, "You can wear white shoes into the mine but you will not wear them white out of the mine." God said in the Proverbs, "Can a man take fire in his bosom, and his clothes not be burned?" (Prov. 6:27). To which we might reply, "Well, God, canst Thou take a sinner into Thy bosom and not be dirtied?" And God replies, "Yes, I can."

CREATION PERFECT

It will be worth while for us to trace the history of this apparent dilemma throughout the Bible. In the beginning God created the heavens and the earth, and, of course, His creation was absolutely perfect. It would be impossible for God to create anything that was not perfect. There is one cult (Christian Science) in America which has fallen into the most grievous error through its failure to understand the simple logic of the entrance of sin. The argument of these people runs something like this: God is perfect. Everything that God creates is perfect. God created everything. Therefore, it follows, they say, that everything is perfect. From this false sequence, they go on to deduce that what we call sin, sorrow, suffering, sickness, death and anguish, are not reality, but are errors of mortal mind, and that they are to be overcome somehow by playing spiritual ostrich and saying that these things do not really exist. What they fail to see, of course, is that although God created all things, including Lucifer, God did not create sin. Sin originated in the heart of Lucifer when this being, who was perfect in all his ways from the day he was created (Ezek. 28:15), opposed his free will to the eternal will of God.

We have the flat statement of the Scripture that Lucifer was created perfect in all his ways. The same passage continues to state, just as flatly, that iniquity was discovered in the heart of

Lucifer. I do not propose to argue this point here, for it is not pertinent to our main subject. Suffice it to say that the Word of God proclaims the fact, and true spiritual reason finds no difficulty with the statement. It is perfectly comprehensible from every point of view. God in His omnipotence and omniscience created a being of great power, wisdom and beauty, and to this being He gave free will. That will could have acknowledged God, and probably did for a considerable length of time, but there came the moment when, seeing his own beauty and power as compared with the lesser beauty and power of all the angelic creation below him, he fancied that he was great enough, strong enough and wise enough to run the universe beneath him without consulting the God who was above him, and that, in turn, he himself should receive some of the credit for all that was being done. It was the origin of this thought in the mind of Lucifer which was the origin of sin.

JUDGMENT

The God who does all things well, and who does all things perfectly, immediately blasted the world with the perfect judgment which turned this earth ball into a waste and desolation. One of the basic teachings of the Word of God is that there is a great interval between the first and second verses of the Book of Genesis. Much that follows is nonsense if this be not understood.

When we read that "the earth was without form and void" (Gen. 1:2), or that it was "waste and desolate," as the revision has it; or that it was "a wreck and a ruin," as another translator has rendered it, we can understand what happened to the perfect earth which God had originally created. In Isaiah 45:18, the Hebrew distinctly states that God did not create the world as we find it in the second verse of Genesis: He created it not "in vain." This is the same word that is translated "void, desolate, or ruin." The R.S.V. translates it perfectly, "He did not create it a chaos." The explanation is, of course, that the creation became a ruin by the perfect judgment of God, who does all things perfectly.

All this is a prelude to that which happened when the Lord God reformed and refashioned His creation in the six days of the re-ordering of the universe. Satan by then knew the nature of

God, and that God was forced to strike sin in its every appearance. Thus, when God created man Satan's thought was to seduce him from God in order to have one more creature under his sway and to frustrate the plan of God.

SATAN'S WARFARE

But God's plans are not to be frustrated. Satan has a wisdom that is greater than human wisdom but which is still folly in comparison with the wisdom of God. Satan's logic was this: "If I can succeed in detaching man from God, then God by His nature will have to curse man. Thus my rule over the sphere of the earth will not be disturbed, and I can continue to reign over my province which has never yet been taken away from me."

For God had not thrust Satan down to Hell in the moment of his rebellion. God could have done so, but what He really did, in effect, was to say: "Here is a claim that another will than Mine can order and reign. Here is a claim that some wisdom apart from Mine is capable of maintaining a rightness that can bring peace and harmony. I will allow that claim to be fully tested. We shall see what any other will than Mine can bring to the creation."

That test is still going on. It shall ultimately be realized by men, angels and demons that there is no true power except that from God. It shall ultimately be realized that there is no righteousness, or rightness, apart from God. And this will be demonstrated not by an arbitrary blast of God's fulminating power, which He most certainly possesses, but by orderly procedure of the revelation of the failure of both Satan and man, by the orderly setting forth of divine righteousness through Jesus Christ, and by the ultimate establishment of the divine righteousness in accordance with all of the true principles of holiness and justice.

The whole tone of the Biblical narrative sets forth the thoughts of Satan after the sin of man. He could not comprehend that God could act in any way other than that of blasting judgment. He himself had sinned and God had blasted His universe; therefore, according to his train of thought, God would have to destroy man, or at least curse him in such a way that there could never be any blessing for man again.

But to his utter consternation he sees God coming with a pleading call of love, seeking the erring man and woman. That must have been one of the most startling moments in Satan's history. Instead of striking forth as lightning, the Lord God of creation comes down and walks in the garden in the cool of the day and calls Adam, "Where art thou?" (Gen. 3:9). The tenderness of the call was a revelation of something in the Godhead which was outside of Satan's fallen nature. When pride and arrogance had lifted themselves against God, a sense of His love had been lost. Selfishness and pride consume love as fire consumes a branch.

Satan, confused and frustrated, must have thought: "How can God go seeking man who has so flatly disobeyed Him? How is it possible for that holiness and righteousness to stoop to touch Adam?"

SATAN FRUSTRATED

Satan was, of course, correct in assuming that God must blast all sin. He was correct in assuming that the grace of God, like a great Niagara, falls perpendicularly upon that which is beneath, and that all who are in the place of that blessing receive the cascade of blessing from the grace of God. He was correct in assuming that the wrath of God, like a great Niagara, falls upon that which is beneath in an acid fall of corroding judgment, and that all who are in that place of judgment must receive the cascade of judgment from the wrath of God. He saw that Adam had, by his sin, departed from the place of blessing to the place of wrath, but to Satan's amazement, the acid of judgment did not fall upon Adam as he had expected. Instead, God is seen talking with the sinner in a kindly way. There is a judgment upon the ground, a judgment upon the animals of the earth, and a certain change in the man and the woman, but God continues to deal with them in kindly fashion. He takes the fig leaves from them and covers them with coats of skins. He continues to speak softly to them, and tenderly. The acid of His wrath does not seem to burn them as it should. Abel dies and God takes him to Paradise in triumph. And the actions of God, which appear so strange to Satan, seem to have something to do with a blood sacrifice.

But how can God be just and the justifier of them that believe His word about the blood sacrifice? There seems to be a contradiction some place. Just and the justifier?

Satan would have it that God must pour all of the acid of wrath upon the sinner, or else, Himself, cease to be God. He must either turn off the cascade of grace and blessing upon the righteous, or continue to pour forth righteousness in a limited circle and wrath outside that circle. But for God to come into the acid of His own wrath, to speak love to sinners, and to pour forth blessing upon some individuals in the place of wrath, is incomprehensible and disconcerting.

BALAAM'S CURSE

That Satan did not understand is demonstrated by an incident which occurred centuries after the fall. The people of Israel had been chosen as a special people and God had thrown all of His love around them. He had brought them forth from Egypt, and had made a path for them through the Red Sea, even while they were blaspheming His name and when they had idols of Egypt packed in their baggage while eating the passover sacrifice. All around them other nations had given themselves over to the control of Satan and worshiped various demons in the guise of gods.

There came the day when the children of Israel arrived at a certain place in their wilderness wanderings and were camped in the plains of Moab, not far from the Jericho crossing of the Jordan. They had just destroyed many of the Amorites, and the people of Moab were in consternation. They thought that the children of Israel would advance on them and lick them up as an ox licks up the grass of the field. The king of Moab was one Balak, and in the emergency he turned to a man named Balaam, who had some local reputation as a prophet. The king said to Balaam that he knew his reputation, that whosoever was cursed by Balaam was really cursed, and whosoever was blessed by Balaam was truly blessed. This, of course, is not to be considered as a true blessing from the living God or a true curse from the living God.

Balak offered riches and honor to Balaam if he would curse the people of God. The Lord appeared to Balaam and told him not to go to Balak. A second time the princes came with offers of reward, and the Lord permitted Balaam to depart with the princes. He showed that there is a great deal of difference, however, between His directive will and His permissive will, for this time he stopped Balaam and spoke to him through the ass that he rode, ordering him to speak only the things which He should command him. All who follow in his way, to speak pleasant words to people instead of the true word of God, are said to have gone in the way of Balaam (II Pet. 2:15).

THE LORD HATH NOT CURSED

This hireling prophet went to Balak, who prepared the blood sacrifice of the demon gods, and took Balaam to the top of a hill where he might see all of the children of Israel encamped below on the plain. After certain preparations Balaam went to seek the power of cursing, but God appeared to him and gave him a prophecy which he was forced to speak by the power of God. Balak said, "Come, curse Jacob for me, and come, denounce Israel" (Num. 23:7). And Balaam answered, "How can I curse, whom God has not cursed? or how can I denounce, whom the Lord hath not denounced? For, from the top of the rocks I see him, and from the hills I behold him; lo, the people shall dwell alone, and shall not be reckoned among the nations. Who can count the dust of Jacob, and the number of the fourth part of Israel? Let me die the death of the righteous, and let my last end be like his!" (Num. 23:8-10).

Balak in his desperation still thought that some word might be spoken against Israel and took Balaam to a second of the Devil's temples on a high hill. A second time the Word of the Lord came upon Balaam, and in spite of himself he prophesied blessing upon a sinful people. For the whole point of the story will be found in the fact that the people of Israel were a sinful people and that God was blessing them in grace instead of cursing them in righteousness. It was the failure to understand the reason for this that kept Balaam seeking after a word of curse upon them. The second time he said, "God is not man, that he should lie; neither the son of man, that he should repent; has he said, and shall he not do it? or has he spoken, and shall he not fulfil it? Behold I have received commandment to bless: and he has blessed; and I cannot reverse it" (Num. 23:19, 20). And in the next verse there comes the astounding statement: "He has not beheld iniquity in Jacob neither has he seen perverseness in Israel: the Lord his God is with him, and the shout of a king is among them" (23:21).

What an amazing verse! Though there was iniquity upon Jacob, God refused to look at it; and though there was perverseness in Israel, God would not see it. In fact, He *could* not see it. He will not look upon the sins of those who put their trust in Him, nor can He see any sin in those whom He hath declared to be righteous. He is the justifier of them that believe in Jesus Christ, and He is just in justifying us.

ABOUNDING GRACE

A third time Balak took Balaam to one of the high places of Baal, and a third time the Spirit of the Lord came upon him and forced him to bless the people which God had chosen. But Balaam still wanted to earn the money that Balak had given to him, so he brought forth the old idea that God had to curse those who got into the place of cursing, and that it would be impossible for God to be just and the justifier of the believer. The record of this is revealed to us in the last book of the Bible. To the church of Pergamos (and the name of this city means "intermarriage, or mixed marriage"), the risen Lord Jesus Christ wrote: "But I have a few things against thee, because thou hast there them that hold the doctrine of Balaam, who taught Balac to cast a stumblingblock before the children of Israel, to eat things sacrificed unto idols, and to commit fornication" (Rev. 2:14).

The idea back of this was the following: God will not let the children of Israel be cursed because He has chosen them to be His people. But He is a God of justice; and, if you could seduce the children of Israel so that they would leave the place of blessing for the place of cursing, then God by His very nature would have to curse them. So Balak was taught to put women of his tribe where the children of Israel could take them and commit fornication with them, and be seduced by the women to go into the temples of Baal to offer sacrifices to the devil gods. This would, he reasoned, make it necessary for God to put a curse on Israel instead of a blessing, and Balak would have the result that he desired.

Now, if we read the narrative closely, it would even appear that the Lord allowed conditions to ripen to the point where it would seem that He had cast off His people. The doctrine of Balaam (Rev. 2:14) is the doctrine that grace cannot operate where there is sin. It is contrary to all of Scripture. Where sin abounded grace did much more abound. And this does not mean that God does not chastise His people. For in the case of those that went astray after the error of Balaam, God slew twenty-four thousand of them at Shittim for joining themselves unto Baal-Peor. But it would be an error to think that these people were necessarily lost. They were joined to God in the covenant of grace. They had the priesthood, the altar, the shedding of the blood. They had kept the passover, and the lamb of the day of atonement had died for them, in their place. We do not know the mind of God, but it will not astonish me to find these people in Heaven, especially when I have looked upon the cross of Jesus Christ and know that God not only is just but the justifier of them that believe. If any are astonished at the fact that such people might be in Heaven, they have never truly comprehended the fact that the only great astonishment is not that others will be there but that we ourselves will be there.

In the midst of our Christianity there are many who follow the terrible error of Balaam. They rob Christian people of the hope of the gospel by distorting the nature of the gospel. They make salvation partly by the grace of God and partly by works. Just recently I ran across a man who attempted to argue that while a man had nothing whatsoever to do with his first birth, he did have something to do with his second birth. That, of course, is not true according to the Word of God. And this man went on in his error to argue that because he had something to do with his salvation he retained the right to uncreate the new life which God creates within those who are born again, for if any man be in Christ, he is a new creation (II Cor. 5:17). All of this work of the creation of new life in the justification provided in the redemption set forth upon the cross of Calvary is the work of the Lord, the quickening, life-giving Spirit.

ALL BY GRACE

Do not let Satan rob you of your peace by taking your eyes from Christ, the surety and bond of your hope, in order to put your eyes on your own sinfulness. God has manifested Himself at the cross and He is seen to be both just and the justifier of him that believes in Jesus. There is no difference in the method whereby He declares man to be lost and the method whereby He declares Him to be justified. Salvation is all by grace.

And here it is necessary to inject a word of warning lest anyone think that I am teaching that as long as one believes he may do as he pleases. That teaching is furthest from my mind, and as we go on to study the further chapters it will be seen that the basis of a true life of holiness is nothing more nor less than a firm foundation in the doctrine of the sovereign grace of God.

Any attempt at creating a life of holiness by human effort is repugnant to God, but every attempt to yield self to Him for crucifixion death, so that the new life, joined to Him, may be flowing as a stream from the fountain of Calvary, is that in which He delights.

CHAPTER XVI

No Pride in Heaven

"Where is boasting then? It is excluded. By what law? of works? Nay: but by the law of faith" (Rom. 3:27).

WHAT A triumphant conclusion. The Spirit has used Paul to carry on the argument like a duelist who gets his confident adversary off guard in order to deliver the *coup de grace* and finish the combat. All phases of human religion have an element of human pride: Christianity alone—that is Biblical Christianity—has no place for pride. Phillips has translated this same verse in a trenchant way: "What happens now to human pride of achievement? There is no more room for it. Why, because failure to keep the Law has killed it? Not at all, but because the whole matter is now on a different plane—believing instead of achieving."

NO PLACE FOR SELF HELP

Man is almost incurably addicted to the principle of doing something toward his own salvation. I will change that and make it even stronger. It is not that man is almost incurably addicted to self-help in salvation, but that by himself he is absolutely and unchangeably addicted to that principle of lifting himself by his own bootstraps. The fact that no man has ever succeeded in doing it does not seem to deter him. It is all an illustration of the nature of the human heart and an example of the distance to which sin has flung man from the righteousness of God. When man thinks that he can do something to bring himself nearer to God he is thereby confessing his unawareness of his true distance from God. And when he thinks that God could be satisfied by something that comes from the human heart he is showing that he cannot comprehend the true holiness of God.

I have illustrated the great principle that is set forth here by an example that I have often preached and have now made into a colored motion picture, "The Geography of Salvation," because I know of nothing that can more clearly illuminate the divine principle of salvation by grace apart from the works of the law, and demonstrate the folly of boasting, since the principle of grace excludes it with finality.

OUT — NOT UP

One of the simplest of the lessons of geography is that altitude has no connection with latitude. I was brought up, for example, in California where there are the widest variations in altitude to be found in this country. Within a few miles of each other there are points that are well below the level of the sea and others that are the highest in the United States. Suppose a man were living down in the Salton Sea region and he desired to leave California. And suppose he said, "I will go over to Carmel. There I shall not be below sea level." But we inform him at once that though he has come to the level of the sea, he is still in California. "Well, then," he replies, "I shall go to the top of Mt. Whitney. You will admit, will you not, that there I shall be on the highest peak in the country?" We grant readily enough that no man can go higher on land in the United States, but we insist that he is still in California. The veriest child can understand the principle that a man cannot leave a state by going up. It is necessary to go out.

Now Scripture teaches expressly that all men are born into the country of death. Some gravitate to the penitentiary, or to skid row, far below the level of common decency. Others are far better than these and have reached a respectable altitude that may even be above the level of the average. Others reach the great heights of the finest in human morality and achievement. They may become professors of ethics, and write books on the difference between that which is good and that which is bad. But they are still in the same locality of death. A man who has descended to the lowest levels and has been a convict, a criminal of the lowest degree, does not change his status in the sight of God by reforming and becoming a respectable citizen.

The Lord Jesus Christ, when He came to this earth, came

into the country of death. The Scripture record is very plain—
Christ associated in general with the lowest levels of the popula-
tion, and the "good" people put Him to death. There are several
verses which speak of His associations and the criticism which
He received from the so-called "good" people because of it. The
Pharisees said, "This man receiveth sinners, and eateth with them"
(Luke 15:2). Our Lord knew the gossip that was circulating
concerning Himself, and made reference to it on one occasion.
Speaking of the difference between His own ministry and that of
John the Baptist, which had been an austere, severe, ascetic
ministry, the Lord said, "John came neither eating nor drinking,
and they say, He hath a demon." Then, contrasting His own message of high joy, and the sociableness which marked His nature
and being, He continued: "The Son of man came eating and
drinking, and they say, Behold, a man gluttonous, and a wine-
bibber, a friend of publicans and sinners" (Matt. 11:19).

THE BOASTFUL PHARISEES

That the Lord Jesus Christ associated with the common outcasts of society was one strong factor in His rejection by the
leaders of the people. The reason is to be found in their own
terrible pride and boasting. They thought that they were something special because they kept the semblance of the law. They
had built up an artificial idea of the law and were living up to this
counterfeit concept. They thought that because they satisfied their
own low requirements, they would also satisfy God. They had not
learned that boasting was excluded. They were still attached to
a system of law-works and had not even the remotest concept of
salvation by grace apart from the deeds of the law. This is why
they were so outraged when the police officers that were sent to
arrest the Lord came back without Christ, saying: "Never man
spake like this man" (John 7:46). "Then answered them the
Pharisees, Are ye also deceived? Have any of the rulers or of
the Pharisees believed on him? But this people [and it must be
read with a sneer to understand their true meaning] that knoweth
not the law are cursed" (John 7:47-49).

Their attitude was revealed from the very beginning of the
ministry of our Lord. It comes out clearly in the so-called Sermon

on the Mount. There the Lord certainly had in mind the truths which we are illustrating by our comparison of altitude and latitude. He saw all men in the country of death and did not care in the slightest on what level they lived or thought they lived. He turned to the common crowd, the average men who lived on the level of common decency and said to them, in the presence of the Pharisees, "I say unto you, That except your righteousness shall exceed the righteousness of the scribes and Pharisees, ye shall in no case enter into the kingdom of heaven" (Matt. 5:20). This must have been one of the most astounding phrases which the leaders of Israel had ever heard. By the time of Christ the entire revelation of truth which God had made through Moses had been corrupted by the leaders to teach a religion that was entirely alien to that faith which is the faith of Abraham, and which is the faith of all those who put their trust in Abraham's greater Son, the Lord Jesus. Little by little, through the years, they had come to the place where they had whittled down the provisions of the law of God, and had built themselves up in pride, until in their arrogant presumption they had come to think that they passed all the requirements of the Holy God. They were aware that their moral dwelling was mountains above the people who lived in the morass of sin, and they wanted credit for their attainments.

Suddenly, to hear this man, Jesus, address himself to the common herd and tell them that they would never see the kingdom of Heaven if they did not produce a righteousness superior to anything that the scribes and the Pharisees had produced, not only killed their hopes of salvation through their works, but was a death blow to their boasting. Practically speaking, the Lord Jesus was as good as crucified. Their hatred was now engendered, and would smolder until the moment when it would break forth to consume Him. The hatred of the leaders for the Lord Jesus was the hatred of outraged and injured pride.

There is a bottomless pit between the country of death and the country of life. It is totally impossible for any man to pass from one to the other by any means other than that which God has provided in Christ. The whole reason for the coming of the

Lord Jesus was to build a bridge across that abyss by dying in the place of sinners. It makes no difference whether a man has climbed to the highest peaks of earthly attainment and can see so far across into the country of life that he can discern some of its principles and even talk about preaching them and living by them. What is necessary is that a man commit himself to the one bridge across that gulf of death—the cross of Jesus Christ.

It should, perhaps, be pointed out that we are not saying at all that if a man crosses the bridge of faith in Christ, out of death and into life, he does not have to seek to change his moral altitude. The truth is that as soon as he passes across the bridge of redemption and finds himself in the land of life, he discovers that the soil is conducive to good works, and that he was saved in order that he might pursue the good works in the land of faith. The works that are roots, planted in self, can never produce anything that is satisfactory to God. If a man should receive anything because of what he had done for God, he could claim the reward, even Heaven itself, as something rightfully due him.

OUT OF DEATH

If we think of this whole matter as fitting on a map, it may become simple to every mind. You are born into the country of death, and there is only one passageway to the country of life, the bridge established by God Himself across the death of the Saviour. The purpose of God's salvation is to provide a way whereby the sinner might cross out of death and enter into life, and into a life of constant growth in Christ. Moral altitude in the country of death is not a factor in salvation. As a matter of fact, moral altitude in a non-Christian may be an obstacle to salvation.

The truth that human honor and integrity may be barriers against reaching Heaven was set forth by the Lord Jesus Christ in one of His oft-quoted and oft-misunderstood statements. I follow the King James Version here, and reject the revision. The rich young ruler came to Christ and said, "Good Master, what good thing shall I do, that I may have eternal life?" (Matt. 19:16). We must understand that this was a technical question and was answered by the Lord in a technical way. He knew the heart of the young man and wanted to bring him to see the folly of his whole way of thinking, so that he would leave the high peaks of his human honor in order to cross over by the bridge of redemption into the country of eternal life. The problem was to bring the young man down from the peaks of his pride so that he would be willing to take the steps of faith that were necessary to salvation. He had to be brought to see that his position was one that was cursed, and that there could be no salvation for him, whatsoever, if he chose to remain in the place that satisfied his pride but which could never satisfy the righteousness of God.

In order to bring this about it was necessary for the Lord to dynamite the young man's thinking so that he would abandon his natural sense of values and accept the divine standard of values. In order to do this, he had to be brought to the place where he realized that every thought which he possessed was no more than a human thought, and that it was vanity. The Lord, therefore, said, "Why callest thou me good?" The young man knew, of course, that measured by his human standards, Jesus Christ was the only good man he had ever seen, and, to him, it was an honorable recognition of worth on a human standard for him to call Christ *good*.

ONLY GOD GOOD

Christ knew, however, that He Himself was God, and that His goodness was not to be sullied by calling it good by human standards. There is a moral agreement in spiritual grammar, where words must be brought to agree in gender, number and case in a spiritual way. Hidden in Christ's question is the thought that a man must come to the place where he calls Christ "good God" or else He must be called "bad man." If His claims are studied closely, it is impossible to conceive of Christ in only His manhood as being good, even by human standards. For He claimed to be God, and taught men that they were to be willing to break up their homes in order to follow Him. He taught that loyalty to Himself took precedence over any human loyalty. And if Christ is nothing more than a man, then He is responsible for more evils than the originators of the concentration camps of Poland and Germany, and the instigators of every war. It is only by placing Christ in the right perspective that the light will fall on all human problems, and it will be seen that boasting is excluded, and that no man can reach the heights of God by climbing up the mountains of human righteousness.

Our Lord then said to the young man, "If thou wilt enter into life, keep the commandments." Now the Lord knew when He said it that it was impossible for the young man to do what He was being told to do. The purpose of setting the task before him was to reveal to him his need, so that he would climb down from his pretentions and come to the bridge of grace out of death and into life. For if a man is to attain to life eternal by keeping the commandments, he must pile mountain upon mountain until he has reached Heaven itself by his own doings. And, indeed, he must find a way to go back into his mother's womb and be born again with a different nature, with one that is without original sin.

The young man in his blindness, however, asked which of the commandments he had to keep. This was, of course, a revelation of his ignorance, for he should have known at once that he should love the Lord his God with all his heart, soul, mind and strength. The young man in his blindness, however, looks back over his artificial concept of the law, knows that he has never actually put poison in anyone's drink, has never actually commited adultery, has never actually stolen anyone's property, and he thinks that this is enough. He therefore asks, "What lack I yet?"

It is necessary at this point to reveal to him that he is on lost ground and that nothing that he can do in the country of death can take him across the abyss into the life of God and into the standards of God. Jesus has to show him that his heart is a human heart, a heart of selfishness, a heart of pride of possession. He, therefore, says to the young man, "If thou wilt be perfect, go and sell that thou hast, and give to the poor, and thou shalt have treasure in heaven: and come and follow me."

THE RESPONSIBILITY OF RICHES

Now with all the force of my being I wish to repudiate the idea that the Lord was teaching communism. There have been those who have taken this verse, and similar passages, and have attempted to teach that the Lord was requiring a redistribution of capital among men. This idea deserves nothing more than ridicule from anyone who knows and understands the teaching of the Word of God. When any man attempts to decry the profit motive from a Christian point of view he is playing fast and loose with the Word of God. Inherent in the commandment, "Thou shalt not steal," is the right of private property, just as surely as there is the prohibition of usury and extortion in the same commandment. If a man has secured property honestly, it is his, and the Holy Spirit has issued an injunction to preachers that they are to instruct the rich as to the manner in which they are to use their riches. "Charge them that are rich in this world," the Word of God says, "that they be not highminded, nor trust in uncertain riches, but in the living God, who giveth us richly all things to enjoy; that they do good, that they be rich in good works, ready to distribute, willing to communicate; laying up in store for themselves a good foundation against the time to come, that they may lay hold on eternal life" (I Tim. 6:17-19). Another translation renders the phrase, "Tell them to do good, to be rich in kindly actions, to be ready to give to others and to sympathize with those in distress. Their security should be invested in the life to come, so that they may be sure of holding a share in the life that is permanent."

The Lord concludes His teaching with a brief parable that has been distorted again and again to meanings that are alien from its true purpose. He looked after the young man who had departed sorrowing because he had great riches, and said to his disciples, "Verily I say unto you, That a rich man shall hardly enter into the kindom of heaven. And again I say unto you, It is easier for a camel to go through the eye of a needle, than for a rich man to enter into the kindom of God." When the disciples expressed their amazement, Jesus replied, "With men this is impossible; but with God all things are possible."

RELATIVE MARKS

When this parable is rightly understood there could be no better illustration of our text in Romans. "Where is boasting, then? It is excluded." The reason that it is difficult for the rich man to enter into the kingdom of Heaven is that he has climbed so high above other men in the country of death, that from his place of eminence and power he begins to look upon himself as something special. He has risen above the mass of men. Is he not better than they? In the language of the street, is he not what he is because he has what it takes? And if he has what it takes to get by with men, should he not expect to get by with God? For is it possible for the human mind to conceive of God's requirements as being other than human requirements on a little higher scale? A teacher never flunks the entire class. Marks are given on a relative basis in proportion to the attainments of the class. Marks are not given in any relationship with absolute knowledge. Therefore, when God marks men in the final examination, there will surely be the great majority of passing marks and a few with *cum laude,* fewer with *magna cum laude,* and a very few with *summa cum laude.* That is the way the rich man thinks. And when he was in college he got through, didn't he? He passed with a gentleman's marks—three C's and a D. And the man who was at the head of the class came to work for him at $3,600 a year and now has risen all the way to $6,000. Well, he thinks, somehow, perhaps it will be the same with God.

It is against this mentality that the Lord Jesus Christ says, "A rich man shall hardly enter into the kingdom of heaven." For if he is going to be saved, he must first abandon all the principles of living which put him where he is. He must curse his own zeal, he must deride his own ability as a go-getter. He must look down upon that factor in himself which furnished the inner drive that lifted him above other men. He must, in short, see himself as a bankrupt in the sight of God. "Where is boasting, then? It is excluded."

HOW THEN?

How can a camel pass through the eye of a needle? There have been scholars who have refused the validity of the explanation that has been given; but whether or not the detail is true in the field of architecture, it is true in the field of theology. The city gates were closed at sunset, and beside the great gates there were small gates which, it is said by some, were called the needle's eyes. If at the close of day the great gates were closed, and a shepherd and his flock came shortly afterwards, he could turn aside from the main way and easily enter the city by the small gate nearby, the gate called needle's eye. But if a caravan of a rich merchant came after the gate was closed, the camel upon which he rode had to be maneuvered through the gate also. To think of the man's riding through the gate in stately pride is out of the question. If he had come earlier, he would have ridden his beast with high disdain, and flipped a coin to a cringing beggar. But now the camel must be brought to its knees. The rider must dismount and walk through the gate like any lowly peasant. The camel, kneeling on a carpet, will be dragged through the gate, the frightened animal barely squeezing through.

This is the position of every man before God. The way of entry by works has been closed. The righteousness of God has barred the gates of pride. No man will enter into Heaven with the rich doings of his own life, and with the disdain and hauteur that accompany human pride. There will be no pride in Heaven except the proper pride of God, who alone is perfect, and who can alone rejoice in His own being because there is no lack in Him whatsoever. If we may change the parable, it is necessary for every man that he come down from his high horse. The Russian peasant has developed a proverb, "The man on horseback doesn't even recognize his own father."

Boasting has been excluded by God Himself. If you will get down into the place of bankruptcy, God will save your soul and take you across the bridge safely, out of death and into life through faith in the blood of Jesus Christ

CHAPTER XVII

Boasting Excluded

"Where is boasting then? It is excluded. By what law? of works? Nay: but by the law of faith. Therefore we conclude that a man is justified by faith without the deeds of the law" (Rom. 3:27, 28).

SALVATION is not vertical; it is horizontal. Unless that fact can be well comprehended salvation will never be understood. In our last study we saw that all men were born into the country of death and that every man sought his own moral level in that country of death. The convict who sinks below the level of common decency is in the country of death, but no more than is the ethical leader, or even the religious leader, who has climbed to great heights in the attainments of human character.

A NEW LIFE

When God moves to save an individual, He does not lift him to a better life, but takes him out of death and into life; and the new life is not merely a better life but an absolutely different, new, and, of course, better life. Man can move himself vertically to a better life or to a worse life, but God alone can take the man horizontally into an entirely different creation.

When this fact is understood the remainder of our text becomes very plain. "Where is boasting, then? It is excluded. By what law? of works? Nay, but by the law of faith." If salvation were vertical a man might boast. Here is a convict who has learned a hard lesson in prison. He comes out of the penitentiary with the firm resolution to lead a better life. He goes to work, toiling with his hands, and saving every penny that he can acquire. He is finally able to buy a small business, and does well in it, making a good profit and expanding the business until he is able to take his position as a substantial person in the community. If he did all that by the strength of his own resolution and the iron discipline of his own will, he could say that he had done well and that he had a right to boast about it. And he would probably boast, if the matter were ever brought up, among those of his friends who knew of his past. He had paid his debt to society and had demonstrated that he had the ability to lift himself out of the muck and to plant himself solidly among the best of the good citizens. His worth would have been proved by what he had done for himself. He would have a right to boast, for the law of works would give him that right.

But such strength of will and determination of resolve are not enough to take a man from the depths of sin to the heights of God. It is a short step from the depths of sin to the heights of man; that step has been taken by many. But no man has ever taken the step from the depths of sin to the heights of God. That can only be done by virtue of the death of the Saviour.

BOOT STRAPS

Perhaps this can be best illustrated by a story. Years ago, in California, there was a family consisting of a father, who had been born in Virginia, and a mother, who had been born in New York, and several small children. The grandfather was in Virginia and had never seen his daughter-in-law or his grandchildren. He determined to visit the West and see his family. The news of his approaching visit brought great joy and great preparations to that household. The house was painted, the curtains were cleaned, and everything was pointed to grandfather's visit. Grandfather would be here in two months. Grandfather would be here in one month; in two weeks; in a week; in three days; tomorrow. And then he came, the handsome old gentleman of the South with a white beard like General Robert E. Lee's, and a twinkle in his blue eyes.

The small grandson took a large share in the old gentleman's interest, and, of course, the boy was greatly impressed. One thing which he never forgot was a pair of slippers which the old gentleman wore. They were made with soft leather tops, and there were loops in the front and in the back by which they were pulled on the foot. Inevitably the little boy, five or so, put his feet, shoes and all, into the strange slippers, and reached down and put his fingers in the loops. The old grandfather said, "Pull hard, my boy, and see if you can lift yourself off the ground." When there was a great effort and, of course, failure, the old man said, "Well, that's too bad. You'll have to eat some more oatmeal, and then we will try again tomorrow." The little boy, who had been so overawed by all the excitement and the arrival of grandfather, had stopped eating each morning in the midst of his breakfast, for there were more important things than food to the curious mind. The parents had, at first, urged him to eat, and then the grandfather took charge. He reminded the boy that the slippers were waiting, and that there would be another trial when breakfast was over. If the movement of the spoon stopped for too long a period, the old man would wink at the boy, make a gesture toward his room where the slippers were, and the boy would speedily go to work on his oatmeal. When the breakfast was concluded the pair, age and youth, would go solemnly into the bedroom where another trial would be made. The little boy would pull and tug, but could never lift himself from the ground. At a convenient moment the old gentleman would say, "Well, we didn't make it this morning, but we'll try again tomorrow."

DOWNWARD PULL

You are inclined to smile at the lad and say, from the height of your superior knowledge, "Poor little boy! You were not aware that the law of gravity is pulling downward with greater force than you can ever exercise in an upward direction. That is why you cannot lift yourself, and you never will be able to lift yourself by your own power, because of that downward drag of gravitational pull." But though you use all of those long words on the boy, I tell you, straight, that you do not have too much right to talk. For many of you are guilty of greater folly than that of the boy. You take hold of your life and you pull and strain and tug and lift. The veins in your forehead stand out with the energy of your effort and the purple of your face witnesses to the fact that you are using all the force that you can muster. I come along and say to you, "What are you doing?" You give one more fren-

zied tug and say, "I'm lifting myself to Heaven, I hope . . . I hope
. . . I hope . . ." And I have every right to say to you, "Poor
child of Adam. You do not know that the downward pull of
sin and the force of your evil nature are exercising a greater downward force than you can ever overcome. You will never, never
be able to lift yourself from this earth to God. It is totally impossible because you do not have the force to overcome sin unto
righteousness."

The cases are absolutely parallel. If you could lift yourself
by your bootstraps, you would have something to boast about.
But if someone comes along and lifts you, then boasting is excluded. By what law? By the law of your struggling? Of course
not. It is excluded by the law of the outward force that lifted you.

LIFTED BY HIM

This is the case of the sinner. He cannot lift himself, but the
Lord Jesus Christ lays hold upon him and lifts him. We read it
in one of the Psalms: "He brought me up also out of an horrible
pit, out of the miry clay, and set my feet upon a rock, and established my goings. And he hath put a new song in my mouth, even
praise unto our God" (Ps. 40:2, 3). And what is that song that
the lifted man has learned to sing? Most certainly he is not going
to sing

"Unto me, myself, who got here by lifting myself by my
    own bootstraps."

There will be no such song in Heaven. The song that the redeemed
sing has no reference to what we were in ourselves, nor to anything that we have done for ourselves. Our song that He puts in
our mouth is a song of praise unto our God, "Unto him that
loved us, and washed us from our sins in his own blood" (Rev. 1:5).

> In loving kindness, Jesus came
> My soul in mercy to reclaim;
> And from the depths of sin and shame,
> Through grace He lifted me.
>
> From sinking sands He lifted me;
> With tender hands, He lifted me;
> From shades of night to plains of light,
> O, praise His name! He lifted me.

He sought me long before I heard,
Before my sinful heart was stirred;
But, when I took Him at His word,
Through grace He lifted me.

His brow was pierced with many a thorn,
His hands by cruel nails were torn,
When from my sin and guilt forlorn,
In love He lifted me.

Where is boasting then? It is excluded. By what law? By the law of lifting yourself? No, by the law of being lifted by the Saviour who came down from Heaven in order to perform exactly that work of redemption.

This plain setting forth of the difference in objective of a system built on works and a system built on faith brings with it certain positive conclusions. A man who is attached to a system of salvation by works may be lifted morally, and may change his altitude for a higher position in the country of death, but he will ultimately land in the lake of fire according to the just judgment of God. The man who is attached to the Biblical system of salvation by faith will be lifted spiritually across the bridge of the cross of Christ, out of death and into life. He will be placed on a new foundation from which the slow process of spiritual growth in this world will begin, but his eternal destiny is settled in the very moment of his transfer, and he is bound for Heaven and the glories of the Lord forever.

EXCLUDE—CONCLUDE

Verse 27 states positively that boasting is excluded, and verse 28 draws from this the conclusion that we are justified by faith without the deeds of the law. It should be noticed that the words *exclude* and *conclude* that are used in these neighboring sentences are from the same root. The English forms are almost pure Latin. The word *claudere* means "to shut." The prefixes give the variations of meaning: *include* to shut something within; *exclude* to shut something out; *conclude* to shut something up closely. An illustration of how language grows, often through the ignorance of people using words they do not really know, is the now famous phrase used by the Hollywood producer from eastern Europe who has done amazing things to the English language. He made his decision as to whether he would go along on a certain deal, by saying, "Include me out." In the language of the New Testament the word for "exclude" has exactly the same meaning as that of the Latin and the English. But the revision correctly translates the second word by "reckon," "figure it out; it really adds up." Salvation is by grace apart from works.

In our text the boasting is barred, shut out, made absolutely impossible. We are, on the other hand, shut up closely to the idea that justification must be entirely by faith without the deeds of the law. There is no possibility whatsoever of mixing the principles of salvation. You are lost by works or you are saved by grace through faith.

It is, perhaps, necessary, to erect one more barrier against the charge that we teach that if there is true faith then there need be no care about the state of one's actions. We repudiate that idea with horror. We remind you merely that the word "works" is used twice in one passage in Ephesians, and that in one case the works are excluded as a means of salvation and in the next lines they are demanded as the fruit of salvation. "For by grace are ye saved through faith; and that [faith] not of yourselves; it is the gift of God: not of works [underline it, *not of works*], lest any man should boast. For we are his workmanship, created in Christ Jesus unto good works [underline it, *created unto good works*], which God hath before ordained that we should walk in them" (Eph. 2:8-10).

JAMES VS. PAUL

The most common objection raised against the doctrine of salvation exclusively by faith is brought out of a misunderstanding of the Epistle of James. Even Luther, great man that he was, and great Christian, fell into the trap of the obvious, and called the Epistle of James an epistle of straw because he did not understand the simple relationship between the two points of view.

Our text in Romans states flatly, "We conclude that a man is justified by faith without the deeds of the law." The Epistle to James says something that seems to contradict this, though it will be seen that it truly corroborates and establishes the idea which is set forth in our text. James writes: "What does it profit, my brethren, though a man says he has faith, and has not works? can [that] faith save him? . . . Faith, by itself, if it has no works, is dead. But someone will say, you have faith and I have works. Show me your faith apart from your works and I by my works will show you my faith . . . faith without works is barren, dead" (Jas. 2:14, 17-20).

James is not contradicting salvation by faith, he is illustrating it. Salvation is not by words, whether they be mumbled or spoken clearly. If a man says that he has faith, there is only one way to prove that it is saving faith, and that is for it to show its fruit. The contrast between James and Paul is really an illustration of the truth that was set forth at the time Samuel went down to the house of Jesse to anoint a king. The choice finally fell upon David, but at the beginning the older brothers were presented. The first was a magnificent specimen, every inch a king, by human standards. But the Lord refused to permit Samuel to anoint him, saying, "The Lord seeth not as man seeth; for man looketh on the outward appearance, but the Lord looketh on the heart" (I Sam. 16:7). In much the same way we could say that James looks upon the outward appearance, but Paul looks upon the heart.

Salvation, so far as God is concerned, is entirely by faith. Works do not play even the fraction of a fraction of a per cent in procuring salvation for a man. God is able to see if the soul has looked away from self in despair and has fixed the entire hope of the being on the sinless Son of God as the substitute provided by God. But how can such a truth become manifest to men? There is only one answer to that question. It is by our outworking of the inward life that man shall see our good works and glorify our Father which is in Heaven. If faith is true faith, it must produce life, and life consists of living works that glorify God. All of these things can be counterfeit, and that is why God alone is capable of telling whether the faith be real or an illusion. We shall see in a later chapter that the Holy Spirit makes known to the individual, in harmony with the Word of God, the reality of His presence in the heart of the believer, and that presence must produce a life and works that are consonant with the holiness of that Holy Spirit.

LIFE THE TEST

I once read a story of a Bavarian wood carver who saw a piece of wood in the mouth of a sack of grain. The wood was the precise color of the grain. The man took the wood and began to carve imitation grains of wheat. Finally he had a small handful of them, and, mixing them with real grain, defied his friends to tell them apart. In fact, his artistry had been so fine that he, himself, was not able to tell the natural from the artificial. Ultimately, the only way to tell the two apart was to put them in water for a day or two. The grains that were from nature sprouted. The ones that had been carved remained exactly what they were—dead imitations.

God has created life within the hearts of those who have been born again. There is the possibility that men may imitate the life of the Christian by copying some of his ways and echoing some of his words. But, in the long run, the difference between the two shall be made manifest by the gaze of God who can tell the difference between the real and the false. In the meantime, we who are Christians must be "careful to maintain good works" (Titus 3:8, 14).

Justification in the eyes of men may be according to a thousand different standards. Justification in the eyes of God will be according to His own being and righteousness. "Therefore we conclude that a man is justified by faith without the deeds of the law."

The passage that we have before us is a conclusion, stated to be a conclusion. The truths have been set forth in part in previous portions of the epistle, but now the matter is summarized and stated in a fashion so definite that there is no means of getting away from the thunder of the judgment of God. Boasting is excluded; justification is by faith. The reason why it is so necessary to spell this truth out in words of one syllable, and even in simplest letters, is that man is so prone to see good in himself and to seek reward for something that he has himself produced. Some time ago in one of my Bible classes where there was a question-box period preceding the study, the following question was asked: "Since all our sins that have been committed before we received Christ are washed away when we are saved, the question arises as to whether the good works which we have done before we were saved can remain to be counted to our credit for reward?" The answer, of course, was that all that are named by the name of good works in the unsaved man are really sin.

An example can be brought to us from the dairy farm. Men milk cows that are infected, and the milk contains the germs of tuberculosis or undulant fever. A scientist who tests the liquid knows that every part of it is infected. But a man, unacquainted with the ways of science, might place the milk in a centrifuge and separate the cream from the skimmed milk. He then would argue that the cream was worth something because it had a high butter fat content, but the scientist knows that the infection can be carried by the cream as readily as by the skimmed milk. It is only by man's judgment that the deeds of the race may be divided into cream and skimmed milk, or good deeds and bad deeds. In the sight of God it is all infected. He must reject everything that has ever touched man. That is why boasting is excluded. A Jersey cow might furnish more butter-fat than a Holstein, but if both were infected there would be no boasting for either of them. Both would have to be dealt with lest the poison within them be spread to the detriment of all.

FAITH'S LAW

Finally, it should be noted that the word *law* is used here in connection with the word *faith*. To make the passage more striking, we may place the word in the possessive case and read it: Boasting is excluded. By means of what law? Of works? No, but by means of faith's law.

What, then, is faith's law? What is this that shuts out boasting? It is the principle which sets forth that we are not to deserve, but that we are to trust. If it is possible for you to learn that lesson, you will have entered into the very rest of God. There is no truth more wonderful than that which is set forth in the Epistle to the Hebrews, which states: "He that is entered into his rest, he also hath ceased from his own works, as God did from his. Let us labor therefore to enter into that rest" (Heb. 4:10, 11). A rabbi may write about peace of mind, a priest may write about peace of soul, but there is no true peace, no peace of heart or

of spirit or of the whole being unless faith's law has been understood. We must labor to enter into the rest of God. We must
force ourselves to appraise our very goodness as evil in the sight
of God though it will still be goodness in the sight of men. We
must force ourselves to understand the nature of the separation
that is involved in this reckoning.

Bishop Moule has a beautiful paragraph with which we may
conclude: "And who can analyze or describe the joy and rest
of the soul from which at last is 'shut out' the foul inflation of
a religious 'boast'? We have praised ourselves, we have valued
ourselves, on one thing or another supposed to make us worthy
of the Eternal. We may perhaps have had some specious pre-
texts for doing so; or we may have 'boasted' (such boastings are
not unknown) of nothing better than being a little less ungodly,
or a little more manly, than some one else. But this is over now
forever, in principle; and we lay its practice under our Redeemer's
feet to be destroyed. And great is the rest and gladness of sitting
down at His feet, while the door is shut and the key is turned
upon our self-applause. There is no holiness without that 'exclusion'; and there is no happiness where holiness is not. . . . So
here we conclude, we reckon, that the justification of fallen man
takes place, as to the merit which procures it, irrespective of his
well-doing. It is respective only of Christ, as to merit; it has to
do only, as to personal reception, with the acceptance of the
meriting Christ, that is to say, with faith in Him."

Wesley sang it:

> And can it be that I should gain
> An interest in the Saviour's blood?
> Died He for me, who caused His pain?
> For me, who Him to death pursued?
> Amazing love! How can it be?
> That Thou, my God shouldst die for me!
>
> 'Tis mystery all! The Immortal dies;
> Who can explore His strange design?
> In vain the first-born seraph tries
> To sound the depths of love divine.
> 'Tis mercy all! let earth adore,
> Let angel minds inquire no more.

He left His Father's throne above—
So free, so infinite His grace—
Emptied Himself of all but love,
And bled for Adam's helpless race.
'Tis mercy all, immense and free;
For, O my God, it found out me!

Long my imprisoned spirit lay
Fast bound in sin and nature's night;
Thine eye diffused a quickening ray—
I woke; the dungeon flamed with light;
My chains fell off, my heart was free,
I rose, went forth, and followed Thee.

No condemnation now I dread;
Jesus and all in Him, is mine!
Alive in Him, my living Head,
And clothed in righteousness divine,
Bold, I approach the eternal throne,
And claim the crown, through Christ, my own.

CHAPTER XVIII

Two Families — Two Fathers

*"Is he the God of the Jews only? Is he not also of the Gentiles?
Yes, of the Gentiles also: seeing it is one God, which shall justify
the circumcision by faith, and uncircumcision through faith. Do
we then make void the law through faith? God forbid: yea, we
establish the law" (Rom. 3:29-31).*

T HE THIRD chapter of Romans comes to its close with what
Bishop Moule has called "a short 'coda' following a full musi-
cal cadence." There are "two brief questions and their answers,
spoken almost as if against a Rabbinist in discussion."

URGENT NEED

To any Jew who might read these lines we make a heart-
searching appeal. We need these truths that are set forth here.
We need them desperately. For we stand before the Old Testament to acknowledge that there is but one God, and that He is
the God of Abraham, the God of Isaac, and the God of Jacob. As
we stand there, afar off, we realize that we are, by race and
heritage, the *goyim*, the Gentiles, members of the outcast nations,
and that we were so placed originally by the God of Israel. We
accept as a fact that we do not have, by nature, a priesthood, an
altar, a blood sacrifice. We accept that we have no means of
access to the holiest of all, that we are godless, hopeless, and
Christless by nature.

Therefore we stand in the most urgent need. Unless some
way can be found to bring us in, we are doomed to be outside
with the unclean, and forever. The problem to us is one that
tops all others. We do not come with brazen face knocking at
the wall of partition and asking that we be admitted of right.
We stand in the place of penitence, far off from God. We are like
Ruth, the Moabitess, half way between the Gentile world of the
curse and the altar of Israel. We look back into our own heritage

and proclaim its bankruptcy. It has nothing that can satisfy our hearts, and we realize that it was a man-made substitute. We know that it is not true in physics that nature abhors a vacuum, but we know that spiritually a vacuum is intolerable. Because our fathers did not have the truth they took the counterfeit. We are, indeed, the children of the uncircumcision. If God is a national God, then I am lost and going to spend eternity in Hell. Therefore it is of great importance to me to establish the fact that God is universal.

NO PROMISE CANCELED

In demonstrating that God is for all men, it does not follow in logic that the particular promises which He has made to an individual people are thereby canceled. The rest of the epistle will show beyond question that God has made definite promises to the people of Israel, and that the day will come when He will fulfill those promises to the last iota.

We shall now set forth the following truths: We shall show that God was the God of the Gentiles even during the age of Moses, and that there was provision made for the salvation of Gentiles at all periods of history. We shall then show that God has a certain relationship to all men and a special relationship to some men. When those principles are understood, the Bible revelation will be much clearer.

In the first place, then, we turn to the Old Testament and find that during the reign of the law of Moses there was provision made for the approach of the Gentiles. Part of the difficulty that has arisen stems from the fact that some people have thought that salvation was by character, and that there was some connection between keeping the law of Moses and being saved. That, of course, is not true. At no period in history have men been saved in any other way than by faith in the grace of God, manifested in His own sovereign way, and conditioned only on believing His Word about the shedding of the blood of the sacrifices which He commanded.

It is very unfortunate that there have been those who have set forth legal obedience as a condition of salvation. Take, for example, an unhappy line in a note by Dr. Scofield in the edition of the Bible whose references bear his name. Under the first chapter of John's Gospel we read, "As a dispensation, grace begins with the death and resurrection of Christ. The point of testing is no longer legal obedience as the condition of salvation." I am still convinced that the Bible with the references by Dr. Scofield is the quickest way of bringing a spiritual baby to spiritual maturity, but that particular sentence is most unfortunate. It has bothered me for years, for I know from the rest of his writings that Dr. Scofield never for one moment intended to teach that works were a part of salvation at any time or in any age. Perhaps he meant that obedience to the law of the offerings was a condition of salvation—that a sinner had to bring a lamb and have its blood shed by the priest. If that is so the line may stand. But most certainly obedience to the moral law was never a condition of salvation. If it had been no man would ever have been saved. None but the Lord Jesus ever presented God with obedience to the moral law. It would have been much better if he had written "legal obedience as the *evidence* of Salvation." That is true.

THE GENTILE UNDER LAW

Since salvation was through grace, since that grace was furnished the sinner on the grounds of the death of the atoning sacrifice, and since that sacrifice could be offered only at Jerusalem and only by a son of Aaron, it is obvious that there was no method for a Gentile to be saved except through the Jewish priesthood. And there was no approach to the Jewish priesthood except by a circumcised member of one of the thirteen tribes of Israel—the twelve tribes that had land and the thirteenth tribe, Levi, whose portion was the Lord.

The law made provision for the entrance of a Gentile into the tribes of Israel, and this was God's provision for salvation for any individual in the age of Moses. Thus we can understand that Ruth, daughter of the tribe of Moab, but widow of a Jew who had dwelt in her land, made her decision to return with her mother-in-law, Naomi, and become a Jewess. Thus she said, "Intreat me not to leave thee, or to return from following after thee: for whither thou goest, I will go; and where thou lodgest, I will lodge: thy people shall be my people, and thy God my God" (Ruth 1:16).

Note that she claimed kinship with the people before she claimed relationship with God. It had to be that way; that was the way that God had made salvation possible to the Gentiles. If someone should ask why God would have demanded a change of nationality before salvation, the answer is simple: the Lord was showing that salvation could be obtained only through Israel, and that the blood had to be shed in Jerusalem. It was a pageant of the exclusive finality of salvation through Jesus Christ, in the death which He accomplished on the hill of Calvary, outside the city wall.

OLD TESTAMENT GENTILES

The words of our Lord to the woman of Samaria should be remembered in this connection. He had revealed to her the depths of her sin, and she had sought to change the subject by asking a theological question concerning the place of sacrifice. "Our fathers [the Samaritans] worshipped in this mountain [Gerizim]; and ye say, that in Jerusalem is the place where men ought to worship" (John 4:20). It is very fortunate that the Lord Jesus lived before Emily Post, for He would never have been permitted to answer in the abrupt and dogmatic fashion which He chose if He had lived in our more enlightened days! He replied with a finality that condemned her utterly, "Ye worship ye know not what; we know what we worship; for salvation is of the Jews" (v. 22). This is to say that there was but one sacrifice and one place of sacrifice, just as He would later transfer it all to Himself and say, "I am the way, the truth, and the life: no man cometh unto the Father, but by me" (John 14:6).

Still another illustration of God's provision for the salvation of Gentiles in the Old Testament days is to be found in the Book of Esther. A nasty bit of anti-Semitism had developed, and by the providence of God and through the instrumentality of Esther, the people were saved. The gallows which had been prepared for Mordecai the Jew, bore the swinging body of Haman. And then we read: And in every province, and in every city, whithersoever the king's commandment and decree came, the Jews had joy and gladness, and a good day. And—note this—it says many of the people of the land became Jews; for the fear of the Jews fell upon them (Esther 8:17). Now it is the Biblical way of saying

that multitudes of the people were saved. They became Jews—
they were circumcised and admitted to one of the tribes—and
now they could bring a lamb and offer the sacrifices at Jerusalem.
God had made provision for them thus.

NAAMAN

The final example that we bring of this Old Testament provision for salvation of the Gentiles is that of the Syrian general,
Naaman. He was the Hitler of his day. He led the armies that
entered and devastated Palestine, killing the men, ravishing the
women, and taking many slaves back to Syria. Among these was
a young Jewish girl who was installed as a slave in the home of
Naaman. When the latter developed leprosy, the young maiden
testified that there was a prophet of God in Israel who would be
able to heal him. She had no evidence to go on other than the
accounts in the Word of God which made provision for the purifi-
cation ceremony of a healed leper. She had never known of anyone to be healed, for Christ Himself said that there were many
lepers in Israel in the days of Elisha, but not one of them was
healed except Naaman, the Syrian (Luke 4:27). At all events,
Naaman went on a pilgrimage to the home of Elisha who told
him to go and wash seven times in the Jordan. The general was
annoyed that the prophet had not acted in some flamboyant
fashion, and complained that the rivers of Damascus, Abana and
Pharpar, were better rivers than the Jordan. But when one of his
followers suggested that it would do no harm to test the prophet,
Naaman obeyed and was healed.

There then follows a very illuminating paragraph in the story.
Naaman ordered his followers to pack several sacks of dirt, enough
to load two mules. And the Scripture continues the story with
a conjunction joining up the act with the purpose, "For thy servant
will henceforth offer neither burnt-offering nor sacrifice unto other
gods, but unto Jehovah" (II Kings 5:17).

We can see the caravan returning to the home of Naaman.
The news has gone ahead that the master is arriving and that
he has been healed. He dismounts from his camel, and his chief
concern is that the precious loads of dirt shall be cared for. They
are carried into his house and poured out within a framework

that has now been made for them. No one is allowed to go near this corner; but Naaman stands on it, as though he were standing on the soil of Palestine, and prays to Jehovah, he a Gentile without any promise from God, but relying on the same grace that healed him.

He who had loudly protested the superiority of Damascus water now openly proclaims the superiority of Jewish dirt. He stands upon it as though he were a Jew, and claims the grace of the great God of all grace.

If Naaman possessed a copy of the Psalms he could well have sung, "I will praise thee with my whole heart: before the gods will I sing praise unto thee. I will worship toward thy holy temple, and praise thy name for thy lovingkindness and for thy truth: for thou hast magnified thy word above all thy name. In the day when I cried thou answeredst me, and strengthenedst me with strength in my soul. All the kings of the earth shall praise thee, O Lord, when they hear the words of thy mouth . . . Though the Lord be high, yet hath he respect unto the lowly; but the proud he knoweth afar off" (Ps. 138:1-4, 6).

RELATIONSHIP

Having established that the God of Israel had, indeed, a method for saving Gentiles before the time of Christ, we now turn to the fact that God has a certain relationship to every child of Adam, and a special relationship to some.

God is the Creator of all men and therefore has a Creator's interest in His creation. His certain relationship to all beings is the relationship of creation. His special relationship to some is that of the Father. We are aware of the implications of our manner of expression and we shall show, specifically, from the Word of God that the Lord Himself declares that He is not the Father of all men, though He does become the Father of some.

Since God created the first pair and gave to them their attributes, it follows that He has a certain relationship to this pair and all their progeny. This truth was set forth by Paul in his address to the Athenians on Mars' Hill. "As I passed by, and beheld your devotions, I found an altar with this inscription, TO THE UNKNOWN GOD. Whom therefore ye ignorantly worship, him declare I unto you. God that made the world and all things therein, seeing that he is Lord of heaven and earth, dwelleth not in temples made with hands; neither is worshipped with men's hands, as though he needed any thing, seeing he giveth to all life, and breath, and all things; and hath made of one blood all nations of men for to dwell on all the face of the earth, and hath determined the times before appointed, and the bounds of their habitation; that they should seek the Lord, if haply they might feel after him, and find him, though he be not far from every one of us; for in him we live, and move, and have our being; as certain also of your own poets have said, For we are also his offspring. Forasmuch then as we are the offspring of God, we ought not to think that the Godhead is like unto gold, or silver, or stone, graven by art and man's device" (Acts 17:23-29).

We are, then, the creatures of God. But in admitting this relationship it is very important that we do not presume upon it and claim something that God has not given to the race inherently. Apes are also creatures of God, but they cannot be placed in the category of His offspring, let alone in the category of His children.

THREE CATEGORIES

We are noting three categories: creatures, offspring, and children. And we shall show from Scripture that God is in a different relationship to each of these three. We can dismiss the relationship of the animals with a single sentence: God created them; they are mortal; they are creatures for the moment; and they have no life beyond death. They have body and individuality, but they are in no wise in the image of God, and are made for man to dominate and use as he will as God said when He brought them before Adam for him to name them.

The human being, however, was made in the image of God. There was something of God in man when God created man. We use the past tense with careful thought, for the Bible tells us that the divine in man was lost in the fall. It is stark heresy to claim that there is even a spark of the divine within the human being apart from Christ. The unregenerate world contains no more than the burned out cinders of a fire and light that have been long lost, and that God Himself declares never can be re-lighted. If ever there is to be spiritual life within man, it must be the result of a new creation, a regeneration.

The Lord Jesus Himself made a most careful distinction be-tween men who were merely the offspring of God and those who had become His children. During His ministry the Lord faced a group of people who had begun to follow Him, and said, "If ye continue in my word, then are ye my disciples indeed; and ye shall know the truth, and the truth shall make you free" (John 8:31, 32). It should be noted that this does not mean that what men *think* to be truth at any given moment shall make men free from what some call the shackles of faith. This means that the truth as it is in Christ shall make men free from sin and the results of sin. Those to whom He spoke were offended because He said that they should be free. There is a proverb which says that one should never speak of a cord in the house of a hangman. Christ's hearers did not wish to be reminded that they were in bondage to the Roman Empire at that moment. In pride, therefore, and in lying, they answered Him: "We be Abraham's seed, and were never in bondage to any man: how sayest thou, Ye shall be made free?" It was a preposterous statement; they had been slaves in Egypt for 400 years, slaves to the Philistines on a score of occa-sions during the period of the Judges, slaves to Babylon for seventy years at the time of the captivity, and had finally returned, only to become the slaves of Alexander the Great, and later of the Romans. They had Caesar's image on the coins in their purses even as they spoke. Christ passed over the matter, however, and gave further teaching on the subject of sin and the slavery of the soul. He said, "I know that ye are Abraham's seed" [note the word "seed" and see it contrasted in a moment with "children"]. "I know that ye are Abraham's seed; but ye seek to kill me, because my word hath no place in you. I speak that which I have seen with my Father: and ye do that which ye have seen with your father. They answered and said unto him, Abraham is our father. Jesus saith unto them, If ye were Abraham's children [see that distinc-tion between "seed" and "children"] ye would do the works of Abraham . . . Ye do the deeds of your father."

SEED AND CHILDREN

This distinction between seed and children is one of the most important in all the Scriptures. The former word implies a physical descent, the latter implies a spiritual likeness. Paul's address on Mars' Hill might be summed up: "Ye are the offspring of God, but you should become His children, for He is offering you the privilege and has opened the way for you to become His sons." Christ's address to these early followers is even more categorical. For He denies that the physical relationship conveys any privileges and teaches flatly that a spiritual relationship is the one that is important. Adam was created in the image of God, but he begat sons and daughters in his own image, as we read in the fifth chapter of Genesis. Adam passed on to them from the genes and chromosomes of his body the physical pattern of the human race. But the entrance of sin from the Devil introduced a new spiritual potentiality, and all those who are not redeemed through faith in God's sovereign grace are seen to be children of another father. Thus Christ continues, "Ye do the deeds of your father." When they protested, "We be not born of fornication; we have one Father, even God," Christ denied the claim most vehemently. He said to them, "If God were your Father, ye would love me: for I proceeded forth and came from God . . . Ye are of your father the devil, and the lusts of your father ye will do. He was a murderer from the beginning, and abode not in the truth, because there is no truth in him. When he speaketh a lie, he speaketh of his own: for he is a liar, and the father of it" (John 8:42-44).

So much for the general relationship of God to the human beings who are His creatures, but who are in the wretched, debased state of being rebels who refuse the righteousness which He offers through Christ.

SONS

The special relationship of sons is that which He reserves for those who, believing the divine verdicts concerning sin and salvation, turn away from self and its works and trust His justifying work as provided in Christ.

Our text, then, may now be simply understood. God is the

God of all men, without respect to race. All men are therefore
totally responsible to Him and will be judged by Him on His
own terms. But sin has entered and all men have fallen to the
level of creature-offspring, who have the seed of Adam within
them, but not the life of God. He is, therefore, not their Father
and they are not His children. He has provided life through Jesus
Christ which He will give in grace to those who abandon all hope
of providing for their own salvation and will accept as bankrupts
that which He gives through grace. To these He gives life, justifies
them freely through grace, and counts them as sons, giving them
the right to call Him their Heavenly Father, which right belongs
to none save those who thus believe in Christ.

There are, therefore, in this world two families and two father-
hoods. There is the great family of the unregenerate, children
of the Devil, who refuse to repent and surrender unconditionally
to the grace of God as set forth in His plan. There is also the
great family of the redeemed, who have seen their lost condition
and accepted all that God has to say about their nature, and all
that God has to say about His Son Jesus Christ. By faith, God
justifies all who thus believe, and becomes their Father. How
wonderful is such a plan!

But does such a plan make void the law of God? Not at
all. For, as we shall see, it really establishes the law.

CHAPTER XIX

The Law Established

"Do we then make void the law through faith? God forbid: yea, we establish the law" (Rom. 3:31).

DOES FAITH make void the law? Never. Faith establishes the law. This is the expression of the doubt that might rise in the minds of some and the positive way in which God treats that doubt. Through three chapters, the Holy Spirit has established the fact of man's complete ruin in sin; and now, for the last ten verses in the third chapter, He has presented the summary of the arguments that salvation is by faith alone apart from the works of the law. The question then rises: Are you then teaching that the law was worthless? Or are you teaching that the law is now made void? And the answer comes: God forbid; what we are saying really establishes the law.

The law is established in several ways: as an expression of the holiness of God; as an expression of the righteousness of God; as the revelation of the sinfulness of man; and as a sword to slay man. But the entrance of faith's law—the law of righteousness through Christ—established the law forever as a demonstration that God demanded its fulfillment to the last iota and exacted its extreme penalty from Christ.

HOLINESS AND RIGHTEOUSNESS

First, the law is established as an expression of the holiness of God. God demands what He is intrinsically in Himself. The setting forth of the law is the manifestation of the principles of honor, honesty, integrity, justice, truth, purity, virtue, equity, and loyalty; and it is the manifestation of all these to the highest degree. When we look at the law we can understand that the seraphs before God must veil their faces as they fly, crying, "Holy, holy, holy, is the Lord of Hosts" (Isa. 6:3). The moral law is like a coin that comes out of the mint, revealing that hidden away

184

in the recesses of the great presses is the invisible die which is minted into the coin which we hold.

And, second, if one side of the coin reveals the holiness of God, the other reveals His righteousness. The law is a demanding thing. God must require righteousness of His creation even as He is all righteousness in Himself. It makes no difference that no member of the creation is able to fulfill the righteousness that is required. The demand is a part of the essential nature of God. He would have been forced by His very being to demand righteousness, positive righteousness and perfect righteousness, even if thereby no soul could have approached Him. It was His love that made it possible for a way to be found whereby those who had fallen short of His holiness and righteousness could be brought into His presence with joy and peace. But the demands were always there, and the law is the perfect expression of that righteousness which we worship and adore.

MAN'S SINFULNESS

In the third place, the law is the revelation of the sinfulness of man. Though there are ten of the commandments in the moral law, they have been summed up by the Lord Jesus in two commandments. A man once asked the Lord Jesus which was the greatest of the commandments, and His reply was, "Thou shalt love the Lord thy God with all thy heart, and with all thy soul, and with all thy mind. This is the first and great commandment" (Matt. 22:37, 38). Now if a man had broken only the fourth commandment, he might be called a fourth commandment sinner. If he had broken only the sixth commandment, he might be called a sixth commandment sinner. Then what shall we call a man who has broken what the Lord has called "the first and great commandment"? Shall we not say that he is the first and great sinner? And is it not true that no man has ever lived up to the provisions of that commandment? Is it not true that you, and every member of the human race, have sinned both in omission and commission? We have left undone the things we ought to have done and have done the things that we ought not to have done.

For several years I acted as pastor in one of the French Protestant churches, l'Eglise Réformée Evangélique. There was a set liturgy for the services each Sunday morning. At the point following the reading of the summary of the law, the congregation sang a French hymn, the translation of which is "O God, Thy law is holy; and Thy commandment is holy, just and good. And if Thou shouldst mark iniquity, O Lord, who could stand before Thee?" It was a solemn moment in each service, and the congregation, it seemed to me, always did some of its best singing at that point. Here was something that each heart knew to be true, and each voice could put strength into such a sentiment because it was something that the heart and the mind joined together in acknowledging as true, as most certainly true. Sometimes it seemed as though some of the people did not dare to sing out as lustily on the free promises of the gospel, and on the setting forth of assurance and trust in the promises, as they did on this acknowledgment of sin. It is, perhaps, good for men to be willing to acknowledge, freely, the existence of their sin; but God wants us to know our sin only in order that we may step forth on His righteousness and sing the song of praise which He has put in our mouths, and which He has given us strength enough to sing.

The existence of laws prohibiting certain actions is always the proof that there are many transgressors. A hundred years ago there was no law in the world which said that a man might not travel at sixty miles an hour. The reason that such laws did not exist is because nobody in the world at that time ever did travel 60 miles an hour. And the reason that such laws have been passed is because there are men who go sixty miles an hour in places and at times that create danger for other people. Therefore, the legislative bodies passed laws prohibiting speeds that were perilous to others. And it follows, therefore, that the giving forth of the decree, "Thou shalt have no other gods before me," demonstrates the existence of people who had put other gods in the place of the one living and true God. When it is declared that no graven images should ever be made, it demonstrates that there were people at that time who had made graven images and were bowing themselves down before idols to worship them. When the law declared "Thou shalt not kill," there was set forth, at the same time, the fact that there were murderers who would think nothing of slaying one of their fellow men. The existence of the law, then, establishes the fact of man's sinfulness.

FALSE HOPE GONE

Again, fourth, the law is established as that which slays men. It is the law which dooms the hope of the sinner to attain salvation by his own efforts. If the commandment proclaims the holiness of God and the sinfulness of the sinner, all at the same time, it thereby removes the hope of the sinner to attain salvation by some means other than the grace of God. As long as there is no law, a sinner might cradle himself in the false hope of salvation by something that can proceed from the human heart. The moment that the law is given, however, it shuts every mouth and brings all the world guilty before God. The law, as we have seen, is like a mirror in that it can show you that you are dirty but it cannot cleanse you from the dirt. The purpose of the mirror is to drive you from itself to the water; and the purpose of the law is to drive you to the Lord Jesus Christ. It is a sword that slays the sinner, but it places the sinner where he can be made alive through the death of the Saviour.

The most important of all phases of the establishment of the law by the new principle of the law of faith is that the final authority of God and the setting forth of the nature of His judgment is firmly established. There is a page in Newell that illustrates this fact very strongly. He says:

"It is the constant cry of those who oppose grace, and most especially that declaration of grace that our justification is apart from law—apart from the works of the law—apart from ordinances, that it overthrows the Divine authority. But in this verse Paul says 'we establish law' through this doctrine of simple faith.

"To illustrate: In the wilderness a man was found gathering up sticks to make a fire on the sabbath day. Now the law had said, 'Ye shall kindle no fire throughout your habitations on the sabbath day.' How, then, was this law to be 'established'? By letting the law-breaker off? No. By securing his promise to keep the law in the future? No. By finding someone who had kept this commandment always, perfectly, and letting his obedience be reckoned to the law-breaker? No, in no wise.

"How then was the law established? You know very well. All Israel was commanded by Jehovah to stone the man to death. We read, 'And they that found him gathering sticks brought him unto Moses and Aaron, and unto all the congregation, And they put him in ward, because it had not been declared what should be done to him. And Jehovah said unto Moses, The man shall surely be put to death; all the congregation shall stone him with stones without the camp. And all the congregation brought him without the camp, and stoned him to death with stones; as Jehovah commanded Moses' (Num. 15:33 ff).

"Thus and thus only was the commandment of Jehovah established—by the execution of the penalty."

THE PENALTY EXECUTED

As soon as the law has slain the transgressor the law is established. Justice is seen to be triumphant. The law of faith, therefore, establishes the law known as "the Law of Moses" by executing Christ in conformity with that law. The Holy Spirit everywhere presents Christ as crucified; announces that Christ died for our sins; that He tasted death for every man. This is presented in the Old Testament in pageant and object lesson and in the New Testament in the exhibition of Christ on the cross and in the doctrinal statements referring thereto. Every lamb that died on the altars of Israel was the establishment of the law and the announcement of Christ's death. The serpent lifted up on the pole in the wilderness was an exhibition of the destroyer destroyed. When the Passover was established the lamb was taken into the house and kept there alive until the fourteenth day of the month when it was killed. It was not the sweet and pretty lamb alive in the house, probably the pet of all the children in every family of Israel, but the lamb put to death and the blood put upon the door posts that made it possible for God to pass over their sins. Remember that there was death in every house in Egypt. In the homes of the Egyptians, there was the death of the elder son; in the homes of Israel, there was the death of a lamb. In all cases the penalty was executed. God provided a substitute for Israel because He knew that He would not spare His own Son, but would deliver Him up to bear the sins of those who obeyed His command to put the blood on the door.

In the New Testament, Christ announced that He came to give His life a ransom for many (Matt. 20:28; Mark 10:45). Christ redeemed them that were under the law by being made a curse for them. Thus the death of Jesus Christ fully established the law by admitting its righteousness and by paying the penalty that it demanded. This was not done according to any thought of man as to what the penalty for sin should be, but according to that which has been set forth by the eternal Judge Himself.

The Apostles suffered great criticism, even to the point of persecution and death, because it was said that they spoke against the law. When Paul was arrested by the Romans in order to protect him from the Jewish mob in the temple in Jerusalem, the cry against him was, "Help! This is the man, that teaches all men every where against the people, and the law, and this place" (Acts 21:28). As a matter of fact Paul was not teaching against the law; he was announcing the one truth that vindicated and established the law forever. The men who argued against him had whittled down the law's demands for generations until, by the time of Christ, the practice of the law had so fallen off that they were no longer stoning sinners to death. The men of that time had cut down the law until it was a thing that they only made a pretense of observing, and thus they satisfied their hearts by disestablishing the law. It was the work of the Holy Spirit through Paul to re-establish the law by announcing that it must bring death, and that the death demanded by it had been paid. Christ had died and the penalty was now executed in Him.

FAITH OF A BLANK

There are men living today, mostly in the midst of Protestantism, who have done far worse than the men of Paul's race who sought to kill him for proclaiming righteousness through faith in Christ's death. These men are worse because they do not even show concern about the law. They believe that they have a spark of the divine within them. They talk about the natural good that is in man, denying the law's position to measure them and

find them wanting, and therefore denying the need of salvation
from sin. Their position has been clearly and terribly set forth in
a book by an Englishman now dead, John W. Graham, M. A.,
Principal of Dalton Hall, University of Manchester. The title is
The Faith of a Quaker, which I had to mention on the radio as
The Faith of a Blank. There is, perhaps, a considerable truth in
that rendering of the title, for they most certainly are blank so far
as knowledge of the righteousness of God is concerned, but far
from blank so far as their antagonism to the law is manifest. The
book, published in England some thirty years ago, was so blatant
in its denial of Christian truth that it drew forth castigation even
from such a liberal as James Hastings. The author had asked why
there were so few members of his denomination, and Dr. Hastings
points out that the reason was deep in the doctrine set forth in the
book. "If the reader concludes that it is the absence of the sense
of sin he will be confirmed by the index. In the index there is one
reference to sin. It is to a single short paragraph on a single page.
Throughout the book there is no recognition of disagreement with
God. That every man is out of harmony with his Maker, through
his own conduct—for we need not ask Mr. Graham to entertain
the idea of inherited sin—that is not taken account of. It is not
denied. It is simply ignored. The whole book—this modern exposition of the creed of the Quaker—is written on the assumption
that man is right with God and has nothing to do but recognize
his rightness."

It is not a new idea. Let me quote a paragraph from the book
itself. "It is remarkable," the author says speaking of George Fox,
"that confession of sin, pardon, conscious weakness, repentant re-
tracing of error, are wholly absent either in his times of darkness
or of light. He says, 'When I came to eleven years of age I knew
pureness and righteousness, for while I was a child I was taught
how to walk to be kept pure.'" What gross deception poor George
Fox was in, and in what gross deception walk all men who do not
understand the law of sin and death!

And Mr. Graham goes on to fight bitterly against the doctrine
of the atonement. Somewhat jealously and enviously he speaks
of the fact that Wesley and Methodists grew in numbers far beyond
his own denomination. The author resents this and says: "It has

sometimes been said that the failure of Quakerism to reach the masses led to the ground being covered by the Methodist Revival. However efficient Friends had been in their own line of service, I do not think they offered milk for babes. John Wesley, with his terrible preaching of Hell, his cheap salvation (cheap in theory at least), by escape through the merits of another, his stimulating hymns, and his verbal Biblical interpretation, widespread and popular as his teaching has become, could not have done his particular work through any Quakerism true to the name."

Having rejected all this it is not amazing that Mr. Graham goes on to speak against the atonement. He writes, "The evangelical doctrine of Atonement, as I am using the word historically, ascribed the salvation of mankind here and hereafter to their annexing for themselves, even while yet sinful, the infinite merits of the crucified Redeemer, whose shed blood was regarded as the equivalent in the Divine sight for the sins of the world. This doctrine most people now find incredible, unspiritual, and even immoral."

FALSE PREMISES

Thus we see how Satan blinds the minds of men that they should believe the lie. For in such a book as that from which we have quoted, there is a total disregard for the law of God, and thus, departing from false premises, the author reaches a set of wrong conclusions. Now, if a man is merely spending his time playing around with a set of philosophical ideas, it does not make much difference whether he has good premises and right conclusions or whether he lands in some morass of thinking. But the moment that he brings his specious reasoning over into the field of theology, there are eternal implications. The difference between spending eternity in the lake of fire or in the Heaven of God is the difference between denying the law of God and establishing the law of God.

We now bring to a close our study of the third chapter. We have considered in the course of the last thirty-two studies, the great declarations concerning man's sin in the first part of the chapter, the declared verdict of God that man is lost and can do nothing for himself, and, in the final section which sets forth Jesus Christ as the one Redeemer, the one possible means of satisfying both God and man. Before leaving this section, I wish to set forth once more the great fact that God has declared that righteousness for man is apart from his own works. I have found a page in one of the commentaries that expresses so well what I want to reaffirm and reiterate that I transcribe it here. Newell writes:

THE UNGODLY JUSTIFIED

"If God announces the gift of righteousness apart from works, why do you keep mourning over your bad works, your failures? Do you not see that it is because you still have hopes in those works of yours that you are depressed and discouraged by their failure? If you truly saw and believed that God is reckoning righteous the ungodly who believe on Him, you would fairly hate your struggles to be 'better'; for you would see that your dreams of good works have not at all commended you to God, and that your bad works do not at all hinder you from believing on Him, that justifieth the ungodly!

"Therefore, on seeing your failures, you should say, I am nothing but a failure; but God is dealing with me on another principle altogether than my works, good or bad—a principle not involving my works, but based only on the work of Christ for me. I am eager, indeed, to be pleasing to God and to be filled with His Spirit; but I am not at all justified, or accounted righteous, by these things. God, in justifying me, acted wholly and only on Christ's blood-shedding on my behalf.

"Therefore I have this double attitude: first, I know that Christ is in Heaven before God for me, and that I stand in the value before God of His finished work; that God sees me nowhere else but in this dead, buried, and risen Christ, and that His favor is toward me in Christ, and is limitless and eternal.

"Then, second, toward the work of the Holy Spirit in me, my attitude is, a desire to be guided into the truth, to be obedient thereto, and to be chastened by God my Father if disobedient; to learn to pray in the Spirit, to walk by the Spirit, and to be filled with a love for the Scriptures and for the saints and for all men.

"Yet none of these things justifies me! I had justification from God as a sinner, not as a saint! My saintliness does not increase it, nor, praise God, do my failures decrease it!"

And we shall see, as we go on, that the true comprehension of these attitudes is that which will make it possible for the Holy Spirit to bring forth His fruit in us and for the life of Christ to be formed in us. We must not think that because the law is established that it has any power to effect righteousness within us. We shall see, the Lord willing, when we come to the eighth chapter, that there are some things that the law cannot do in that it is weak through the flesh, but that *these very things* can and will be fulfilled in us who walk not after the flesh but after the Spirit, and that they shall be fulfilled by the greater law, the law of the Spirit of life in Christ Jesus, that will ever continue to make us free from the law of sin and death. May God make these truths fruitful in every heart to which these words come.

CHAPTER XX

Abraham's Faith

"What shall we say then that Abraham our father, as pertaining to the flesh, hath found? for if Abraham were justified by works, he hath whereof to glory; but not before God" (Rom. 4:1, 2).

W E COME now to the fourth chapter of Romans. The scholar who divided the New Testament into chapters saw, indeed, that there was a division of thought *here*, even though a proper division of the spiritual lesson might also have made an entire chapter of the eleven preceding verses. From what we have seen so far, it has now been established that justification is by faith alone, and that by the deeds of the law shall no flesh be justified in the sight of God. God is no respecter of persons, and there is no difference between the method by which He declared man to be sinful and the method by which He now declares man to be righteous in Christ. Boasting has been excluded. Thus the claims of pre-eminence which were so strongly set forth in the beginning of the third chapter are now seen to be vain in the sight of God. What was a man's proud position by race and heritage is seen to be of no worth in Christ. Finally, the argument has shown the complete ruin of mankind by sin, but it has also shown the believer's complete identification with Christ in His righteousness. Such doctrine is the unmitigated delight of the true believer. We revel and rejoice in the truth for it establishes us at once as children of God, heirs of His grace, and joint heirs with Christ. We are accepted in the Beloved and are objects of God's highest plans and tenderest love.

SOME OBJECT

But at the same time this doctrine raises some objections in the minds of those who do not understand the eternal nature of grace. I have had people object to the doctrine of salvation by faith in the grace of God, as manifested in Jesus Christ alone, on the grounds that it did not touch the vast number of people who had lived before the time of Christ. The answer, of course, is that it did touch those people and that salvation through Christ was just as possible hundreds of years before He appeared on this earth as it has been since He has come and performed the actual work of expiation for our sins through the shedding of His blood. If Christianity were a religion founded by Jesus Christ a bare nineteen centuries ago, then it would not be worth the trouble of considering it for a moment. But if it were founded by God the Father in conjunction with His eternal Son before the world began, then it is an entirely different matter. Herein, of course, lies the fact of the exclusive finality of revealed Christianity as the only true faith. All other religions are the gropings of man after God. The faith that is in Christ is God's revelation of truth from Himself, in the terms and in the manner He wished us to have the truth.

ABRAHAM AND DAVID

Just as there are people today who attempt to disclaim their responsibility before God in Christ because of some fancied difficulty concerning men of previous ages, so there were men in Paul's day who claimed that there was a serious obstacle to their acceptance of salvation through Christ because of what they had been taught to believe concerning their special rights and privileges inherent in their natural birth. They had been taught from infancy that they had a distinctive place as a nation because of their physical descent from Abraham. This was, of course, absolutely true. But they had also had their vision clouded from infancy by a haze of traditions and legal ordinances which blinded them to the true meaning of Abraham's calling and their position as his natural children. The arguments that are about to be expounded in this fourth chapter of Romans will dissipate their claims and shatter their pretensions still further. The two principle examples that would have risen to the minds of these children of Israel were those of Abraham and David. The one was established as the friend of God, the other was the type of royalty which God had established over them. These men, Abraham and David, loomed large in their thinking, but we shall see that the lives of both demonstrate the truth of the doctrine of justification by grace apart from the works of the law. Far from weakening the argument, these two men by the nature of their relationship with God are proofs of the doctrine of grace alone.

Abraham, of course, was the patriarch and founder of his nation. Those who, in the days of Paul, were living in the pride of a racial heritage alone could never have considered themselves as superior to the founder and father of their faith and their nation. Therefore, if Paul demonstrates that there was no intrinsic righteousness in Abraham, he has shut the mouths of Abraham's descendants so that they may not boast in their own righteousness. If he shows that Abraham was not saved by works, then he demonstrates that his descendants could not be saved by works. If he proves that religious rites had nothing to do with the salvation of Abraham, then he proves that they cannot hope to be saved by the observance of religious rites. The greater includes the lesser. If they were going to accept, as they had to, that the Old Testament was the Word of God, then they would have to bow before its testimony concerning their ancestor, Abraham; they would have to see themselves lumped together with him in the work of God, and would be forced to realize that their salvation had to be on the same basis as the salvation of their father Abraham. As Calvin puts it: "Since it is then evident that he (Abraham) was justified freely, his posterity, who claimed a righteousness of their own by the law, ought to have been made silent even through shame."

NO GOOD IN ABRAHAM

This first verse of our chapter has been translated and interpreted in several ways by various writers, but the sense adds up to the same total in the end: there is no good in Abraham any more than there is good in any member of the human race. In some of the Greek manuscripts, the text reads, "What shall we then say that Abraham our father has found pertaining to the flesh?" Others read it as our foremost English versions have it: "What shall we say that Abraham our father according to the flesh hath found?" No matter which road we take we shall come out at the same end. Some have thought that the verse was speaking of the fleshly relationship of Abraham as the physical father of his race; others have thought that the flesh referred to the circumcision by which his physical flesh had been cut; some have thought that the flesh referred to the good works which were the product of his human character; still others have thought that it referred to the performance of the moral and ceremonial requirements of the law which was not yet given. But no matter which one of these you take, and no matter if you invent some other idea that might be drawn from the words, the result is the same. The essential idea is this: Did Abraham receive any benefit whatsoever from anything that found its source or spring in himself or in his own character and doings? The context shows clearly that this is the meaning of the question and then proceeds to devastate the idea, almost with contempt, as being utterly ridiculous. If you think that Abraham gained anything before God by anything that he was or did or that he could be or could do, you have failed to comprehend the truth. That is the sense of the verse, and the proof is now set forth in the following verses. And when the demonstration is made, the conclusion will be that the entire history of God's saving work is a great unity. There may be a change in the method by which truth is presented, and there may be apparent differences between the outward forms of the law and the inward form of the new covenant, but fundamentally they are the same if we go to the roots of both. All is to be found in the truth of grace. Everything must depend upon the goodness of God and the grace which He has provided through the Lord Jesus Christ by the shedding of His blood.

The second verse now enters into the answer to the question which has been set forth. If Abraham had had anything in himself, he would have had something to boast about, but that boasting could not have been before God. But was Abraham declared righteous on any principle of works? Search the Scriptures and you will discover that there is not even the remotest hint that such was the case.

There are men in the Bible whose *character* is mentioned without any reference to their faith but not so with Abraham.

Take as an example of this, some of the kings of Israel who are mentioned as performing good works and as fighting against idolatry. It is said of some that they did "right in the sight of the Lord." But there is no mention of their faith. With Abraham, however, there is mention of wrong things that he did in the sight of the Lord, and then the flat statement that he was saved, reckoned righteous, because he believed God. Though his works are faulty, yet his faith was the basis and ground of his salvation.

ONLY FAITH SAVES

In the same way, we have some men in the Bible who were famous for their *place* or *position* before God, but whose faith is not mentioned at all. Such were men like the High Priests or King Saul. Were these men saved? The question frequently comes up; but since Scripture is silent on the details, we may not go beyond that which is written. Yet since Scripture is a book of principles, and not a book of rules, there is evidence that throws light on the problem. There were High Priests who were evil, but who were the priests of the Lord. Are they in Heaven? Here is a question we cannot answer, simply because there is no reference to their faith. King Saul was the anointed of God. He died under dramatic and terrible circumstances. Was he saved, and is he in Heaven today? We may not answer with positive assurance because there is no mention of his faith. We can leave such questions to God, trusting in His infinite mercy. But with Abraham the matter is entirely different. More definitely than the word on any other man in the Bible, we are told that Abraham had saving faith, and that this faith was accounted unto him as righteousness. His works were spotty; he did a very dishonorable thing on two different occasions, when he was willing to sacrifice the honor of his wife to save himself in a moment of possible danger. But without question we can say that he was and is a saved man because God flatly declares him so.

Now if the salvation of Abraham had been on the basis of his works, he would have been able to boast before other men and say something like this: "I am saved and will be in the Heaven of God because I have been able to do something which has put

me in the place of blessing. I have achieved a righteousness which
is acceptable to God, and thus I am accepted in my works." Such
boasting would have been possible before men but not before
God. Even the best of men would be forced to recognize the
infinite distance that separates the highest man from the lowest
step of the footstool of God. But Abraham was able to look to
God and to approach Him on the basis of the friendship which
God announced, because he took everything from the grace of God.

A GIFT TO FRANCE

A recent incident in my own experience will set forth this
truth. I have long been interested in the work of the evangelical
church in France. In my student days I was pastor of a French
church for four years and formed many friendships with the
godly men who were spreading the gospel in that needy country.
When the second world war came, I could do nothing but pray.
When the war was over and the curtain was lifted, I began to
find out what were the needs of the little French church in order
to help where I could. At first we sent many tons of second hand
clothing to the leaders, and hundreds of boxes of food. There
were three financial projects which interested me in connection
with the church. I knew that they needed strengthening in their
theological seminary, in their preparatory school and in their whole
pastoral body, and I set myself to help meet those needs. Without
any knowledge on their part—and that is the point of my story—
without any knowledge on their part I secured twenty thousand
dollars in this country and went to Europe in connection with my
ministry in England, with the intention of telling them about it.
At the English Keswick I met one of the professors of the French
theological seminary and told him, casually, that I intended to
pass by Aix-en-Provence where the Seminary is situated in connection with the university of that city, because I had a gift for
them of twenty thousand dollars. His jaw dropped at the mention of the sum—about six million francs—and he was amazed
and delighted at the prospect of the development of the school.
I went down to Aix in 1948 and told them that the money was
in the bank in Philadelphia, awaiting their need. We have since
been able to increase this sum and buy the property that enables

them to be lodged in their own enlarged building instead of a tenuous hold on a rented property.

Now as soon as the fact of this gift became known in France, I began to be besieged by letters from other works asking me to raise funds for them. Would I rebuild an orphan asylum? Would I help with a hospital and school in the Pyrenees? Would I help with an old folks' home? Would I help rebuild a summer vacation colony in the Jura? The answer in all cases was that I would not be interested. But a year or two after the beginning of our relationship, as I was teaching for some weeks in the Seminary I went for a day's trip with three of the professors. They deprecated the conduct of some of the people who had been insistent in their desires to get money from America through me. Then I pointed out the great difference that there existed between themselves who had asked for nothing but who had received everything, and the others who were willing to ask for everything but who had received nothing. Because these men had asked nothing of me, and because the movement for their help had begun with me, they could look me in the eye on the basis of equality. There was a basis of true friendship established with real dignity possible between us. Some others who came as beggars came fawning. But those who were the objects of an unasked grace could stand as equals in an enterprise of mutual aim and method.

ABRAHAM BELIEVED

Thus it was with Abraham. He had no claim whatsoever upon God, but when God came to him and made great promises to him, Abraham simply believed God, and it was counted unto him as righteousness. The blessing had no reference to himself but came entirely from the sovereign grace of God. This is set forth by an immediate appeal to Scripture. "Abraham believed God, and it was reckoned to him as righteousness."

There should be an application of this principle to the individual case of each reader of these lines. We must realize that our position, like that of Abraham, is one of imperfection, and that signifies a state of separation from God and of just condemnation. To be less perfect than God is to be a sinner. We stand bankrupt before Him with no coin of divine righteousness to pay our entry into Heaven. There is no possible exchange rate and God has declared our currency debased and unacceptable. We stand, therefore, in a hopeless situation. It was before such a condition that God acted. He came to us with a proffer of free grace, and provided full payment in Christ. He speaks to us today and tells us that He is willing to declare us righteous, even while we are ungodly, if we will simply believe Him.

Several years ago I was speaking with a man about his soul. The conversation had gone on for some time and the man seemed to be in total darkness. All that I would say to him failed to penetrate the murk of his fallen spirit. Finally he said to me, almost in a desperate tone, "But what does God want? Tell me, What does God want?" And the answer was given to me in a coruscating line, as I said to him: "God wants to be believed. More than anything else, God wants to be believed. If you sandpaper your life until you have taken off all the surface roughness and yet do not believe Him, He will have to cast you into outer darkness. But if you will understand that He longs, and yearns with deep desire that men shall simply take Him at His Word and believe what He says, then He is satisfied to completion, and will declare you as righteous as Himself. God wants to be believed."

THE HONOR OF GOD

There was a dawning wonderment in the face of the man and he said, "I begin to see. After all, the honor of God is involved." "Precisely," I answered him. "Since it is totally and utterly impossible for us to furnish the righteousness which His nature demands that He require of us, there is only one way for Him to do it, and that is to provide it Himself and give it to us as a gift. That which we can never attain we may obtain. That which we cannot earn we may receive. And it must be done outside of our being and beyond our reach or doing. God must do it all." The whole matter became clear to him and he entered into that saving faith that was willing to turn away from everything in himself to cast himself utterly upon the promise of God and upon the God of the promise. And the angels rejoiced in Heaven because the heart of God was made glad that one more child of

Adam had seen the brilliance of the light that is salvation and had turned away from the darkness of self in order to enter into the life that is the life of faith, the life of resting in God.

Over two hundred years ago, Johann Andreas Rothe expressed it in a great hymn:

Now I have found the ground wherein
  Sure my soul's anchor may remain—
The wounds of Jesus for my sin
  Before the world's foundation slain;
Whose mercy shall unshaken stay,
When Heaven and earth are fled away.

Father, Thine everlasting grace
  Our scanty thought surpasses far,
Thy heart still melts with tenderness,
  Thy arms of love still open are
Returning sinners to receive,
That mercy there they may taste and live.

O Love, thou bottomless abyss,
  My sins are swallowed up in thee!
Covered is my unrighteousness,
  Nor spot nor guilt remains in me,
While Jesus' blood through earth and skies
Mercy, free boundless mercy, cries.

With faith I plunge me in this sea,
  Here is my hope, my joy, my rest;
Hither, when Hell assails, I flee,
  I look into my Saviour's breast;
Away sad doubt and anxious fear!
Mercy is all that's written there.

Though waves and storms go o'er my head,
  Though strength, and health, and friends be gone,
Though joys be withered all and dead,
  Though every comfort be withdrawn,
On this my steadfast soul relies—
Father, Thy mercy never dies!

Fixed on this ground will I remain,
  Though my heart fail and flesh decay;
This anchor shall my soul sustain,
  When earth's foundations melt away:
Mercy's full power I then shall prove,
Loved with an everlasting love.

That is all that God demands of the sinner. Believe Him, believe His Word, and He will put down to your account that you are righteous in Christ, even at the moment of your ungodliness. Then He will begin all His work in you to bring you on, experimentally, day by day, into the image of His likeness, to be conformed to the image of His Son.

THE APPEAL TO SCRIPTURE

It is to be noted that the whole argument of the passage again turns on the quotation of a verse from the Old Testament. There can be no doubt that Paul turned to the Old Testament as being the Word of God. This was final. This was a citation from the supreme court to show that the case had been judged, and that there was the legal reference to cover the matter so that there could be no further ground for discussion. Oh, that we might hear more of this turning to the Word of God. If our pulpits would ring with this question and with the answers that would be thus called forth, we would be in the midst of real revival. What saith the Scriptures? This must ever be our cry. And, when we have asked the question, we too have revealed an attitude that is like the attitude of Abraham which God found so delightful to His own heart, and on the grounds of which He counted Him among the righteous.

It is very important to notice this connection between belief and the Scriptures. The Word of God may have been spoken to Abraham, but it is not spoken in our ears. It is written in a Book. The Bible never tells us that men were inspired; its constant declaration is that the Scriptures were inspired. And the word *Scriptures,* of course, is the Latin word for "writings." It has come down to us in the word *script.* This means then that the writings were the Word of God. And if we are to be the spiritual children of Abraham, we must believe the Word of God that has come to us through the Scriptures even as he believed the Word of God that was spoken to him in one of the theophanies that at times accompanied the giving of the revelation.

There is nothing in ourselves, any more than there was anything in Abraham. We have found nothing according to the flesh any more than had he. But as he turned away from everything that was in himself in order to thrust the full weight of his confidence and hope on the Word of God, so do we turn away from everything that is in ourselves to thrust the full weight of our confidence and our hope upon the Word of God. It is the written Word about the living Word that brings us life. It is this attitude which God desires us to have. If we turn to Him and believe Him as He presents Himself to us in this Book, we shall be reckoned righteous, even as was Abraham.

CHAPTER XXI

The God of Abraham

"For what saith the scripture? Abraham believed God, and it was counted unto him for righteousness" (Rom. 4:3).

ONE OF THE most beautiful thoughts in the Bible is that which is expressed in our text which the author of the Epistle to the Romans quotes from the Old Testament: "Abraham believed God and it was counted unto him for righteousness." In order that we may understand the real meaning of the phrase which contains so much of grace for us, let us look at the central word which will give us the key to the passage.

Our King James Version says that Abraham's faith was "counted" unto him for righteousness. The revisions change this to read that his faith was "reckoned" to him for righteousness. The recent Confraternity version issued by the Roman Catholic Church translates it, "Abraham believed God and it was credited to him as justice." Segond renders it in the great French translation as "imputed," a word that is used in several other passages to translate the Greek word that is found in our text.

GOD'S BOOKS

Before considering the Greek word, let us look for a moment at the various English words that have been used by the translators. They all add up to the idea of a bookkeeping transaction on the part of God. The idea of a recording angel goes back only to the eighteenth century, so far as I have been able to trace it, for the expression seemingly occurs first in Laurence Sterne's *The Life and Opinions of Tristram Shandy* about 1761. But the idea may surely be deduced from the Scriptures.

It is certain that God keeps books. There are several sets mentioned in the Word. There is the book of life, which seems to be a sort of population roll of all those who have lived in our world. From this, it would appear, some names may be blotted out. There is also the Lamb's book of life, which is the roll of

those who were chosen in Christ before the foundation of the
world. From this no name could ever be erased. Who records
these lists we do not know; the idea that angels have charge of
the work is a mere assumption from the fact that the angels are
said to be the messengers of God, doing His bidding. Then again
there are books in which God records the spiritual actions and
even the spiritual thoughts of those who believe in Christ. Even
if one does no more than to think upon the name of the Lord,
the thought is not lost, but enters into the record (Mal. 3:16).
But there would also seem to be a personal record of the actions
and thoughts which, although recorded, have nothing to do with
the fact of salvation (that is to say, God does not act favorably
toward any man because of any action of the man or because of
any thought in the mind or heart of the man). This personal and
individual account records what each man is in himself, and then
what he becomes in Christ.

If you could look over the shoulder of the angel messenger
(if there is such a being), or, at any rate, if you could see the
account that is held in your name, there would be most certainly
an entry that would show that God had written down on your
account that you were a sinner by nature and a sinner by choice.
The fact is evident, and the record is sure. By the nature of your
being, everything is against you in the record. Nor could there
be anything favorable because the contamination of sin runs
through all the record of any man. The first glance at the record
would show everything against you and nothing for you. There
would be a long list of liabilities, and there would be no assets
whatsoever since all the efforts of man are false currency and not
acceptable by God for the record. The sin of Adam, to use the
verbs of our text, has been counted, reckoned, credited, or imputed
to the account of every individual.

ABRAHAM'S ACCOUNT

But there would be a further recording on the accounts of
some. We are authorized by the text which we are studying to
look at the account of Abraham. What did he find according to the
flesh? The question is asked in the first verse of the fourth chapter

and is immediately answered. He found absolutely nothing before God. But suddenly we note that the account is paid in full and that something is reckoned, or credited, to the asset side of the ledger. There is no effort to hide the fact of Abraham's sin. One of the reasons for believing that the Bible is a divine book is that God never attempts to whitewash the reputations of the men whom he chooses for His purposes. They are all presented as men of the race of Adam with the seamy side of their character well displayed. These men live and breathe, and we find their close kinship with ourselves. They are liars like Abraham, cheats like Jacob, murderers like Moses, and adulterers like David, and the unvarnished tale is told in all simplicity. But then we see that the record has been changed by God Himself. Suddenly there is a declaration that the sponge has been passed over the entire account of those who are His own in Christ. We sing it in one of our great hymns,

> Jesus paid it all;
> All to Him I owe;
> Sin had left a crimson stain;
> He washed it white as snow.

But immediately our text gives us a new angle of the problem. Where we have previously seen that the shedding of Christ's blood does indeed provide the remission for sins, we now have a positive declaration of a bookkeeping transaction on the other side of the ledger. For our text is not now dealing with what happens to our sins, but with the fact that the righteousness of God Himself is written down to our account. For where once nothing was for us, God is now for us, and has accounted us as righteous in His sight. God now tells us that on the credit side of Abraham's account He, God Himself, has written down the entire assets of His own divine being to the credit of Abraham. This has been done because it pleased God to do it, and not because there was or could be anything in Abraham. Our text shows us the finger of God, or the attending and recording messenger of God, putting down to the account of Abraham the perfect righteousness of God. Abraham believed God, and so God puts in the accounting His own righteousness. It is counted, reckoned, credited, imputed to the account of Abraham.

Several years ago my bank account showed a balance of one hundred dollars more than my own records. I went over and over my books but could not find any error. I went to the bank and discovered that their books showed a deposit of which I simply did not have any record. The bank records were brought out and it was found that an anonymous person had brought in the sum and had caused it to be deposited to my credit. I never was able to identify the donor, but I have thought of the motives that must have prompted him as he walked into the bank that day. There must have been some blessing received, either from a radio sermon, or from something of mine that had been read or heard, and the giver decided to express an appreciation that would be known to God, and that would come to me in due course. It was in such a way that God moved toward Abraham. His motive, of course, was love.

GOD MOVED

No man ever moved toward God. The impulsion has always come from the seeking God. The day came when, in the accounting of God, ungodly Abraham was suddenly declared righteous. There was nothing in Abraham that caused the action; it began in God and went out to the man in sovereign grace. Upon a sinner the righteousness of God was placed. In the accounting the very righteousness of God was reckoned, credited, and imputed. The Lord God Himself, by an act of grace moved by His sovereign love, stooped to the record and blotted out everything that was against Abraham, and then wrote down on the record that He, God, counted, reckoned, credited, imputed this man Abraham to be perfect even at a moment when Abraham was ungodly in himself. That is justification.

There is a remarkable passage in the footnotes of the Confraternity edition of the New Testament published recently by the Confraternity of Christian Doctrine of the Roman Catholic Church. This edition bears the imprimatur of the Bishop of Paterson, where the St. Anthony Guild Press printed the book, and reproduces a letter from Rome, signed by Eugene Cardinal Tisserant, President of the Pontifical Biblical Commission, congratulating the American committee on their splendid work. In view of these endorsements, it is more than interesting to find this version abandoning all of the false translations of the old Douay version, and accepting the translations that are correct, and which have already been current for generations in the great versions which we have possessed in Protestantism. And while the footnotes in many places take the recognized Roman Catholic position of interpretation on many moot points, there is the flat acceptance of the true Biblical doctrine of justification by faith alone in the footnote on our present text though modified somewhat by the false doctrine of falling from grace. The full note is as follows: "We should distinguish between justification and salvation. We cannot be saved without good works, and accordingly St. Paul repeatedly insists on the necessity of avoiding sin and doing good. But justification, that is the infusion of sanctifying grace, cannot be merited by us; it is an entirely gratuitous gift of God." A parallel note on another verse (3:20), includes the further statement: "The justification of which St. Paul here speaks is the infusion of sanctifying grace which alone renders a person supernaturally pleasing in the sight of God. This cannot be obtained either by the observance of the law or by any other work of unregenerate man."

The whole essence of Reformation theology is to be found in the last half of the first note and in the part which we have quoted from the second note. The only error which we would point out is that which sees a distinction between justification and salvation. For certainly if God has infused sanctifying grace into the heart of an unregenerate man, and if that sanctifying grace "alone renders a person supernaturally pleasing in the sight of God," then we may say, by faith, that such a man has indeed been rendered supernaturally pleasing in the sight of God. With all our heart, soul, mind, and strength we would declare that such a man is, therefore, saved, and that there can never be contradiction between justification and salvation.

CREDITED AS JUSTICE

Further, my heart was delighted when I read the footnote on the phrase "credited to him as justice." The Catholic commentator says, "When God, who is infinite truth, credits some-

thing to a man, it is equivalent to saying that He imparts it really
to the man; for there is no make-believe with God."

It would almost seem that the writers of these notes saw
clearly that which the Bible teaches. Their honesty forced them
to write down the true interpretation, and then, apparently, they
were frightened at what they saw. Like someone who is learning
to swim they stepped off the ledge of human doing and found
themselves in the profound depths of full salvation by free grace.
They wrote that a man was by justification "alone rendered a
person supernaturally pleasing in the sight of God." Then, gasp-
ing for breath because they found themselves out of their depth,
they cry out: "But surely, but surely we have to do something
ourselves, do we not?" Oh! if they had only possessed the faith
of Abraham to believe God. How is it possible to say: "All our
sins are blotted out through Jesus Christ"; and to say: "We have
been made supernaturally pleasing in the sight of God"; and then
to say: "But of course we have to do something in order to be
saved." There is the great illogic of the lack of faith. Let us
rather say: "God has blotted out all my sins, and God has written
down on my side of the ledger the righteousness which is His
very own, crediting it to me, imputing it to me, reckoning it to
me. Therefore, I have been made supernaturally pleasing in the
sight of God, and that is what I am. I am redeemed, justified,
and saved. From now on I must recognize the nobility of my
position and live in the light of that grace."

LOGIZOMAI

After having looked at the meanings of the English words of
our various translations, and drawn the joy from them, let us turn
to the great word which Paul used in the Greek and see how strong
the statement really is. The word that is translated "counted,
reckoned, imputed, credited," is in the original, *logizomai*. It is
used forty-one times in the New Testament, thirty-five times by
Paul, and nineteen times in this epistle. In fact, it is a word that
we are going to meet eleven times in this fourth chapter alone.
It is necessary, therefore, that we understand rather fully its meanings and implications. Mark uses it for the statement that Christ
was "numbered" with the transgressors (15:28). In the Book of

the Acts, in the account of the harangue which Demetrius made to the silversmiths of Ephesus, he said that it was no small thing that Diana should be "despised," or literally, "counted" as nothing. In the fourth chapter of Romans alone it is translated "counted" (vv. 3, 5) "reckoned" (vv. 4, 10) and "imputed" (vv. 6, 8, 11, 22, 23, 24). In the eighth chapter, it will be found as "accounted," and in the fourteenth chapter as "estimate." It can readily be seen, therefore, that there is an idea of mathematical reckoning and the application in the depths of its meaning. Thayer's lexicon defines it: "To reckon, count, compute, calculate, count over."

We have, therefore, as plain as it is possible to express it, the truth that God has with fixed determination made a precise and mathematical calculation in which He has written off as gone forever all of the sin of the one who trusts in the vicarious atonement which He has provided in Jesus Christ, and that He has with thought and care placed the deposit of His own righteousness to their credit so that the books which once declared them bankrupt now manifest them as the possessors of all that God could ever require of them.

NOT A REWARD

Before leaving this sentence it may be necessary to point out that the imputation of righteousness was not a reward for faith. When God counted Abraham as justified, when He reckoned Abraham's sin as being upon the Saviour and credited the account of Abraham with divine righteousness, it was not because He had looked down upon the earth and found Abraham as possessing something that no one else had, and decided to reward him in this divine manner. There is no merit in believing God any more than there is in believing in a twenty dollar bill. It is not believing in a bill that makes the bill good. It is the fact that the United States Government has issued the bill and stands back of it that gives value to the bill. Faith in itself in worthless. True faith accepts the unsupported promise of God as being the very reality itself. When this is the heart attitude, then God looks upon the individual and accepts as reality the belief that is in the heart. Thomas well says in his devotional commentary: "Abraham did the only righteous thing possible; he believed in God, and thus the question of verse 1 is answered. Abraham 'found' justification by faith. Let it be said once again that there is absolutely no virtue or merit in faith. Trust is man's answer to God's truth. Faith is the condition, not the ground of salvation. God is the One whom we trust, and it is His free grace that warrants and elicits our confidence."

More than a century ago Thomas Bradbury put together eight verses from the Bible which show the various phases of the doctrine of justification. First, we may conclude that the believer is justified in the sovereignty of God, wholly because of His will. This is deduced from the statement: "Who shall lay anything to the charge of God's elect? It is God that justifieth" (Rom. 8:33). In the second place, we are justified without a cause in us by His grace. This is set forth in the statement, "Being justified freely [without a cause] by his grace, through the redemption that is in Christ Jesus" (Rom. 3:24). In the third place, we are justified meritoriously by the virtue of the blood of the Lord Jesus Christ. This we find set forth in the following statement: "Much more then, being now justified by his blood, we shall be saved from wrath through him" (Rom. 5:9). Fourthly, we are justified, imputatively, by Christ's obedience, as we read, "By the obedience of one shall many be made righteous" (Rom. 5:19). Fifthly, we are justified authoritatively by the resurrection of Jesus Christ from the dead; we read, "Who was raised again for our justification" (Rom. 4:25). In the sixth place, we are justified efficaciously by the work of the Holy Spirit, according to the Word, "justified in the name of the Lord Jesus, and by the Spirit of our God" (I Cor. 6:11). In the seventh place, we are justified experimentally by the faith of the Lord Jesus Christ, as it is written, "Knowing that a man is not justified by the works of the law, but by the faith of Jesus Christ" (Gal. 2:16). And, finally, the evidence of our justification is to be found in our works, as we read, "Ye see then how that by works a man is justified, and not by faith only" (Jas. 2:24).

A GREAT SALVATION

When all of these phases of the truth are seen, some of the greatness of our salvation can be comprehended. It was a magnificent task that confronted our God, and He alone could have found the way whereby He could touch dirty sinners without Himself becoming contaminated. He alone could have found the way to declare ungodly men godly and justified. He alone could have taken fallen children of Adam and made it possible for them to sit upon the throne of the universe with Himself. He alone could have taken those who were joined to the harlotry of sin and turned them into the pure bride of Christ. He alone could have taken that which was nothing in itself and made of us that which is declared to be "the fullness of him who filleth all in all." He alone could have condescended to our depth in order to raise us to His height. He alone could have imagined the way whereby the guilty could be counted as justified, the impure could be looked upon as pure and holy. He alone was in a position to stride through Heaven to the record hall of creation, dip his garment in blood and wipe away the stains of sin from our record, and, then, in the majestic gesture of Deity, write down on our credit account that we were declared wholly righteous, and justified in His sight, made supernaturally pleasing before Him. He alone, who is all knowledge and all intelligence, could say that He would perform the miracle of forgetting our trespasses and sins, so that that which had appeared before Him as the greatest offense should henceforward be considered as though it did not exist, yea, as though it never had existed. He it is alone who could have looked down upon a race totally estranged from Himself, gone aside after the worship of devil gods, and could have picked a man like Abraham, and declared him to be righteous and the father of all them that would believe in His Word. Is it any wonder that the church sings:

> The God of Abraham praise
> Who reigns enthroned above,
> Ancient of everlasting days,
>   And God of love.
> Jehovah! Great I AM!
> By Heaven and earth confessed;
> I bow and bless the sacred name
>   Forever blessed.
>
> The God of Abraham praise,
> Whose all sufficient grace
> Shall guide me all my happy days

In all my ways.
He calls a worm His friend,
He calls Himself my God;
And He shall save me in the end
    Through Jesus' blood.

He by Himself hath sworn,
I on His oath depend;
I shall on eagles' wings upborne,
    To Heaven ascend;
I shall behold His face,
I shall His power adore,
And sing the wonders of His grace
    Forevermore.

He keeps His own secure,
He guards them by His side,
Arrays in garments white and pure
His spotless bride:
With streams of sacred bliss,
With groves of living joys,
With all the fruits of paradise,
    He still supplies.

The whole triumphant host
Give thanks to God on high;
Hail, Father, Son, and Holy Ghost!
    They ever cry.
Hail Abraham's God, and mine!
I join the Heavenly lays;
All might and majesty are Thine,
    And endless days.

And surely our worshipful hearts will sing the praise of the God of Abraham who called Abraham His friend, and declared him righteous when he was yet ungodly, and who credits to you and to me the very righteousness of God when we believe in the Lord Jesus Christ as our Saviour.

CHAPTER XXII

The Serpent in the Wilderness

"Now to him that worketh is the reward not reckoned of grace, but of debt. But to him that worketh not, but believeth on him that justifieth the ungodly, his faith is counted for righteousness" (Rom. 4:4, 5).

THERE IS a vast difference between wages and a gift. The law recognizes the right of the laborer to collect his wages, and a worker who has not been paid may cause a lien to be placed on land, goods, or money until his account is satisfied. In our study of Abraham as an illustration of justification by faith apart from the works of the law, God now invokes this principle to demonstrate that salvation is by free grace and that a man's being and doing cannot have anything to do with the matter.

We read: "Now to him, indeed, who works, the reward is not reckoned as of grace but as of a debt. But to him who does not work, but who believes on him that justifieth the ungodly, his faith is reckoned for righteousness" (4:4, 5).

JUST PAYMENT

If a man can produce a character or a quantity of works that can meet the demands of God, then it goes without saying that the man can go to Heaven with all boldness in himself, and can claim the right of entrance. He can go to Heaven's gate with the boldness with which a workingman lines up at the cashier's window to receive his pay envelope. He knows that he has punched the time clock and that he has put in a full number of hours, and he knows that, therefore, he has every right to walk up and receive his pay. The solid mass of all the other laborers would be on his side in any contest over the wages if it is known that he has done the work. In all countries where the reign of law dominates, the power of the state would be firmly behind the

215

man who had done the work. He must receive his pay. Likewise should any man produce works that are worthy of Heaven, God Himself would have no right to keep that man out of Heaven. A creature no longer comes, under such circumstances, as a suppliant, demanding a favor, but comes as a claimant, seeking his own. Such a man need not say, "Lord, have mercy on me," but he may say, boldly, "Make place, O Lord, I have now arrived and must receive that which is my own."

Such an argument can never be brought over entrance into Heaven. The first chapters of this epistle have demonstrated abundantly that all have sinned and are falling short of the glory of God. A chain has been forged against the sinner that binds him to doom without a breath of hope in his favor. In his commentary on Romans, Anders Nygren, Lutheran Bishop of Lund, Sweden, shows that there are two chains of three links, the one binding the lost soul to wrath and the other chain binding the believer to salvation. The first chain is that of law, transgression, and wrath. God has given His law, man has transgressed that law, and the wrath of God must necessarily flow out against the transgressor. The course of events is as inevitable as the unchanging nature of God Himself. On the other hand God has forged the chain of grace, the promise, and faith. Nygren writes: "The promise is given by grace and can therefore be accepted only by faith. But the operation of the law is the precise opposite: 'The law brings wrath.' As to that it is not necessary for Paul to speak at length here. He has done that earlier in discussing the old aeon. He has pointed out that the wrath of God is revealed not only against unrighteousness, but also against righteousness through the law. The wrath of God is, of course, revealed against sin even when the law is not known. But the idea that through the law one can escape the wrath of God is the more unreasonable . . . because the law does not remove sin, but makes it greater. Sin does exist even where the law is not known; but there cannot be transgression, because that implies a law which is transgressed. What happens, when the law is made known, is that sin is intensified to transgression. Therefore the law also intensifies the wrath of God.

FAITH, GRACE, AND THE PROMISE

"Thus Paul shows the connection within the one series; the law, sin, and wrath are inseparable. Now he turns to the other series, showing concisely that an unfailing unity exists here, too, and that this unity demonstrates the necessity of faith. That is why it depends on faith, in order that the promise may rest on grace and be guaranteed to all his descendants. The three links in this series—faith, grace, and the promise—are closely joined in the Greek. Literally translated it would read, 'Therefore by faith, in order that by grace, to the end that the promise may stand fast.'"

Paul presents us with a paradox of absurdities. He first shows that it is absurd to believe that a man can be saved by works, and then, what might seem to some equally impossible, shows that salvation is by simply resting on the promises of God. The example that he takes in Abraham is all the more striking since this founder of the faith, who was called the friend of God, had to be saved in exactly the same way as the vilest transgressor of the law. The argument runs: if a man who had such nearness to God that God was not ashamed to be called the God of Abraham, and to call the man His friend—if such a man could not be saved by works, how then do little people who know their own distance from God expect to be saved by their works? If Abraham, close as he was to God, had possessed good works, he would have come to God by right and not by the grace of unmerited favor. But Abraham did not work in order to be saved. He walked closely because he was saved, but his salvation was entirely through faith in the promise.

SALVATION WITHOUT WORKS

The principle of salvation by works having been destroyed, the apostle now proceeds to establish the principle of salvation without works. The characteristic that gave to Abraham the particular position which he held in the history of his people was this simple characteristic of faith. He believed God. It was that which was accounted to him for righteousness. Illustrations from his life will fill the remaining portion of this fourth chapter. At this point the principle is being established.

Years ago I read an article in which the writer took as his subject the incident from the life of the children of Israel in the desert which best showed the utter bankruptcy of salvation by works. The argument was developed somewhat as follows. The Lord Jesus sets forth as the example of salvation that, "As Moses lifted up the serpent in the wilderness, even so must the Son of man be lifted up: that whosoever believeth in him should not perish, but have eternal life" (John 3:14, 15). This verse precedes the statement, probably the best known in the Bible, that "God so loved the world, that he gave his only begotten Son, that whosoever believeth in him should not perish, but have everlasting life." Now, how does the example of Moses, lifting up the serpent in the wilderness, illustrate the doctrine of salvation by grace through faith?

The people had journeyed from the Red Sea to the borders of the land of Edom. They were much discouraged because of the way and began to murmur against God and against Moses. The Lord sent fiery serpents among them, and they bit the people, and many of the people died. The repentant people came to Moses, acknowledged their transgression and asked him to intercede for them with the Lord. When Moses did so, the Lord answered in a manner that seemingly is one of the most absurd examples of all of the divine revelation. When it is looked at closely, however, we can understand why the Saviour Himself chose this as the perfect example of salvation through faith apart from the works of the law. Moses was told to make a serpent of brass and expose it upon a pole in the middle of the camp. God told him that it would come to pass that every man who was bitten by one of the serpents and who would look upon the serpent of brass would be healed.

NO HUMAN REMEDY

It goes without saying, that, naturally speaking, the proposition is exceedingly absurd. We can comprehend the wonders of sulfa drugs, penicillin, and the other antibiotics that are coming from the medical laboratories, but no one would suggest, even for a moment, that there was any therapeutic value in looking at a serpent made of brass and hung on a pole in the midst of the camp.

The force of the whole story lies in a comparison of the methods of cure that might have been told to the people and which were not mentioned at all, but were relegated to the sphere of the useless by the bringing in of a totally irrelevant matter, from the human point of view, to take the place of all the methods of man's doings. The nature of that divine remedy will become apparent after we have noted the things that were not prescribed. God was preparing the way for the teaching of the true absurdity of faith.

First of all, the people were not told to make for themselves any remedy. The brewing of potions and the making of salves would have given them all something to do and would have satisfied every natural instinct of the heart to work on behalf of its own cure. There was nothing of the kind mentioned. They were to cease from human remedies and turn to a divine remedy. The fact that they were not told to make a human remedy is indicative of the greater fact that there is no human remedy for sin. Men have been bitten by the serpent of sin. How are they going to be cured of its bite? There is nothing but death awaiting them as a result of their wound unless God Himself shall furnish a remedy. Men rush around in the fury of human religions seeking a palliative for sin. They perform all sorts of rites, chastising the flesh, humbling the spirit. They undertake fasts and pilgrimages. Like the man in Israel's camp who refused to look at the brazen serpent, but spent his time brewing concoctions for ameliorating his own conditions, they are carried off to spiritual death through the poison that is in their being. The man who trusts in religion instead of looking to Christ will be eternally lost.

In the second place, the men in the desert were not told to help each other. They were told to look at a brazen serpent fixed to a pole. In our day, there would have been eager recruits for works of social service to aid those who had been bitten. Those who had been recently bitten might rush to help the advanced cases, thinking that by their activity, good in itself, and satisfying to the pride that wants to be active, they would somehow help themselves. It was Harry Elmer Barnes, liberal professor of social sciences at Smith College several years ago, who said that there was a great rush of students to the courses that prepared them for welfare services because they had such problems of their own they thought that they might find some personal solution in preparing themselves to help others. But such a solution is not possible. A man who does not know how to swim cannot dive into the water and save a drowning man. He will merely add his own death to that of the one he is seeking to save. And the man who thinks that he can save himself through social service has never understood the nature of the snake bite and the nature of God's remedy.

It must not be thought for a moment that I am decrying works of social welfare. The true reality of social Christianity began with fundamental believers. Hospitals, asylums, and similar works of mercy are all by-products of fundamental Christianity. These works did not exist before the stream of mercy that accompanied grace was set free in the world. They sprang out of faith, and the endowments that buttress most of the great social works of our country were the gifts of fundamental believers of the past generations. And the great movements for freedom stem from Protestant history as has been abundantly demonstrated by J. Wesley Bready's book, *This Freedom—Whence?* Out of the great awakening in England under the Wesleys and Whitefield came the movements that freed the slaves of the British Empire and started the chain reaction in other countries. We do not deny the validity of such works of mercy and welfare. We point out, merely, that these works cannot save the soul. Giving to such causes and working in these causes must be the *fruit of faith* and not a work in behalf of salvation. Not by helping others is the poison of our sin-bite cured.

NO FIGHTING SIN

In the third place, the men in the desert, dying of the venom of the snake bites, were not told to fight the serpents. If the incident had been met after the fashion of our day, there would have been a rush to incorporate the Society for the Extermination of the Fiery Serpents, popularly to be known as SEFS; and there would have been badges for the coat lapel, cards for district workers, secretaries for organization of branches, pledge cards, and mass rallies. There would have been a publication office and a weekly journal to tell of the progress of the work. There would have been photographs of heaps of serpents that had been killed by the faithful workers. The fact that the serpents had already infected their victims would have been played down, and the membership lists would have been pushed to the utmost.

Let us accompany one of the zealous workers as he might take a pledge card into the tent of a stricken victim. The man had been bitten and the poison has already affected his limbs. He lies in feverish agony, the glaze of death already coming to his eyes. The zealous member of the Society for the Extermination of Fiery Serpents tells him of all that has been done to combat the serpents, and urges the man to join—as a life member if possible (fee $10,000), a sustaining member (fee $1,000), contributing member (fee $25), or annual member (anything the organizer can get). The dying victim fumbles in his pocketbook for money and takes a pen in hand. His fingers are held by the worker who helps him form his signature on the pledge and membership card, and the man signs in full—and dies.

It is possible that I may be misunderstood in the following, but it is something that must be said. There is never one line in the Bible that teaches us that we must fight against sin. That statement may startle some, but a dispassionate reflection on the whole of the sweep of the divine revelation will quickly make us aware of the truth of the statement. Enoch did not fight the ungodliness of his cousins, he exposed it and pronounced judgment upon it. Noah did not fight the evil that was in the world in his day; he built an ark to carry him and his family over the flood of judgment that was to come upon the world because of its sin. Moses did not fight against sin, except in Egypt in his youth when he murdered a man and had to flee into the desert for forty years until God could teach him truth and bring him back in the right way. Moses declared the law; and, when it had been set forth in all its deadening force, slaying every man that came in its shadow, he announced that salvation would be by virtue of the death of a blood sacrifice which would be provided by God, and acceptable to Him, and that would be administered by the priests who would stand at the altar on behalf of the sinner.

HATRED OF SIN

This does not mean that the true Christian will not hate sin, for the more he is like the Lord Jesus the more he will hate sin. Of the Saviour it is written, "Thou hast loved righteousness, and hated iniquity; therefore God, even thy God, hath anointed thee with the oil of gladness above thy fellows" (Heb. 1:9). But the hatred of Christ did not manifest itself in crusades against sin. Half the world was in slavery to the other half when the Lord was here, but never once did He lift up His voice to speak against slavery as an institution. The tramp of Roman legions was always in the ears of the Saviour while He was here on earth, but never once did He speak against war. He went to the cross and died, and thereby set in motion a doctrine and a set of principles based on that atoning death that would make peace possible in hearts that believed in Him and would make peace impossible where those principles were not accepted. Christ's hatred of sin was manifested in dying on the cross in order to furnish life to those who would believe His Word. His life, freely given, would enable the believer to partake of the Lord's nature and furnish the base from which sin could be overcome. Thus, only, would the Lord fight sin. And we are to fight it by lifting up the cross and proclaiming the gospel which takes men out of death and into life.

In the fourth place, the men on the borders of Edom, bitten by serpents, were not told to pray to the serpent on the pole. Nor is the sinner told to pray for salvation. Christ has died and salvation is to be believed, not prayed for. How often sinners are told to pray "God be merciful to me, a sinner," when the true translation of that passage is "God be mercy-seated to me, a sinner,"—that is, deal with me on the basis of the shed blood of the propitiation. God has already been merciful to the highest degree. There is nothing more to be prayed for.

In the fifth place, the bitten man was not told to bring an offering to the serpent. Nor is the sinner told to bring an offering to God. The one was told to look at the serpent; the other is told to look at Christ on the cross and risen from the dead, and to believe the promise of grace. An old Scotch evangelist, James McKendrick, a real man of God now alive forever more, spoke of his impressions of some American evangelistic meetings. "And they are always telling the sinner to do something," the old man complained. "They tell the sinner to give his heart to God. And what would God do with the dirty thing anyway? No unbeliever is told to give his heart to God; he is told to believe God's Word about the blood of the cross. Only the Christian is told to give his renewed heart to God." And, of course, he was quite right. As our text says, "And to him that worketh not, but believeth on him that justifieth the ungodly; his faith is counted to him as righteousness."

STUPIDITY OF INCREDULITY

In the sixth place, the bitten men were not told to get some relic of the serpent or a splinter of the pole on which the serpent was lifted up. Of all the foolish things in religion the most foolish of all is the idea of merit by relics. That the powdering dust of some skeletal death has the power to do something for a sinner is an idea so utterly pagan to the believer's mind that it is almost inconceivable that men should hold to it for a moment. But the evil heart that wishes to cling to something that can be seen is unwilling to turn utterly to Christ and look to Him, believing God's Word about His death. Relics came into Christianity at the time of the crusades, a dozen centuries after the time of Christ. Just as G. I.'s were asked to bring a souvenir from the war, a button from a German coat, a Japanese flag, or some other item, so the men of the crusades were asked to bring back the bones of a saint, or a piece of the true cross. And where there was a tremendous buyers' market there was an equally great source of supply. The Arabs, tongue in cheek, found bones of all the apostles, and so many pieces of the supposed cross that ecclesiastical authority had to issue a statement that the wood had the power of reproducing itself. To such lengths will go the stupidity of incredulity. Unwilling to believe in salvation by free grace apart from works, men are forced into the extremity of absurdity.

It is very interesting to note the terrible indictment of God against those who made off with the very serpent that was erected in the midst of the camp. Somehow—we are not given any details—

but somehow, somebody made off with the brazen serpent and it
was carried through the desert, across the Jordan, and kept around
for hundreds of years. When Hezekiah came to the throne we
read (II Kings 18:4) that "he brake in pieces the brazen serpent
that Moses had made; for unto those days the children of Israel
did burn incense to it; and he called it *Nehushtan.*" This last word
is a great sneer, and might well be translated, "piece of brass."
It is thus that the Holy Spirit would speak of the supposed bones of
St. Peter, or the supposed pieces of cross, shroud, and other items
in a sensory and vain religion. Piece of bone . . . rotten death . . .
dirty cloth . . . stinking candles.

LOOK TO CHRIST

The real value in the serpent on the pole was the picture it
portrayed of Christ lifted up on the cross to die for sinners. They
had been bitten by serpents; we have been bitten by sin. They
were dying; we are dying. That which was exhibited in the camp
was the likeness of the thing that had bitten them, but in a destroyed
state; that which was on the cross was Christ made in the likeness of
sin's flesh (Rom. 8:3), and made sin (II Cor. 5:21) for us. And as
God told the wounded Israelites to do a thing that was humanly
absurd, so the whole of the gospel message is that which is humanly
absurd. That is why it is said that "the preaching of the cross is
to them that perish foolishness" (I Cor. 1:18). Yet, I dare to say
today that which is very similar to that which Moses spoke in the
desert. I tell you, whoever you are, that if you will turn away from
your wounds, from your sin, from your self, from your works, from
your prayers, from your religion, and from everything, and look
away to Christ dying on the cross and believe God's unsupported
Word about that shedding of blood for the remission of sins, I
assure you, on the authority of that Word, that God will create an
absolutely new life in you, justifying you freely by His grace. "To
him that worketh not, but believeth on him that justifieth the ungodly, his faith is counted to him as righteousness." James Proctor
has put it very simply in a hymn that is often sung by certain
groups in Great Britain.

Nothing, either great or small,
  Nothing sinner, no.
Jesus died and paid it all,
  Long, long ago.

When He, from His lofty throne,
  Stooped in love to die,
Everything was fully done;
  Hearken to His cry.

Weary, working, burdened one
  Wherefore toil ye so?
Cease your doing, all was done,
  Long, long ago.

'Till to Jesus' work you cling
  By a simple faith,
  "Doing" is a deadly thing,
  "Doing" ends in death.

Cast your deadly doing down
  Down at Jesus' feet;
Stand "in Him," in Him alone,
  Gloriously complete.

It is finished, yes indeed,
  Finished every jot,
Sinner, this is all you need,
  Tell me, is it not?

CHAPTER XXIII

For the Ungodly

"But to him that worketh not, but believeth on him that justifieth the ungodly, his faith is counted for righteousness" (Rom. 4:5).

WHEN I was in my teens, I saw a booklet with a message of the gospel, and the title struck me immediately. I read the booklet, but I remember nothing but the title and the text. The text was the one we have before us today, and the title was *Ungodly People: the Only Kind God Saves.* It is indeed striking, and, what is more, it is absolutely true. The text from which the idea was taken is here in the fourth of Romans: "But to him that worketh not, but believeth on him who justifieth the ungodly, his faith is credited to him as righteousness."

It is an amazing thought, because it is so contrary to most of the religious thinking of humanity. Almost every man, if not every man, naturally thinks that God wants good people in Heaven, and that the way to get there is to be as good as possible and cross your fingers for the rest. It is, of course, true that that is the way to get by in the world. There are multitudes that say, "I'll do my best and carry a rabbit's foot for the rest." The rabbit's foot wasn't very lucky for the rabbit in the first place or it wouldn't be in your pocket, and it certainly will not do any more for you.

ELIGIBLE FOR SALVATION

If you really want to be saved, just realize that you are ungodly, accept the fact, and then you will find that you have thereby become eligible for salvation. If you picked up a newspaper and found an advertisement saying that $25 a day would be paid for six hours of work for all who applied, providing they were red headed, it would not do you any good to apply for the job if you were a brunette or a blonde. But if your hair were red, you could say, "I meet the condition and I will go and apply

for the job." Now, in a human offer there are many things that
can come up to make the realization impossible, but with a divine
offer there can be no possibility of slip-up. The note on this verse
in the Roman Catholic Confraternity version is excellent. There
we read, "When God, who is infinite truth, credits something to
a man, it is equivalent to saying that He imparts it really to the
man; for there is no make-believe with God."

Therefore, when we read that God justifies the ungodly, all
we have to do, in order to be justified, is to admit that we are
ungodly, and to fling ourselves on the grace of God. Salvation
is as simple as that. If you accept God's verdict as to what you
are in yourself, and accept God's verdict that He is satisfied with
that which Christ did in dying upon the cross, you can know that
your account has been met, and that you are looked upon as being
in Christ, saved and safe, justified and declared righteous.

NONE GOOD

Can the title of the booklet mean what it says, that the ungodly
people are the only kind God saves? Does this mean that God
never declares righteous the godly and the good? The answer
is exactly that. God utterly refuses to take into Heaven anyone
who claims to be godly or good on the basis of some supposed
godliness or goodness. The explanation is, of course, that there
are no godly, and there are no good. There may be some who
pass these tests from the point of view of purely human definitions;
but when the words are seen from the divine point of view, it will
be realized at once that there are no godly and there are no good.
You must understand that all this question of grading sinners is
an abomination before a God who is absolutely holy. Who are
you to declare that one man is better than another? Is it not
true that a man who is sober, so far as alcohol is concerned, may
be very drunk with pride? And who can discern the shades of
honesty or chastity in a human being? It takes just as much of
the grace of God to save what we call a "good" person as what
we call a "bad" person.

Another may wish to reject the truth of our text by saying
that not even God can call something that is black by the name
of white, and that He cannot proclaim that a man is godly when

at the same time He declares the man to be ungodly. But, like most of these difficulties in the Bible, it is not there when you look closely. God does not say that an ungodly man is declared godly, but he says that the ungodly man is declared righteous. In a man declared righteous, God will work a continuing work of godliness, so that the Christian will become more and more godly as the years pass; but from the first moment the believer has been declared righteous even when he is ungodly.

MANY WILL NOT COME

In that which is set forth here we find one of the greatest reasons, if not the greatest, as to why many people will not become Christians. They refuse, absolutely, to admit that they are ungodly; and, since God will not justify any but the ungodly, they thereby shut themselves away from salvation. Newell has a paragraph or two that present this truth in the strongest fashion. "It cannot be too much emphasized," he writes, "that the words, 'the ungodly,' wholly shut out any other class from justification. If you say, God, indeed, has in some special cases justified notoriously, openly, evidently ungodly ones; while His general habit is to justify the godly (which is what human reason demands), then you at once deny all Scripture. For God says, 'There is no distinction; for all sinned; there is none righteous,—not one.' And if you claim that God justifies the godly, we ask,—on what ground? If you say that it is on the ground of their godliness, you have left out the blood of Jesus Christ,—on which ground alone God can deal with sinners; and you have really denied this so-called 'godly' man to be a sinner before God at all, since he is to be justified on another ground than is the openly ungodly sinner, the shed blood of Christ. The burning question is, have you and I been really convinced of the fact of our sinnerhood and guilt, and of our utter helplessness, and lost state, so as to be able to believe on a God who can and does 'declare righteous the ungodly'—those who believe, as ungodly, on Him?"

The English word, "ungodly," means "not god-like." There should be no argument on that score, for we are creatures and He is the Creator; we are finite and He is infinite; we are imperfect and He is perfect; we are sinners and He is holy. In no

phase of comparison can we be said to be like God, even though
it is written that our first parent was created in the likeness of
God. The fall and the consequent entrance of sin and death
destroyed that likeness, so that man can be described best by the
simple word, "ungodly." The Greek word has a slightly different
connotation. It means "destitute of reverential awe toward God,
contemning God, impious."

HOW UNGODLY?

Now if it be asked how we are ungodly, there are several
ways of answering the question. In the first place, we are ungodly
by heritage. No matter what lineage you may claim, you came
from ungodly parentage if you go back a few generations. The
Lord Jesus took the mask from the religious leaders of His day
by demonstrating this fact to them. He said, "Woe unto you,
scribes and Pharisees, hypocrites! because ye build the tombs of
the prophets, and garnish the sepulchres of the righteous. And
say, If we had been in the days of our fathers, we would not have
been partakers with them in the blood of the prophets. Wherefore ye be witnesses unto yourselves, that ye are the children of
them which killed the prophets. Fill ye up then the measure of
your fathers" (Matt. 23:29-32). And if any man today attempt
to get away from the accusation, we point to the fact that he is
out of the loins of Adam and Noah, to say nothing of barbarian
ancestors within a few generations past.

In the second place, not only are we ungodly by heritage, but
we are ungodly by birth. An individual has two parents, four
grandparents, eight great-grandparents, sixteen great-great-grand-
parents, and then, multiplying by two for each generation, it is
technically possible that a man have over a million ancestors if
you go back only twenty generations. And the reality is that the
whole mass of humanity is a mixture of distant cousins, and we
are all bound together in the common sinfulness of the race.
Theologically speaking, the matter has been set forth in the Psalms,
"Behold I was shapen in iniquity; and in sin did my mother conceive
me" (Ps. 51:5). Now this verse is not even remotely teaching
that there is anything sinful in marriage, begetting and conception,
which are, of course, established by God and are holy to the highest

degree. But this verse in the Psalms is teaching that original sin is transmitted by the process of the begetting and that a sinful parent cannot pass on to his offspring anything other than his sinful nature. Thus, we are all ungodly in our birth.

In the third place, we are all ungodly in our choices. We have not obeyed the law of God, nor even the natural law of our hearts. We know that our desires turn to self, and the very words that indicate our self have a pejorative meaning that our thoughts are not naturally toward our Creator. *Self* and *selfish; ego, egoism* and *egotist; will* and *wilful;* all are words that refer to our own being, and all of which show a bad meaning. It is put in the Scriptures, "We have turned every one to his own way" (Isa 53:6). And there are many other words in our language which show that our whole being is corrupt and sinful.

Almost any emotion has a word in our language that is used in a bad sense. Thus our wills have given us *wilful,* our senses, *sensual,* and even the highest feeling, which in Christ's sufferings could be called His passion, has become a wretched word to describe the basest feelings. Our emotions have given us *emotional;* and a word which once had nothing but a good meaning for a desire has fallen to a state where it has nothing but a bad meaning, *lust.* This is not the end of the list, but this vocabulary is sufficient to demonstrate that our very language carries within it the proof that we are ungodly, and that anything that touches us is thereby contaminated.

GOD LOVES THE UNGODLY

Ungodly in our heritage; ungodly in our birth; ungodly in our choices. We have, indeed, departed from God from the beginning, and can never bring ourselves back by our own efforts. But it is precisely the ungodly person whom God is willing to declare righteous. It is the ungodly whom God has loved. In the fifth chapter of this epistle we shall come to the phrase which declares, "For when we were yet without strength, in due time Christ died for the ungodly" (5:6). We need not, therefore, despair of our lot. If we are by heritage, birth, and by choice ungodly, our very condition is our recommendation for salvation. It is the ungodly for whom Christ died, and it is the ungodly whom He declares righteous, without any cause in us, simply because it pleases Him to do so. And the hinge that binds the ungodly man to God is simple faith in the promise about His love, mercy, and grace, and a confident trust in the death that He died for us on the cross.

Let no man feel left out. You are ungodly, but you have been loved. You are ungodly, but God is willing to declare you righteous in Christ. Think not that the promise is for another; it is for you. How fortunate that we are not mentioned by name, for then we would be in doubt; we would be sure the promise must be for another of the same name. If the Bible said that God so loved John Smith, each one of that name would be sure that there was a lack of identification and that it was talking about some other John Smith. I note in the Manhattan telephone directory that of all the hundreds of Smiths there is hardly a single name that is not duplicated. Why even a name as rare as Donald Barnhouse would not satisfy me if I found it in the divine revelation. When I first began speaking on the radio more than twenty years ago, I went to Chicago for a meeting and a young man came up to me and said, "My name is Donald Barnhouse." I looked at him in some surprise, for my branch of the family has come down by a long line of only sons, so that there are no cousins by the name; but here was a Donald Barnhouse in the flesh, and telling me that in the bank where he worked he was now being called "deacon" by his friends because someone with his rare name was preaching on the radio!

POSITIVE IDENTIFICATION

But I have another name that is in the Scriptures, and a description of me that is so accurate that I can never mistake the identification. My first name, my middle name, and my last name are in the Bible, and so are yours—and a perfect description of your being. Christ said one day, "The Spirit of the Lord is upon me, because he hath anointed me to preach the gospel to the poor" (Luke 4:18). There is my first name, and yours—Poor. In another place our Lord said, "The Son of man is come to seek and to save that which was lost" (Luke 19:10). There I find my middle name, and yours— Lost. And on another day our Lord said, "They that be whole need not a physician, but they that are sick [do need a physician]. But go ye and learn what that meaneth, I will have mercy, and not sacrifice: for I am not come to call the righteous, but sinners to repentance" (Matt. 9:12, 13). And there is my last name, and yours—Sinner. So the whole name is written out, Poor Lost Sinner, and I know that my name is written there as the one for whom the Lord Jesus Christ came to die. I know that it means me, and I can lay hold upon the promise because my name is there. And if there were any further doubt, as an identity card contains not only the signature but also the portrait, my picture is drawn and my nature portrayed, and my description is put down as ungodly.

I can testify personally that it was when I accepted that identification that God transformed my life, and I began to be aware of the fruits of faith. It was long afterwards that I grew into the knowledge of what He had done indeed, when I accepted His verdict about my sinful name and station, and believed what He Himself said about His love and grace to me in Christ. Though I did not know what He had done when I believed His Word, any more than I knew anything about obstetrics on the day I was born, yet the Lord did justify me on that day; and even while I was yet ungodly, He accounted me righteous in Christ. By the time I was four or five years old I knew I was alive and that I was a human being. By the time I was in my teens I knew the facts of life and how I had come into this world. After I had been saved some time, I knew that I was alive in Christ; and after I had been saved several years, I came to know the process of what I might call spiritual biology, by which God counted ungodly me to be righteous before Him.

There are two conclusions to this messsage. The one is for those who are ungodly even by the world's definition, and the other is for those who are good according to the world's definition but ungodly according to God's definition.

For those who are considered ungodly even by the world's standards I wish to recount an incident that occurred in the ministry of W. R. Newell, that great Bible teacher of the past generation. He tells it as follows:

THE MOST UNGODLY MAN IN TOWN

"Years ago in the city of St. Louis, I was holding noon meetings in the Century Theatre. One day I spoke on this verse—

Romans 4:5. 'To him that worketh not, but believeth in him who justifieth the ungodly; his faith is reckoned unto him for righteousness.' After the audience had gone, I was addressed by a fine looking man of middle age, who had been waiting alone in a box seat for me. He immediately said, 'I am Captain G——,' (a man very widely known in the city): And when I sat down to talk with him, he began: 'You are speaking to the most ungodly man in St. Louis.' I said 'Thank God!' 'What!' he cried. 'Do you mean you are glad that I am bad?' 'No,' I said, 'but I am certainly glad to find a sinner that knows he is a sinner.' 'Oh, you do not know the half! I have been absolutely ungodly for years and years and years, right here in St. Louis. I own two Mississippi steamers. Everybody knows me. I am just the most ungodly man in town!' I could hardly get him quiet enough to ask him: 'Did you hear me preach on "ungodly people" today?' 'Mr. Newell,' he said, 'I have been coming to these noon meetings for six weeks. I do not think I have missed a meeting. But I cannot tell you a word of what you said today. I did not sleep last night. I have hardly had any sleep for three weeks. I have gone to one man after another to find out what I should do. And I do what they say. I have read the Bible. I have prayed. I have given money away. But I am the most ungodly wretch in this town. Now what do you tell me to do? I waited here today to ask you that. I have tried everything; but I am so ungodly!' 'Now,' I said, 'we will turn to the verse I preached on.'

"I gave the Bible into his hands, asking him to read aloud: 'To him that worketh not.' 'But,' he cried, 'how can this be for me? I am the most ungodly man in St. Louis.' 'Wait,' I said, 'I beg you to go on reading.' So he read, 'To him that worketh not, but believeth on him that justifieth the ungodly.' 'There!' he fairly shouted, 'that's what I am—ungodly.' 'Then, this verse is about you,' I assured him. 'But please tell me what to do, Mr. Newell. I know I am ungodly; what shall I do?' 'Read the verse again, please.' He read: 'To him that worketh not'—and I stopped him. 'There,' I said, 'the verse says not to do, and you want me to tell you something to do; I cannot do that.' 'But there must be something to do; if not I shall be lost forever.' 'Now listen with all your soul,' I said. 'There was something to do, but it has been done!' Then I told him how that God had so loved him, all ungodly as he was, that He sent Christ to die for the ungodly. And that God's judgment had fallen on Christ, who had been forsaken of God for his, Capt. G——'s sins, there on the cross. Then, I said, 'God raised up Christ; and sent us preachers to beseech men, all ungodly as they are, to believe on this God who declares righteous the ungodly, on the ground of Christ's shed blood.' He suddenly leaped to his feet and stretched out his hand to me. 'Mr. Newell,' he said, 'I will accept that proposition!' And off he went without another word.

"Next noon day at the opening of the meeting, I saw him beckoning to me from the wings of the stage. I went to him. 'May I say a word to these people?' he asked. I saw his shining face, and gladly brought him in. I said to the great audience, 'Friends, this is Captain G——, whom most, if not all of you, know. He wants to say a word to you.' 'I want to tell you all of the greatest proposition I ever found,' he cried. 'I am a business man and know a good proposition. But I found one yesterday that so filled me with joy, that I could not sleep a wink all night. I found out that God, for Jesus Christ's sake, declares righteous any ungodly man that trusts Him. I trusted Him yesterday; and you all know what an ungodly man I was. I thank you all for listening to me; but I felt I could not help but tell you this wonderful proposition; that God should count me righteous. I have been such a great sinner.' This beloved man lived many years in St. Louis, an ornament to his confession."

And after such a story I want to say to any who read these words, and who know their own ungodliness, that God makes the same proposition to you in this moment. "To him that worketh not, but believeth on him that justifies the ungodly," his faith is counted unto him as righteousness.

A DREAM WORLD

And now the conclusion for those who are living in the illusion that they are godly when in reality they are ungodly. You are deceived or deluded by appearances. When you think you are good, you are bad. You have an error of mortal mind, You are calling some supposed godliness real when it is very unreal. Your conceptions are false. You are living in a dream world of fantasy and delusion. Your mind is spiritually deranged. You must repent of your fixed false opinion about your own goodness and come to accept the reality as it is declared in the Word of God. Turn the garment of your thinking right side out and accept the facts as they are, and as they are set forth in the Word of God. I was ungodly, but am now declared righteous before God, even though the threads of the ungodliness are the very woof of the fabric of my being. God has given me a new warp, twisted harder than the weft, and He is at work in the weaving of His sanctification, but the justifying work has been done. Will you join me in this moment in casting yourself upon Him who justifies the ungodly when that ungodly one ceases from working and trusts in Christ alone?

CHAPTER XXIV

They Whose Iniquities are Forgiven

"Even as David also describeth the blessedness of the man, unto whom God imputeth righteousness without works, Saying, Blessed are they whose iniquities are forgiven,· and whose sins are covered" (Rom. 4:6, 7).

THE WHOLE argument of the fourth chapter of Romans is an illustration from the life of Abraham to show that the famed patriarch, father of his nation, was not saved by the rites and ceremonies of the law, since he lived and died several hundred years before Moses received the law, but that he was justified by grace through faith, apart from the works of the law. In the midst of the story of Abraham a quotation from David is given, as if to show that at the mouth of two witnesses the thing should be established. Alongside the first witness, Abraham, the father of the faithful and called the friend of God, Paul now quotes David, the great king, to whom was given the promise that the Messiah should be raised up from his seed to sit upon the throne of Israel. If a politician in America, to prove his point, were able to quote both Washington and Lincoln, even then his case would not be as strong as Paul's case in setting before them the fact that both Abraham and David were saved by grace without the work of the law.

DAVID'S DECLARATION

The interjected passage, in the midst of the story of Abraham, to which we will return, is as follows: "Even as David also declares the blessedness of the man to whom God credits righteousness apart from works: Blessed are they whose iniquities are forgiven, and whose sins are covered; Blessed is the man to whom the Lord will not credit sin." The quotation is from Psalm 32, and in the Hebrew the word *blessedness* is in the plural. It would be correct to translate it: O the blessedness of the man to whom the Lord will not credit sin.

We have here a wonderful example of the way in which the Holy Spirit interprets the Scriptures. The Old Testament passage is in three phrases, all having to do with the negative aspect of sin. The New Testament passage sums it all up with one statement concerning the positive aspect of righteousness. In this and the next studies, we shall consider the three parts of David's declaration and the New Testament summary of the doctrine.

First, then, is the statement, "Blessed are they whose iniquities are forgiven." God's people have often had many accusations brought against them, but God looks at us through Jesus Christ. We admit immediately that a thousand people attending the garden party of the royalty in Buckingham Palace will have more elegance than a thousand people in a church service. We accept the fact that a thousand lawyers in convention have much more brains than a thousand ministers in convention, and we sadly admit that sometimes they even have more ethics. We know that the average Rotary or Kiwanis Club meeting in the average town will assemble more men of push and vigor than are generally gathered at a luncheon of some Christian laymen's organization. Furthermore, we know that the more devoted to the Lord a group of Christians may be the more likely they are to appear drab and dull to the world.

GOD'S ACQUIRED PEOPLE

Some time ago I was speaking with a friend from another city about the possibility of influencing a well-known citizen, owner of a great radio station, to allow our program to go out over his station. I outlined the approach I had in mind, and said that I would tell the man that theologically my messages were of the doctrine for which a certain church in the city was famed. It is a church that draws many thousands of people. But my friend immediately said, "I wouldn't mention that church if I were you. It wouldn't be too good a recommendation in our city. The people that go there are rather colorless; and, if you wished to obtain a favor from such a man, it would probably be best not to mention that particular church."

It was good worldly wisdom, and probably was important in view of the nature of the man in question and his outlook and attitudes on worldly affairs. But I knew that church, and I knew the sacrifices that were involved in its great missionary offerings. I knew the number of its sons and daughters that were serving God in far places of the earth, helping to draw men out of death and into life. And I knew that the drab congregation had for the most part been made white through the blood of Jesus Christ. And I knew that those whom the world called colorless were looked upon by God in all the glorious colors of the virtues of the Lord Jesus Christ. It is the Lord who said in the Old Testament, "Fear not, for I have redeemed thee, I have called thee by thy name, thou art mine" (Isa. 43:1); and it is the Lord Jesus who said in the New Testament, "Fear not, little flock; for it is your Father's good pleasure to give you the kingdom" (Luke 12:32).

The principal characteristic then of this people of God, taken as a group, is not a characteristic of this world. God Himself has said, "For ye see your calling, brethren, how that not many wise men after the flesh, not many mighty, not many noble, are called: but God hath chosen the foolish things of the world to confound the wise; and God hath chosen the weak things of the world to confound the things that are mighty; and the base things of the world, and things which are despised, hath God chosen, yea, and things which are not, to bring to nought things that are, that no flesh should glory in his presence" (I Cor. 1:26-29). The principal characteristic of this group of believers is a Heavenly, a spiritual one. We are, as Peter says, "a chosen generation, a royal priesthood, a holy nation, God's acquired people, that (we) may declare the wonderful excellencies of him who hath called (us) out of darkness into his marvelous light" (I Pet. 2:9).

SPARROWS

All of this high position is ours because of the grace of God in Christ. It has nothing to do with worldly being or doing. It is not measured by human attainment, human gifts, or human graces. It comes entirely from the fact that the Lord has set His love on us. In the eighty-fourth Psalm, David sings one of his most beautiful songs, and says, "Yea, the sparrow hath found her an house, and the swallow a nest for herself, where she may lay her young, even thine altars, O Lord of hosts, my King and my God" (Ps. 84:3). Now the sparrow is the Bible symbol of worthlessness. The little boys who caught sparrows in the streets of Jerusalem sold two for a farthing and five for two farthings, if any customer had so much to spend for meat. Yet, the Lord Jesus said not one of them could fall to the ground without the knowledge of His Heavenly Father. And now we see that this little bird, symbol of all that is worthless, found its house at the altar of the Lord.

The humble soul finds its worth at the cross of Jesus Christ. Here is a true indication of the worth and value of the group of God's own who are truly born again. At times I see pictures of church pageantry with richly-gowned prelates and with the bowing and scraping of underlings giving deference to human beings, and I think how far removed this is from the humble Christ who walked the roads of Galilee healing the sick and cleansing the lepers. I see the poor deluded people pushing and shoving to get near some man to kiss his ring or stand beneath the shadow of his blessing, and I think how far removed from the Spirit of God all such trumpery really is. And then I look down some little street and see a humble chapel where a group of simple people worship the Lord in the beauty of holiness, despised and rejected of men, even as was their Lord, and I know that this is the rich reality of spiritual truth. Here are the sparrows who find their nest at the cross of Jesus Christ. Here is worthlessness that finds its worth because the Saviour died. And thus you may find your worth.

SWALLOWS

And as the sparrow is the symbol of worthlessness, so the swallow is the symbol of restlessness. Winging its way from dawn till dusk, flying high to greet the sun even before its rising, the bird seems never to alight for a restful moment but goes on its way—a way so unending that it finally wearies the watcher who would follow its soaring grace. But suddenly the mating urge comes upon it and it swings to its nesting, there to rest in periods of peace and quiet, periods as long as it once spent aloft in the blue. And God says that this is what He offers the restless soul, weary of its wanderings. And thus you may find true peace. Yea, the swallow hath found a nest for herself where she may lay her young—even Thine altars.

This group of sparrows and swallows, with an occasional eagle called in by God to condemn all the other eagles who trust their pinions instead of their Maker, forms the Church of Jesus Christ. This is the group included in the word "they" of our text. "Blessed are they whose iniquities are forgiven." For now that we have identified the group, we see that the stamp upon them is an invisible one. The hallmark of the atoning blood has been engraven upon them by God. Men cannot see that their iniquities are forgiven but God can see it, for it is He Himself who has done it, and not we ourselves. Could you have told from their outward appearance when they were dying on the cross which one of the two thieves was on his way to Hell and which was on his way to Heaven? It would have been impossible for the outward eye to determine a difference, but man looks upon the outward appearance, and God looks upon the heart. You should be in great fright of the fact if you are not born again, and we who are born again may be in restful calm because we know that we have been accepted in the Beloved and that we are looked upon through Christ.

ORGANIZATION VS. ORGANISM

The change from the plural to the singular in the midst of this quotation from David is one that has tremendous import. "Blessed are they . . . blessed is the man . . ." God is teaching us something about the collectivity of believers and something about the heart of the individual. It will be well to explore this difference a little more before seeing the individual application in our next study. The plural in the quotation refers to what the Bible calls the Church. I must put it that way because the world uses the word *church* quite differently from the sense in which the Bible uses it. The Bible never refers to an organization as the Church; the word is reserved for the organism.

The difference between the organization and the organism is the difference between a watch and your heart. You may wear a watch just a few inches from your heart or a few inches from the heart's pulse in your wrist. The watch ticks and the heart throbs, but there is a vast difference between the two. The watch is an organization and the heart is an organism. The watch is a machine, made by man: the heart is life, given by God. The only church that God knows anything about is the organism. The organization is a necessary thing, perhaps, but a bastard thing, in which death and sin are mixed up with life in a way that cannot be discerned by man but can be seen only by God.

The words that were used in antiquity for the Lord's people soon took on a variety of meanings, as words skip around from one idea to another and from one object to another. In our own time we have seen the word *bottleneck* get out of the bottles and into the production line of factories. The word *ceiling* which comes originally from the Latin word for Heaven, moved through its meaning for the covering of a room to become attached to a set of prices on commodities, but many would argue that a government price structure was a long way from being Heavenly.

THE CHURCH

Our English word *church* has had a vast history and there have been students who have sought its derivation in many directions. Scholarship is now pretty well agreed that the word is a corruption of the Greek word *kuriakon,* an adjective meaning "of the Lord." The word *church* in half a hundred forms is found in all the languages of the Germanic and Slavic tribes which had seen and sacked Roman and British churches in Gaul and Britain for centuries before they had any of their own. And we have every reason to believe they had known and spoken of them as *cirican* (from which *church* and *kirk* are derived) during the whole of that period.

The New Testament word that is translated *church,* however, is *ecclesia,* from which we get our common word *ecclesiastical.* It derives from a preposition *ek* meaning "out of" and a verb *kalein,* meaning "to call." It always refers to persons and never to buildings or organizations. Moreover, it always refers to *saved* persons and never to a mixed multitude that would include both wheat and tares. The true church is the group of individuals, some of them now in Heaven, some of them living on the earth, some of them not yet saved but who will one day believe. The true church is known only to God, and man has absolutely no knowledge of its real composition. The true church is entered by the work of the Holy Spirit in the heart of a man, quickening him, making him alive in Christ. It is quite comprehensible that the Devil, who is always the author of confusion, should seek to devitalize the word and make it apply to buildings, or to groups of people that include some of his own children instead of only God's children.

If this distinction is thoroughly understood, there will be no deception as to the place of the Church in the world and as to the nature of the people who compose it. Anyone who comprehends this truth will laugh, sadly perhaps, but, nevertheless, laugh at the pretensions of any group which claims to be the authentic church, founded by Jesus Christ. When you read an advertisement in the papers put in by some group which seeks to tell you that Christ founded their particular branch of Christianity, you can know that someone is trying to impress the ignorant and the unlearned. Those who have even the slightest knowledge of etymology, church history, and of the theology of the New Testament will know that the Lord Jesus Christ built His true Church, the assembly of all believers who have been made alive by the Spirit on the grounds of faith in the atonement provided by the death of Christ, and that He builded it upon Himself. The attempt to establish patent rights on God through somebody's supposed bones, for example, is a trick that could never have originated with the God of all truth and grace. The organism, the body of true believers, the true Church, is composed of some who are in the Roman Catholic organization, but not all, of course; of some who are in various Protestant organizations, but not all, of course; of some who are in the Eastern churches, but not all, of course, and of some who have never belonged to any organization, but who are true believers. This is the true Catholic Church of which we speak when we say in the creed, "I believe in the holy Catholic Church." We make no reference, of course, to the Roman, Greek or other churches which wish to usurp the word *catholic* for themselves alone.

The organizations are entirely the outgrowth of man's doings. That one should claim to be older than another brings a shrug of the shoulders to those who are concerned with life and not with organization. Only in a world that is dominated by the go-getter principles that animate Hollywood and advertising agencies could anyone be impressed by the statistics of membership or by pretentions to position and power. For example, I recently read an estimate of the membership of various communions based on the recent census. What difference does it make whether this or that number of people belong to this or that organization? In the first place, the different groups have different ways of counting their parishioners. The Roman Catholics, for example, count the entire number of their families, including the new-born babies who have been baptized. And once they are counted, they are never dropped from the list, even if thousands leave that organization and join another, as, for example, some seventeen thousand Roman Catholics were baptized into the Lutheran Church alone in a recent year, not to mention the other thousands that went to other denominations. And there were, of course, certain numbers of thousands that went in the other direction also, since the movement of conversions from one organization to another has always been a two-way street. Protestant organizations do not count children in the membership until they are old enough to have made their own public confession of faith in Christ. A figure that would be expressed, for example, as twenty-five millions belonging to some Protestant organizations, would be about thirty-four millions if reckoned by the Roman Catholic method of counting; while the Roman figure of twenty-five millions, if reckoned by the Protestant method, would shrink to seventeen or eighteen millions. And the Christian who holds to Bible truth and who has been delivered from the pride of statistics, would shrug his shoulders at either set of figures, and would say, "Man looketh upon the outward appearance, but God looketh upon the heart."

BLESSEDNESS

Turning from all thoughts of organization to the living, vital body of true believers, our text sets forth their condition in these beautiful words: "Blessed are they whose iniquities are forgiven,

and whose sins are covered." What is the nature of this blessedness that belongs to the collectivity of the true believers? First
of all, let us distinguish this usage of the English word *blessed*,
as applied to human beings, from the same English word which
we have seen applied to God in the first chapter of Romans (v. 25).
In the earlier chapter we read of those who "worshipped and
served the creature more than the Creator, who is blessed forever." The Greek word that is applied to God is one that indicates
that all praise is to ascend to Him, and is the word which has
come down in our language as *eulogy*. But the word that is used
in our text, applied to the true and invisible Church of Jesus Christ,
makarios, indicates that all joys are placed upon us. When God
is blessed, the soul rises to Him in thanksgiving; when the believers
are blessed, the love and grace of God are poured forth upon
them. Once more we see that all things center in Him, who is
the object of our praise and the source of our joys. It is for this
reason that the center of the worship of the true believers has
always been accompanied with music. In the Old Testament the
center of worship consisted in the singing of the Psalms. In the
New Testament the Lord tells the believers that they are not to
be drunken with wine, wherein is excess, but that they are to be
filled with the Spirit, "speaking to yourselves in psalms, and hymns,
and spiritual songs, singing and making melody in your heart to
the Lord" (Eph. 5:19).

A NOTE OF TRIUMPH

It is a matter of church history that music has been the hand-
maiden of the gospel. In religions where Christ is not known
at all the music is always a dirge. In branches of Christianity where
liturgy, form, and ceremony largely replace the warmth of the
gospel, the music tends to be slow and mournful. Where modernism
and liberalism have taken hold, the hymns become a part of the
service where the organ plays loudly, a paid choir sings without
heart, and faint murmurs come from parts of the building where
spiritual life struggles to express itself in spite of the circumstances.
But wherever there is the warm knowledge of sins forgiven,
wherever Christ is exalted in His grace and saving power, then
the singing takes on a note of triumph. Luther sang:

> A mighty fortress is our God.
> A bulwark never failing.

Isaac Watts, when the eighteenth century was beginning, taught the church to sing:

> Come, let us join our cheerful songs
> With angels round the throne;
> Ten thousand thousand are their tongues,
> But all their joys are one.

The Wesleys added a thousand songs to the hymnody of the church, and every evangelical revival has brought its quota of praise and melody. At times the words and music have come from various groups that have not known the refinements of taste, but the beating, pulsating melodies of the Salvation Army in the gutters of the world, or the heart-moving hymns of Moody's day have all expressed the joy of a redeemed people singing praise to God for His love and grace in dying for us on the cross. At times the words and music were in high poetry and distinguished rhythm, and the church sang:

> O could I speak the matchless worth,
> O could I sound the glories forth,
> Which in my Saviour shine,
> I'd soar and touch the Heavenly strings,
> And vie with Gabriel while he sings,
> In notes almost divine.

At times the words and music are in trashy verse and barbarous beat, as a group of young people in some youth meeting may tuck their chewing gum to one side of their mouths and burst forth in:

> Hallelu, hallelu, hallelu, hallelujah,
> Praise ye the Lord.

But the impulsion in it all comes from the fact that there is a sense of freedom because a burden has been lifted. The Lord Jesus Christ is in the midst of His people, and He is leading the singing. That is not an extravagance, but a direct statement of Scripture, for we read that Christ is not ashamed to call us brethren, saying, "I will declare thy name unto my brethren, in the midst of the church will I sing"—oh, lay hold on that wonderful truth—"in the midst of the church will I"—Jesus Christ—"sing praise unto thee" (Heb. 2:12).

The singing Christ in the hearts of the people is the source of our blessedness and our joy. We are redeemed, we are His. Why should we not sing? For good and just reasons most of evangelical Christendom begins worship services with the doxology:

> Praise God from whom all blessings flow,
> Praise Him all creatures here below;
> Praise Him above, ye Heavenly host,
> Praise Father, Son, and Holy Ghost.

And somewhere in the service there is the *gloria*:

> Glory be to the Father, and to the Son, and to the
> Holy Ghost;
> As it was in the beginning, is now, and ever shall be,
> World without end. Amen.

And thus our hearts sing. The Holy Spirit in every believer who reads these lines will exalt Christ in praise because of all our joys. And the Holy Spirit will heighten the gloom that foreshadows the doom of everyone who has no song in his heart. He will give you a song today if you will believe His Word and trust in the Saviour who brings the song.

CHAPTER XXV

Sin and Iniquity Gone

"Blessed are they whose iniquities are forgiven, and whose sins are covered. Blessed is the man to whom the Lord will not impute sin" (Rom. 4:7, 8).

DAVID sang to the Lord in a Psalm that is quoted in our text in Romans four: "Blessed are they whose iniquities are forgiven and whose sins are covered. Blessed is the man to whom the Lord will not credit sin."

Each one of us can well understand that which speaks to us individually. We have already looked closely at the collectivity of the believers who form the blessed "they" whose sins and iniquities have been dealt with by God. In this study we shall look closely at our text and discover the difference between iniquities and sins, and the difference between something that is forgiven and something that is covered. Then we shall examine the fact that the Lord, in His bookkeeping, simply does not write down sin against the account of certain people.

DEFINITIONS

We can begin by saying that although all iniquity is sin, not all sin is iniquity. That is something like saying that all cats are animals, but not all animals are cats. Sin is a much larger term than iniquity. Perhaps the difference can be illustrated simply. A child is told that he may not steal a cooky from the kitchen. He disobeys and steals the cooky. The act was wrong; it was a sin. It was disobedience and a theft. But certainly it was not an iniquity. No one would suggest cutting the child's hand off, as thieves are treated in barbarous countries. No one would suggest putting the child in reform school. No one would suggest calling in the officials of the juvenile courts. Certainly the matter should be dealt with, and a good sound application of a strap is highly important. God Himself has said, "Foolishness is bound in the heart

of a child, and the rod of correction will drive it far from him"
(Prov. 22:15); and, "He that spareth the rod hateth his son" (Prov.
13:24). If the sin is not dealt with, it may well blossom into
iniquity as the child grows older.

In the Greek of our text the difference between the two words
is very interesting. Just as we change the meaning of a word by
adding a prefix, thus bringing in the exact opposite by the addition of a letter or two, so the Greeks did in their language. We
speak of "possible and impossible," "movable 'and immovable."
The Greeks canceled out a meaning and brought in the opposite by
adding the letter *alpha*, equivalent to our *a*, in order to negate
the meaning of a word. We have several examples in English that
have been brought straight out of Greek. A theist is someone
who believes in God; an atheist is someone who denies the reality
of God. A person who is moral has a set of standards and lives
úp to them in considerable measure; a person who is amoral has no
standards at all.

The word used for "sin" in our text is *hamartia,* "missing the
mark," and consists of the aspirated *alpha* before a word meaning
"to share": the idea being that the man who missed the mark in a
contest would not share in the prize. The sinner, therefore, would
not partake of the rewards which God has prepared for those who
love Him and believe His Word. The word that is translated
"iniquities" is formed in the same fashion. The common noun for
"law" is *nomos* and the word for "iniquity" is *anomia*—"lawlessness." Seen in this light our text would read: Blessed are they
whose transgressions of God's law are forgiven, and whose falling short of His righteousness is covered.

UNIVERSAL REBELLION

We do not need to labor the fact that all have sinned, coming
short of the glory of God. Our study of the whole first section
of this epistle has abundantly demonstrated the rebellion of the
human race and its consequent judgment by our Holy God. Now
the group of justified men are seen as blessed because their transgressions and their sins have been dealt with by the grace of God.
We are all in the place of need, and the famous line in the prayer
book of the Church of England covers both phases of our incom-

pleteness, positive and negative: "We have left undone those things which we ought to have done and we have done those things which we ought not to have done."

FORGIVEN — COVERED

Let us now turn our attention to the difference between that which is forgiven and that which is covered. In the Greek of the New Testament, there are fourteen different verbs used for the idea of "send" and "sent." The word that we have here for "forgive" is one of these. When the Lord Jesus was speaking His parables, He preached to the multitude from a boat during the first part of the discourse; and then we read that he sent the multitude away and went into the house. The word that is there translated "sent away" (Matt. 13:36) is the word that is used in our text. "Blessed is he whose iniquities are sent away." In our civilization when a man has committed some crime the authorities send the man away. We have slang phrases for this idea: one that has developed in New York where they send a man up the river to Sing Sing prison. Almost any criminal would understand a warning which said, "You will be sent up the river," or "You will be put away." It is a happy man who knows that he is a criminal and who finds that, instead of being sent away himself, he is kept in the place of joy and privilege and that a method has been found whereby it is his iniquities that are sent away.

Many men do not understand the doctrine of salvation by grace simply because they do not realize that God has made it possible to separate the sin from the sinner and to deal with the two separately and on different principles. Man cannot separate the sin from the sinner, and therefore he locks the sinner up and makes him pay for his sins. God has taken the sins from the believer and has put them on the Lord Jesus Christ, and there on the cross has punished Him instead of the sinner, and therefore the sins have been dealt with. We sing in one of our great hymns:

> Living, He loved me; dying, He saved me;
> Buried, He carried my sins far away.

THE SCAPEGOAT

The reference in this verse is to one of the sacrifices that had

been established under the law of Moses. The high priest took two
goats and one of them was slain in the place of the shedding of
blood. The blood of the goat that was slain was an atonement
for the sins of the people. The live goat was then brought before
Aaron, and he laid his hands upon the head of this goat and confessed over him all the iniquities of the children of Israel, and all
their transgressions, even all their sins. The description of the
scene, as it is recorded in Leviticus, continues: "And he shall put
them upon the head of the goat, and shall send him away by
the hand of a man that is in readiness, into the wilderness; and
the goat shall bear upon him all their iniquities unto a solitary
land; and he shall let go the goat in the wilderness" (Lev. 16:21-22).
This was, of course, a beautiful pageant of the death of the Lord
Jesus Christ, and His complete dealing with our sins for us. He
was the sin-bearer; He was the scapegoat.

The expression, "scapegoat," was invented by Tyndale when
he translated the Bible into English in the early sixteenth century.
Some have imagined that the live goat, which in Hebrew is called
Azazel, is the name for a being, a demon, or even the Devil, but
the best scholarship repudiates this. If such were the case, the
hymn would read something like this:

> Living, Christ loved me; dying He saved me;
> But the Devil carried my sins far away.

Wilhelm Moeller, in the *International Standard Bible Encyclo-
pedia*, perhaps the greatest of all Biblical encyclopedias, says:
"The goats represent two sides of the same thing. The second is
necessary to make clear what the first one, which has been slain,
can no longer represent, namely, the removal of the sin." He
further says: "The fact that the goat is accompanied by somebody
and that it is to be taken to an uninhabited place is to indicate
the absolute impossibility of its return, *i.e.*, the guilt has been
absolutely forgiven and erased, a deep thought made objectively
evident in a transparent manner and independently of Azazel . . .
In the personal interpretation, we could have in addition to the
idea of the removal of the guilt, also a second idea, namely, that
Azazel can do no more harm to Israel, but must be content with
his claim to a goat which takes Israel's place."

SIN TAKEN AWAY

That there is definitely this idea of a removal of the sins of the individual believer is further indicated by the great verse in the New Testament, "Behold the Lamb of God which taketh away [or beareth away] the sin of the world" (John 1:29).

And the cleansing of the leper contains the parallel idea in the use of two birds for the cleansing ceremony. The first bird was killed and the blood was caught in a bowl. The second bird was dipped alive into the blood and then allowed to go free. As the bird soared into the blue sky the cleansed leper could look at the spot of scarlet against the blue and could rest in perfect confidence that his iniquity had been sent off or away forever. If he had been asked: "How do you know that your sin has been dealt with?" he could have answered, "I rest secure in the sacrifice that was made for me. And the fact that it has been accepted as a sacrifice by God is shown by the blood that is being carried into the Heavens by the free-flying bird. There is my guarantee; there is my surety." And if I be asked why I can rest quietly in the finished work of the Lord Jesus Christ, I can point to the fact that on the third day He arose from the dead and ascended into Heaven. He bore with Him the marks of His death. It is no wonder that the disciples in the room whither they had fled after His death for fear of their enemies were glad when He showed them His hands and His side. For in the fact of His resurrection after His death, there is the guarantee that God the Father is perfectly satisfied with that which His Son did when He died for us on the cross. Our sins are removed from us as far as the east is from the west (Ps. 103:12). How blessed, then, is the man whose sins are removed far from him, placed upon the substitute, and there dealt with fully, so that the one who was the ungodly sinner is now accepted in the Beloved of the Father.

SINS COVERED

The second verb in this verse sets forth that the sins of the blessed man, the believer, have been covered. In our text in the New Testament the word for "covered" is used only here, being one of that class of words, quite large, that are used only once

in the Bible. Theologically, it would not ordinarily have been in
the New Testament for it is a word that belongs in the Old Testament, and is found here only because it is in a quotation from the
Psalms. For in the Old Testament times sins were covered, but
in the New Testament, since Christ has died and risen again, sins
are never covered any more, for they have been put on Christ
and dealt with once for all, and forever.

But before the Lord Jesus Christ came into the world and
died, it was necessary for God the Father to treat sins in a different fashion. If Abraham and Moses and David, and millions
of others who lived before the time of Christ, are in Heaven today,
it is because of the fact that God dealt with them in a special way
in view of the death of Jesus Christ which was a fact in His mind,
but which had not become a fact in human actuality. The word
covered is the term that is used in the Bible to denote this method
of dealing with the sins of men in the Old Testament. Thayer,
in the famous lexicon of the New Testament, defines the word
in a beautiful phrase, "they are covered over so as not to come to
view, *i.e.*, are pardoned."

When we come to Scriptural ideas, there is no way of understanding them except through the Scriptures. There are no human
analogies which can set forth truth that is completely divine.
Almost a century ago A. A. Hodge, in his magnificent work, *The
Atonement*, wrote as follows: "The plan of redemption, the office
of our Surety, and the satisfaction which He rendered to the claims
of justice against us, have no parallel in the relations of men to
one another. We are carried above the sphere of the highest relations of created beings into the august counsels of the eternal and
independent God. Shall we bring our own line to measure them?
We are in the presence of Father, Son, and Holy Spirit; one in
perfections, will, and purpose. If the righteousness of the Father
demands a sacrifice, the love of the Father provides it. But the
love of the Son runs parallel with that of the Father; and not
only in the general undertaking, but in every act of it, we see the
Son's full and free consent. In the whole work we see the love
of the Father as clearly displayed as the love of the Son: and
again, we see the Son's love of righteousness and hatred of iniquity
as clearly displayed as the Father's in that work of which it were

impossible to tell whether the manifestation of love or righteousness is more amazing. In setting out upon the undertaking we hear the Son say with loving delight, 'Lo, I come to do Thy will'; as He contemplates its conclusion, we hear Him say, 'Therefore doth My Father love Me, because I lay down My life, that I might take it again.' They are one in the glorious manifestation of common perfections, and in the joy of all the blessed results. The Son is glorified by all that is for the glory of the Father. And while, in the consummation of this plan the wisdom of God —Father, Son, and Holy Spirit—shall be displayed, as it could not otherwise have been, to the principalities and powers in Heavenly places, ruined man will, in Christ, be exalted to heights of glory and bliss, otherwise unattainable."

NO HUMAN ANALOGY

In order to find the meaning of the covering of sin, we are forced to go to the Bible. In any human analogy a thing which is covered is still there, but in the Bible the covering of sin was a temporary thing until God could take it out and deal with it in Jesus Christ. Sometime ago in one of my Bible lectures a written question was handed in which set forth the following difficulty that was in the mind of the questioner. "If men were saved before the time of Christ, then why should the cruel reality of the death of the Saviour on the cross have been necessary? Why could not God have kept on saving men in the same way that He saved them before Christ came to this earth?" It was a good question, but it revealed the ignorance of the questioner on the most important nature of the salvation that was provided in the time of the Old Testament. No man before Christ was saved apart from the death of Jesus Christ. Their sin was covered, but the day came when it was uncovered and placed on Christ. It was then that the full satisfaction to God was made for the sins of those who had lived before Christ and for us who have lived since.

Summarizing a long passage in Hodge on the use of the proper words, we find that during the latter part of the nineteenth century the word *atonement* became commonly employed to express that which Christ wrought in order to complete the salvation of His people. But before then, the term, used since

Anselm (1274), and habitually employed by all the Reformers, was *satisfaction*. This term is much to be preferred, first, because the word *atonement* is ambiguous. In the O. T. it is used for an Hebrew word which signifies, "to cover by making expiation." In the N. T. it is used but once, and then as a translation for a Greek word meaning *reconciliation*. But reconciliation is the effect of the sin-expiating and God-propitiating work of Christ. On the other hand, the word *satisfaction* is not ambiguous. It always signifies that complete work which Christ did in order to secure the salvation of His people, as that work stands related to the will and nature of God.

When Abraham or David, or any other believer of the Old Testament time, believed God's Word about the sacrifices that were prescribed through Moses for Aaron and his house to offer before God, the Lord God counted the sins of such an individual to be covered until the time when the Lord Jesus Christ should come and die on the cross. Then the meaning of the sacrifices could be seen. Then the object lessons which God had set before His people found their fulfillment. Then the sins which had been covered by God throughout the Old Testament time were uncovered and placed on the Saviour in order to be expiated completely and sent off forever from the one who had committed the sins. It was on this ground that an individual believer could know that his own sins were dealt with.

AN OMISSION

There is a beautiful indication of how intimately personal are these promises in the Psalms from which our text is quoted. If you read the verse in the Hebrew, there is no subject whatsoever for the verb. The English has drawn attention to this by printing three words in italics, which procedure is followed whenever English words have been added to complete the thought of a text. In the phrase, "Blessed is he whose transgression is forgiven, whose sin is covered," there are three words omitted. It is startling to see the implication. You often see forms printed in which you may add your name. On a check are printed the words, "Pay to the order of —————," and there is a blank after the phrase. What a delight to find your own name in the blank space! I suggest that you put your own name here in the blank which is in the Hebrew. I would have to read it, "Blessed is Donald Grey Barnhouse whose transgression is forgiven"; my sin is covered. And you may put your name in that place also, if you believe that Jesus Christ is God, that He came from the love of God in order to pay the fine that was demanded by the justice of God.

Do you now begin to see the force of the argument? O the blessedness of the man whose sins and iniquities have been dealt with by God Himself at the cross of Christ! O the blessedness of the man to whom the Lord will not reckon, or credit sin.

THE G.I. AND THE CHASE NATIONAL BANK

Perhaps the best way to set forth the truth that is in the last clause is to recount a charming little story that appeared in the New York papers a few years ago. An ex-G.I. went into the Chase National Bank in New York in order to get a loan from their small loans department. The Chase National is one of the two or three largest banks in the world and negotiates loans of many million dollars with great industries. But it also has a small loans department, instituted a few years ago, which will lend a few hundred dollars to a working girl or a laboring man. The former soldier had to fill out a lot of forms because the government was guaranteeing the loan, and it was necessary for him to come back a second day.

When he came to the window the teller kept him waiting a long time, finally leaving the window, saying he would be back shortly. There were several people in line, but the teller was gone almost ten minutes. Just as some impatience was beginning to make itself manifest there was quite a commotion around the window. The president of the bank walked through the great hall, came to the G.I., introduced himself, and asked to have him turn to be photographed. Newspapermen were there, and the amazed G.I. learned that his loan was quite special. The day before the bank records had indicated that sometime on the following day the total loans made by the small loans department would reach the sum of one billion dollars. The bank authorities had decided to publicize the fact by giving as a gift the amount of any loan requested by any customer who happened to apply at the very moment when this billion dollar figure was reached. The soldier was the fortunate man. He had signed all the papers and had obligated himself to repay the sum of six hundred dollars in certain installments. But now, before the news cameras, he was given the sum of six hundred dollars and his note and other papers were returned to him. The bank, of course, got much more than six hundred dollars' worth of publicity on the transaction, but we might well say, "O the blessedness of the G.I. to whom the Chase National Bank will not impute or debit his loan." The bank had effectively said, "This one is to be placed to our account. You will never have anything to pay."

GOD'S SOVEREIGN PLAN

This is precisely the situation for those who believe in the Lord Jesus Christ. We have sinned, make no doubt about that. We agree that there is absolutely no difference between us and any other sinner when seen from God's point of view. The customer before or after the happy G.I. who got the free gift might have been more deserving than the one who actually received the money without obligation. It was the bank's choice to make him the recipient of its grace. God has declared that it is His sovereign plan to credit to the account of Jesus Christ the sins of all who will admit that they are personally spiritually bankrupt, and who will throw themselves upon His grace to save them. If you will believe God's Word he will justify you, just as you are. He will credit all of your sin to the account of Christ and will credit His own righteousness to your account. Then you will know what it is to cry, "O the blessedness that is mine because my transgressions were put upon Christ, because my sins are blotted out. O the blessedness that is mine because my sins are not credited to my account but to the account of Christ." Then you may sing one of the greatest verses in all our hymns:

> My sin, O the bliss of this glorious thought,
> My sin, not in part, but the whole
> Is nailed to His cross, and I bear it no more,
> Praise the Lord, praise the Lord, O my soul!
>
> It is well . . . with my soul . . .
> It is well, it is well with my soul.

CHAPTER XXVI

Abraham's Example

"Cometh this blessedness then upon the circumcision only, or upon the uncircumcision also? for we say that faith was reckoned to Abraham for righteousness. How was it then reckoned? when he was in circumcision, or in uncircumcision? Not in circumcision, but in uncircumcision" (Rom. 4:9, 10).

THERE are some truths in the Bible that can be understood only by studying the time element involved, so that it can be determined when an event happened in relationship to some other event. For example, two men asked the same question concerning salvation but the answer was quite different because of the difference in time. The Lord Jesus was asked: "What must I do to inherit eternal life?" (Luke 10:25; 18:18), and the Apostle Paul was asked, "What must I do to be saved?" (Acts 16:30). Christ gave one answer and Paul gave another. And if any Christian were asked the same question today, he would give Paul's answer and not Christ's. The reason for this is that Christ gave His answer *before* He went to the cross and died, while Paul gave his answer *after* the Lord Jesus Christ had died and risen again from the dead. The difference in time is the reason for the difference in the answer.

There is the same explanation for a whole line of argument in the fourth chapter of Romans in our study of the life of Abraham as it is set forth there. Abraham is, from many points of view, the most important character in the Old Testament, even surpassing Moses and David in the importance of the revelations of truth made about him and his relationship to God. Abraham is called the father of many nations, and he is looked upon as being the father of all who believe God's Word about the Messiah. The teaching about Abraham is brought out in many different parts of the Bible. The story of his life is recorded in the Book of Genesis, but the explanation of the spiritual meaning of his life

257

is to be found in Joshua, in Jeremiah, in the Gospel of John and in the epistles.   The eleventh of Hebrews gives the longest of its paragraphs on faith to the analogies from the life of Abraham. The Epistle to the Galatians has two of its six chapters centering in the lessons to be drawn from the life of Abraham, and Paul devotes a large section of Romans, his greatest epistle, to lessons from the life of Abraham.

WHEN WAS ABRAHAM SAVED?

The meaning of Abraham and his faith, as set forth here in Romans, is to be understood only by a reference to the calendar of the events in his life and the order of those events.   Paul has set forth that salvation is entirely by grace and totally apart from the works of the flesh.   Man's complete ruin in sin and God's perfect remedy in Christ has filled the first three chapters of the epistle.   Now Paul must proceed to show the people of Israel that salvation is apart from mere law-observance, and Abraham is used as the example.   When was Abraham saved?   The answer shows, of course, that he was saved several hundred years before Moses and the giving of the law.   It is evident, then, that Abraham cannot have been saved by the law.   But, someone might argue, God gave to him the rite of circumcision, and thus Abraham was identified with the chosen people and the law that should be given to them, and through them to the world, much later.   But now the calendar is brought out in proof that this argument is not true.   When was Abraham counted as justified?   The scheme of events shows that he was saved long before God revealed to him the sign of circumcision that was to mark his body as faith in God's word was to mark his soul and his spirit.

This teaching is of great importance to me as a Gentile who has become a Christian.   I can show this to you by setting forth a conversation that took place recently.   I had come out of a store across from my church and was on my way to my office, walking with an associate in our work.   A well-dressed gentleman asked the way to Arch Street.   I replied with brevity that he could follow the sidewalk on Seventeenth Street until he passed through the tunnel under the Pennsylvania Railroad tracks, and that Arch Street would be the first main street after the tunnel which had not been removed at that time. The stranger said, "I am certainly thankful to get such definite and direct information. Most people are unable to give proper directions." I replied that I spent my life giving people directions on how to get to Heaven, and that I liked the directions to be plain and complete. Learning that I was the pastor of the church across the street, the man began to talk and soon I learned that he was a Jew, who had come to this country from Vienna. He was a cultured, educated gentleman, and by his guidance the conversation turned on spiritual matters. He put pointed questions that demanded plain answers. I replied by quoting passages in the Scriptures, and one of them I quoted to him in Hebrew, which he understood. He began to manifest great interest because he saw that I could talk to him on his level. I spoke to him of the exalted position of the Jews and the great place they have in the future plan of God, and how they are now back in Palestine in readiness for the fulfillment of prophecies on their behalf which have been written for centuries.

We spoke of the fact that the apostles were Jews and that the Lord Jesus Christ Himself was a Jew. I told him that this was one of the reasons why I loved the Jews so much and why I did everything that I could to fight anti-Semitism and to further their spiritual interests. "But," I said to him, "I want you to realize how important one thing is to me. Remember that I was a Gentile. Under your law I had no access to God. There was a curse upon me from the day of Moses. If we stop there, I am without hope and cursed forever. So if you have any love of humanity, realize that I must either have a Saviour or be lost according to your law. So do not take my Saviour from me. To me He must be my Jehovah, my Saviour, my Sin-bearer, or I am condemned by the just condemnation of a holy God." I believe that this kind man saw the point and comprehended the state of my necessity. Every Jew must realize that if he refuses to accept the fact that Jesus Christ is God's Son and our Saviour, he thereby condemns every non-Jew to perdition.

GENTILE FAITH

Our text in Romans substantiates my position and solves my problem. After speaking of the blessedness of those whose ini-

quities are forgiven, and whose sins are covered, and after saying, "Blessed is the man to whom the Lord will not credit sin,"
the inspired writer then draws the great conclusion by putting
a pertinent question. "Cometh this blessedness [of God's gift of
divine righteousness to all who have faith alone] then upon the
circumcision only, or upon the uncircumcision also?" And the
answer is found in the statement that follows: "for we say that
faith was reckoned to Abraham for righteousness."

Stifler has an interesting comment on this sentence. He writes,
"Paul has turned the Jew's boast upside down. It is not the Gentile
that must come to the Jew's circumcision for salvation; it is the
Jew who must come to a Gentile faith, such faith as Abraham had
long before he was circumcised . . . When Isaac was saved he was
not saved by his circumcision any more than was his father before
him. God never promised salvation except by faith. He never
promised a perpetual nationality except to circumcised men who
believe."

SYMBOL VS. REALITY

How the heart of man shows its perversity by man's desire to
seek salvation in the symbol of the reality rather than in the reality
itself. Most certainly we can never, never criticize the Jew for
clinging to circumcision rather than to the simplicity of faith when
we have in the midst of churchianity thousands of people who seek
salvation in baptism, the symbol of salvation, rather than in the
simplicity of faith alone.

There recently came across my desk a small book of meditations by a French religious leader, the title of the book being,
Some Rare Virtues. One of the rare virtues was that of gratitude,
and the writer has some beautiful things to say about the necessity
of thanking the good Lord for everything in life. But to my horror,
after a wonderful passage on the necessity of thanking God for
His providence in maintaining us in life, breath by breath, the
writer says, "If from this example taken in the natural order we
pass to the supernatural order, who thinks at the time of a child's
baptism of an unheard-of marvel? The blessed Trinity comes to
take its abode, without a sound, but nevertheless really, in this
weak, whimpering creature! A priest consecrates and the little bell

rings for the elevation. I ask you, who, even among the fervent, realizes fully the sublime beauty of what has taken place?" And thus the horror of the false doctrine of baptismal regeneration is set before men as an example of the work of God. But the Scripture teaches us in every part that the baptism is not the salvation, and has nothing to do with the salvation, any more than a wedding ring has anything to do with the consummation of a wedding. The latter is a symbol of a very beautiful thing, and baptism can be a symbol of a very beautiful thing, but most certainly the baptism itself could never wash away the sins of the soul.

It should be realized that the argument of the epistle is being carried forward in a devastating fashion. First, the apostle shows that there is no possibility of salvation through works performed by any individual. Now he is proceeding to show that there is no possibility of salvation through ordinances practiced by any individual. It is a very important section of the Word of God for Christians because there has been so much emphasis placed on ordinances, or as they are sometimes called by many branches of the church, sacraments.

CHRIST ALONE SAVES

Newell has a good paragraph on this point, saying, "After the same manner with the Jews, the vast majority of those calling themselves Christians place reliance today, alas, on some ordinance, or sacrament, saying, 'Christ told us to repent and be baptized, did He not? Christ commanded us to take the Lord's supper.' But remember that God justifies not those observing ordinances, but the ungodly who believe. If you are still regarding baptism, or the Lord's supper, or 'the Mass,' or 'christening,' or 'confirmation,' as having anything whatever to do with God's declaring you righteous, you do not understand being declared righteous as an ungodly one. And in the gospel, since the cross, you are not told first to cease being ungodly, and then believe; but as ungodly, to believe!

"Neither baptism nor the Lord's supper (upon both of which, in distorted form, thousands have rested as 'sacraments' commending them unto God), has power to give any standing whatever before a righteous God: that belongs only to the shed blood of the Redeemer of guilty and hopeless ones such as we are all!"

As a matter of chronology, Abraham was not circumcised until he was ninety-nine years old. He was saved by faith and declared righteous some fifteen years before the revelation of the sign and symbol of the circumcision.

THE IMPORTANCE OF ABRAHAM

In all the Bible there is no man, except the Lord Jesus Christ, who was much more than man, who should attract and hold our attention more than Abraham. He is certainly the most illustrious person of Biblical history. With him there is a beginning as important as the beginning with Adam, and even more important than the beginning with Noah. It is impossible to understand human history from the divine point of view, which is, of course, the real point of view, without understanding the reasons behind the call of Abraham from a family of Devil worshipers to become the father of the faithful and the founder of the Jewish and Arab races. His life is all the more important when we read at the end of this chapter in Romans that "it was not written for his sake alone . . . but for us" (4:23, 24). Furthermore, one of the foundation truths of Christianity is found in the Epistle to the Galatians where we read, "And if ye be Christ's, then are ye Abraham's seed, and heirs according to the promise" (Gal. 3:29).

DEVIL WORSHIPERS

Years afterwards, when the children of Israel had finished their forty years of wandering in the desert, when they had passed safely over the Jordan into the promised land, when they had occupied that land under Joshua and were beginning to be at peace, God gave further parts of the record concerning the circumstances of Abraham when he was called to become the father of his people. Joshua was about to die, and in his farewell address to the people he had so well led for so many years, he said under the inspiration of the Holy Spirit: "Thus saith the Lord God of Israel, Your fathers dwelt on the other side of the River [the Euphrates and Tigris], even Terah, the father of Abraham, and the father of Nahor and they served other gods. And I took your father Abraham from beyond the River, and led him throughout all the land of Canaan, and multiplied his seed . . . Now therefore, fear Jehovah, and serve him in sincerity and in truth; and put away the gods which your fathers served beyond the River and in Egypt, and serve ye Jehovah" (Josh. 24:2, 3, 14, R. V.). Here is the proof that Abraham came from a family of Devil worshipers, and this fact is confirmed by two other passages of Scripture.

The one is in the story of his grandson who went back to his grandfather's home to get a wife. After Jacob had visited with his cousins for some time, he fell in love with Rachel. There is a full account of his experiences with his father-in-law Laban, and finally the story comes to the point where Jacob determined to leave the land of Ur of the Chaldees, from whence his grandfather had been called, and return to the land of Canaan to the land which God had promised to him also. Because there was some bad feeling between Laban and Jacob, the latter decided to move suddenly when his father-in-law was away on a journey. When Laban returned home and found that his daughters and his son-in-law, taking all their goods with them, had left the country, he pursued them. He had noticed that the household idols, most precious possessions of a Devil-worshiping family, had disappeared with his children. When he overtook the fleeing party, which was forced to travel slowly because of the flocks and herds, he chided Jacob for having stolen the idols. When a search was made the idols were not found because Rachel had taken them and hidden them under the camel saddle upon which she sat. This incident shows clearly that there were idols, that they were cherished, and that Abraham's cousins remaining in the land of the Chaldees had continued to follow the Devil gods from which Abraham had been called.

Further confirmation of this fact is found in the statement in Isaiah (51:1,2): "Hearken unto me, ye that follow after righteousness, ye that seek the Lord, look unto the rock whence ye are hewn and to the hole of the pit whence ye are digged. Look unto Abraham your father, and unto Sarah that bare you." When we put two phrases of that text close to each other, we find that he tells them to look at the hole of the pit from which He had removed Abraham. Israel is called upon to remember that it had what might be called a pagan ancestry and that it was the grace of God to them through Abraham that made it possible for them to be saved.

SOVEREIGN GRACE

Up until the time that Abraham was seventy years of age he had no knowledge whatsoever of the true God. He was brought up in a heathen land among Devil worshipers, he dwelt in a large city that was entirely heathen, and undoubtedly lived after the manner of all the other heathen boys, young men, and men during the various stages of his growth. God did not appear to him because there was anything good in his character, but because it pleased God to come to him. One of the fundamental truths of the Bible is set forth in the fact that God did not choose Abraham because there was anything whatsoever in him that could have recommended him above his fellows, but only because it pleased God in His sovereign grace to appear to Abraham and call him out for His own eternal purpose.

One writer has put it thus: "One thing stands out with unmistakable clearness, namely, that the call which Abram received from God, was one of pure grace, sovereign grace, amazing grace. What was there in him to attract the notice of God? What was there in his circumstances to cause the great Jehovah to appear unto him? What had he done to entitle him to the inheritance which was given him? Nothing, absolutely nothing. It was grace and grace alone that moved God to act."

There is one more word in the prophecy of Isaiah which shows the sovereignty of this divine grace. After calling upon them to look to the hole of the pit from which they had been digged, to look even to Abraham, the passage continues, "For I called him alone and blessed him and increased him" (Isa. 51:2). Look well to that word "alone." God says, "I called him alone." Why did not God call one of his companions in the city of Ur? Why did not God take Abraham's brother? The need of these others was just as great as Abraham's need.

There are many people who are so blind to the nature of salvation that they will cry, almost automatically, "But surely there must have been something in Abraham that attracted the attention of God!" To hold such an idea for even a moment is to contradict that which the Word of God everywhere teaches about the nature of God and about the nature of sin. If there had been anything,

anything at all, in Abraham to attract God, it would be that the perfection of God could be satisfied with imperfection in a creature. If such were the case, there would be no place to draw the line and a universalism of salvation would be found necessary. Sin could then run unchecked; all the Bible teaching about the justice of God would become nonsense; there would be no place found for the eternal punishment of rebellion; and Satan would have triumphed. But the nature of God demands that His justice be satisfied, and this has been done in the payment by His love to that justice.

IT PLEASED GOD

The race lay in its total blindness, and God stooped from Heaven to appear unto Abraham. If an angel had asked the Lord why He was choosing Abraham He could have well answered: "Because it pleases Me to choose Abraham." If the angel had continued, saying, "But there is no good in Abraham," God could have well answered, "There is no good in any creature; but I choose to set my love upon him." And if the angel had then asked, "But will You not dirty Your Being by folding this Devil worshiper to Your breast?" God could have well answered, "I will go down and give My only Son to die for Abraham, and the blood of My Son will cleanse Abraham of his filth, so that I shall not be sullied when I draw him to Myself." And if the angel had once more asked, "But does not Abraham deserve judgment as much as any other man of Ur of the Chaldees?" God could have well replied, "All of them deserve the same from Me, but I propose to give My beloved son to take the stroke of that judgment, so that I may look upon Abraham as righteous." And if the angel had finally said, "But will not Abraham have to make some steps in righteousness before it is possible to count him as righteous?" God could have well replied, "Never, for it is while he is yet ungodly that I shall account him righteous and it is the power of the new life that I shall plant in him which shall cause his steps to move toward Me, slowly at first and then more firmly as time goes on."

AN EXAMPLE

And we must not forget today that Abraham's case is presented in the Bible as the example and pattern of all salvation. The manner in which God saved Abraham is the manner in which God will save you. If you are not willing to be saved as Abraham was saved, then you cannot be saved. If you insist on clinging to the rags of your own righteousness, you will be carried away with them to the place of judgment and burning. If you are not a believer in the Lord Jesus Christ today, you are not a spiritual child of Abraham.

On the other hand, if you are truly saved it is because you have been saved exactly as Abraham was saved. You were dead in trespasses and sins and by nature a child of wrath. The God of glory somehow appeared to you, most probably through some passage in the Bible, and gave you a revelation of the nature of His love. He showed you that you could never lift yourself by your own efforts but that He would gladly count you as righteous even in the midst of your ungodly state, if you would stop trusting in anything in yourself and put your trust in the Lord Jesus Christ alone. All this was apart from joining anything and apart from having anyone do anything to you, such as baptism, or apart from anything in your character, or apart from any rite, or ceremony, or liturgy, or good work. It was the sovereign God reaching out to you in the heart of His love and in the wonder of His grace and bringing you to life and immortality through the gospel of our Lord and Saviour Jesus Christ.

When we realize the simple wonder of this great fact, our hearts burst forth in praise unto Him who loved us and washed us from our sins in His own blood, and raised us to the rank of sons through faith in the Saviour. We cry out, O the blessedness that is mine because the Lord has forgiven my iniquities and cleansed me from my sins. O the blessedness that is mine because the Lord does not credit my sin to my account but to the account of the Saviour. And all of this happened to me, as it did to Abraham, when I was yet ungodly.

> He saw me ruined in the fall,
> And loved me, notwithstanding all.
> He saved me from my lost estate,
> His loving-kindness, O how great!

CHAPTER XXVII

The Steps of Faith

"And he received the sign of circumcision, a seal of the right-eousness of the faith which he had yet being uncircumcised: that he might be the father of all them that believe, though they be not circumcised; that righteousness might be imputed unto them also: and the father of circumcision to them who are not of the circumcision only, but who also walk in the steps of that faith of our father Abraham, which he had being yet uncircumcised" (Rom. 4:11, 12).

PAUL HAS proclaimed that man was completely ruined in sin. He has demonstrated the total incapacity of any man to save himself or to be saved by anything that men could combine, even in religious or national organization, to do for the outward need of the individual. Relentlessly, he has pursued the argument with divine logic and has closed off every avenue of escape, leaving man bankrupt, but face to face with the love of God at the cross of Jesus Christ, where God is willing to declare an ungodly man to be righteous on the grounds of the satisfaction that was provided in the death of His Son.

He has illustrated his point by citing the work of God in the life of Abraham whom he calls the father of all them that believe, and has demonstrated that God declared Abraham to be righteous while he was in the midst of ungodly surroundings, living with a Devil-worshiping family, and at least fifteen years before he received the seal and sign of God's purpose for him in the act of circumcision. We now read: "And he received the sign of circumcision, a seal of the righteousness of the faith which he had while he was in uncircumcision: that he might be the father of all them that believe though they be in uncircumcision, that righteousness might be reckoned unto them; and the father of circumcision to them who not only are of the circumcision, but who also walk in the steps of that faith of our father Abraham which he had in uncircumcision."

THE FATHER OF ALL WHO BELIEVE

This passage demonstrates that the Lord God has a definite desire for a redeemed people who shall be a spiritual people and live for Him spirtually, but it also demonstrates that God wants a physical nation, the Jews, and that He Himself has called them through Abraham, has given them promises, and intends to keep them separated from the world so that He may fulfill His purposes through them. Of both these groups Abraham is the father.

The text sets forth that Abraham is the father of all who believe, even though they be not circumcised, and that Abraham is the father of all who have been circumcised and who in addition to the bodily mark of the covenant follow in the steps of the faith of Abraham.

As we are going to spend our time in this study in setting forth the steps of the faith of Abraham, we wish to say in passing that there is here a very important revelation as to God's national purpose for the nation Israel. I tremble when I hear some Protestant theologians attempting to say that there is no national purpose for the Jews. Such men have denied the Word of God and are flying in the face of the evidence set forth therein.

God is not going to allow the United Nations to succeed. I have maintained for many years that any such attempt to unite the nations of the world in a bond of brotherhood or in a bond of self-government is doomed to absolute failure. I proclaimed it throughout all the history of the League of Nations, now defunct, and throughout the history of the present United Nations, so far as it has gone to date. If it were possible for the United Nations to succeed, then man could announce to God that the human race had been able to undo the curse that was pronounced at the time of Noah when nationality was created by God as a curse and when God reached out and took Abraham in order to make of him a special nation through whom He intends yet to rule this world.

Make no mistake about it: the little nation of Israel will expand far beyond its present borders. Not only will it control Jerusalem and the part of Palestine that is held by the Arabs, but its territory, according to the promise given by God, will extend from the river of Egypt even to the great rivers, Euphrates and Tigris, and will include Syria and even Asia Minor, the country of the ancient Hittites, promised to Abraham at the time of the confirmation of the deed of the land to him (Gen. 15:20).

But, that I may be faithful to the Word of God, let me add that not all Israel is Israel according to the revelation which we have in the Book. Our text confines the promise to those of the circumcision who walk in the steps of the faith of their father Abraham which he had while yet uncircumcised.

Let us then turn our attention to these steps of his faith, in order that we may see what faith may be ours as Gentiles who have no part in the covenant of circumcision, and in order to see that the same faith must be that of the believing remnant of the ancient people who were his physical descendants.

STEPHEN'S DISCOURSE

The first step of Abraham's faith is revealed to us in the great discourse of Stephen which was given in Jerusalem on the day in which Stephen was killed as the first Christian martyr. Stephen began his address at the time of his arrest in the following terms: "The God of glory appeared unto our father Abraham, when he was in Mesopotamia, before he dwelt in Haran." We do not know the full reality of that vision. We do not know how the appearance took place or what manifestation Abraham had of the God of glory. The very title is awe-inspiring to the one who knows the Bible and who can read between the lines of such a passage. The glory of God is a great and wonderful subject, but the God of glory is even greater than the glory of God.

At all events, we must conclude that Abraham, living among Devil worshipers, as we saw in our last study, suddenly became aware of the living reality of the true God. Perhaps he had thought of the many gods that were worshiped in his city by his contemporaries. Perhaps there had sometime come into his mind the idea that there must be one god more powerful than any of the other beings that were worshiped by his fellow men. He perhaps did not realize that all the rest of the gods were demons, as the Bible later reveals. In Psalm 96:5, we read in the English that all the gods of the nations are idols, and in the New Testament we are told that everything that is sacrificed to idols is sacrificed to demons (I Cor. 10:20). The Hebrew of the passage in the Psalms contains an interesting play on words, for the name for "gods" and the word for "idols" are very much alike—all the *elohim* of the nations are *eleel*, literally, "vanity, good for nothing."

THE REALITY OF GOD

But, though Abraham may not have understood all that was involved in this, he did know that the God of glory had appeared to him, and that all the other gods were vanity and nothing. Never again in his life did he turn for a moment toward any one of them. He knew now that he had found the reality of the living and true God, and this must ever be the first of the steps of faith. The soul who has comprehended God's glory can never turn to lesser things again. Going on our ordinary way, occupied with the things of time and sense, suddenly He makes Himself known to us.

It is a matter of such great import in the life of a soul that the enemy of souls, the Devil, has, of course, sought to counterfeit the glory, and he appears to men as an angel of light (II Cor 11:14). But there is a vast difference between the God of glory, and Satan transformed as an angel of light.

If one wishes to know how to be aware of the difference in order not to be deceived, the answer is that the God of glory will always appear in relationship to the promise of redemption as it is found in Jesus Christ. The angel of light will seek to draw men to goodness, and ethics, and brotherhood without any thought of salvation by blood. By this you shall be able to discern the difference between the two. Also it should be realized that these two lights appear before the closed eyelids of spiritually blind men. A lighted candle held within an inch of the eyelids of men who have some types of blindness will stimulate the rods and cones of the retina to the point where the senses have some awareness of light, and the poor blind man may think that this is the sun. But the true light of God that comes in His sovereign grace will create within the eyes a faith which shall be able to see the sun itself and to bask in the glory of the God of glory.

ABRAHAM'S RESPONSE

Now it should be evident to anyone with spiritual perception that such an appearance as that of the God of glory to Abraham in Ur of the Chaldees had to bring forth a reaction and a response of submission and obedience. If you tell me that you have really come face to face with the true God of glory as He reveals Himself in Jesus Christ today, and if you then tell me that it is not necessary for you to do anything about it, I know that you are living and thinking in the midst of great self-deception. Faith that is true faith will always act, and faith without such action is dead. Here is the true meaning of James' great statement, "Faith without works is dead" (Jas. 2:20). It does not mean at all that faith apart from works is dead, but that true faith must work. If there is to be an argument about the reality of faith, it must be based, first, on its conformity to the standard set forth in the Bible, and second, on the nature of the action it produces in the person who has the faith.

When the God of glory appeared to Abraham, quite naturally Abraham changed his whole way of living. The command of God followed the appearance of glory, "Get thee out of thy country, and from thy kindred, and from thy father's house, unto a land that I will shew thee" (Gen. 12:1). The essential element of this command is one of separation. The God of glory will always begin by saying, "Get out . . ." And the immediate step of faith will be obedience to the command.

STRANGERS AND PILGRIMS

The call which Abraham received was first a call for him to leave the land of his birth and life, and, second, a call for separation from his kindred and his father's house. And since our text says that Abraham is the father of all who believe, we must realize that his is a pattern case in each of these steps. He was to leave his dwelling place and his kindred. And in a spiritual sense we must have the same separation in our lives when we start the walk of true faith. Abraham was born in Ur of the Chaldees; we are born into the world. He was called out to a promised land; we are called out to a heavenly calling (Heb. 3:1). We have been chosen out of the world (John 15:19), and we are told that our citizenship is in Heaven (Phil. 3:20). As far as our earthly walk is concerned, we are henceforth to look for a city that hath foundations, whose builder and maker is God, and not to be concerned about any earthly roots (Heb. 11:10). Our position is that of those who are strangers and pilgrims on the earth (Heb. 11:13; I Pet. 2:11).

This does not mean that a Christian is not to be thrifty; it does not mean that a Christian may not save and purchase his own home; it does not mean that if a Christian is greatly prospered, he may not have a very fine home. There have been those who have thought that any scale of earthly riches is incompatible with the calling of a Christian. The proof that this is not so is to be found in the definite declaration of the Holy Spirit, through the Apostle Paul which says, "Charge them that are rich in this world, that they be not highminded, nor trust in uncertain riches, but in the living God, who giveth us richly all things to enjoy" (I Tim. 6:17). And it is to be noticed that Abraham, in going out to the strange land, became a mighty prince among the tribes and that he possessed great riches and was able to muster a small army among the great number of his servants. But the fact was that Abraham was a stranger and a pilgrim on the earth. He did leave his native land and begin to walk with God. Everything that he owned was now held in the reality of its true and eternal values. Nothing was held for any intrinsic worth. Henceforth all that was touched or possessed was looked upon as a gift from God—of value if it enhanced the glory of God and brought the Lord nearer to the heart, and of no value at all if it caused the light of God to grow dim and the memory of the glory to fade.

If we have seen the God of glory, we will be out of this world in a real sense. Paul wrote to the believers who lived in various parts of the Roman Empire, addressing, for example, those at Philippi as the saints who were "in Christ and at Philippi." "In" and "at" are very different, the one from the other. You may have seen letterheads that gave both a home and a business address. Such is the meaning of the address to the saints. Their business address was at Philippi, but their home address was in Christ. I ever pray that it may be so with me. I do not want to say that I live in Philadelphia; I want to say that I live at Philadelphia and in Christ Jesus. Herein is the significance of the word to the Colossians: Christ "hath delivered us from the power of darkness, and hath translated us into the kingdom of his dear Son" (Col. 1:13).

A CURSED WORLD

Perhaps someone would wonder why the Christian must develop such an other-worldly attitude and hold this world in such contempt. The answer is not far from us as we turn the pages of the Word of God. In an earlier study in this same epistle, we saw that the law was given that every mouth might be stopped and all the world brought guilty before God (Rom. 3:19). We live, then, in the midst of a world that has been cursed by God. John tells us that this world rests in the embrace of the Devil even as a licentious man might rest in the embrace of a prostitute (I John 5:19, Greek). We are told that everything in this world shall be dissolved—its works of art, its works of industry, its works of science, its edifices of religion, its homes and palaces, its halls of learning and music, its places of amusement, all are under the condemnation of God and doomed to destruction. In fact, the divine revelation states: "Seeing that all these things shall be dissolved, what manner of persons ought ye to be in all holy manner of life and godliness" (II Pet. 3:11).

It is for these reasons that we may understand the declaration that our Lord "gave himself for our sins that he might deliver us from this present evil world, according to the will of God and our Father" (Gal. 1:4). And he even goes so far as to tell us that in the new Heavens and the new earth, the former, that is the one in which we now live, shall not be remembered nor come into mind (Isa. 65:17). And if we wish to sum it all up, we may set it forth in the single statement that this is the world that crucified the Lord Jesus Christ, and this is the world that would do it again if He came once more submitting Himself into its hands. This He will never do, for when He comes again, He shall rule it with a rod of iron and dash it into pieces as a potter's vessel (Psa. 2:9).

SEPARATION — THE FLESH

The next step of Abraham's faith which constitutes him the father of all that believe is the command to get out from his kindred and his father's house. And if Abraham's separation from the land of his birth is the symbol of our separation from this world which crucified our Lord, then Abraham's separation from the ties of the flesh may easily be understood as our separation from all ties of the flesh, both around us and within us. It is perhaps very significant that this portion of Abraham's obedience was incomplete, and that the steps in this direction were halting. He evidently let his aged father, an idolator, dominate the first section of the journey, and they dwelt for some time in Haran, even until his father's death. It was only upon the removal of this tie that the obedience of Abraham flowered to ripeness, and he was willing to go all the way through to the land which God had chosen for him and to which He was leading him by faith.

When we were born, we were the children of Adam, and by nature were the children of the curse which came upon him. When we are told to leave our kindred and our father's house, we are being told that we are to realize that our kinship with the old Adamic nature has been broken by the Lord Jesus Christ, and that the body of our flesh has been crucified with Christ. This we shall see at much greater length when we come to the sixth chapter of this epistle. In fact the next three chapters of Romans are largely concerned with the subject of our separation from Adam and our union with the risen Lord Jesus Christ. The unregenerate man is still looked upon by God the Judge as being in Adam and under the curse that rightfully belongs to Adam and all who remain in him. The believer in Christ is now looked upon by God the Redeemer as being *in* Christ, and our standing and position are entirely new because of this change that God has wrought in us. Herein lies the meaning of the great declaration: "If any man be in Christ, he is a new creation; old things are passed away, behold all things are become new" (II Cor. 5:17).

POSITION VS. CONDITION

This great step of faith, like all others, is first seen in our position and then in our condition. In the sight of God we are already

separated from self and the flesh and are already seen as being
in Christ. We were enemies, we are now sons; we were children
of wrath, we are now children of righteousness. We were darkness,
we are now light in the Lord. We were of the family of Adam, we
now are of the family of God. We were unrighteousness, we are
now righteousness. We were of idols, we are now temples of the
Holy Spirit. All of this, and much more, is ours positionally the
very moment we are saved. In sight of God all of this has been
accomplished. But conditionally, the Christian life is to proceed
in the practical transformation of our lives day by day, and over
a long period of years. Justification is a crisis; sanctification is a
process. The word of God declares our position, even as the command of God separated Abraham from his land, his kindred, and
his father's house. We are to lay hold upon the position by faith
and go out, step by step, even as Abraham laid hold upon the
position and entered as a stranger and a pilgrim on the weary,
desert way.

Here is the underlying meaning of one of the difficult passages
in the Gospels. The Lord Jesus said, "If any man come to me
and hate not his father, and mother, and wife, and children, and
brethren and sisters, yea, and his own life also, he cannot be my
disciple" (Luke 14:26). The passage has shocked some because
they knew but one meaning of the word *hate*. We read in Ephesians
that no man ever hated his own flesh (Eph. 5:29), but here we are
told that a man must hate his life. The answer is that in the
Gospels our Lord is using the word *hate* to express the idea that
we must establish a rigorous system of priorities and put the
Lord first. We must never allow any ties of human love to take
precedence over our love for the Lord. We must never allow our
love for our children to condone any false position in their lives,
but must commit them to the Lord and be willing to see them
suffer and fail in everything in life if they are not saved and
surrendered to Him. We must put the Lord before father or
mother. If a young person is called to the foreign mission field and
the parents do not wish the child to go, he must go anyway. If an
unsaved wife wishes a husband to take her into the world in a
frenzied round of fast living, he must put Christ first, even if he
should be abandoned by the one whom he loved with the highest

earth love. We are told in the Epistle to the Galatians that "they that are Christ's have crucified the flesh with the affections and lusts thereof" (Gal. 5:24). The flesh, therefore, has its affections, and they must not be allowed to take precedence over the love that is due to Him who loved us and washed us from our sins in His own blood. So the teachings of the two Testaments balance, the one the other. In the Old Testament Abraham was told to get out from his home, his kindred, and his father's house. In the New Testament we are told to crucify the flesh with its affections.

NAHOR

All who truly believe will discover that this is one of the most important phases of our discipleship. If there is a refusal to follow, we may question if the faith is reality. Perhaps we can close this section of our study by pointing out the case of Abraham's own blood brother, Nahor. The Scripture reveals that Nahor was the son of Terah, even as was Abraham. When Abraham obeyed God and started to get out he abandoned his brother Nahor who stayed on in the land of the Chaldees. The nephew of these two men, child of a third brother, was Lot. He followed Abraham as a true believer, and later was delivered by God and was proclaimed to be a justified man (II Pet. 2:7). Nahor, on the contrary, settled down in the land of the Chaldees; and, like Cain who murdered his brother Abel, he builded a city. Cain called his city after the name of his son, but Nahor called his city after his own name. The God of Abraham was Jehovah but the gods of Nahor (as the margin of the revised version puts it in Gen. 31:53) were the Devil gods whose idols were worshiped by his son Laban (Gen. 31:19, 30, 34).

You today are like Abraham or Nahor. You can remain in the world, settle down, name your city after yourself, live with the gods which are demons. If you thus live like Nahor, you shall die like Nahor. But if you see the God of glory and get out, for you will get out, then you will go from strength to strength like Abraham. May God give you strength to walk in the steps of faith.

CHAPTER XXVIII

Faith Apart from the Law

"For the promise, that he should be the heir of the world, was not to Abraham, or to his seed, through the law, but through the righteousness of faith" (Rom. 4:13).

IN THE thirteenth verse of Romans four the writer sums up that which has been set forth, lest there be any misunderstanding. "For not through the law was the promise to Abraham or to his seed, that he should be heir of the world, but through the righteousness of faith."

A little mental arithmetic and a little knowledge of Biblical history will assure any student that Abraham lived some four centuries before Moses and the giving of the law. The statement, therefore, that Abraham did not receive the promises through the law is as evident as it would be to say that George Washington did not base his decisions on the Atlantic charter. And we have already seen that the sign of circumcision came to Abraham some fifteen years after the receiving of the promise and the announcement of his justification by faith. Paul now sets law and faith opposite each other in a clear fashion in order to enhance the value of righteousness by faith.

When Abraham was justified before God, he had no law and he had no ceremony or sign; he had nothing but faith. This shows us very clearly, then, that faith does not depend on anything other than the pure and unadulterated grace of God.

THE ARGUMENT IN GALATIANS

In order to understand this passage fully, it is necessary that we refer to a parallel discussion of the subject as set forth in the Epistle to the Galatians. The central chapters of that epistle are also built around Abraham and are also concerned with the question of salvation by grace through faith apart from the law or its ceremonies. The argument in Galatians rises out of a triumphant cry in which the apostle states the conclusion at the beginning. "I do not frustrate the grace of God," he says, "for if righteousness come by the law, then Christ is dead in vain" (Gal. 2:21). For the true Christian, and, indeed any intelligent Gentile who wishes to go to Heaven, this is of outstanding importance. We have no place in the law; we are aliens from the covenant and strangers from the commonwealth of Israel. We have no place in any of the tribes, and therefore we have no access to the altar where the high priest of the tribes can shed the blood of a substitute sacrifice in order to set forth the principle of our justification and consequent righteousness in the sight of a holy God. Here is the very core of the New Testament teaching: if righteousness could come by the law, then Christ is dead in vain.

Theologically, we may substitute any other thing or idea for the word law. If righteousness could come by baptism, then Christ is dead in vain. If righteousness could come by ethical struggling, then Christ is dead in vain. If righteousness could come by any manner of form, ceremony, or liturgy, then Christ is dead in vain. If righteousness could be imparted by the dictum of any priest, pastor, rabbi, or religious leader of any name or stamp, then Christ is dead in vain.

Immediately after setting forth this idea, Paul writes in the next verse, "O foolish Galatians, who hath bewitched you?" (Gal. 3:1), and proceeds to show the folly of thinking that righteousness can be secured or maintained on any other principle than that of the sovereign grace of God. Phillips paraphrases it: "Oh you dear idiots of Galatia! who has cast a spell upon you?" And Abraham is brought into the argument again: "Even as Abraham believed God, and it was accounted to him for righteousness. Know ye therefore that they which are of faith"—that is, of the party of those that hold to salvation by faith apart from anything in the one who believes—"the same are the children of Abraham." And the Holy Spirit continues the teaching, saying, "And the Scripture, foreseeing that God would justify the heathen through faith, preached before the gospel unto Abraham, saying, in thee shall all nations be blessed. So then they which be of faith are blessed with faithful Abraham" (Gal. 3:6-9).

ABRAHAM AND HIS SEED

There are two ideas set forth in our present text which introduce entirely new elements in the spiritual teaching of the epistle. The first of these two ideas grows out of the mention of the seed of Abraham to whom the promise was given, and the second arises out of the revelation of the nature of the promise that was given to Abraham and his seed.

It is now seen that the promise was not made to Abraham alone, but to Abraham and to his seed. One of the key verses of all Scripture joins these two names together and identifies them beyond question. Following the great declaration which we have quoted from the third of Galatians, there is a wonderful exposition of the doctrine of the expiation of sin and the satisfaction of the justice of God on the grounds of the substitutionary death of the Lord Jesus Christ. It is a passage that ranks high among all the passages of the Word of God in importance of its revelation. First, there is the announcement that any man trying to be justified by clinging to the works of the law thereby places himself in the position where he stands under the curse of God, since the law carries a curse for even the least deviation from its demands. "For as many as are of the works of the law are under the curse" —not merely *a curse*, which would be bad enough, but *the curse*, which is comprehensive and all-inclusive—"for it is written, Cursed is every one that continueth not in all things which are written in the book of the law to do them" (Gal. 3:10).

CHRIST MADE SIN

The law is an entity, a whole, in the sight of God and was given in order to demonstrate to man that he could never do anything that could satisfy the perfect God who must demand perfection. James has put it, "Whoso keepeth the whole law, and yet offendeth in one point, is guilty of all" (Jas. 2:10). These texts establish that there is no such thing as a moderate sinner or a partial sinner. With God there are no pastel shades—a man is saved or lost; he is under the blessing of salvation or under the curse of the law; he is declared righteous by grace or he is declared accursed by law. There is no third position possible.

After this announcement, the Galatians passage proceeds to set forth the vicarious death of the Lord Jesus Christ in the strongest terms: "Christ hath redeemed us from the curse of the law, being made a curse for us; for it is written, Cursed is every one that hangeth on a tree" (Gal. 3:13).

Here is set forth the *modus operandi* by which the holy God is righteously able to take the sins of men and place them on the sinless Saviour. Back in the Book of Deuteronomy there was the phrase set forth in the law: "Cursed is every one that hangeth on a tree." There is no mention of the righteousness or the unrighteousness of the one who is thus hanged. It is a word in the law of God which pronounces a curse upon one who dies in a certain fashion. And when the Lord placed Himself in the hands of men and allowed Himself to be hanged upon the cross, He became, even in the midst of His spotless perfection, in His sinless glory, a technical violator of that law. It was on this ground that God was able to pour the entire weight of His wrath upon the Saviour. Thus it was that Christ was made sin for us, He who knew no sin (II Cor. 5:21). This is why the Lord Jesus Christ could not have been the Saviour if He had been stoned with stones, as the Jewish law provided death for its violators. This is why the Lord Jesus Christ could not have been the Saviour, if He had been killed, as His fellow-citizens of Nazareth attempted to kill Him, by hurling Him from the top of a cliff. This is why the Lord Jesus Christ could not have been the Saviour if He had died in any other way than by crucifixion death.

But the Galatians text shows more than this method of substitutionary death; it gives the purpose of that death in the next line: Christ has redeemed us from the curse of the law, "so that the blessing of Abraham might come on the Gentiles through Jesus Christ; that we might receive the promise of the Spirit through faith."

The blessings that were promised to Abraham were not promised to him alone, but they were promised to him and to a vast company of human beings who should follow him on the earth, and who should be in number as the sands of the sea— an earthly people—and as the stars of the sky—a Heavenly people.

SEED — NOT SEEDS

But now God introduces another element in the teaching, for He reveals to us the real basis of the promise that was to Abraham and his seed. One day, recently, I was looking into the eyepieces of a very fine Zeiss microscope which a medical student had brought home from Germany. He had adjusted the mechanism and then told me to look. All seemed blurred. He then put my fingers on a focusing knob, and as I turned it slightly, the object began to increase in clarity until I saw it in all the magnificent sharpness of its most powerful definition. The doctrine of salvation is thus brought into focus by turning Galatians 3:15 to bear on the whole of Scripture: "Now to Abraham and his seed were the promises made. He saith not, And to seeds, as of many; but as of one, And to thy seed, which is Christ." Here God has spelled out for us, so that the simplest child may comprehend if he will submit himself to the Holy Spirit's teaching, that the promise was not made to Abraham and his earthly seed alone but that it was made to Abraham and his greater Seed, the Lord Jesus Christ.

The salvation of man is, according to the plan of God, in a covenant that was made within the Godhead. In one of the early chapters of our study of this epistle we set forth the Bible teaching concerning the nature of the Trinity. With all that in mind, we may now say that salvation was a matter between God the Father and God the Son. It was the nature of His love that prompted Him, Father and Son, to conceive such a plan of salvation, and it was the nature of His holiness that made it possible for Him, Father and Son, to fulfill the plan. It might be written in the language of our lawyers today: "Whereas God alone is holy, and whereas there is no good in man that could ever satisfy God, it is now therefore divinely decreed that God the Father, hereinafter called the party of the first part, covenants and agrees with Abraham and Jesus Christ, hereinafter called joint parties of the second part, to redeem and to justify any member of the human race who will turn his faith, hope, and trust away from man or anything in man, and put that faith, hope, and trust in the Word of God about the Lord Jesus Christ, especially in that Word concerning the person of Christ, that He is very God, and in the work of Christ, that He did by His death provide the perfect satisfaction which the justice of God was required to demand of all sinners. It is moreover decreed that nothing in this covenant and agreement shall be voided by any failure, positive or negative, in one of the parties of the second part. And it is finally decreed that any person who would enter a claim to the benefits of this covenant and agreement must, a priori, abandon all claims to worthiness in himself, and that any such claim to worthiness, under whatever heading, shall thereby constitute full grounds of exclusion of that person from any of the benefits of this covenant and agreement."

There is the rock of our salvation—it was planned before the foundation of the world, and it was set forth in the eternal councils of the Godhead as the Father and the Son covenanted together that there should be a vast company of the race of Adam who should be elevated to the position of eternal sons and should be made to participate in the government of the universe with God forever, and all on the basis of faith in God's Word about the Lord Jesus Christ.

ABRAHAM AND CHRIST

God promised Abraham and Christ that all this should be accomplished. But, someone objects, supposing that Abraham goes bankrupt? That would make no difference so long as Christ remains solvent. The promises are sure because they were made between God the Father and God the Son. The promise came to Abraham, "I will bless thee . . . and in thee shall all the families of the earth be blessed." "But, Lord," Abraham might have said, "suppose I get out of Thy will?" God replies: "I will bless thee." Abraham might again ask, "But, Lord, suppose my posterity should become idolators?" God still replies: "I will make of thee a great nation." And again, Abraham might question, "But, Lord, suppose that my descendants should crucify Thy Son?" But God still replies, "I will bless thee."

We look at all the record and say, "Lord, suppose that Abraham becomes a liar, and teaches his wife to lie, and breaks whatever conditions there are to his place in the covenant?" God replies, "I will bless thee." We ask, "But suppose his grandson, Jacob, becomes a crook?" God answers, "I will bless thee." We ask again, "But suppose his greatest son, David, becomes an adulterer and a murderer?" God replies, "I will bless thee." In a voice that is reduced to trembling, we ask, "But why, Lord?" And the answer comes, "Because I am the God who will through My servant one day write, 'If we believe not, yet he abideth faithful: he cannot deny himself'" (II Tim. 2:13). And all that we can say is, "But, Lord, this is grace without merit." And the Lord will reply, "Yes, this is indeed unmerited grace."

Thus we conclude that our salvation is as sure as the righteousness of Christ and that our perserverance is as certain as the holding power of the rock of our salvation. We are in Christ, saved and safe. The promise was made to Abraham and Christ; and as I am, by faith, a child of faithful Abraham, the promise was made to me and Christ.

Finally, then, let us look at the nature of the promise that is set forth here in our text. There is something more here than the promise of salvation from sin and unto the righteousness of the presence of God. The wording of the Scripture is that "he should be heir of the world." If we look closely at the story of Abraham in Genesis, we note that he was first told that in him all the families of the earth should be blessed (Gen. 12:3), and later that all of the nations of the earth should be blessed in Him (Gen. 18:18).

THE PROMISED LAND

There was an earthly promise given to Abraham as well as a Heavenly promise. To him and his physical descendants, there was given a deed by God himself to what is called the Holy Land, and to much of the land surrounding it, even from the river of Egypt to the great river, the Euphrates and the Tigris, and the land of the Hittites which included Asia Minor. Much of what we call the Near East was included in the promise which was never withdrawn. The Israel of our day has taken the first steps in modern times to the occupation of that which shall certainly come to the Jews once more before the end of time, and the promise is as sure as any promise that is made in the Word of

God. Not all the Arab peoples of the world, and not the power
of the north, will serve to stop the steady advance of the people
of God when once He begins to make good the fulfillment of the
earthly promise which comes to Abraham and his seed.

But there is an even larger sense in which there was a promise
made to Abraham that he should be the heir of the earth. Abraham
was chosen, nationally, at a moment that was very important in
the history of the human race. Mankind had just united itself at
the tower of Babel and had declared itself independent of God
in a special way. God had intervened and had created diversity
of language and nationality as a curse to divide men and separate
them so that they could not carry on their warfare against Him
as they would desire. It is for this reason that we know that any
attempt to unite the nations of the earth is doomed to ultimate
failure. Whether it be League of Nations or United Nations,
God has doomed all such efforts to frustration. The earth shall
one day be united, but it shall come through Abraham's Son, the
Lord Jesus Christ. It was on this planet that sin first began when
the prince of this world became Satan and usurped the place of
God, becoming the god of this age. It is to this earth that the Lord
Jesus Christ shall return and take up the power that has been won
by Him through His triumph on the cross.

When the Lord Jesus Christ came here to live and die, he
announced to God at the end of His life that He had accomplished
one of the important purposes of His coming. In the great high
priestly prayer which is recorded as having been spoken in the
garden of Gethsemane, on the Mount of Olives, the Lord Jesus
said, "I have glorified thee on the earth; I have finished the work
which thou gavest me to do" (John 17:4). We cannot emphasize
the importance of the fact that the Lord, in His humanity, glorified the Father on the earth. The scene of the presumptuous and
prideful rebellion of Lucifer became the scene of the yielded
and humble obedience of the Son of God. It is because of what
He did on the cross that He shall one day return to possess the
crown of the earth. Righteousness shall yet triumph. It will not
come by treaties or victories of men; it will come on the plane of
His deity by the powerful intervention of God. The Hallelujah
Chorus shall yet be sung, as the angelic host will join with the

redeemed of earth in crying, "The kingdoms of this world are become the kingdoms of our Lord, and of his Christ; and he shall reign forever and ever" (Rev. 11:15).

It was at the moment when the earth had followed in the footsteps of Satan and had sought to unite against God that there was the intervention by the true Sovereign of the universe and the call of Abraham. There at Ur of the Chaldees, in sovereign grace, God appeared to Abraham and told him to get out from his land, his kindred, and his father's house and to go to a land which God would show him. Abraham, by faith, followed the command of God, and went out, not knowing where he went, and thus became the father of all the faithful. He entered into Canaan and possessed that land by faith, and it and the surrounding country was given to him and his descendants forever. But there was much more than that involved. The Lord Jesus Christ will one day rule and govern this earth, and will do it by means of those whom He has called out through faith to follow him. To the Corinthians, Paul cries out, "What! know ye not that the saints shall judge the world?" (I Cor. 6:2), and the title *saints* is that which is bestowed upon all who are justified through faith apart from the works of the law. Abraham was a child of Adam, but he obeyed the command of God to get out from his father's land, his kindred, and his father's house. There was a separation from all that was of Adam, and we who were once of Adam's seed by race have become Abraham's seed by grace.

Bishop Moule states it most beautifully. After showing that it was not by works or merit, nor by ancestral or ritual privilege, but simply because Abraham believed God, Bishop Moule then says: "We see him as he steps out from his tent under that glorious canopy, that Syrian 'night of stars.' We look up with him to the mighty depths, and receive their impression upon our eyes. Behold the innumerable points and clouds of light! Who can count the half-visible rays which make white the heavens, gleaming behind, beyond, the thousands of more numerable luminaries? The lonely old man who stands gazing there, perhaps side by side with his

divine Friend manifested in human form, is told to try to count.
And then he hears the promise, 'So shall thy seed be.' It was
then and there that he received justification by faith. It was then
and there also that, by faith, as a man uncovenanted, unworthy,
but called upon to take what God gave, he received the promise
that he should be the 'heir of the world.'

HEIR OF THE WORLD

" 'Heir of the world'! Did this mean of the universe itself?
Perhaps it did, for Christ was to be the Claimant of the promise
in due time; and under His feet, literally all are set already in right,
and shall be hereafter set in fact. But the more limited and
probably in this place the fitter, reference is vast enough; a reference to the world of earth, and of man upon it. In his 'seed,' this
childless senior was to be King of Men, Monarch of the continents
and oceans. To him, in his seed, 'the utmost pats of the earth'
were given 'for his possession.' Not his little clan only, encamped
on the dark fields around him, nor even the direct descendants
of his body, however numerous, but 'all nations,' 'all kindreds of
the earth,' were to 'call him blessed,' and to be blessed in him, as
their patriarchal Chief, their Head in covenant with God . . ."
Think of that "starry night when the wandering friend of God
was asked to believe the incredible, and was justified by faith,
and was invested through faith with the world's crown. Is not
God indeed in the fulfillment? Was He not indeed in the promise?
We are ourselves a part of the fulfillment . . . of whom the great
solitary, Abraham, was then made 'the Father.' Let us bear our
witness and set to our seal."

Yes. This is true. I know that I, for myself, have heard the
same call as that which came to Abraham on that starry night
so long ago. When God told me to get out of the land. I realized
that the world had crucified Christ and that I was to take my
stand with God against the world, and I have done so. When
God told me to get out from my father's house, I realized that I
had to take an active stand against everything that was mine by
inheritance from Adam, and I turned my back on it forever. I
accepted the fact that there is nothing, utterly nothing, of good

that can come to the human race through anything that comes from the human race, but that any good must come all of grace as it came to Abraham that night under the stars. And when I realized my oneness with him in these principles, I was made one with his seed, a sharer in the inheritance of the world which shall be mine forever, as it shall be the part of all who separate from Adam to be joined in the faith of Abraham through the grace of the Lord Jesus Christ.

CHAPTER XXIX

A Sure Inheritance

"For if they that are of the law be heirs, faith is made void, and the promise made of none effect: because the law worketh wrath: for where no law is, there is no transgression. Therefore it is of faith, that it might be by grace; to the end the promise might be sure to all the seed; not to that only which is of the law, but to that also which is of the faith of Abraham" (Rom. 4:14-16)

FROM time to time I am asked my opinion concerning the salvation, or possible salvation, of those who believe one or another system of false doctrine, or those who live at a near or far distance from active espousal of the truth of God as it is revealed in the Word. I am profoundly grateful that the decision concerning the salvation of no man rests in the hands of any other man or group of men. But there are certain principles set forth in the Word of God which show certain classes of people cannot be saved and that show just as clearly that people from any class or section of the population may be saved if they will abandon all in their thinking and doing to come by simple faith to the cross of Jesus Christ.

PRETENSIONS

In studying the pretensions of men, there are some principles set forth that will lessen the surprise that you may have at the judgment bar of God when you see some people admitted whom you did not expect to enter Heaven and see others excluded who may have talked much of religion and worked hard within its outer courts. We must not forget that it was to religious leaders that the Lord Jesus announced that He would one day turn against them with great wrath, saying, "I never knew you: depart from me, ye that work iniquity" (Matt. 7:23). I anticipate that there will be many in Heaven who have been looked upon as pariahs and outcasts while they lived upon this earth. I will not be astonished

to see in Heaven such women as the prostitute in Feodor Dostoevsky's *Crime and Punishment*, and to see such well received
by the Lord Jesus Christ in that day, even as the thief who
believed on the cross. And while we shall not expect to see in
Heaven those who have been openly defiant of the Saviour, and
who come under the verdict of God against those who have
trodden under foot the Son of God, who have counted the blood
of the covenant wherewith they were sanctified as an unholy thing,
and who have despised the Spirit of grace (Heb. 10:28, 29), there
is another category of people who I think will be absent from
Heaven and who will be the angriest of all at their exclusion.
These are those who say that they believe that Jesus Christ is
God, and that salvation is by His death upon the cross, who hold
to the fact of the miracles and believe in the inspiration of the
Holy Scriptures, but who add some other condition to salvation
than that of sheer unmerited grace.   There are those who are
orthodox as to the person and the work of the Lord Jesus Christ
who say, for example, that in addition to such faith one must
observe Saturday as the sabbath instead of Sunday.   There are
still others who are orthodox as to the person and work of Christ
but who hold that the waters of baptism take away original sin,
or that there is some sin that the individual must suffer for himself, in spite of the fact that God declares that all was done through
the work of the Lord Jesus Christ. All such, the Holy Spirit
warns, most solemnly, that Christ shall profit them nothing; that
they have fallen from grace; that they are thereby debtors to keep
the whole law, and that Christ is become of no effect to them
(Gal. 5:2-4).

WHEAT AND TARES

I believe that Christendom is honeycombed with such false
believers who have adopted a mental attitude of acceptance of
the orthodox position about the person of Jesus Christ and the
fact that He is the one and only Saviour, but who, in fact, refuse
to turn away from everything that is of the flesh and of the law,
in order to be saved by Christ alone.   I solemnly set forth that
the Scriptures state that all such who mix the Word of free grace
with the doctrine of law-works are said by God's Word to be

excluded from salvation. These, perhaps, constitute the greatest number of the tares which resemble the true wheat of the real children of the Kingdom, but who do not possess the life of God which He gives only to those who are, like Abraham, willing to turn away from all idolatry of every form of unbelief to be saved by grace alone.

It is right that I should set forth this great teaching at this point in my exposition, for our present text is the final word on this subject as expressed in this epistle. For more than eighty studies we have ploughed a straight furrow across the great plains of these early chapters and have seen again and again the story of man's complete ruin in sin and God's perfect remedy in Christ. We are about to leave the subject of salvation and enter into the great questions of the growth and development of the life of Christ within the life of the individual who has been born again. And after the manner of the man who is making a package, and who ties just one more knot even after the cord seems to most eyes to have made the contents fully secure, Paul adds one great binding argument to establish the divine case, and to destroy the false hope of those who would still trust in something that arises from the flesh.

"For if they that are of the law be heirs," he writes, "faith is made void, and the promise made of none effect: because the law worketh wrath: for where no law is there is no transgression. Therefore it is of faith, that it might be by grace to the end the promise might be sure to all the seed; not to that only which is of the law, but to that also which is of the faith of Abraham."

WORKS VS. PROMISE

There are two ideas about salvation, the human idea and the divine idea. The human idea is salvation by works, the divine idea is salvation by promise. There are the two opposing systems in single words: works or promise, the law or grace. Now the law can be broken, but the promise cannot be broken. The promise was made by God to God. It was confirmed by an oath, and since God could swear by no greater He swore by Himself, so that by two unchangeable things the promise might be made sure. Now no creature is perfect, therefore there has been no fulfillment of the law by any man. Therefore if any man should be saved by his partial fulfillment of the law, it would mean the voiding of the promise and the annulment of the divine idea. It would mean a slip-shod God and a dirty Heaven. It would mean the triumph of half-evil which on close observation is seen to be all evil.

The Greek words for "void" and "annulled" in our text are in the perfect tense, and have, therefore, a very strong meaning. Bishop Moule does a very interesting thing in translating these two words. He wants to put some of the strength of the Greek into the English, so he translates it: "For those who belong to law inherit Abraham's promise, faith is ipso facto void, and the promise is ipso facto annulled." Phillips in his paraphrase puts this idea into even more simple language, "The ancient promise given to Abraham and his descendants, that they should eventually possess the world, was given not because of any achievements made through obedience to the Law, but because of the righteousness which had its roots in faith. For if, after all, they who pin their faith to keeping the Law were to inherit God's world, it would make nonsense of faith in God Himself, and destroy the whole point of the Promise."

For law and grace are opposites as much as are night and day. Bring in day and you banish night. The light must ever exclude the darkness. For not through darkness did the promise come to Abraham and his seed that they should inherit the world, but through the light of righteousness. For if those who belong to darkness inherit the promise, then light is thereby shut out and the promise is thereby annulled.

NO LAW — NO TRANSGRESSION

"Because the law worketh wrath" is the next flat statement of our text. The effect of the law is not peace but wrath. And this fact is amplified by the additional phrase that "where no law is, there is no transgression." We can comprehend this statement and its enlargement by a very simple illustration. Fifty years ago there was no law in the United States against traveling at high speeds along the roads and streets of our country. Not one of the forty-eight states had laws at that time against traveling at seventy or eighty miles an hour. If any man had possessed a car capable of such speed, and he could have found a stretch of road that physically would have permitted such a speed he could have proceeded without interference. Even if the pedestrians had been forced to flee in consternation and if the horses had been frightened to such an extent that they dashed into the walls of greenhouses, leaving a trail of flying glass, there would have been no law under which the driver of the car could have been arrested for speeding. There would have been folly but no transgression. As the speeds of cars increased, the various legislative bodies began to make laws against these speeds. As soon as these laws were passed the excessive speed became a transgression, and it was then possible to arrest the driver and bring the wrath of the court to bear upon him. He could be fined to the full extent of the law's provision. This is the simple principle that is set forth in the text we are considering. There was a time before Moses and Mt. Sinai when God had never expressed the principles of holiness in a series of edicts concerning the righteousness of His being and the consequent demands of that righteousness upon every one of His creatures. Cain killed Abel, and it was the evil of murder, but the commandment had not been given; therefore there was no transgression of the law in the case of Cain. Ham dishonored his father but this was before God had expressed through Moses the great command, "Honor thy father and thy mother." Therefore there was no transgression of the law in the case of Ham. Similar illustrations might be multiplied from the sacred history, but these will suffice.

Sin was present before Moses but there was no transgression because there was no law. In later studies, we shall see that this does not teach that Cain and Ham were saved, for we shall see that death reigned from Adam to Moses, even though there was no law. But the coming of the law brought man's guilt before him in a definite way, and made it possible for the Holy Spirit to charge the individual with the transgression which was set forth in the statute books of God.

The fact that law works wrath, and the fact that we are the objects of promise, lead us to the conclusion that we are not under law. At the very first setting forth of this notion which shall dominate much of our future study, we must protect ourselves again by crying out with all our force that we are not saying that a man may live in lawlessness because he is not under law. God deals with His creation in different ways at different times. Paul is teaching us that God, after the death and resurrection of the Lord Jesus Christ, is now entering into a phase of His dealings with man whereby all should be on the principle of grace. Now we must not be understood as teaching that man was ever at any time saved by law. Works have never entered into the principle of salvation at any age of God's dealings with men.

GRACE AS OLD AS ADAM

If fallen Adam reached Heaven, it was entirely because God the Creator and Judge of man determined within Himself that in sovereign grace He would justify Adam on the grounds of His own divine love toward that fallen creature. If God determined similarly to save Abel and condemn Cain, it was once more on the ground of His own sovereign love, for neither of the two brothers deserved anything but death at the hands of a righteous God. Within the bounds of salvation by grace alone, God has established different tests to demonstrate to man that there is no good in man whatsoever. The period of law was one of these tests; when it came to an end, and the full flow of grace was established at the cross and the open tomb, then it was manifest that the law could do nothing but work wrath, and that where there was no law there was no transgression. That phase of God's dealings with man had a definite beginning, which anyone can see in the history of Moses; and it also had a definite end, which should be as easily seen in the outworking of the whole principle of grace in the epistles. But man is incurably addicted to doing something for his own salvation, and, therefore, it is most difficult for him to accept the doctrine of pure grace. If it were not for the intervention of the Holy Spirit to create a new life within the believer capable of comprehending grace, no man would understand the principle at all.

Now the object of all of God's teaching through Paul is to bring believers into a place of victory and power where they shall be able to live a life of triumph. Entering into the victory of Christ, accomplished historically, nineteen centuries ago, we are able to arrive at personal victory in this twentieth century. This is the aim of the Christian life, and all of this will be brought out in detail as we proceed. But now God is teaching us that the period of law from Moses to Christ could bring nothing but judgment to those who tried to hold to the law alone, and that the bringing in of a better hope in Christ ended the reign of law.

INHERITANCE BY FAITH

Finally, this passage teaches that the two methods of attaining righteousness are mutually exclusive. If you are going to establish your righteousness by your own efforts, then you are not going to commit yourself fully to the grace of God. And, on the other hand, if you once commit yourself fully to the grace of God, you have thereby stepped out of the realm of trying to do things for yourself, and have come to rest in the work which Christ performed for you when He took your place on the cross as your substitute.

"For this cause," we read in the sixteenth verse, "the inheritance is by faith that it may be according to grace; to the end that the promise may be sure to all the seed." It goes without saying that every man in his right mind wants the inheritance of eternal life. A man would have to be insane to believe that there was a difference between Heaven and Hell and then not desire Heaven. Satan, the enemy of souls, has, however, brought confusion into the minds of men by holding before them the idea that they must do something themselves in order to obtain the inheritance. In our text we see, plainly, that the inheritance must be by grace through faith. For if, for a single moment, we should look upon the inheritance as obtainable by anything that comes from man, there would, henceforth, be no place of security for any man. Always there would be the wonder if enough had been done to meet the requirements for the inheritance, if there were any standard of requirements set up. Perhaps this can be illustrated by a simple story.

I was riding recently with two young members of my church who are approximately of college age. The girl brought up the fact that a certain Christian woman had a beautiful mink coat and wondered how a Christian woman could spend so much money on a coat when there were people starving in Europe and when there were so many Christian missionary works that are in real need of financial support. The young man, who is older, and a clearer thinker, pointed out to her the error in her thinking. She had no right to judge the owner of the coat, because she did not know the circumstances of her life and needs, and the state of her heart relationship with God. He transferred the argument to automobiles and asked if she would question the fact that an aunt of hers drove a Cadillac. The girl, forced into a corner by the logic, made a rash conclusion and said that the aunt should probably not drive a car that was better than a Buick. The young man pursued the logic still further and asked, then, why the aunt should not drive a Chevrolet. When the girl was forced by her own untenable position to agree with this, he pursued the logic relentlessly and asked why there should be any car at all and why the aunt should not depend on trains and walking. The girl saw the position into which she had been pushed, and going back to the mink coat question, immediately concluded that if anyone were to start drawing lines he would be forced to reason that one should go around dressed in Burlap sacks, and that no refinement of dress could be sought at all.

Now, turning the process upside down, and applying it, not to coats and automobiles but to the question of law and the keeping of law, we can see where an argument about salvation by works would lead us. Has a man been a rather good man? Well, has he been good enough to get into Heaven? Could another man who has told one less lie than he be admitted to Heaven? Suppose someone has two less lies to his account? Or suppose a man has two more lies? Or, again, suppose a man has made certain sacrifices in his giving to worthy causes? Has he made sacrifices enough? Is there a percentage that may be established? If a man gives a tithe, is he thereby satisfying God? If that is so, what about a poor man and a rich man? A poor man may have five children and fifty dollars a week. Is he supposed to give five dollars a week to Christian causes? And if another man has a thousand dollars a week and only a wife and one child, can he get by with God by giving a hundred dollars a week to charity and

keeping nine hundred dollars a week for his own uses? The absurdities of the comparisons become evident the further we push
them to logical conclusions.

If a man is to be saved by any system of works, he is never
going to have any assurance of salvation and never will he have
any security before God. All of his time will be spent in anxiety.
Assurance and security are possible only on the basis of the grace
of God. If any man wants to do his part, or attempt to do any
part, he will never known whether he has done his part or has
reached the measure of the percentage that would be necessary
to get him over the line, out of the field of the condemned, and
into the group of those who are saved.

Faith in the grace of God does not turn its attention to anything that man has done, or to anything that man could do. Faith
has but one object for its gaze, and that is the promise which
God has made in His grace to do everything for the sinner, to
reckon sin to the account of the Saviour, and to credit the righteousness of God to the account of the believer. As soon as we
realize that the work of the Saviour is a finished work, then there
is nothing left for the sinner to do. The promise is by grace
through faith, unmixed with anything that arises out of the being
or the doing of man.

Thus the solid foundation of our salvation stands squarely
on the basis of the work that has been done by Christ at Calvary.
Thus it is possible for a believer to be safe as well as saved. It is
possible for the believer to be in the center of full assurance,
joyfully and quietly resting in an unchangeable position of
security, because the inheritance is by grace through faith.

The law is the womb of doubt, and anyone who is attached
to the law or its works is going to be besieged by all of the doubts
which are born from the law. Any individual who has his eyes
upon himself will be miserable. The man who walks by the law
walks in the night, and his footsteps echo against the walls of the
darkness that goes with the law. These echoes rise to his ears
and each sound from all the troop of doubts gives him fear upon

fear. If he pauses, he is in the silence of dread fears, and as he runs from them his footsteps echo all the faster with the increasing tempo of his hysteria of doubt. The marching battalion increases; the reverberations of his doubts multiply, and finally he goes to his doom to the accompaniment of the tramp of an army of doubts and fears. This is the inheritance of the law.

But the man who walks by the promise of grace walks in the broad day. His footsteps echo against the light of the promises of God, and he feels himself to be surrounded by the angels of blessing. His eager steps press forward to claim the blessings, and the increasing tempo of his footsteps sets up the echoes of further blessings. If he stops, he finds himself in green pastures and beside still waters. When he walks again he is in the paths of righteousness. He hastens on to the golden city and the brightness of its prospect takes away any sense of fatigue that might naturally rise from the length of the road. And when the road ends, he finds that he has been supplied with grace at every step and brought on to the triumph of life eternal, and all because of the grace of sovereign love. This is the inheritance of Grace.

THE PROMISE SURE

Safety, certainty, and enjoyment. These are the prerogatives of every child of Abraham. The promise is sure to all the seed. Those who are of the circumcision and who believe, are sure of their part in the inheritance because the promise was by grace through faith to their father Abraham. Those of us who are by nature children of wrath, but who have become children of faithful Abraham through simple faith, are guaranteed our part in the inheritance forever because of the nature of the covenant and the promise. Abraham is not the father of one nation, but of many nations. That is why God gave him the promise out in an open field, under the starry hosts. God had in His mind the salvation of an innumerable company of men who would have the simplicity of faith that was Abraham's that night under the stars. It makes no difference what your background may be, for God saves men from every kingdom, tongue, tribe, and nation; yes, He saves some men out of every religious background. All that He asks is that there be a complete turning away from everything that finds its source in man, and a complete turning to all that finds its source in the grace of God. Any man who thus turns, God writes down as a child of Abraham, counts his portion in the inheritance and gives the right of assurance, safety, and certainty, and thus prepares the ground for his moment by moment joy.

CHAPTER XXX

Things That Are Not

"(As it is written, I have made thee a father of many nations,) before him whom he believed, even God, who quickeneth the dead, and calleth those things which be not as though they were" (Rom. 4:17).

THE PRESENT passage we are studying in the fourth of Romans bring us to a change of atmosphere in the thinking of the Apostle. Until now we are constantly aware of the fact that Paul knew there were those who did not agree with him. He has been taking the several possible objections against the truth of salvation by grace and has been destroying the foundation of such false arguments. The atmosphere of the epistle up to this point has been the atmosphere of the debating hall. Paul has set forth the truth of Christianity as it is revealed by God and has spent a good portion of his time in the rebuttal of the false positions of those who trust in character, in works, in human merit, in ritual ceremonies, in race, or in some other false hope. He has been showing that the truth of God is a vital system and has been setting forth the logic of that system.

ALIVE FROM THE DEAD

But speaking about Abraham as the father of us all, that is of all who believe, has carried Paul in his thinking into the group of those who do believe. There is no possible difference of opinion concerning the nature of salvation among those who have truly been born of the Spirit into the family of God. All who believe and who are truly born again think alike on this subject. The supernatural work of God is such that it brings new life with it, and those who have been the objects of the miracle work of grace must be aware that they are alive from the dead.

Bishop Moule expresses the change in a beautiful paragraph. "Here the great argument moves to a pause, to the cadence of a glorious rest.   More and more, as we have pursued it, it has disengaged itself from the obstructions of the opponent, and advanced with a larger motion into a positive and rejoicing assertion of the joys and wealth of the believing.   We have left far behind the pertinacious cavils which ask, now whether there is any hope for man outside legalism, now whether within legalism there can be any danger, even for deliberate unholiness, and again whether the gospel of gratuitous acceptance does not cancel the law of duty.   We have left the Pharisee for Abraham, and have stood beside him to look and listen.   He, is the simplicity of a soul which has seen itself and seen the Lord, and so has not one word, one thought, about personal privilege, claim, or even fitness, receives a perfect acceptance in the hand of faith, and finds that the acceptance carries with it a promise of unimaginable power and blessing."

I am quite in accord with the Bishop, but I would point out still further that the change takes place not so much by the transfer of the thinking from the Pharisee to Abraham, but from the Pharisee to the God of Abraham.   The seventeenth verse of this fourth chapter carries over the previous thought, pointing out that Abraham is the father of all who believe "before God," or in the sight of God, "whom he believed, even God, who quickeneth the dead, and calleth those things which be not as though they were."

SEEING THE UNSEEN

We are asked to walk from our place and position, whatever it may be, and to look in the direction in which we see Abraham looking.   We see this man, who came from a background of idolatry, looking with such a fixed and intent gaze that we are forced to stop and look in the same direction.   Whether we see what he saw depends on our answer to the divine call and our acceptance of the responsibility which God places on us.   It is possible for men to look and see nothing because there is nothing to see—but it is also possible to look where there is something and to see nothing because of a lack in your eyes.   Let me show you the difference.

Many years ago in my teens, I was with a group of friends and we decided to play a practical joke on the unthinking people passing along the streets. We went near a busy intersection and started to look up at a certain point where there was absolutely nothing to be seen. One of us pointed and another one said, loudly enough to be overheard by the passers-by, "It is not." Another one of our group said, "It is so." One or two people stopped and began looking in the same direction in which we were looking and pointing. We let our argument grow heatedly for a few moments and by that time there were perhaps ten people gazing fixedly in the direction we had been looking. Then one by one, we slipped out of the crowd and regathered a few yards down the street to watch the result of our strategem. By this time about fifteen people were looking and talking, and we heard one man who left the group say to another, "I think it is a balloon." Remember that this was about 1915 or 1916. The crowd continued to change as new passers-by joined the group and those who had been staring longest left. Twenty minutes later there were still several people looking, though some of them had drawn away from the spot where we had started the little show and were leaning with their backs to the wall of a building trying to see something that was not there and which never had been there.

That little incident is a good illustration of all the earth-born religions. People talk about having faith and they tell you to look in a direction where there is absolutely nothing. There are people so desperately in need of seeing something that they will look till they are almost blind, and yet will never catch a glimpse of anything real. In fact, their persistence in staring in the direction of something that does not exist reduces the powers of their vision to see the truth which they really do not want to find. But it is also possible, I say, to look where there is something and to see nothing because of a lack in your eyes.

When Abraham looked up from his life in Ur of the Chaldees, he was not looking at the non-existent. Stephen tells us in his great discourse before martyrdom, "Men, brethren and fathers, hearken; The God of glory appeared unto our father, Abraham" (Acts 7:2). We do not know the nature of that vision, but we know that it was a gaze into glory, one which transformed the life of Abraham, and that has transformed the lives of all who have ever caught the same vision. It is not the open-jawed empty stare of the curious passer-by looking for some novelty of the moment. It is the vision that sets a man to walking stedfastly in the path of God and which leads the believer into the obedience of faith.

A TWOFOLD REVELATION

Our text describes God in two phrases. He is the "God who quickeneth the dead," and He is the God who "calleth those things which be not as though they were."

In the texts that follow, the second of these two descriptions is first explained, and then the first is explained by the great act of faith in the life of Abraham. We will also look at them in this reverse order.

Abraham is called the father of all who believe because he believed in the God who calls things that are not as though they were. Let us note, first of all, that the phrase shows us that God is altogether on another plane than that of His creatures. We dare not call things that are not as though they were. Any man who does so will soon get a reputation for being a liar, and the reputation will be an accurate description of his character.

Several years ago I was preaching in a certain city in the middle west. A church in that city was without a pastor, and the officials asked me some questions about a man who was on their list of possible candidates. I did not know the man personally, but I was well acquainted with a Christian leader in the distant city where this possible candidate was located. The men suggested that I telephone my friend and get them the information which they desired. I soon put through my long-distance call and the conversation went something like this: "I am in such-and-such a city, and I am in a room with several of the officials of a church which is considering Dr. Blank of your city for their vacant pulpit. What do you think of him, privately and confidentially?" My friend replied, "Well, he is a conservative. That is to say there is nothing in his preaching that is a violation of the conservative position. And he has a pretty good church, but . . ." And the trailing voice of my friend let me see that there was some serious question as to the man's qualifications for the position that was open.

I pressed him, and he finally answered, "Well, the main difficulty is his relationship with all his colleagues and fellow-workers. You might describe him best by the Biblical phrase that he 'calleth the things that are not as though they were.' I secured my friend's permission to quote the phrase to the men who were in the room with me, and the conversation ended. The men shook their heads and crossed this man off their lists. They did not want a man whose veracity was questionable.

THE QUESTION

How, then, is this a title of honor for our God when it is a description of dishonor for man? The answer lies in the eternal nature of God. We are creatures, He is the Creator. We are in time, with a beginning and an ending, so far as this earth life is concerned; He is the Lord of eternity, without beginning and without ending. I have frequently used an illustration, which has its imperfections, but which shows the difference in our viewpoint with that of God. I have spoken of a man in a canoe on a river who sees nothing but wheatfields around him. He remembers that twenty-four hours before, he was in the midst of a forest, and could see nothing but trees. He sees by a map that in another twenty-four hours he will be in a large city, where he will see nothing but buildings. For him there is a past, a present, and a future. An aviator, flying at 20,000 feet above him can see the forest, the wheat fields, and the city in the same glance. They are all present for him. I am aware of the imperfections of my illustrations, for the aviator in my story is also a finite being with a past, a present, and a future, but in a small way it may enable us to realize that there is a point of view vastly different from our own, and that God, in eternity, has always seen all things, past and future, as eternally existing in His sight.

The man in the canoe cannot speak of the city or the forest as being present, but the man in the plane can. A human being, bound by earth, time and space may not call things that are not as though they were, but God, who knows the end from the beginning, and who has decreed all things, can do this. Abraham understood this about God, so that when God made him specific promises he believed them without any other evidence, since the Word of the only Being in the universe who cannot possibly be mistaken is the perfection of evidence. Thus faith becomes the substance of things hoped for and the evidence of things not seen (Heb. 11:1).

THE COVENANT

If we turn back to the story of Abraham as it was first given in the Book of Genesis, we discover some interesting shades of truth in the verb tenses of God's promises. Take, first of all, the promises to Abraham concerning the land. When the God of glory first appeared to Abraham in the land of the Chaldees, the promise was set forth in the future tense: "Get thee out . . . unto a land that I will show thee" (Gen. 12:1). When Abraham finally arrived at the borders of the land after the hesitancy on the road in Haran, God appeared to Abraham again and said, "Unto thy seed will I give this land" (Gen. 12:7). It should be noted that Abraham moved from Ur toward the promise of the land. Now that he sees the land, there is a further promise of posterity. And it must be remembered, most importantly, that Abraham was an old man and that he had no children at the time this promise was given.

Sometime later Abraham asked God a question. It was at the moment that God had told him that the number of his seed should be as the stars of the sky and the sands of the sea; it is at this moment that it is said that Abraham believed God, and that it was counted to him for righteousness. Then the faithful old man said to God, "Lord God, whereby shall I know that I shall inherit it?" (Gen. 15:8). In answer God set before Abraham the pageant of a blood sacrifice, picture of the sacrifice of the Lord Jesus Christ, and changed the tense of the verb, in the most solemn terms binding Himself to perform that which He had promised. We read, "In the same day the Lord made a covenant with Abram, saying, Unto thy seed have I given this land, from the river of Egypt unto the great river, the river Euphrates; the Kenites, and the Kenizzites, and the Kadmonites, and the Hittites, and the Perizzites, and the Rephaims, and the Amorites, and the Canaanites, and the Girgashites, and the Jebusites" (Gen. 15: 18-21). Someone may wonder why we have set forth this list of the names of the people who were to be dispossessed. We answer that we have the same faith that God gave to Abraham, and that we believe that the young nation of Israel, now in part of Palestine, will possess all of this land that was promised to them in Abraham, even from the river of Egypt, through the modern countries of Jordan, Syria, Lebanon, that part of Turkey that is in Asia Minor, and that part of Iraq which goes up to the great river. This covenant was put in the past tense by God, who calleth things that are not as though they were. We believe that this promise is one of the fundamental reasons why Satan, the author of anti-Semitism, stirs up such hatred of the Jews. He knows that the promises have been made to this ancient people, even through Abraham, and that he, the Devil, who is now the prince of this world, will one day be forced to yield his control of earth government to Abraham's seed. He knows that the Jews will be the colonial administrators of God, taking their orders from the reigning Lord Jesus Christ, and His bride, the true Church.

Thus, we see how God described the land He had promised to Abraham in terms of complete possession at the moment when it was occupied by a host of Hamitic peoples, under the spiritual leadership of the Devil. Incidentally, we must never be confused by the popular misconception that would make the Negro the son of Ham. The Hamites were the Egyptians, the Hittites, the Babylonians, the Canaanites and the Carthaginians. For two thousand years of history they blocked the way of God' people, but the promise was fulfilled even as God had pronounced it; and the Hamites were finally overthrown by Japheth when Rome destroyed Carthage. Today we are at the end of the second great period in human history—that dominated by the peoples of Japheth, but we hold with Abraham in his faith that the things which are not shall be sure, yea, that they are sure, because they have been spoken by God. Thus we expect to see the nation of Israel the possessors of the land and the focal point for the witness of the righteousness and power of God throughout all the earth.

In our next study we shall see how the resurrection promise —God's ability to bring life out of death—is bound up with this other description of our God, namely, that He calls things that are not as though they were. In the remaining paragraphs of this study, I want to turn your attention to some of the things which God has put down to our account and has promised us in no uncertain terms. The inheritance of Abraham included a land. Our inheritance from the God who calls all things that are not as though they were includes all this and Heaven too—a phrase that belongs only to those who have been born again through faith in the blood of Jesus Christ. There are many people who are enjoying the beauties of earth and the joys of this life of whom it would have to be said, in truth, that they would have nothing but this, and this only temporarily, until they enter Hell forever.

PROMISES

There are many who read these words who truly believe in the Lord Jesus Christ as personal Saviour. Let me point out some of the promises that God has given to you the moment you believe. There you are, man or woman, member of the human race, with a slowly dying body, facing a narrow grave according to all of the human evidence that we have obtainable. Outside the Word of God there is not a line, not a breath of evidence that there is any ultimate difference between your life and the life of a dog. From the point of view of human philosophy a living dog is better than a dead lion, a living moron better than a dead Einstein, a living pauper better than a dead Rockefeller, a living criminal better than a dead saint.

But at this point God intervenes. He speaks words of promise, and we who are blessed with the faith of faithful Abraham know differently. On the Word of God who calls things that are not as though they were, we claim that we have a life that can never be forfeited. We have been given eternal life. On this same Word of God we declare that we have a relationship that can never be abrogated. We who were sons of wrath have been declared to be sons of God. We have a righteousness that can never be tarnished. That righteousness has been declared to be ours by the Word of our God. We have an acceptance that can never be questioned. No angel or demon—not Satan himself— can stand between us and the accomplishment of the promise. We have been judged in a judgment that can never be repeated. He who calls the future as the past is the One who cried out, "It is finished." We have a title that can never be clouded. This has been given to us concerning our eternal place with our God. We have a position that can never be invalidated. God has seated us with Christ in the Heavenlies. So here are seven gifts of God that are without repentance. We have a life that cannot be forfeited, a relationship that cannot be abrogated, a righteousness that cannot be tarnished, an acceptance that cannot be questioned, a judgment that can never be repeated, a life that can never be clouded, and a position that can never be invalidated.

OUR POSSESSIONS

But in addition to this we have a standing that can never be disputed. No one can ever bar us from our right to rest in His presence. We have a justification that can never be reversed. We have been declared just, and there is no court to overrule our God. We have a seal that can never be violated. Our God has placed us in Christ and put upon us the seal of the Holy Spirit. We have an inheritance that can never be alienated. The Lord who died to give us the promises, rose from the dead to be the executor of His own estate. We have a wealth that can never be depleted. God has with Christ freely given us all things. We have a resource that can never be diminished. God's fountain will flow to us forever. We have a bank that can never be closed. Our God is able to keep that which we have committed unto Him. There is a second set of seven promises that are not and yet which are by the Word of God.

We have a possession that can never be measured. The eternal Heavens are ours and eternity itself. We have a portion that can never be denied. God who gave His Son gives us freely all things with Him. We have a peace that can never be destroyed. There is no foe that can break through the hedge that He places about us. We have a joy that can never be surpassed. As water must seek its own level, so the pressure of our joy which is from God must ever burst forth in us. We have a love that can never be abated. This is true because His very name is love. We have a grace that can never be arrested. Nothing can stop the flow of that which is God's very nature. We have a strength that can never be weakened. For it is His strength that is made perfect in weakness. And that makes a third set of seven promises that are ours from Him who calls things that are not as though they were.

We have a power that can never be exhausted. We have a salvation that can never be annulled. We have a forgiveness that can never be rescinded. We have a deliverance that can never be thwarted. We have a preservation that can never be hindered. We have an assurance that can never be dishonored. We have a new nature that can never be changed. And there we have seven more promises that are ours from Him who calls things that are not as though they were.

We have a fruit, the fruit of the Spirit, that can never be destroyed. We have a hunger that can never be unsatisfied. We have an approach, an access, that can never be blocked. We have a blessing that can never be interrupted. We have an attraction, Christ, that can never be surpassed. We have a good that cannot be adulterated. We have a comfort that cannot be absent. And in our multiplication we have reached five times seven.

But we have, also, a persecution that can never be evaded. We have a suffering that can never be omitted. We have a warfare that can never be shunned. We have a ministry that can never be shifted. We have a message that can never be repressed. We have a walk that can never be neglected. And we have a service that can never be unrewarded.

But if we have those seven obligations that are put upon us by the Word of God, we have a seventh seven of triumph, to which we hold as Abraham held to the promises that were given him. He walked slowly along the pathless desert, for he looked for a city that hath foundations, whose builder and maker is God. Thus he had, and thus we have, all of the future to which we move in our pilgrim pathway through the desert of this life step by step. And for that walk, we have a Bible that can never be destroyed. We have an intercessor who can never be disqualified. We have a victor who can never be vanquished. We have a resurrection that can never be prevented. We have a destiny that can never be changed. We have a hope that can never be disappointed. And we have a glory that can never be dimmed.

There are seven times seven great promises and if I ever run short of sermon texts, I can take 49 sermons right there on those great possessions which are ours from the God who calls the things that are not as though they were. And yet we walk through the streets and lanes of our land outwardly like the others around us who do not possess these promises. "Man looketh upon the outward appearance but God looketh upon the heart." You may see two men, and the one may appear to you to be a nobleman and the other to be a nobody. But the God who calls things that are not as though they were may have set the eternal values in the reverse order. The prince may be lost and the peasant saved. The judge may reach Hell and the convict may reach Heaven.

You have the right to turn away from all of the criteria that are set up by man and his feeble ways of perceiving and judging, and to call things that are not as though they were. For if you put your trust in the Lord Jesus Christ, you are then in Christ, and in Him all things are yours, and ye are Christ's and Christ is God's (I Cor. 3:22, 23).

CHAPTER XXXI

God Who Quickens the Dead

*"(As it is written, I have made thee a father of many nations,)
before him whom he believed, even God, who quickeneth the dead,
and calleth those things which be not as though they were" (Rom.
4:17).*

ABRAHAM'S God is the God who calls things that are not
as though they were; and the reason that Abraham is called
the father of all who believe is because he had faith to believe in
this God who calls things that are not as though they were, even
when it involved the question of bringing life out of death.

In order that we may understand the nature of Abraham's
faith, let me recount some of the details of it in his life and the
circumstances which led up to the promise and the fulfillment
of the promise.

FATHER OF MANY

Abram was his name in its earlier form, and the name Abram
means "father of many." The key to the story is that this man,
even though he had a name like that, was the father of none.
At the age of seventy the Lord God of glory appeared to him
when he was yet an idolator, living in the midst of a family of
people of idolatry, and told him to get out from his country, and
from his kindred and from his father's house unto a land that
God would show him. The vision must have been one of great
glory and power, for Abram started moving with his flocks and
herds, and with his wife and servants, and kept on traveling, at
least a thousand miles, until he came to the land that God had
promised to show him, and which God now promised to give him,
and which, later, God said He had given to him and his seed
forever.

When this promise of the land was given to Abram, it was
stated that the gift was not only to him but to his seed after

him. And the point of the story lies in the fact that Abram had no seed. This may not be a disaster in our western lands, but in the Orient it must have been particularly galling. The Orientals are a most polite people, and their politeness manifests itself in asking you many personal questions which would be considered impolite in our culture, but which must be asked in the Oriental culture. Several years ago I was in a remote village of north-western China. I had been told that I should expect the most personal questions, and they were not long in coming. The chief elder of the church in the village in which we arrived sat politely by me as we were waiting for dinner. The conversation went something like this: "How old are you?" I told him, and asked his age. He answered me and we compared our ages. His next question asked if I were married. I answered that I was. He asked me my wife's age, and how many children we had, and their ages. He asked me if my wife were beautiful, and I replied that she was. He answered that I was fortunate, and that my parents had chosen well for me. I did not get involved by telling him that I had picked my own wife, and that I had been married for almost three years before my parents even saw her. He then wanted to know about my house, how large it was, how many windows, and if we kept servants. The fact that he could not have had any frame of reference for our western life made no difference to him. He was showing his personal interest in us. He was being very polite.

Now Abram was an Oriental. He was used to the palaver of the Orientals. Furthermore, he was strategically located athwart the roads of the camel caravans that carried the commerce of the ancient world between Egypt and the North and East. He owned the wells, and his flocks and herds were great. The Scripture says that "Abram was very rich in cattle, in silver, and in gold" (Gen. 13:2). When the caravans of the rich merchants came into the land, either from the north or from the south, they stopped at Abram's wells. The servants of Abram took good care of the needs of the camels and the servants of the traders. Food was sold to the travellers. And in the evening time the merchants would have come to Abram's tent to pay their respects. The questions would have followed a set pattern. How old are you? Who are you? How long have you been here? When the trader had introduced himself, Abram would be forced to name himself: Abram, father of many.

It must have happened a hundred times, a thousand times, and each time more galling than the time before. "Oh, Father of many! Congratulations! And how many sons do you have?" And the answer was so humiliating to Abram: "None." And, many a time there must have been the half concealed snort of humor at the incongruity of the name and the fact that there were no children to back up such a name. Abram must have steeled himself for the question and the reply, and have hated the situation with great bitterness. I once knew a man whose name was Wrench was told me that he divided all of his acquaintances into two classes: those who did not make wisecracks about his name and those who did. He said that he automatically cringed when someone would hear his name and begin one of the wisecracks which he had heard in every possible variety: was he related to monkey wrench; was he the lefthanded wrench, and all the others. I knew a Mr. Meek who had been asked a thousand times if he had inherited the earth.

Abram would have understood him very well. Father of many —father of none. The possibilities were varied, and I believe that it is possible to detect in the psychology of the narrative the fact that there was much gossip about it. The servants who heard the jokes and who saw Abram's embarrassment repeated the details with embroidered variations. It was a world of cloth and goat skins, where all lived in tents, and where there was little privacy from the eyes and none in the realm of the ears. There must have been many conversations on the subject—who was sterile, Abram or Sarah? Was he really a full man? Oh, he was the patriarch; his word was law; he had the multitude of cattle and the many servants, but—he had no children, and his name was "father of many."

ABRAM AND HAGAR

If someone thinks that I am imagining all this let me present in proof the psychology of his wife, Sarah, who finally came to him and suggested that he take her servant girl, Hagar, and have a child by her. Sarah must have sensed that it was she herself who was barren. She was a very proud woman, and very sensitive, as the sequel shows, and she must have been goaded to her action by a desperation which forced her to push her husband into the arms of another woman.

Remember, I say, that it was a world of cloth and skins—they lived in tents, surrounded by servants. The offer is made —Abram is presented with the slave girl as a concubine. The news must have spread with rapidity; the tent was prepared for the master and the slave girl; the servants who did the work and who surrounded the group must have greeted one another with smirks and winks—old Abram, father of many, father of none, had gone into the tent with a concubine.

Days passed, while the idle speculation of the womenfolk fanned into greater gossip as the news was finally confirmed that Hagar was with child by Abram. Sarah saw herself despised in the eyes of the woman of Egypt. The news spread in the camp, for it was a matter of great importance, involving the inheritance of great riches. There was going to be an heir. Abram was looked at with a little more respect—at least it was now certain that he was a real man—here was the proof of it. And he had fathered a child in advanced age. Then it was Sarah after all—it was she who was sterile—a woman who could not fulfill the functions of a woman.

And then the child was born—it was a boy, and his name was Ishmael. The birth of a son is a very important event in the life of any man. A man who has only daughters, even feels himself slightly cheated, as the jokes of Eddie Cantor about his family of girls have shown the nation. Abram was proud of that son; he was proud of himself. All the natural rising of the flesh was his. He was a man, and the little baby boy was the proof of his virility. He partook of the universal feeling of manhood. This feeling was expressed, a few years ago, by a song-lyric that came over the radio. Oscar Hammerstein set for the feelings of a man when he learned that he was going to be a father:

> I wonder what he'll think of me!
> I guess he'll call me "the old man"!
> I guess he'll think I can lick

Every other feller's father;
Well, I can.
    I bet that he'll turn out to be
The spit-an' image of his Dad—
But he'll have more common sense
Than his puddin'headed father ever had—

I'll teach him to wrassle,
And dive through a wave,
When we go in the mornin's for our swim.
His mother can teach him the way to behave,
But she won't make a sissy out o' him.
Not him! Not my boy! Not Bill!
My boy Bill! I'll see that he's named after me.

He'll be tall and as tough as a tree, will Bill!
Like a tree he'll grow, with his head held high
And his feet planted firm on the ground,
And you won't see nobody dare to try
To boss him or toss him around . . .

Say, why am I takin' on like this?
My kid ain't even born yet!

And at the end of the next verse the prospective father suddenly faces the awful thought that the child might be a girl!

THE CONTRAST PRESENTED

Well, that was the popular song and Abraham understood this pride of fatherhood. Several years passed and the Lord God appeared to Abram and reminded him of the previous unchangeable promise that he should have seed as the stars of the sky and the sands of the sea. Abram cried out: "Oh that Ishmael might live before thee" (Gen. 17:18). It was a cry of ignorance, and sets the scene for the background of the faith that followed in the life of the patriarch. In the New Testament the contrast between the son of the slave and the son of the wife is set forth in the Epistle to the Galatians. We read in Galatians 4:21-31: "Tell me, ye that desire to be under the law, do ye not hear the law? For it is written, that Abraham had two sons, the one by a bondmaid, the other by a freewoman. He who was of the bondwoman was born after the flesh; but he of the freewoman was by promise. Which things are an allegory: for these are the two covenants; the one from the Mount Sinai, which gendereth to bondage, which is Hagar. For this Hagar is Mount Sinai in Arabia, and" the Bible continues, "corresponds to Jerusalem which now is, and is in bondage with her children. But Jerusalem which is above is free, which is the mother of us all. For it is written, Rejoice thou barren that bearest not; break forth and cry, thou that travailest not; for the desolate hath many more children than she which hath an husband. Now we, brethren, are the children of promise as Isaac was. But as then he that was born after the flesh persecuted him that was born after the Spirit, even so it is now. Nevertheless, what saith the scripture? Cast out the bondwoman and her son for the son of the bondwoman shall not be heir with the son of the freewoman. So then, brethren, we are not the children of the bondwoman, but of the free."

Now the teaching of this paragraph in Galatians gives us the sure meaning of our passage in Romans, and of the whole significance of the historical incident as it is recorded in the Book of Genesis. There is every indication that Ishmael was born of the natural virile powers of Abram. That child was born as all other children are born. There was no miracle connected with his birth. Abram was eighty-six years old, but it was a child of his natural powers.

Now, when the travellers came to the wells to camp and came to call upon Abram, the question of the name was not quite so difficult as before. What is your name? Abram, father of many, Oh, congratulations! And how many sons do you have? I have one son. True, it was not very many, but it was enough to keep the smirk off the faces of the strangers and the winks from the glance of the servants who stood nearby. Abram had a son. He was a man.

THE COVENANT CONFIRMED

Thirteen years passed thus. Abram had declined in health, and was now feeble. He was ninety-nine years old when God appeared to him and reminded him of the promise which had been made to him. Abram's first reaction was to remind God that, after all, he did have a son, Ishmael, and that the existence of this one son was enough to keep God from being a liar. Even if Abram died then, God could give Ishmael a multitude of sons and fulfill the promises. But God does not work in that fashion. The line of the Messiah was not to come through the womb of a daughter of cursed Ham by means of the finagling of Sarah trying to help God out of a fix.

God said unto Abram, "I am the Almighty God; walk thou before me, and be thou perfect. And I will make my covenant between me and thee, and will multiply thee exceedingly" (Gen. 17:1). Now observe well that this covenant which established the Hebrews as a race and gave them the start of their religion took place at least fifteen years after Abraham had been been called and had left his land. His was salvation by grace, and now God proceeds to elaborate on the covenant. Abram fell on his face before God, and God continued, saying, "As for me, behold my covenant is with thee, and thou shalt be a father of many nations. Neither shall thy name any more be called Abram, but the name shall be Abraham, for a father of many nations have I made thee" (17:4, 5).

There are some things in the Bible that cause me to chuckle, and there is a thought in connection with this verse that always has had that effect on me. I cannot help but think of what must have happened when Abraham broke the news to his family and servants that he was now changing his name. They all knew that his former name was Abram, father of many, and they knew it had been somewhat of a thorn to him. So we can imagine the stir of interest and curiosity when he announced, "I am going to change my name." Were there some who said to themselves with a laugh, "The old man couldn't take it. It finally got under his skin. After all, to be father of nobody for eighty-six years, and then to be the father of only one, with a name like he has—father of many—must have its rough moments. So he is going to change his name. I wonder what it will be."

And then the old man spoke. "I am to be known as Abraham —father of a multitude." We can almost hear the silence of the stunned moment as the truth breaks upon them. Father of a mulitude? Then the laughter broke forth behind the scenes. "The old man has gone crazy. He had one child when he was eighty-six, and now at ninety-nine he is beginning to get ideas. Father of

a multitude! was there ever anything more ridiculous for a man
of his age?"

CONQUERING FAITH

From a human point of view there can be no doubt of the
fact that the idea of a change of name in that direction was a little
queer at that age. If it had been a human idea, product of human
desire or human thought, it would have been what is called wishful
thinking or the result of advanced senility. But this was an order
from God. The thought originated in the divine mind and not in
the human mind. Nothing is foolish when it comes from God,
"because the foolishness of God is wiser than men; and the weakness of God is stronger than men" (I Cor. 1:25).

Faith never looks at the obstacles, faith looks at God. If
there is ever to be a real deliverance from God, the atmosphere
of our problem must be one of great difficulty. If there is to be a
miracle work of God, the atmosphere of our problem must be that
of total impossibility. The Lord does not tell His people to jump
through literal stone walls, but He is constantly permitting the
Devil to work in the middle of the road in which we must travel.
Satan loves to erect facsimile walls that frighten the timid, walls
of *papier-maché* to test our faith. When we know that God has
told us to move forward, we hurl ourselves at the seeming obstacle
and find that it rips apart at our touch, and we have learned once
more the wisdom and power of God, the fact that He knows the
way in which we are to go and has no difficulty in caring for us
in that way. We also learn to know that the enemy of our souls
is a weakling whose efforts are puny and meaningless when we
walk by faith and not by sight.

The God who calls things that are not as though they were
had spoken. Abraham, father of a multitude, for that was now his
name, believed God who had announced that out of the dead
womb of Sarah and the dead glands of Abraham He was going to
bring a child that would be born of the miracle power of God.
That is why this child, Isaac, is so sharply contrasted with Ishmael.
This wild child of the desert was a child of natural generation;
Isaac was a child of supernatural generation. Abram begat Ishmael
in the power of his manhood; Abraham begat Isaac in the power
of the resurrection that God worked within his being.

This is why the New Testament tells us that Ishmael, as a type, corresponds to Mt. Sinai: Ishmael is the natural fruit of the law. And Isaac, it is said, corresponds to Jerusalem, the place of the grace of God. Sinai and Calvary; these are the two mountains that show the workings of God. On the one, the stone of the tables of the law; on the other, the wood of the cross of Jesus Christ. On the one, the finger of God writing in justice; on the other, the blood of God, seeping from His wounds of love. Justice versus mercy; wrath versus grace; hatred of sin versus the love of the sinner; law versus grace; Ishmael versus Isaac.

QUICKENING THE DEAD

Isaac is the proof that God can bring life out of death. This, our text says, is the quality in God which Abraham believed. God quickens the dead. The words *quick* and *quicken* are old English words which mean to be alive and to give life. We still have this meaning in the modern usage that remains in the creed: He shall come to judge the quick and the dead. When we read that Abraham believed "God who quickeneth the dead," we understand that Abraham comprehended that life was in God, that life was of God, and that God could do as He pleased in matters of life and death. If Abraham had been thirty years old and God had told him he was to have numerous children, Abraham could well have trusted in the force of his own virility. He might have comprehended in a vague way that God is all-powerful, but in his case it would have been believing that God brings life out of life. But when the final test came, Abraham was ninety-nine years old; and he was forced to lay hold on that quality in God which is the power to bring life out of death, and to call the nonexistent as actually being. All that he had in his loins was death, and there was no Isaac nor any other seed. But he believed that God was able to bring life out of his loins, and call Isaac, who was not, as though he were. He believed that God was able to bring Isaac into being in the same fashion that He had once said, in the midst of darkness, "Let there be light" (Gen. 1.3). So now in his loins, God said, "Let there be Isaac."

The Greek word that is translated by this old English word *quicken* is worth looking at with care. It is really a combination of two Greek words, the noun for *life* and the verb for *make*. Abraham placed his faith in the God who is life, and believed the promise that was made to him. It should be recognized clearly that whenever God makes a promise, the *fulfillment* of the promise does not exist at the time the promise is made, but the *guarantee* of its fulfillment exists the moment that God makes the promise, otherwise God would be a liar. Thus every promise that God has ever made must come to actual fulfillment. We have only to consider this from one point of view to see how wonderful this quality of God really is. We have seen that God justifies the ungodly while they are ungodly. God declares a man to be righteous at a moment when there is no righteousness in the man. But the fact that God has made such a declaration forces God to bring that man to spiritual life in Christ, and will ultimately demand the fulfillment of our glorification in Heaven. Abraham was told that he should have a child; therefore the child had to be born. Likewise, we are told that we have been declared righteous in Christ; therefore we must one day be brought to perfect righteousness before God and all the hosts of Heaven. God is bound to carry through to the utmost of perfection every promise that He has ever made. We shall see how Abraham believed this in a continuing process of laying hold on the life of God, but we must also see how it applies to ourselves.

COMPREHENSION OF FAITH

In the eighth chapter of Romans, we shall come to the series of verbs where God declares us to be foreknown, predestinated, called, justified, and glorified. The very nature of God demands that all of these verbs be put in the past tense. In the chain of promises as they involve you and me, we have been foreknown of God; our destination has been mapped out; we have been actually called—though in the case of some who read these lines the call may come at this very moment; our justification becomes a fact in our own lives, even as it is a fact in the promise; and, finally, in the text we are declared to be glorified, although the actual fulfillment of our glorification will not take place until the second coming of the Lord Jesus Christ. The nature of the faith that comprehends these things, and the nature of the process by which

God brings us thus into His very being, is a most important study, and we shall have to look at it more closely. Abraham's faith was much greater than is ours, for he believed the promise of God concerning something that God said He would do. We look back to the cross of Christ and rest on something that God has done. But although the faith of Abraham was so great, God makes us heirs together with him in the promise, and we shall see the glory of Heaven, and touch it with our hands, just as much as Abraham saw the body of Isaac and took that body into his arms. God always produces what He promises. He cannot lie and He is our God.

CHAPTER XXXII

Alive from the Dead

"Who against hope believed in hope, that he might become the father of many nations, according to that which was spoken, So shall thy seed be" (Rom. 4:18).

THE GREATEST human character in the Bible is Abraham. He stands out among all the men of the Bible as a mountain stands out above the hills. His stature surpasses that of Moses and of Paul. These other men were great, and were mightily used of God, but they would have called Abraham their spiritual father without a moment's hesitation. The promise of God to him was that he would become the father of many nations—not the father of one nation, but the father of many nations. His physical descendants have given us Israel on the side of Isaac and many tribes of the Arabs on the side of Ishmael, but among the Gentile host around the world his children have become as the stars of the sky because these Gentiles dared to follow him in the fearless path of faith in the God who brings life to the dead and calls the nonexistent things existing.

No one can fully understand the New Testament without understanding Abraham, just as no one can understand Abraham and the Old Testament without understanding the New. It is in this chapter that we have been studying in the Epistle to the Romans that we are given a vantage point where we can truly get a vision of the stature of this great man of God, who was the first great man of faith. In our text we read, "Who against hope kept on believing in hope, to the end that he might become a father of many nations, according to what was spoken: So shall thy seed be!"

As we look more closely at the faith of Abraham, we shall see that its main characteristic was that he trusted in God to the extent that he believed that God could bring life out of death. In his particular case it was a belief that God could bring life out of his sterile body. True faith applies the same principle to all of the

Word of God. Let us look back through the history of the universe and see some of the manifestations of this power of God to bring life out of death.

A DEAD EARTH

"In the beginning God created the heavens and the earth" (Gen. 1:1). These are the words that open the Bible. We do not know how long that perfect creation existed, millions or billions of years, perhaps—we have no way of telling. But if we believe what the Bible teaches, we come to know that after a certain period— long or short—the great catastrophe of sin occurred in the universe, and the shining cherub, Lucifer, who had been created by God to act as prime-minister of the universe, conceived in his heart the desire to originate ideas in the government of his province, and to take some of the worship or credit to himself. The perfect God, who does all things perfectly, immediately acted in judgment and blasted the universe with a curse which reduced the world itself to waste and desolation, without form and void, a wreck and a ruin, and darkness covered the face of the deep. It was as though God had said to the universe of spirits, "Here is a power who believes that he has life. We will give it a complete test. He has announced that he will ascend into Heaven and be like the most High God: the first problem on which he can exert his fancied powers is the problem of restoring life to a dead planet." It was an engineering job, if you like, but proud Lucifer could do nothing about it. How long this earth lay in the darkness of judgment, we do not know, but science has pushed back the curtain a little and we can catch a dim view of the rise and fall of glacial periods, and we can see the dim forms of great beasts roaming the continents of earth. There was no power in the universe that could do anything about the condition of the earth except that of the only Being who can bring life out of death, He who is our God.

In the fullness of time He acted. In Isaiah 45:18 God tells us that He had not created the earth "in vain"; [The R.S.V. improves this greatly by saying that He did not create the earth a chaos]. The same Hebrew word is used that is found in the first verses of Genesis where He tells us that the earth was without form and void. He did not create chaos, but brought it in judgment. God now was to demonstrate that He alone had life and the power of bringing light out of darkness, life out of death. "Let there be light: and there was light" (Gen. 1:3). The darkness that had enshrouded the earth for so long was drawn back, and the death of the planet was fully revealed. Then in swift moments He ordered, He commanded, and the creation came back to its pristine beauty and perfection. Thus it would have remained had not sin entered once more in the fall of man.

A DEAD PEOPLE

Here, again, was a scene of death, in the garden of Eden, only this time it was death in the heart of humanity. Can life be brought out of that death? The answer to that question, and the attempts of man to settle it without God, gives us the key to all of human history. Man has persistently acted in blind unbelief on the principle that it is possible for him to do something about the condition of sin in the world. Men have attempted individual reformation only to discover that they had wells of sin and despair within them that poured forth vile waters to contaminate the heart more rapidly than any work of reformation could stanch the flood. Mankind was organized in families, and the parents wept as they saw Cain murder Abel. Parents have seen their children grow up throughout the centuries, with the same seeds of sin growing wild; and wilder fruits within the succeeding generations. When all of mankind was together on the plain of Shinar at the tower of Babel there was an attempt to govern man by the authority of human power, but all human government has grown increasingly corrupt through the ages, and it is common knowledge that righteousness is perverted and justice mocked on every level of human affairs. Behind the walls of our city halls, our county court houses, our state legislatures, and our national administrative offices, there is a power of trickery and chicanery that is matched only by the ruthless forces of high crime which swarm outside these walls. What power can bring life out of all this death?

MADE ALIVE

Abraham believed in the God who could make life out of death, and thus it is that we believe. Individually we have dis-

covered that the new birth is the work of God whereby He creates
within individuals, within the dead Adam of our natures, the new
life of Christ so that we have been made partakers of the divine
nature (II Pet. 1:4). There was nothing within us that could have
been used for the task any more than there was any physical life
within the loins of Abraham or the womb of Sarah that could have
produced a child when they were at the century of their living.
But as Abraham believed God for his body, so we have believed
God for our souls, and God has given us eternal life, and this life
is in His Son. "He that hath the Son of God hath life, and he that
hath not the Son of God hath not life" (I John 5:12).

The whole of the Christian hope partakes of this same nature
of faith in the God who brings life out of death. It is the province
of a minister to stand beside many a coffin and see the last remains
of men and women who have gone down into death. The body
is a decaying, dying thing at the best, and when the life spark has
gone there remains nothing but death. As early as the Book of
Job, which was possibly the first book of the Bible to be written,
there is evidence of simple faith in the immortality of the soul and
spirit, and of the certainty of life after death. This, once more, is
faith in the God who brings life out of death. Job wrote, "For I know
that my redeemer liveth, and that he shall stand at the latter day
upon the earth; and after my skin hath been thus destroyed, yet
in my flesh shall I see God: whom I shall see for myself, and mine
eyes shall behold, and not another" (Job. 19:25-27).

THE POWER OF GOD

The individual who has believed in the God who brings spiritual life in the midst of his spiritual death, through faith in the Lord
Jesus Christ, may hold fast to the hope that God will bring physical
resurrection life out of the death of our bodies at the return of the
Lord Jesus Christ. Have you ever noticed that the Biblical account
of the resurrection has two verbs describing the scene that are
verbs of motion in opposite directions? There is a verb which
states that we shill arise and a verb that states we shall descend.
The resolution of the paradox is found in the nature of death.
When the soul and spirit move out of the body which has been their

residence throughout this mortal lifetime, the invisible being of the believer goes directly to the presence of God.

Scripture puts it: "absent from the body, to be present with the Lord" (II Cor. 5:8), and again "to depart is to be with Christ, which is far better" (Phil. 1:23). Thus we see that the spirit and soul are conscious with the Lord in Heaven, while the body, of course, has decayed and gone back to the primal elements of its dust. Now listen to the word of the Lord (I Thess. 4:13-18) concerning our resurrection: "I would not have you to be ignorant, brethren, concerning them that are asleep [i.e. the body]; that ye sorrow not as others which have no hope. For if we believe that Jesus died and rose again from the dead, even so, them also which sleep in Jesus will God bring with him [note the direction of the verb—He will bring with. The Lord is in Heaven; the souls and spirits of the believers are in Heaven. They whose bodies sleep in the dust of the earth shall be brought in their souls and spirits back to this earth at the time of the resurrection of the believers. He shall bring with]. For the Lord himself shall descend [note the direction of the verb, descend] from heaven with a shout, with the voice of the archangel, and the trump of God; and the dead in Christ shall rise first [note the direction of the verb rise] then we which are alive and remain shall be caught up together with them in the clouds, to meet the Lord in the air; and so shall we ever be with the Lord. Wherefore comfort one another with these words."

When the two directional verbs are examined, there is found the teaching that the souls and spirits of the believers who have gone into Heaven shall come down to be joined to the bodies that shall rise from the dust of the ground, and that the resurrection shall be the triumph of immortality over mortality, of incorruption over corruption, of life over death. Let no one argue about the difficulty of resurrection on the grounds of the dissipation of the chemical elements that formed the body, for God takes care to tell us that the resurrection will take place by the working of the powers whereby He is able to subdue all things to Himself (Phil. 3:21). You will have no difficulty with the working of the power of God when you come to know the God of all power.

Furthermore, the Bible goes on to describe another great working of life out of death in the account of that which is to come to pass at the end of the age. We live in the midst of a disintegrating civilization. Oswald Spengler has described "The Decline of the West." Toynbee has set forth the dissolution of our civilization. A thousand prophets of doom have played Cassandra in total ignorance of what the Bible teaches concerning the future of this world. The Christian is the only one who knows, for he is in the position described by Amos, "Surely the Lord God will do nothing but he revealeth his secret unto his servants, the prophets" (Amos 3:7). We look out over the world today with the only optimistic eye to be found among the commentators of our generation. A few years ago when we preached the judgment of God upon a sinful world, men were ready to belittle our ideas on the grounds that we had been reading too much in the Apocalypse. Now all of our magazines, our scientists, our various commentators describe the supposed destruction that is to come with the atom bomb and the hydrogen bomb, and we are forced to be the one who restrains them by saying that they have not been reading the Apocalypse enough. Man is not going to destroy the human race, but he is going to bring it down only to that disintegration of death out of which the Lord, who brings life out of death, will by the power of His Word, in the midst of His own appearance on the scene, bring that life out of death. The kingdoms of this world will yet become the kingdom of our Lord and of His Christ (Rev. 11:15). He shall reign forever and ever, and the Hallelujah Chorus shall yet be sung throughout the universe. In Abraham's seed, the Lord Jesus Christ, the promised Messiah, shall bring life out of the death of man's efforts.

OUR SURETY

The proof and guarantee of all these workings of life out of death are to be found, of course, in the resurrection of our Lord Jesus Christ. If there is no resurrection of the body of Christ, then there is no Christianity. But He had announced, constantly, that He would die and rise again, and on the third day His tomb was empty, and He was seen of hundreds of witnesses. He had said, "Destroy this temple and in three days I will raise it up" (John 2:19). He was speaking of the temple of His body. Again the Lord Jesus announced that He was going to lay down His life so that He might take it again (John 10:17-19). He said, "No man taketh my life from me, but I lay it down of myself. I have power to lay it down, and I have power to take it again."

The narrative of His death is surrounded with every care to show that it was a real death. His veins were opened so that the blood might be drained from His body. The soldiers who were accustomed to executions came to the crosses to expedite the deaths of the victims by breaking their legs, and, when they came to the cross of Christ they testified that He was dead already. Spiritually, of course, He had dismissed His spirit. The body was then taken and anointed for burial, with heavy weights of spices wrapped in the scores of yards of burial cloth again and again around the body. He was put in a tomb that was covered with a great stone and sealed with the seal of the Roman Empire, to break which was death, and guards were set to watch before the door. But as He had said, He came forth from the dead. His resurrection body was a real body. He ate broiled fish with his disciples on the shore of Lake Galilee (John 21:10-13). He came into the upper room where the disciples were gathered together in fear, and to their frightened senses made Himself known unto them. "Behold my hands and my feet, that it is I myself; handle me, and see; for a spirit hath not flesh and bones as ye see me to have. And when he had thus spoken he shewed them his hands and his feet" (Luke 24:39, 40).

It was a resurrection right enough, and because He lives I live already in the newness of my spiritual life. He is alive, and because He lives I draw my daily strength from Him. He is alive, and because He lives He shall come again and receive us unto Himself (John 14:3). Our bodies shall triumph over the tomb. Our spirits may even now triumph over sin and come to the day when they shall be like unto Him, the Lord. Life from the dead. This is what we believe in Him who brings life out of death and calls the things that are not as though they were.

Abraham was chosen by God to illustrate this great principle in his own body. God was going to bring from the death of the human race the life of the Son of God, the Messiah. That is why it is so important to understand that Jesus Christ was born of a mother who was human as every other woman is human. The virgin Mary was conceived in sin and shapen in iniquity, even as every other member of the human race. We believe, of course, in the Virgin Birth of

Christ, but the doctrine of the immaculate conception of Mary prepares the groundwork for the denial of the nature of the redemption that was provided by the Lord Jesus Christ, as it nullifies the principle of His divine life coming out of the womb of a member of this corrupt human race.

THE TRIUMPH OF FAITH

In Abraham, this birth, and all of the other phases of the principle of life out of death, were to be illustrated in a pageant of triumphant faith. God had told him that he would have a son. There was no natural possibility of fulfillment. But against all human hope Abraham believed in the divine hope. He knew that He was dealing with God who brings life out of death. And we are children of Abraham when we believe in simple faith that God is the life for all our problems of death.

Newell has an interesting paragraph and comment on a page from John Bunyan. Newell writes, "Satan hates active faith in a believer's heart, and opposes it with all his power. The world, of course, is unbelieving, and despises those who claim only 'the righteousness of faith.' The example of professing Christians generally is also against the path of simple faith. Among the 'seven abominations' that Bunyan said he still found in his heart, was 'a secret inclining to unbelief.' 'Against hope,' against reason, against 'feeling,' against opinions of others, against all human possibilities whatsoever, we are to keep believing."

There follows the quotation of the wonderful contrast of faith and unbelief in John Bunyan's *Come and Welcome to Jesus*. Bunyan says,

Let me here give the Christian reader a more particular description of the qualities of unbelief, by opposing faith unto it, in these particulars:

1. Faith believeth the Word of God, but unbelief questioneth the certainty of the same.

2. Faith believeth the Word, because it is true; but unbelief doubteth thereof, because it is true.

3. Faith sees more in a promise of God to help than in all other things to hinder; but unbelief, notwithstanding God's promise, saith, How can these things be?

4. Faith will make thee see love in the heart of Christ when with His mouth He giveth reproofs, but unbelief will imagine wrath in His heart when with His mouth and word He saith He loves us.

5. Faith will help the soul to wait, though God defers to give, but unbelief will snuff and throw up all, if God makes any tarrying.

6. Faith will give comfort in the midst of fears, but unbelief causeth fears in the midst of comforts.

7. Faith will suck sweetness out of God's rod, but unbelief can find no comfort in the greatest mercies.

8. Faith maketh great burdens light, but unbelief maketh light ones intolerably heavy.

9. Faith helpeth us when we are down, but unbelief throws us down when we are up.

10. Faith bringeth us near to God when we are far from Him, but unbelief puts us far from God when we are near to Him.

11. Faith putteth a man under grace, but unbelief holdeth him under wrath.

12. Faith purifieth the heart, but unbelief keepeth it polluted and impure.

13. Faith maketh our work acceptable to God through Christ, but whatsoever is of unbelief is sin, for without faith it is impossible to please Him.

14. Faith gives us peace and comfort in our souls, but unbelief worketh troubling and tossings like the restlessness of the sea.

15. Faith maketh us see preciousness in Christ, but unbelief sees no form, beauty, or comeliness in Him.

16. By faith we have our life in Christ's fulness, but by unbelief we starve and pine away.

17. Faith gives us the victory over the law, sin, death, the devil, and all evils: but unbelief layeth us obnoxious to them all.

18. Faith will show us more excellency in things not seen than in them that are, but unbelief sees more of things that are, than in things that will be hereafter.

19. Faith makes the ways of God pleasant and admirable, but unbelief makes them heavy and hard.

20. By faith Abraham, Isaac, and Jacob possessed the land of promise; but because of unbelief neither Aaron nor Moses, nor Miriam could get thither.

21. By faith the children of Israel passed through the Red Sea, but by unbelief the generality of them perished in the wilderness.

22. By faith Gideon did more with three hundred men and a few empty pitchers than all of the twelve tribes could do, because they believed not God.

23. By faith Peter walked on the water, but by unbelief he began to sink.

Thus might many more be added, which, for brevity's sake, I omit beseeching every one that thinketh he hath a soul to save, or be damned, to take heed of unbelief, lest, seeing there is a promise left us of entering into His rest, any of us by unbelief should indeed come short of it.

CHAPTER XXXIII

The Nature of Abraham's Faith

"An being not weak in faith, he considered not his own body now dead, when he was about an hundred years old, neither yet the deadness of Sarah's womb" (Rom. 4:19).

THE ESSENCE of any religious thought is what is called faith. We who study the Bible know that there is a great difference between the faith of some and the faith of others. The savage who has what is called faith in his witch doctor is far removed from the true saint who lays hold on the living God and secures the triumph of inward joy and power for the outworking of that faith in a life of devotion to God and service for others. The Bible is *par excellence*, the book of faith. Its principles set forth the meaning of true faith and also show the various shades of credulity as exhibited by those who put their trust in false gods.

The principle of believing God, and the nature of that belief, form a great part of the teaching of this book of Romans, and much of the teaching on faith centers in the examples of the men and women, common sinners like ourselves, who have gotten through to God and believed him unto salvation from the sins of the past, unto power for the life of the present, and unto hope for the life to come. Of all the individuals that are presented to us in the Bible, the greatest human being is Abraham, and he stands out above all the others in such a way that he is called the friend of God, and the father of all who believe.

I think that I may say that I have never known Abraham until recently. I had read my Bible, of course, and knew the general outline of the story of his life, but I did not know Abraham. Then three things combined to bring me to focus much of my attention on this great figure. In my Sunday morning sermons I began to retell the great stories of the Bible. I came down through the stories of Genesis: the creation, Adam, Eve, Cain, Abel, and the others, and ultimately I reached Abraham. At the same time I was

writing short ten-line paragraphs for daily meditations to be published in our magazine of Christian truth, *Eternity*, beginning with
the first line of Genesis. I reached the chapters on Abraham at
the same time. And finally, having begun the study of the Epistle
to the Romans eighteen months before, I came again at the same
line to the exposition of the fourth chapter of the epistle, which
is all about Abraham. I can estimate roughly, that I spent several
hours a day with Abraham during more than three months. It was
a thrilling companionship for me, and I am sure that the effects of
knowing this man and the principles which God has set down concerning the nature of his life, his growth, his faith, his failures, his
restoration, his perseverance, his triumph, and his reward have
been profound in my life.

In this study I direct your attention to the details of the nature
of Abraham's great faith in God, reminding you that verses 23 and
24 of this fourth chapter of Romans read: "Now it was not written
for his sake alone, that [his faith] was reckoned unto him [for
righteousness] but for us also, to whom it shall be reckoned [or
credited] if we believe on him that raised up Jesus our Lord from
the dead." With that in mind, let us watch this man, about a
hundred years old, as he reacts to the promise of God that his
sterile body shall be revivefied so that he may beget a child who
shall continue the line of the Messiah and bring to fruition all of the
redemptive promises of God.

SEVEN ASPECTS OF HIS FAITH

If we read closely, we shall see that there are seven phrases
which characterize the reactions of Abraham to the situation as it
was presented to him by God. These are far too important to treat
in one study. We shall come back to some of them in detail, but
we set forth all seven here in order that we may get the whole
picture before putting it under the microscope. When the astounding promise was given to him, we find that, first, Abraham was not
weak in faith. Secondly, he did not look within his own body at
his personal weaknesses. Thirdly, he did not look around him at
the difficulties presented by outward circumstances. Fourthly, he
did not stagger at the promise because of its seeming impossibility.
Fifthly, he was strong in faith. Sixthly, he thanked God for the

answer before it had arrived. Lastly, his whole attitude was that of the fully persuaded man who knows something without question, who lives with it and acts upon it as a *fait accompli*, something that is already done.

SUBSTITUTES FOR FAITH

Before we look at the nature of true faith, let us glance at some of the substitutes which have been circulated among men, just as real value always draws forth an effort to counterfeit.

There is one school of thought which holds that by denying reality it is possible to do away with it. It is a form of escapism which is not unlike that of the man who wishes to flee to a lonely island in order to get away from the complications of modern life. I remember well the first time I ever ran up against this sort of thing in the religious field. As a boy in my teens I lived in a small town outside of San Francisco, and during my high school years I owned the agency for one of the San Francisco newspapers. I had four boys working for me who delivered the papers in the residential areas, while I took Main Street, and once a month I did all of the money collections. It was at a time when I was growing rapidly, and one of my customers was a little woman who was greatly deformed. Some malady of the spine had bent her low, so that she was only about four feet ten inches tall. One day the woman remarked upon my increasing height, and I, in a boyish fumbling way, started to say some word of sympathy for her in her stunted condition. To my amazement she looked up at me and said, "You must not be deceived by outward illusions. What you see is an error of mortal mind. I am as straight as you are and there is absolutely nothing wrong with me at all." I was too ignorant to cope with the situation, and I said something which expressed my stupefaction at such an attitude toward life. One day, in a group of older people, this woman's name was mentioned, and I blurted out all that she had told me. They were aware of her delusion, and one of the gentlemen in the group told a story in a kindly way that settled my mind on the subject. He told of a colored man who was taking care of a lawn in the cemetery and came across a gravestone on which was the inscription, "Not dead, but sleeping." The man read it, scratched his head reflectively, and said, "He sure ain't foolin' anybody but hisself." Someone else remarked that the line could be true about the man whose body was asleep and whose soul was alive in Christ, but that the poor woman was surely fooling nobody but herself.

THE ERROR

Before we leave this point, that self-deception is not to be confused with faith, it may be well to answer the underlying fallacy of a philosophy that can produce such false thinking. The argument goes like this: God is perfect, is He not? And the answer is, Yes. A perfect God could not create anything imperfect, could He? And the answer is, No, He could not. Well, God created all things, did He not? And again the answer is, Yes, He did. Well, then, does it not follow logically that all things are perfect, and that anything that seems not to be perfect must be an illusion that rises from mortal mind?

Such a philosophy fails to take account of the historical fact of the origin of sin in the heart of Lucifer, who, the Bible says, was perfect in all his ways, until iniquity was found in him (Ezek. 28:15). There had been no sin whatsoever in the universe before this wonderful being, created by God in perfection, and given a free will—mark that fact—given a free will, decided that he could perform the tasks appointed to him without seeking power from God, and that he could take the credit for it, from the angels that were below him in power, and not pass that credit, or worship, on to God. Thereupon, the perfect God perfectly blasted the universe and set up all of the perfect laws of disintegration, decay, erosion, death, and the like, in order that men might learn that the essential law of all being was to know that there was no good outside of the Creator, that we had to be utterly dependent upon Him, and take none of the credit whatsoever for ourselves. Failure to take account of the entrance of sin and death into the world and divine judgment at the fall will lead to delusion, and self-deception.

PRESUMPTION

Another substitute for faith that is frequently encountered is presumption. There are those who exalt the human mind to the place of deity and take its findings as infallible. Some have even gone so far as to rule God out altogether and to rest the framework of their life and living on nothing more than what they think is right. There are many ramifications of this practice, and a little thought will seek them out and dispose of them. All are marked, however, by a fundamental rationalism, which is the opposite of true faith. One school of presumption sits in judgment upon the divine revelation, picks and chooses that which suits its purpose, and ultimately arrives at the nebulous idea that inspiration is to be judged by that which inspires the reader. If something should rise from the pages of Scripture which judges and condemns, it will be rejected as uninspiring and therefore uninspired. But if something is found that tickles the fancy of the reader, even though it be twisted from its context to make it fit his purpose, he finds it inspiring and proclaims it loudly as his faith. Such faith, I repeat, is presumption. There is a supreme example of this in those who claim that God is the father of all men. The Lord Jesus Christ in the course of His ministry probably hit the doctrine of the fatherhood of God and the brotherhood of man harder than He ever struck at any other false concept. He said, "I speak that which I have seen with my Father: and ye do that which ye have seen with your father." When they replied with the arrogance of presumption which they thought was faith, their words were, "We have one Father, even God." Jesus Christ replied, "If God were your Father, ye would love me: for I proceeded forth and came from God; neither came I of myself, but he sent me." And the terrible effect of their presumption is revealed by His next word: "Why do ye not understand my speech? even because ye cannot hear my word." Presumption sets up a mental block, or a spiritual block, which makes it impossible for a man to receive reality. And the Lord Jesus Christ, continuing His argument, brings it to its devastating conclusion: "Ye are of your father the devil, and the lusts of your father ye will do. He was a murderer from the beginning, and abode not in the truth, because there is no truth in him. When he speaketh a lie, he speaketh of his own: for he is a liar, and the father of it" (John 8:44).

Any man who sets his own mind above the divine revelation

that was given to us from God, concerning Christ, and recorded in the Word, is guilty of presumption and must one day suffer the condemnation that Christ has announced, when He declared that He would say, even to those who will claim to have done many mighty works in His name? "I never knew you: depart from me, ye that work iniquity" (Matt. 7:23).

CREDULITY

There is a third substitute for faith that is quite common in the world, and that is the substitute of credulity. A person that will hand his mind, or any section of it, over to someone else who is to do all the interpreting of the facts of life for him, will find that he is the victim of an exploitation which would be bad enough if it concerned nothing more than this life, but the consequences are disastrous when they are seen to be eternal. In the dark places of this world, we know there are those who follow the mumbo-jumbo of the witch-doctors with a blind credulity, unreasoning and unwavering. They have no other hope and thus they grasp at any straw as would a drowning man. But in the midst of our civilization, we see the same thing taking place with results that are just as fearsome. In the political realm we have fought and are fighting wars against the ideologies which ask men to hand the political section of their brains over to some group which undertakes to do their thinking for them.

The sad thing is that there are those who deprecate such practices in the realm of political thought but who turn their minds over to a group or organization or party in the theological world and think nothing of it. If their particular authority has spoken, then it is a statement that must be accepted. Their credulity will accept any dogma that is promulgated for them, and will seek to justify it, even at the expense of reason, not to speak of historical facts.

These three fields of thinking, then, delusion, presumption and credulity, have furnished patterns that go by the name of faith, but they are not faith even though their devotees would call them by that name. A stone, a block, or a piece of moss are not oranges, even if someone wished to call them oranges.

TRUE FAITH

In returning to the first phase of Abraham's life with God, we see that he was not weak in faith. Someone may say that I have shown conclusively that certain actions and thoughts are not true faith, but I have not shown what the reality is. Perhaps I can illustrate it by the following. There is an ancient tradition in India that some magicians have been able to uncoil a rope in an open field, throw it toward the sky, aid a boy to start climbing it, and see him disappear into the air above. It has been conclusively demonstrated that the story is a table to be compared with that of our own Paul Bunyan and his blue ox. But if I may use it as an illustration, I would say that there are hundreds of people, perhaps multitudes, who sit working on their rope which they call faith. They have it in a neat coil beside them, and seem very proud of their handiwork. Should I come along questioningly and ask them what they are doing, they would reply that they are working on their faith. When I would want to know how it operates they reply that they expect, when the time comes for them to die, to uncoil their rope of faith, throw it skyward, and climb it into eternal life. I ask them what the upper end is tied to in order to give it strength and security. Immediately they fly into a towering rage and accuse me of being narrow-minded, bigoted, medieval, and any number of other characterizations. But long acquaintance with the Bible has made me an intensely practical person. I want to know to what the upper end of that rope is fastened.

Now the life of Abraham shows us the direct opposite of these fantastic persons, with their weaving of delusion, presumption, and credulity. I find him standing calmly by a rope that has been let down from Heaven. I look closely at it and see that it does not touch the earth, but that it is a few feet off the ground. I question Abraham about this and discover that he has learned that a man is to turn away from everything that has its source and strength upon this earth, and that he is to live his life by that which comes down from Heaven. "But the rope does not touch earth," I exclaim, and he lays his hand upon it and shows me that his body forms the contact, and that all that comes from Heaven can pass into the earth through the lives of those who reach up to lay hold, by what is true faith, upon that which God Himself has given us from Heaven. The first element of true faith, then, is that it originates with God and not with man. Unless that is seen, there is no real faith. Any movement that begins in the heart of man is, necessarily, not to be considered as faith. That is why the Holy Spirit says, in Ephesians 2:8, 9, "For by grace are ye saved, through faith; and that not of yourselves, it is the gift of God; not of works, lest any man should boast." True faith, then, is the gift of God. We admit that human reason cannot furnish the answers, and turn toward God our empty hearts. Only God fills us with true faith, and enables us to grow in grace and in the knowledge of our Lord. We acknowledge the emptiness of all of earth's cisterns, and God opens up the never-failing spring of faith within us. Abraham had passed by this way. He had seen the vision of the glory of God and had learned, therein, the nothingness of man. From that moment his heart was turned toward God, and he was not weak in faith.

In the second place, we see that he was not troubled by inner doubts. His own condition did not affect the picture. It is interesting to note that the different versions of our text have translations that come from sets of manuscripts which say two opposing things but which mean, on close analysis, exactly the same thing. In the King James Version we read, "He considered not his own body, now dead." Many other translations accept this rendering. But there are other translators who have followed a reading that is to be found in some manuscripts, versions, and ancient citations, and who translate it, "He considered his own body, now dead." At first glance it would appear to be a great contradiction. He did not look at his body; he looked at his body. Well, did he or didn't he? It does not make any difference. The meaning in both cases is the same. If you wish to follow the King James Version and say that he did not look at his own body, the meaning would be as follows: God told Abraham that he would have a child that would fulfill the promises which had been made to him. Doubt might have whispered, Look at your body! It is dead! And Abraham would have brushed the argument aside, saying, in effect, What has that to do with it? I am not looking at my body, and its weakness, I am looking at the promise of God.

Now if you wish to follow the other translations and read it that he did look at his own body, the explanation would be as follows: God told Abraham that he would have a child that would fulfill the promises which had been made to him. Doubt might have whispered, Look at your body! It is dead! To which Abraham would have replied, All right; let's look at it. It is dead. So what? It isn't a talking bird that has come to tell me that I shall have a child. It isn't a fortune teller trying to mulct a piece of gold from a credulous old man who wants to see his estate established in a solid line through a son that shall come from his loins. It is God Himself who has said that I shall have a son. So I look at my body and say that it doesn't enter into the consideration of the question. When God speaks, that is enough.

AN APPLICATION

Because of the limitation of time, let us stop and make a personal application of these two points, bringing them down to our century and to our own need. I am now presuming that you have turned away from the false and that you are desiring with all your heart to have the real. You are not enmeshed in delusion and self-deception. You see yourself clearly as a sinner in a world of sinners, born of a judged race, and hastening on toward the end of life and, unless the Lord shall come, a place for your body in the cemetery. You admit the facts and step out of your dream world to face the reality of yourself alone with God. You are no longer in the world of presumption. You realize that the ego wants to be god in your life, and you have faced that fact and come to the place where you are willing for God to deal with it. And you are no longer in the maze of credulity, following whatever will-o'-the-wisp that some group or party would set before you in order to count you as one of theirs. You have taken your place as a needy sinner in the sight of God and you look toward Him. Immediately He places before you the cross of Jesus Christ, and you see there the answer to your need, since the death of the Saviour, first of all, satisfies the holiness and justice of God and, then, makes it possible for His love to come through to you in effective salvation. You are, therefore, no longer weak in faith, and you find yourself in the path that was marked out for you by God with the feet of Abraham.

Immediately doubt will come whispering to your heart. And when that happens you must take the second step with Abraham and refuse to look within you. Doubt will whisper, "But you are not good enough to go into a perfect Heaven with a perfect God!" Faith will look away from your accusing conscience and sing:

> Come ye sinners, poor and needy,
> Weak and wounded from the Fall;
> If you tarry till you're better,
> You will never come at all.
>
> Let not conscience make you linger,
> Nor of fitness fondly dream;
> All the fitness He requireth
> Is to feel your need of Him.

Oh, turn your heart away from your own need, your own sin, your own conscience, your own lack, and come to Him just as you are. He will meet your need and you will walk as a child of faithful Abraham, living and walking by faith in Him who loved you and washed you from your sins in His own blood.

CHAPTER XXXIV

The God of Abraham

"And being not weak in faith, he considered not his own body now dead, when he was about an hundred years old, neither yet the deadness of Sarah's womb: He staggered not at the promise of God through unbelief; but was strong in faith, giving glory to God" (Rom. 4:19, 20).

IT IS ONE of the great qualities of faith that it looks past all external circumstances and sees God alone, who is the author of the promises. This is the third of faith's characteristics: Abraham did not look at the deadness of Sarah's womb (Rom. 4:19). God had promised them that they should have a child; and Sarah was past ninety years of age and Abraham had reached the century mark. But since God said it, that was enough for true faith.

A GREAT GOD

Men are always in difficulty with their faith because their God is too small. If they can once see the true God, and get the perspective that sees Him as filling all in all, then the difficulties of life will rapidly diminish to their proper proportions. I learned of the idea of a great God and a little god from my old professor of Hebrew, Robert Dick Wilson, who was one of the intellectual glories of Princeton Theological Seminary in the great days of Warfield, Davis, Machen, and the others. After I had been away from the Seminary for about twelve years, I was invited back to preach to the students. Old Dr. Wilson came into Miller Chapel and sat down near the front while I set forth the Word of God. At the close of the meeting the old gentleman came up to me, cocked his head on one side in his characteristic way, extended his hand, and said, "If you come back again, I will not come to hear you preach. I only come once. I am glad that you are a big-godder. When my boys come back, I come to see if they are big-godders or little-godders, and then I know what their ministry will be." I asked him to explain, and he replied: "Well, some men have a little god, and they are always in trouble with him. He can't do any miracles. He can't take care of the inspiration and transmission of the Scripture to us. He doesn't intervene on behalf of His people. They have a little god and I call them little-godders. Then there are those who have a great God. He speaks and it is done. He commands and it stands fast. He knows how to show Himself strong on behalf of them that fear him. You have a great God; and He will bless your ministry." He paused a moment and smiled, and said, "God bless you," and turned, and walked out.

I am certainly glad that I do have a great God. I have the God who knows all, is all-powerful, unchanging, eternal, never-failing. My God has never made a mistake. He has never been surprised by anything that happened, for He has always known and decreed all things. He knows the end from the beginning.

THE FRIEND OF GOD

Now Abraham had this same God. He knew Him well, and God condescended to call him His friend. It is one of the marks of wonder in the Scripture that the God of the universe should feel the need of a friend. But when that need is understood the mercy, and grace, and love of God begin to stand out, and we realize why He was willing to come to this earth and undergo the torments of the cross in order to redeem us to Himself. Abraham was not weak in faith; he did not take the weakness of his body into consideration. The outward circumstances of earthly impossibilities were nothing to him, as he knew that with God all things are possible.

All through the Word of God we find this same disregard of circumstances on the part of those who believed God. Noah did not pay any attention to the fact that it had never rained upon the earth, but went ahead and built a vessel the equivalent of an 18,000 ton ship. He did not look at the circumstances; he looked at God. Gideon did not pay any attention to the fact that his little army was outnumbered many to one. He did not look at the circumstances; he looked at God.

Caleb and Joshua furnish us with one of the most remarkable illustrations of this point of view. Twelve spies went into the land of Canaan from Kadesh Barnea. They were all in agreement that it was a beautiful land, flowing with milk and honey. The grapes of Eshcol were brought back as samples of the fertility of the land. But all of the twelve also concurred that there were giants in the land. In our English version the story can be placed around three words, all beginning with the letter G. If you want to teach this lesson to your children, draw a large capital G and write after it the three words: God, giants, grasshoppers. The ten said that there were giants in the land, and beside them the Israelites were as but grasshoppers. The two, Caleb and Joshua, did not look at themselves, but they looked at God. They said that there were giants in the land, but that with God they could easily be overthrown.

The lesson is stupendous when it is realized that God is teaching us thereby that it is impossible to see both God and yourself in the same glance. You can only stand on one side of your circumstances. Your point of view is such that you look over the top of your circumstances and see your pygmy self in the background, or you walk around your circumstances and look over them to the great God who overshadows them and makes them appear as nothing.

ON TOP OF THE CIRCUMSTANCES

Many years ago I told a story over the radio that has been picked up and printed in many places since then. In the early part of the great depression, I knew a certain man who had undergone severe losses. In addition, his health had been touched and he had sickness at home in another member of his family. I met him on the street and asked him how things were. He replied, "Well, under the circumstances they are not too bad." I asked him another question and got the same introduction to his answer: "Well under the circumstances . . . " A third time I spoke of something else and received the reply, "Well, under the circumstances . . ." I answered him and said, "What on earth are you doing under the circumstances? God never meant a Christian to live under the circumstances." We have been placed on top of the circumstances. It is always our gracious privilege to live out of this world. If you will get out from under the circumstances and put the circumstances under, you will discover that you can answer that "on top of the circumstances everything is going very well." It might be worth while for you to consider for a moment the meaning of the word *circumstances*. The word comes from the Latin *circum*, which means "around or round about," joined to the verb *stare*, "to stand." We know the prefix in such words as *circumnavigate*, to sail around the world, and the verb has come to us in a score of other forms. Our circumstances are the things of life which stand around us—the details, the events that make up life. God has so ordered our being that every event, yes, every detail, can be a circumstance that may be used to bring us closer to Him, if we are willing to stand on the circumstances, instead of getting under them.

This was the lesson which Abraham learned so well, and which is set forth here as one of the qualities of his faith. Within him was death, around him was death, but then there was God, who brings life out of the dead. What then is the place of death in this story? It is the cup in which God shall pour life; it is the framework that shall exhibit the picture of God's power; it is the dust in which the seeds of glory shall bud and flower by the intervention of the Lord God, who is life, and in whom there is nothing of death. Let us learn the lesson well: doubt looks at circumstances; faith looks to God in Christ.

A STRAIGHT FURROW

Another quality of faith is now set before us in the life of Abraham. It is said that "looking unto the promise of God, he wavered not through unbelief (4:20). I have quoted from the Revised Version as it gives the extra verb that is omitted in the King James Version. For though all translations say that Abraham did not waver, or stagger, in the Greek and the revisions it is set forth that this unwavering walk of Abraham took place with his eyes fixed upon the promise of God. Here is one of the greatest lessons of faith. If we are not to waver, we must have our eyes fixed steadfastly upon the Lord Jesus Christ. Perhaps I can best illustrate the meaning of this verse from an incident that happened to me when I first learned to plow.

I got on the seat of the tractor, pulled the lever that dropped the plow into the ground, and started across the center of the field, hoping to plow a straight furrow and then continue the work of preparing the land for the seeding. After I had gone a few feet, I turned around to look at the furrow, and was entranced at the rushing flow of top soil along the plow share. Rich and black, the soil turned over and I then turned to look where I was going. When I had turned around the first time, I had unconsciously carried the wheel of the tractor with my movement and gotten away from the straight line. I pulled the tractor back into line and then, a moment later, I looked back at the furrow once more. I became more and more distressed at what I saw, for behind me, wavering across the field, was the undulating line of my furrow which revealed, as though etched in the earth, the wandering vision which I had had. I soon learned that there was only one way to plow a straight furrow. When you are about to accelerate the tractor and pull the lever that sinks the plow into the ground, you must sight across the field at a distant point and keep the nose of the tractor squarely on the sighting point. You must not turn around to see how the furrow is coming, or if you do give a hasty glance to see that all is well, it must be done after making certain that the fixed point is straight ahead, and the eye must be brought immediately back to it. Now I can take a plow across a field and leave a furrow a quarter of a mile long, black and straight, simply because I have learned that when the guide furrow is being laid in the field the plowman must keep his eye on a fixed point, whether it be on a tree, a barn, a distant hill, or some other point. Woe unto the man who plows his furrow looking aside, or looking behind him, or looking at a crow that may fly across his line of vision.

LOOKING TO THE PROMISE

This is what the Scripture says about Abraham. Looking unto the promise of God, he wavered not through unbelief. In the early part of his story we may see a bit of crooked furrow, but as time passes we see the line, straighter and straighter, and the whole of his life is fixed at a dead set upon his Lord. His eyes were fastened upon the promise and nothing else mattered. He did not deviate because he had the unchanging gaze. There was no staggering, no wavering, but the steady walk, step by step, plodding along the way. More and more his eyes were filled with the vision of the God of the promises, and nothing in the world mattered any more. He was born into a world of death, he was living in the midst of death, and he knew that death would one day engulf his physical body. But his eyes were on the promise and he looked for "a city which hath foundations, whose builder and maker is God" (Heb. 11:10). Lot had his eyes on the lush grass in the plain of Sodom, and his furrow was a crooked one. Peter had faith to step out of the boat when he saw the Lord Jesus come walking upon the sea; but as soon as he took his eyes away from the Saviour and let them rest upon the waves around him, he began to sink. That contrast between Abraham and Peter is one that is multiplied a thousand times in life around us today, and in the lives of many of us. It is a glorious truth that the Lord is always ready to stand before us in His promises so that we may see Him plow the straight furrow, that we may see Him and walk in the path of the sea. Do you have your eyes filled with that Heavenly vision and the great promises of God today? Can you walk the road of life, if need be, a plodding road, but one that is daily filled with glory because of the One who fills your vision?

You may complain that you cannot see God. That is true for the eyes of the flesh. But Abraham looked at the promise and that was sufficient. You have the Word of God in your hand, and it is the Word of God that conveys life to the believer. We are not speaking of the binding and the paper and the ink, but the Word itself, the Scripture of truth, is the means whereby God conveys life to us. Abraham was not so fortunate as we are to have this Word in form that could be seen with the eyes. But the eyes of the spirit had seen the God of glory; the ears of the spirit had heard the command to get out from land, home, and kindred. The heart had laid hold upon the truth of the promise, and when the Lord further appeared to Abraham and spoke to him concerning the child that was to be born to him, the heart of Abraham laid hold upon the promise, and the eyes of his spirit left the object of faith and the ears of his spirit never stopped listening to the promise echoing through his mind. Thus it was that the walk of Abraham became an unwavering walk.

TRUE HOLINESS

These truths are of great importance to every Christian. Men long for righteouness and true holiness and seek them in multiple ways. There is only one way to find righteousness and true holiness, and that is through the Word of God, and the applications of its principles to the life by the Holy Spirit. I know that I risk being greatly misunderstood when I say that no one will ever be separated unto God and that no one will advance definitely in spiritual ways apart from the promise of God. It is through the sanctifying power of the Word of God that spiritual life is communicated to the believer. It will never be given in any other way than through the truth of the Scripture. No one was ever sanctified through attending a prayer meeting, even if he labored in prayer all night. Someone may wish to controvert that by pointing to the fact that it was in the Aldersgate prayer meeting that Wesley felt his heart strangely warmed, and went forth to be the great instrument for the spiritual revival of England. But you have only to read a little deeper into the history in order to learn that it was while someone was reading the preface to one of Luther's commentaries that Wesley felt his heart strangely warmed. Turn back to the work of the great reformer, and we discover that what Wesley heard was a tissue of quotations from the Word of God, and that this was the means that God used to reach the heart of Wesley. I go so far as to say that no man has ever been saved apart from some definite truth out of the Bible and that there is no possible growth in Christian life apart from the depening knowledge of this Book.

A few years ago I was invited to give a series of lectures at the English Keswick, which might be called the mother of all Bible conferences. Thousands of people gather there in the beautiful lake district for a Bible conference on the deepening of the spiritual life and the study of the teaching of the Word concerning the work of the Holy Spirit in the Christian life. I had several months in which to prepare for these studies, and I read and reread the Word of God to find the Scriptural methods for holy living. I found four verses which presented methods of growth in spiritual life. The most important, because it contains the others, is the Word of Christ, "Sanctify them through thy truth; thy word is truth" (John 17:7). This coupled with a verse in Peter, shows that the sanctifying process is by means of the promises of God. Peter writes, "As newborn babes, desire the sincere milk of the word, that ye may grow thereby" (I Pet. 2:2). Therefore, we see that the basis of spiritual growth is through the promises of God.

The other methods develop out of this. Paul tells us that "the love of Christ constraineth us; because we thus judge, that if one died for all, then were all dead, and that he died for all, that they which live should not henceforth live unto themselves, but unto him which died for them and rose again" (II Cor. 5:14,15). Here the constraining power is the contemplation of the love of Christ. But where shall we contemplate it apart from the promises of God? If we would listen to it explained, it is the Word that is back of the explanation. If we would see a picture of the death scene of the Lord, it is the Word of the Lord that gave the artist the incentive to set down on canvas the truth that might help an illiterate, at least a spiritual illiterate, who would then have brought to his mind the things that had been told him from the Word.

The third method for holy living is the work of the Spirit within us. Some might argue that I am defeating my argument, for here, they would say, is another force that is apart from the Word of God. But the heart of Bible truth is that the Holy Spirit never works in any man apart from the truth that is in the external Word. The key passage on the subject is in Corinthians, where we read, "But we all, with open face beholding as in a glass the glory of the Lord, are changed into the same image from glory to glory, even as by the Spirit of the Lord" (II Cor. 3:18). Those who know the symbolism of Scripture will soon see that the glass in which we behold the glory of the Lord is none other than the mirror of His Word. God will not communicate with a lost soul apart from the truth that is set down in the Bible. And the Lord, even the Holy Spirit, will bring a child of God along the pilgrim way only by means of the Word of God.

The fourth method for holy living that I find in the Word of God is the contemplation of the truth that the Lord Jesus Christ is coming again. After describing the second coming of Christ, especially in its transforming relationship to the whole body of believers, the inspired writer says, "And every man that hath this hope in him, purifieth himself, even as he is pure" (I John 3:3). But if you attempt to lift your eyes to the sky to see the coming Lord Jesus, you will not behold Him as yet, for not yet are all things put under His feet. But what we do see are the promises of God concerning that coming, and filling our eyes with the promises, we see the glorious vision as it is painted by the Spirit in the Word, and our hearts are purified by the thought of the glory and the holiness that shall be ours when we are like Him—not merely in His attributes of power and possession, but above all in His attributes of holiness and yieldedness. These are the things that shall be ours, and as we look upon them we find them growing within us with an ever increasing desire.

And what joy it gives us to recognize that there is growth in our spiritual life. Some months ago I was looking through a box that contained several hundred snapshots, mixed together without any design, except that they were various scenes that had been snapped over the years and had never been placed in albums. I found among them some pictures of myself taken when I was about twenty years old. I looked at them and saw a startling resemblance to my younger son. I took them to him and said, "What do you think of these pictures?" He began to look at them, thinking that they were pictures of himself. He began talking about his aspect in one of them, and then said, "I don't remember having these pictures taken. Where was I? What is this background?" He began examining the background and could not identify it. I ended his puzzlement by telling him that the pictures had been taken out in California. He had not been in California within the last two or three years, and suddenly it dawned upon him that these were pictures of his father. We had a good laugh about it, and I can remember that when we were through we looked at each other with a look that did not find expression in words, but which was deep in both of our hearts; we realized that we were one in many ways, and the knowledge drew us still closer together.

As I set before you the picture of Abraham, who is called the father of all them that believe, I trust that you can begin to find some family resemblance to that portrait which is painted here. Do you have real faith, and not delusion, presumption, or credulity? Have you ceased any introspection, ceased looking within yourself for things that might nullify the promise? Have you stopped looking at the circumstances that are round about you? Have you turned to the promise in order to fasten your eyes upon it so that you may plow a straight furrow across the field of life with the certainty that you are marching toward a goal that has been set before you as the object of your faith, and the stabilizer of your daily walk? If you can find any traces of such reality of faith, you can look at the portrait of Abraham that is set before us in the Scripture and say, "I am a little like him. There is a family resemblance. He took it from the Lord. And some day I shall see Him and be like Him, for I shall see Him as He is."

Near the end of the Epistle to the Hebrews there is a great gallery of the portraits of the men of faith throughout the Old Testament. After the whole length of the corridor has been walked, and the remarkable faith of this pantheon of the patriarchs and prophets has been seen, the Holy Spirit says, "Wherefore, seeing we also are compassed about with so great a cloud of witnesses, let us lay aside every weight, and the sin which doth so easily beset us, and let us run with patience the race that is set before us, looking unto Jesus, the author and finisher of our faith; who for the joy that was set before him endured the cross, despising the shame, and is set down at the right hand of the throne of God" (Heb. 12:1, 2). The great word there is "looking unto Jesus." Weymouth, in his translation, has rendered it, "simply fixing your gaze upon Jesus." If you will ask the Lord today to give you the knowledge of the promises concerning His Son, He will do it. You will see the promises concerning His death. You will see the promises concering His resurrection. You will see the promises concerning His present power and authority upon the throne of God. You will see the promises concerning His return in glory and triumph. And the promises will fill your being and you will never be the same again.

CHAPTER XXXV

Strong in Faith

"He staggered not at the promise of God through unbelief; but was strong in faith, giving glory to God; and being fully persuaded that, what he had promised, he was able also to perform" (Rom. 4:20, 21).

THE GREAT example of faith in the New Testament is that of Abraham, whose story is told again and again.

I was driving along the road recently with my radio tuned in to a quiz program. A candidate was trying to "Strike it Rich," and had to identify a person whose first name was John. The quizmaster told the competitor that the man was a New Testament character, who had baptized Jesus, that he had had his head cut off for Salome, but still the man couldn't get the answer and when the quizmaster gave him the hint by saying John the Ba . . . the man replied, "John the Butcher," and lost fifty dollars. It might be argued that the man had no religious background, or was of a faith that did not know the New Testament. I am going to put a question about men in the New Testament that I believe would be missed by ninety per cent of the Christians in the country, and perhaps by half the preachers.

Put the question this way, and try it on your Sunday-school class: By actual count what men's names are mentioned the most often in the New Testament? Paul's name is found a few more times than that of Peter; John the Baptist's name is third. But the question that will stump most people is: Whose name is found the most ofter Paul, Peter, and John the Baptist? You may dismiss the names of James, John, and the other disciples. Their names do not occur half as often as that of another man. And if you think that it may be a woman's name, you are wrong again; there are five women in the New Testament named Mary, but that name does not occur half as often as the name of the man who is number four in the name count. The answer to the question is: Abraham.

That name is found sixty-four times in the New Testament. Abraham is one of its most important characters, though he lived 2000 years before the New Testament. In this listing I have purposely omitted the count of verses quoted with "Moses said," or "Moses wrote."

THE GREATEST JEW

Some time ago, on the occasion of the grouping of several Jewish feasts—Yom Kippur and the Jewish New Year—*Life* magazine published an article by the President of the Conference of Jewish Rabbis, which set forth the creed of modern Judaism. Twice in the article the rabbi said that Moses was the greatest Jew who had ever lived. I would have said the same thing myself several years ago, excepting, of course, the God-man, the Lord Jesus Christ who was not only made flesh, dwelling among us, but who was made Jewish flesh, as the Scripture plainly states (Rom. 9:5). But as time has passed, and as I have spent more hundreds of hours with the Word of God, I have changed my opinion. Not Moses, but Abraham is the greatest Jew who ever lived. It is the error of thinking Moses to be greater than Abraham that has oriented Jewish thought to legal righteousness instead of to salvation through faith in, what the theologians have called, the vicarious, substitutionary sacrifice, presented to God as the satisfaction for all His righteous demands against the sinner. When Abraham is seen as the greatest human character of the Bible, overshadowing even Paul and Moses, then it will be understood how even Moses, who received the law from God, was saved because of faith in God's Word about the blood sacrifice presented through his brother Aaron.

We have seen, in previous studies, that Abraham was not weak in faith; he did not look within his own body at his personal weaknesses. He did not look around him at the difficulties presented to him by outward circumstances. He did not waver when confronted by the seeming impossibility of the promise. Our text now states that he was strong in faith, and that he thanked God for the answer before he had any evidence that it would be accomplished. These two strands of faith go together in the great unbreakable cord that can bind a man to God forever.

It should be noted that the preceding verse states that he was not weak in faith. Now we read that he was strong in faith. When a believer has come to the knowledge of the reality of divine inspiration, he learns that God is not working at literary effect, but that every word, every change of expression, carries with it a great weight of importance. God is seeking to build us in Himself, and the slightest shade of meaning is of great importance. What is the difference between the negative and the positive expression of faith? Perhaps I can illustrate this from a simple example which would have been understood by all who lived in Palestine in the Old Testament days.

THE HYSSOP

There is a plant that grows in Palestine called hyssop, that was used in the ritual of the Mosaic worship, which is a great illustration of the nature of faith. Botanists have not been able to agree on the identification of the plant that is mentioned in the Scriptures, and certainly it has no relationship to the plant of the same name that has been domesticated in parts of our country. But from a verse in the Kings, which speaks of the wisdom of Solomon, who studied many things, we learn that the great king was wise concerning "the hyssop that springeth out of the wall" (I Kings 4:33). There is a plant which fulfills this descripition which I saw in Palestine under interesting conditions. The first time I was in Jerusalem I was taken into the palace of the Grand Mufti, and then into the Hall of the Sanhedrin, where few tourists ever penetrate. In his room is a window that looks down upon the wailing wall, and we stood there and photographed the scene below in considerable detail. It was a moving sight. At the foot of the wall, beating their heads slowly against it, were groups of Jewish rabbis, mostly from central Europe, and as they bowed forward they were wailing, reciting the Book of Lamentations over and over again. Above their heads was the high expanse of wall, and from it was growing the long trailing plant that was identified to me as the hyssop of the Bible. The remarkable thing about this particular plant is that it has a very short root—sometimes not over half an inch long. It can cling to the surface of the rock, drawing its sustenance from the air, from the wind, from the rain when there is any, from what bits of dirt fall from above or are borne on the wind to the meager roots, or from what particles of nourishment there are in the rock itself. From that tiny root the plant flourishes, sometimes twelve and fourteen feet in length. What a great plant to grow from such a slender root! This is one of the reasons why the plant can be such a symbol of faith. For when we cling to the rock, though our faith may be small, it can be strong, and a whole life can grow from the shortest root, provded it clings to the rock.

Abraham was not weak in faith. He did not have the faith that believed in itself. Faith, in itself, is worthless, just as a root is worthless if it is unattached. If one grasps the branch and pulls the root away from the rock, the branch will soon die. Faith, to be of any value, must cling to the Rock. Our faith, nothing in itself, becomes everything when it clings to the Lord Jesus Christ, the Rock of Ages. I have pointed out earlier in these studies that you may have faith in a bridge and drive your car across it at fifty miles an hour, but if a freshet has washed out the foundations of the bridge, you will go down in its wreckage, and be killed. Your faith was all right, but there was nothing underneath that faith. Faith without a foundation is nothing but stupid credulity. But true faith, like the hyssop, though its roots be short, will produce great fruit if fastened to the rock. Abraham's faith was like that.

Before we leave this illustration of the hyssop, it will be well to point out another passage in the Old Testament which refers to it. Pieces of this plant were plucked and made into what we would call a brush, to be used in the ritual of the blood sacrifices throughout the Levitical worship. The pieces of hyssop were used for the part that is the brush proper, instead of bristles which we would use today. A piece of wood, that of the sweet-smelling cedar, was used for what we would call the handle of the brush. The two were attached by a small piece of scarlet cord, and the whole was hung at the side of the altar and used for the sprinkling of the blood. When a leper was cleansed, or when there was some other part of the service that demanded sprinkling, the priest used this little brush of hyssop. It was dipped in the blood of the animal that had been sacrificed, and then shaken upon the one who was to be cleansed. David, in his great Psalm of repentance, speaks of it in terms of his own cleansing: "Purge me with hyssop, and

I shall be clean: wash me, and I shall be whiter than snow" (Ps. 51:7). In other words, "Deal with me on the basis of the blood sacrifice." Hyssop was the plant, then, which applied the work of redemption to the one who needed salvation. Thus it became a further picture of faith, which is that which lays hold on the life that God communicates to us through the cross of Jesus Christ, and applies it directly to our need.

STRENGTH OF FAITH

Abraham had such a faith. Our text tells us, indeed, that he was strong in faith. I have tried to analyze what strength of faith really means. After eliminating all of the counterfeits—credulity, superstition, presumption, and the like, we come to the simplicity of understanding that strength of faith is the reality of believing with all your heart and acting upon that belief. There is an example that lies under our observation almost every day. It is the way a girl will commit her whole life and being into the hands of a man. Put aside all of the false cases where the very degradations of what should be true faith are illustrations in themselves of the spiritual fornications that are being committed by souls that go a whoring after strange gods, to use the phrase that the Word of God often employs (Exod. 34:15, 16; etc.). But when a good woman commits herself into the heart of a good man who loves and respects and honors her, there is a perfect illustration of faith. He tells her that he loves her. She believes him. There is faith. She loves him in return and tells him so. He believes her. There is faith. She begins to alter the course of her life. All of her efforts are put into the preparation of her trousseau and the other needs of her new life. He turns his thoughts to the purchase of a ring, and begins to look over the housing situation. And all of this transformation of action takes place because two people have faith in the word of each other and proceed to act upon the implications of a question and answer such as: "Will you marry me?" "Yes, I will."

We have all seen girls who were very strong in that type of faith which includes a large proportion of love; and when a good woman loves she is willing to go to death for that love and the faith that is bound up in it. Abraham had a faith like that. There is one thing further that should be said about the illustration of the girl loving the man with that love and faith which are interchangeable at times: a human love and faith can be deceived, but that which is centered in the Lord God almighty can never be deceived. Human beings have flaws and may fail, even where they are greatly loved, but God cannot fail. He is the faithful one. "It is of the Lord's mercies that we are not consumed, because his compassions fail not. They are new every morning: great is thy faithfulness" (Lam. 3:22, 23). Abraham had looked upon the God of glory and knew His faithfulness. He was cleaving to Him without wavering, and his faith was strong because his faith was centered in the God who is all strength.

THANKS IN ADVANCE

The next part of our text shows that Abraham gave thanks to God before he saw or received the answer to the promise that had been given. We read that he gave glory to God. As soon as God made the promise, Abraham laid hold upon it and knew that the promise was secure. He thanked God from the first instant. To have taken the attitude that he would have to see the answer before he would believe would have been doubt, and doubt in such a case would have been an insult to the one who made the promise.

Several years ago an incident took place which will illustrate this point. In 1939, on the day that Chamberlain declared war on Hitler, I began a city-wide meeting in Belfast, Ireland. Scores of churches were united for the meeting, and the chairman of the commitee which invited me to the city, was the late Robert Clyde, Esq., one of the outstanding business men of the north of Ireland. There was naturally great confusion in the city because of the declaration of war. My family was in France, staying at a little beach town in Normandy, and I wanted to communicate with them, in order to tell them that they should leave for America on the *George Washington,* which was going to Havre, to evacuate American citizens. Thousands of people wanted to send telegrams, and the censors, fearing spies, discovered that the best way to circumvent spies was to hold all telegrams for several days so that the importance of any communication would be lost in the delay.

Mr. Clyde took me to the Postmaster General in order to get a telegram through to the American Consul at Havre. When this gentleman agreed to see that a telegram should go to the Consul, there was a question of credit for extraordinary expenses. Mr. Clyde saw my hesitation and put his hand over my arm and said, "Now if there is an question of funds you can draw on me any moment up to a thousand pounds, if that will help you." In those days a thousand pounds was almost five thousand dollars. Fortunately, I did not have to avail myself of the offer, and my family was able to get transportation on that overcrowded ship and get safely home. But the offer was real and I turned to Mr. Clyde with some emotion to thank him for his kindness. He gripped my hand and told me that it was nothing. But I knew that there was a heart of Christian love and confidence behind the offer and I gave him all the thanksgiving that I could bring from my heart. If I had sneered and said, "I will believe that when I see it," I would have been an ungrateful churl.

My thanks to Mr. Clyde at the moment the promise was given was an evidence of my opinion of him; of my opinion of his character, his ability, his word, and his honor as a gentleman and a Christian brother. It should be remembered, as I pointed out in a previous study, that our English word *opinion* is used to translate the Greek word *doxa,* from which we get *paradox, orthodox,* and *heterodox,* meaning "contrary to opinion," "straight opinion," "other opinion." But the connection of this idea with our text is that the word *doxa* is the Greek word in our text for "glory." Glory is your opinion about God. Abraham gave his opinion to God. All his opinion was good. There was no shadow on his mind concerning the nature and character of the God who had given the promise. Thus his whole heart was filled with good opinion—a good *doxa,* and that was his doxology.

GOD IS ABLE

The heart of Abraham was as sure that God could and would fulfill His promise of a child to be born to him even though he were a hundred years old, as I was sure that Mr. Clyde would advance me five thousand dollars in my emergency if I needed it. I could have been mistaken; Mr. Clyde could have dropped dead; or he could have changed his mind because of the entrance of some new factor of knowledge yet unknown to him. With God there could have been no such difficulty. When God has spoken it is impossible to be mistaken about the reality of His promise. He is eternal, and as the prophet Habakkuk put it, "Thou shalt not die" (Hab. 1:12, Heb.). God could never change His mind. When it was spoken, the promise was as good as accomplished. No new factor of knowledge as yet unknown to Him could enter into the picture, for He knows the end from the beginning, and there is all knowledge with Him forever.

Thus it was that the whole attitude of Abraham was that which is described in the next verse: "Being fully persuaded that what God had promised, he was able also to perform" (4:21). His life became an attitude. That is the important part of the life of faith: the life of faith is an attitude. We must be careful on this point because there have been attempts to capture the word *faith* and make it mean something quite different from that which is set forth in the Word of God. During the past generation there have arisen a group of missions which have become popularly known as "faith missions." Understand well that I am not speaking against them in any way; I happen to be on the committees of some of these works, and have been able to channel large sums of money to them at times. Young people from my church have gone to the foreign mission field under some of these missions which are called faith missions, and I am sure that they are leading lives of real faith. The objection that I make is the common usage of the term in such a way that it discriminates against missionaries who have gone to the fields under the denominational boards. In the minds of some people, if two brothers go to China under different boards, one of them may be living by faith and the other may not. The difference is not only imaginary, but invidious, discriminating offensively against some of God's finest saints.

One cannot draw sweeping conclusion and divide Christian people into classes in such a way, any more than you can call all Scotch people stingy, all Jews tricky, or all Negroes inferior. Such qualifications are false to the core, and indicate merely that the person who is doing the talking is covering a lot of ignorance with a few easy words.

There are some people connected with what are called faith missions that have little or no faith in God. If the treasury gets low, they are in a panic and will use any type of worldly means to fill it up again. On the other hand, there are people who may draw regular salaries as pastors or missionaries who are looking by faith to the Lord in every breath that they draw. We must not be tricked into thinking that there is a higher quality of faith in a man who, perhaps, merely wants to be free from the supervision of a committee who might reprove his laziness or audit his books. I know poor people who are Christians who are not living a life of faith, and I know wealthy people who are Christians and who are living a life of faith. The lines of faith-living cut across all the lines of organization, denomination, financial position, age, accomplishment, or any other segregating lines that you may wish to draw. "Man looketh upon the outward appearance; the Lord looketh upon the heart." But the Lord who does see the heart knows where there is saving faith to save us from sin, and further—which is pertinent to the present text—He knows what Christians are living from the breath they draw in earthlife and what Christians are living from the breath that they draw from the presence of God in their lives, moment by moment.

SANCTIFICATION IN CHRIST

We must not forget that the present paragraph in the fourth of Romans is a great transition passage in the epistle. The Spirit is leading us away from the doctrine of justification by faith apart from the works of the law and is leading us into the life of sanctification in Christ. There is a great difference between faith and faith and faith. The three may look alike in print, but their quality is as different as the quality difference in three stones, one of which is paste, another a diamond with a flaw, and the third a flawless diamond of rare value because of the purity of its lights. The first faith is that of the unsaved man who believes in Jesus Christ as he believes in Napoleon or Julius Caesar. The second is the saving faith that has been under study in the first chapters of Romans. But now we are going on to a deeper faith— the faith that lives moment by moment in Christ. If we are to make the transition, we must understand the nature of the thing we are talking about.

Christ once said, "He that believeth on me . . . out of his innermost being shall flow rivers of living water" (John 7:38), and we are told that He spake this of the Holy Spirit. Now it is evident that this statement is not true of the belief of all Christians. Not all believers are fountains of blessing to others. All Christians are like the Dead Sea or the Sea of Galilee. There is a vast difference between the two. The Dead Sea is mineral-filled water that would kill every living thing that was near it. The Sea of Galilee is teeming with fish and supports many people from its depths. Thus it is with Christians. The baby Christian may have faith—saving faith, without which one cannot be standing before God justified; but the advancing Christian will be a spring, or will strike the rock, so that the waters may gush through.

The true life of faith is an attitude. It brings the Lord Jesus closer to us than breathing, and nearer than hands and feet. I find, in my own experience, that I can compare my knowledge of God, and Christ, and the Holy Spirit only with phases of knowledge that I have within myself concerning myself. I might be mistaken by outward appearances that would deceive me along almost any line concerning something in which another human being is involved. About myself I cannot be mistaken in some things. I know that I am alive. I will not argue the matter. I am alive. And I know that I am alive forevermore in Christ. I will not argue the matter. I know some other things about myself— I am a man, I am over six feet two inches tall, I am an American citizen, I am a minister serving a certain church for many years. These are facts. They are incontrovertible. If anyone attempts to question any one of them, I will have an attitude of profound pity toward him. These are facts. I know. I am certain.

And thus it is within my heart concerning the facts of God. He exists. I know it. The Lord Jesus Christ is God. I know it. He arose from the dead. He lives within me in a certain sense. The next to the last verse of the first Epistle of John says, "We know that the Son of God is come, and hath given us an understanding, that we may know him that is true, and we are in him that is true, even in his Son Jesus Christ" (I John 5:20). That is the simple fact of it. We know; and we know that we know. It is an attitude. We pity profoundly anyone who does not have it, for we know that they have never understood the life of faith. Abraham and many of us today are able to have the attitude of the fully persuaded man who knows something without question, and who lives with the knowledge and acts upon it. It is something that is done and that cannot be undone. Praise God.

CHAPTER XXXVI

The Progress and Growth of Faith

"And therefore it was imputed to him for righteousness. Now it was not written for his sake alone, that it was imputed to him" (Rom. 4:22, 23).

A BRAHAM has been the central figure of this chapter. The argument has shown that Abraham believed God even when he was living in Ur of the Chaldees, and that he left his pagan surroundings and came through the desert to the promised land, walking by faith. This took place some fourteen years before he was bound to the Lord by the covenant that included circumcision as its seal. Therefore, it was faith, and not rites and ceremonies and the outward forms of religion, that was credited to the account of Abraham instead of the righteousness that he did not possess in himself, but which God must require of men, even though not one man possesses it.

The whole course of his growth in faith has been presented to us and we have examined the parts in detail. But now we wish to assemble the whole of the parts and note the progress and growth of faith in Abraham. The story divides his faith into seven sections: (1) he was not weak in faith; (2) he paid no attention to interior doubts; (3) he paid no attention to the seeming impossibility of outward circumstances; (4) he wavered not at the promises through unbelief; (5) he was strong in faith; (6) he praised God for the answer before there was any evidence of its arrival; and (7) he possessed the attitude of a fully persuaded man.

INSTEAD OF RIGHTEOUS

Because of all this, it is now written, his faith was accounted to him, credited to his account, instead of righteousness. It is the reversal of the process of the fall when Adam sinned through disbelief. For the disobedience of Adam was the last step in a path of departure from God, and the first step was disbelief of the warning of God. In Abraham the process is reversed. Abraham begins by believing God, and the ultimate result is a mental and spiritual giving of himself, utterly, to the promises of God. He yields himself in his heart and mind to the truth of God's word and acts in accordance with that faith. He may stumble in the pathway once in a while, for he still possesses the Adamic nature, but his face is turned steadfastly toward the city of light, and he is accompanied on his pilgrim journey by God Himself, who will never allow him to be cast down, even though he should stumble. Abraham fixes his eyes on the goal, looks not at the obstacles in the path, and goes forward to the end.

In the progressive steps of faith that are set forth here, there is a remarkable quality of faith that emerges above and beyond the details. We know, from our own experience and the experience of others that faith at times grows weak. We know, also, that there are times when our faith grows strong. How do these changes take place? What is it that causes one to grow cold in faith? And how does faith grow strong? We might think that everything depended on circumstances, but the whole point of the present chapter in the epistle is that there is no relationship between the temperature of faith and the intensity of circumstances. We have all seen graphs of a business cycle which show two lines more or less paralleling each other. The one will show the index of prices and the other the index of production, and it can be seen that there is a definite relationship between the two. But if you draw one line showing an increase in difficulties in the life of an individual and an increase of faith you will see that the relationship between the two is a supernatural one and not a natural one. If the relationship were merely natural, we should expect that faith would grow stronger when the obstacles grew weaker. We would think that as the doubts increased the faith would decrease. We would think that the eye of faith would have its vision of the promise obscured by the growth of the mountain of doubt between it and the promise. On the other hand, one might expect that faith would grow strong when the obstacles decreased. We would think that as doubts grew less, faith would grow greater. When the fulfillment of the promise would appear humanly possible, we would think that faith would grow stronger. But the passage before us declares that the opposite is the case. It is when we see the impossibility of our own condition that faith turns to the promise of God to feed upon the Word and grow strong on the heavenly nourishment.

Faith does not build upon impossibilities but upon God and His Word. In the case before us, it was because Abraham did not trust in the natural strength of his own being that he could face the seeming absurdities in his situation and yet not lose faith. He saw the invisible. He held fast to the eternal. He heard the divine promise. He knew the fragrance of God's presence. He had tasted the sweetness of the promise and he knew that here was life. His senses turned away from the base food of nature and turned to the heavenly object which God revealed to the eyes of faith.

FAITH JOINED TO GOD

It is very important to understand that it is impossible to separate true faith from God, the object of the faith. At times we hear people talking about faith, and it would seem that they are thinking in terms of some indefinite, amorphous feeling, that is totally dissociated from God. They think of faith as a function of the soul, or an inner condition in man. But according to the Word of God it is impossible to think of faith without thinking of God as the object of faith. True faith acts because it is joined to God, its object. If one looks away from God, the attitude of the soul turns to sight, and is no longer faith. But when we turn away from the things of sight and look to God, we no longer walk by sight, but are walking by faith, because we are seeing God.

The reason that we stress this point so definitely is because there are false religions that have grown up on the fringes of Christianity, such as Christian Science, New Thought, Unity, and the like, that talk about "faith" with a saccharin smirk that makes the talker look as though he were living in a narcotic world and talking about something that is utterly divorced from the reality of life or the greater reality of God. Upon pressing the point it is discovered that the "faith" they are talking about is not anchored to the God and Father of our Lord Jesus Christ. It's some sort of feeling within them that they call by the name of faith. But such "faith" is not the faith that the Holy Spirit is here describing to us.

But the story of faith's development and maintenance that lies before us contains an even more definite teaching. There are those who may talk about "faith in God" as something different from nebulous feeling that has no object, and yet their "faith in God" is not true faith in the Bible sense of the term. For their supposed "faith in God" is an indefinite and rather vague belief in God, but in a way that leaves out the nature of His being and the reality of His promise. Faith, to be the kind of faith that is set forth in the Bible and illustrated in our text, is that which looks past all outward circumstances, cleaves to God Himself, lays hold upon His Word, and understands that the true God gives life to the dead and calls into being the things which do not exist. It was this God that Abraham glorified by his faith.

In the first chapter of Romans, Paul points out that the pagan world, when it knew God, glorified Him not as God, but changed the glory of God into an image. We would put it that they traded or exchanged the glory of God for an idol. The phrase in the Greek for glory is the same as that which is used in our context. They gave up the glory of God (*doxa theou*). But that which is refused to God by those who substitute idols for the true glory of God, the faith of Abraham gladly renders to Him, and when the old patriarch heard the promise he gave glory to God. He turned from idols to the true God. Again we note that true faith is the reversal of the whole process of unbelief. That is why Abraham's faith was credited to him for righteousness.

FAITH AND GOD

Faith and God. Join them together because they are inseparable, and that which God has joined together, let not man put asunder. Faith and God, and when we see the God of reality we shall have the faith that is real. We shall discover that the cold of the night will cause our faith to grow warmer. The path of the justified one shineth more and more unto the perfect day (Prov. 4:18). He that hath begun the good work in us will keep on perfecting it until the day of Jesus Christ (Phil. 1:6). We turn our eyes to the Lord, and thus we may go from strength to strength (Ps. 84:7). Our last works, like those of the believers who dwelt in the midst of the darkness of Thyatira, are more than our first works (Rev. 2:19). Our force increases as we march. We mount up with wings as eagles, we run and are not weary, we walk and are not faint (Isa. 40:31). This is not because of a vague "faithiosity," but because we have the God-given faith that is joined to Him, and through which He flows to us.

The faith of Abraham was perfect faith when it was still within the mind and heart of God and before it was communicated to Abraham, for faith is ever the gift of God. When Abraham had received this gift of faith he turned it back to God, believing Him, using it toward God. But, of course, the faith lost something by touching human nature, and it was in no wise perfect in itself. This is why we read that the faith was counted to him *for* righteousness. Note that it was not counted to him *as* righteousness. In the Book of Genesis, the chapter after the story of Abraham's exercise of faith shows that the faith was imperfect: that he tried to help God out by begetting a child in his own power; and God had to wait for years until Abraham knew that there was indeed nothing in himself that could fulfill the promise of God. Man is so corrupt that even his faith is not righteousness, but can only be reckoned to him instead of righteousness. I believe that this is why this same thought is repeated three times in this fourth of Romans. For if you will glance back you will see that these same words are found in verses 3, 9, and 22. Why does God repeat this truth again and again? The answer is found in the next verses.

"Now it was not written for his sake alone, that it was imputed to him; but for us also . . ." (4:23, 24). Oh, we are so slow to learn! It is right that we should sing the old gospel song:

Tell me the story often, for I forget so soon . . .

FOR US ALSO

And so the Holy Spirit turns from ancient to modern times; from our father Abraham, long since dead and alive forevermore, unto us, to us also; that is, to the true believers who are blessed with faithful Abraham, and called Abraham's children. The progress of the argument should be noted. The first chapters of the epistle are centered in the discussions with those who bring up objections. The unbelieving skeptics are reading the lines of the main roles, and occupy the center of the stage, as Paul demolishes their arguments, one by one. From them the Holy Spirit turns to Abraham, and the debaters leave the scene, no more to speak in the epistle. But throughout the entire fourth chapter our attention is directed to Abraham, the great man of faith, who is called the father of many nations, because of the great faith which was his, and which would reappear in the hearts of multitudes of believers throughout the centuries. But now at this point in the study the scene is to change again. There will be no more mention of Abraham until we reach the ninth chapter, and then he will appear in a totally different connection. The leading actors on the scene now are those who live in this present age. You may find yourself there if you answer the invitation to believe that which is everywhere between the lines in this passage. It is we, ourselves, who are the objects of the tender solicitation of God. We who believe in this age are linked with the promises of the past and are shown to be one with Abraham in the solidarity of faith.

All that has been written of Abraham, we find, was not written for his sake alone, but for us also. It goes without saying that there was no writing of this story while Abraham was yet alive. The Holy Spirit who was the eager participant in the communication of all truth to Abraham was the one who held Moses' hand as he wrote the story in Genesis. God had indeed appeared to Abraham at several different times and under several different forms. And when the words of assurance passed the lips of God they became the food of Abraham's faith, the foundation of his hope, the cause of his obedience, and the directive of his action.

When finally the words were written in what we know as the fifteenth chapter of Genesis, the definite purpose in the mind of God concerned the company of the believers through all the ages. What is the food that makes our faith strong? The written Word of God. What is the foundation of our hope? The written Word of God. What is the cause of our obedience, and the directive of our action? The written Word of God. This is why we repudiate with horror the papal declarations that flout the Word of God and would exalt the councils of men to a position above the revelation that is written, and therefore above the name of Jehovah, since God tells us that He has magnified His Word above His name (Ps. 138:2).

THE FOUNDATION OF ASSURANCE

We are told here that the written Word of God is to be the foundation of our assurance. How wonderful that God wishes us to have assurance. There are many who do not have it, and there are some who believe that it is not possible to possess it. The Roman Catholic church, for example, holds that a person's eternal destiny depends upon himself right up to the last moment, and that he must die in a "state of grace" in order to be assured of any possibility of future salvation. Even then he is supposed to go to a place of fire to purge his own sins for ages of time, and can never know the wonderful joys of *present* assurance of salvation and justification. For such a one the whole question is like the toss of a coin—heads or tails, or, on his coin, Heaven or Hell. He tosses the coin, and then lives in great fright, telling you that one must die before it shall be possible to know how the coin has fallen. But the true believer who builds upon the written Word of God may know the joy of absolute assurance. I thank God that I know it. Christ tossed my coin for me, and has showed me that He took Hell for Himself on the cross, in order that I might have Heaven forever. This is the present portion of every child of God.

This is not the only place where God tells us that the written record was made for us. It should be realized, first of all, that there is not one promise in all the Bible for an unsaved man. There is not one line in the Book that can be of comfort to a Hindu, a Moslem, or an unregenerate Protestant or Roman Catholic or to any other child of wrath of whatever religion. Remember, there is not one promise to an unsaved man. There is, of course, the offer of salvation, but an offer is very different from a promise. John 3:16 still stands there in the Bible as an offer of salvation, but there is no promise until one has believed, and then all the promises become ours through Jesus Christ. "For the Son of God,

Jesus Christ . . . was not yea and nay, in him was yea. For all the promises of God in him are yea, and in Him Amen, unto the glory of God by us" (II Cor. 1:19, 20).

In another place also, we are told that the things which are written down, even in the Old Testament, were recorded specifically for us who live today. There is a remarkable passage in the second Epistle to the Corinthians that sets forth this truth and establishes the solid foundation of our trust and hope, since we are told that the events which happened to the men of faith in the Old Testament, and the failures of some of the men of that time, were written for our admonition and warning. Recounting the story of those who were overthrown in the wilderness because they failed to comprehend all of the blessing that was for them in the fountain that gushed from the rock, we read, "Now these things were our examples, to the intent we should not lust after evil things, as they also lusted. Neither be ye idolators . . . Neither let us commit fornication . . . Neither let us tempt Christ . . . Neither murmur ye . . . Now all these things happened unto them for examples: and they are written for our admonition, upon whom the ends of the world [that is, the overlapping of the ages] are come" (I Cor. 10:6-11).

A CALL TO STUDY

What a call this should be for us to study the Word of God. If we do not study the Word of God, we can never be approved of Him. We will be shamed workmen at the time of the manifestation of our position in Him if we neglect the revealed Word (II Tim. 2:15).

It was written for us also. How wonderful of our God to have us in mind. We were chosen in Christ before the foundation of the world (Eph. 1:4), and in the fullness of time God proceeded to all the operations of His grace that finally paid the penalty, and ultimately called and justified us. He wrote down in His Word that He had justified Abraham by grace through faith and that He would do the same for all who put their trust in Christ. He gave us the down payment of assurance in order that we might have it as an allowance to live on, day by day, until He shall publicly manifest us, along with Abraham, in the presence of all the universe, as being absolutely righteous because of His work at the cross.

That is why a future tense is introduced in the text at this point. For we read, It was written "for us also, to whom it shall be imputed . . ." "Here the Lord is bidding us look forward to that day when all that has been promised to us shall become actual. It was thus with Abraham. God showed him the stars of the sky and told him that his seed would be as the shining dust of all the galaxies. Abraham believed it, and God counted it unto him for righteousness, and gave to Abraham the confidence of the promise. The patriarch never lived on earth to see it, but it has already come to pass to a great extent, and shall be fulfilled to the end. And then all of us who have turned away from earth and its standards, who have turned away from Adam and his deeds, to put our trust in the Word of God about the Lord Jesus Christ, shall be manifested in one glorious body, the body of the Lord Jesus Christ. Then our faith shall be publicly credited to us, for righteousness, before all the universe.

ONE IN HIM

This verse shows us all the redeemed, apart from time, and apart from any circumstances, presented as one justified body, possessing one justifying righteousness. There are many passages in the Bible that consider all believers in a divine oneness, from Abel, the first to die in faith, down to the last man that shall be redeemed from this earth. No matter what differences God may make between the saved in His intent and purpose to use us for different ends, we are all seen as one great group, the body of the redeemed. It is interesting to note this fact in a famous verse in the Gospel of John, the truth of which is partly hidden from us by the nature of the English translation. We read, "All that the Father giveth me shall come to me; and him that cometh to me I will in no wise cast out" (John 6:37). In the Greek the phrase "all that" and the verb "shall come" are in the singular. It is only in the last half of the verse that the individual believer is seen apart from the collectivity. It is as though God said, "The entire group of believers, given to Me by the Father shall come to Me as My bride; and thus each individual in the whole group may know that, in coming, he will never be cast out, because he is a part of the corporate whole."

It is, of course, another part of the great teaching of assurance, and the security of all believers. Those who teach the horrible doctrine that justification can be undone, and that salvation can be lost, fail to comprehend the oneness of the body of Christ. If even the poorest and meanest believer who has truly trusted in the Lord Jesus Christ could ever fall away and be lost, it would mean that in addition to the wounds which Christ has received on Calvary, there would be another wound, that of an amputation, and that He would appear forever as a cripple, limping, because one foot had been cut away; or it would be seen as he extended a hand, that a finger had been amputated. Such a doctrine is false to the core, and is a denial of Christ and the finality of His redeeming, justifying work.

In another of my books I tell the story of a little boy who was asked if he were not afraid that he might slip through the Saviour's fingers and be lost. He shook his head and said, "No, I can't slip through His fingers; I'm one of the fingers."

All of this is bound up in the future tense that is used in this text. "It shall be imputed to us." The best commentary on this text is found in another part of the Word of God. John writes, "Behold, what manner of love the Father hath bestowed upon us, that we should be called the sons of God: therefore the world knoweth us not, because it knew him not. Beloved, now are we the sons of God, and it doth not yet appear what we shall be: but we know that when he shall appear, we shall be like him; for we shall see him as he is" (I John 3:1, 2).

And to this grace, so great grace, our renewed hearts can only answer by continuing the quotation, solemnly affirming, "And every man that hath this hope in him purifieth himself, even as he is pure" (I John 3:3).

CHAPTER XXXVII

Delivered and Raised

"But for us also, to whom it shall be imputed, if we believe on him that raised up Jesus our Lord from the dead. Who was delivered for our offences, and was raised again for our justification" (Rom. 4:24, 25).

WHY DID Christ die? And why did Christ rise again? There are several different ways of looking at it: among which there is one from the standpoint of the Saviour Himself, and one from the standpoint of God the Father. When these two views are presented in the Scripture they are set forth for a distinct purpose. In our study in Romans we have come to a point where God the Father is now seen as the object of our faith, and the Lord Jesus is set forth as the channel and the way through which we go to the Father.

We believe without question that Jesus Christ is God, the second person of the Trinity, and that He eternally existed in that oneness and equality with the Father which is set forth throughout the Scriptures. But because our Lord Jesus loved us so much, He voluntarily submitted Himself to the subordination that was implied in the incarnation, and there is a sense in which that subordination to the Father shall last throughout all ternity. As our text in Romans 4:24 stresses the activity of God the Father, we must set forth that phase of the truth. But we would safeguard our position from criticism by glancing at another aspect of the truth for a moment.

THE SON'S POWER

Our Lord made definite declarations about His own relationship to His death and His resurrection. He spoke one day to the people, saying, "I am the good shepherd, and know my sheep, and am known of mine. As the Father knoweth me, even so know I the

Father; and I lay down my life for the sheep . . . Therefore doth my Father love me, because I lay down my life, that I might take it again. No man taketh it from me, but I lay it down of myself. I have power to lay it down, and I have power to take it again. This commandment have I received of my Father" (John 10:14-18).

In order to understand this it is necessary for us to go back into the councils of eternity and listen to the Father and Son speaking together. It is possible to reconstruct the conversation because of certain phrases that are revealed to us in various parts of the Bible. When it was determined that there should be a creation, and that the creature should be given a free will, it was known to God, of course, that man would turn that free will unto himself, thereby bringing the condemnation of God upon him. It would be necessary for the God of all holiness and all justice to strike with perfect wrath against the sinner. But the Godhead, Father, Son, and Holy Spirit, decided that the Son should become a man and be perfectly obedient to the Father in everything, and that He should voluntarily submit to the stroke of that divine wrath, placing Himself in the position where God the Father would have to strike Him to death. The Son announced that He would do this thing, and thus He became the Lamb, slain from the foundation of the world (Rev. 13:8). At the time of the incarnation we read, "Wherefore, when he cometh into the world he saith, Sacrifice and offering thou wouldst not, but a body hast thou prepared me: In burnt offerings and sacrifices for sin thou hast had no pleasure. Then said I, Lo, I come (in the volume of the book it is written of me), to do thy will, O God" (Heb. 10:5-7).

It is absolutely impossible to understand Bible Christianity unless we realize that God the Father put Jesus Christ to death on the cross. There have been those who have emphasized the fact that the Jews delivered Him over to the secular arm of the Roman power, and have blamed the Jews for it as a race. Those who have thought such a thing have been theologically ignorant. The fact that the officials of the Jews delivered Christ to the Gentiles for crucifixion is relatively unimportant. Someone may think that I am thereby teaching that the fault lay with the Romans who did the actual nailing of the nails into the hands and feet of Christ. Again this is relatively unimportant. Christ had said, "No man taketh my life from me; I lay it down of myself." It would have been impossible to put Him to death if He had not desired to put Himself in the place of death.

The important thing about the death of Jesus Christ is that God the Father put Him to death. Nothing else is relevant; nothing else matters. All else is purely incidental, and while the incidental may have an importance in certain ways that have but small effects, the great fact is that God the Father put God the Son to death. We read in the prophecy of Isaiah, "It pleased the Lord to bruise him; he hath put him to grief" (Isa. 53:10). And on the day of Pentecost Peter announced, "Ye men of Israel, hear these words: Jesus of Nazareth, a man approved of God among you by miracles and wonders and signs, which God did by him in the midst of you, as ye yourselves also know; him, being delivered by the determinate counsel and foreknowledge of God, ye have taken, and by wicked hands have crucified and slain" (Acts 2:22, 23). The important thing here is the declaration that Christ was delivered by the determinate counsel and foreknowledge of God. The evidence is in the same chapter that the men who were thus accused repented, received Christ as their Messiah, and were the objects of God's saving grace. In all that happened at the cross there was forgiveness for the men; all could be spared except Christ. God did not spare Him; God had to deliver Him up for us all.

THE WORK OF THE FATHER

Our text at the close of the fourth chapter of Romans is based on the theological implications of this fact. Abraham has been described as the man of faith who believed the Word of God without wavering. He looked through to the God who brings life out of death and calls the things that are not as though they were. It was on this ground that God reckoned Abraham's faith to him for righteousness. God then announces that this truth is set down in the Scriptures not for Abraham alone, but for us also, to whom the same bookkeeping transaction is performed if we believe in God who raised up Jesus our Lord from the dead (Rom. 4:24). It must be noted that the emphasis is placed here on the work of God the Father. He is acting in His judicial capacity. It is striking to note the difference in the form of expression concerning the death of Christ as it is used here and as it is used in the third chapter of this same epistle. The last ten verses in chapter three show Jesus Christ set forth as the propitiation—the mercy seat —through faith in His blood. The person and work of the Saviour are shown to us as the objects of our faith. The purpose of this mercy seat sacrifice, we are told, is that God might be just and the justifier of him that believeth in Jesus (Rom. 3:26).

But now, at the end of the fourth chapter, we look beyond Christ to the God and Father who justified us through Christ. To be truly justified we must know not only the Saviour who has paid the price, but the Father to whom the price has been paid. The order must be given here—first Christ and then the Father. Now we can understand why the Lord Jesus said, "I am the way, the truth and the life; no man cometh unto the Father but by me" (John 14:6). So now we are brought face to face with the God who justifies us, and are called to put our trust in Him, as the one who has dealt with our sins in every way. To be truly justified we must know Him who has done the work, and not merely the means He has provided for the work of our justification. And the means provided for dealing with our sins is the death and resurrection of Christ. Not merely the death of Christ, but the death and resurrection. This is why we want more than the crucifix which reminds one of the dead body of Jesus on the cross. We want a bare cross from which that body has been removed. We want a tomb with the stone rolled away from the door. We want to see the Lord Jesus Christ risen and moving among His people. We want to see Him, indeed, seated on the throne of God, clothed in the glory He had with the Father before the world was. And when we thus see Him He will point us to the Father, as to the One who has planned the redemption, and accomplished it in every detail.

Our text does not say that He gave Himself for our sins, but that He was delivered up because of our sins. Our text does not say that He rose because of our justification but that He was raised. In other passages in the Bible the Lord Jesus is the active performer; here He is the passive victim. There is a double cause and there is a double effect.

DELIVERED FOR OUR SINS

First, we read that it was because of our sins that He was delivered. The verb is a strong one, and has been translated by one commentator, "He was handed over because of our transgressions." We can understand the phrase as it is used in certain judicial procedures. A criminal has been found guilty of murder and he is handed over to the hangman for execution. This is the idea that is found in our text. It is the idea that is central in the Epistle to the Romans. Jesus Christ was executed by God. How such a truth destroys all the false ideas that men have attempted to set forth in connection with the death of our Lord. Such a passage as this dissipates forever the governmental theory of the atonement, or the exemplary theory of the atonement. Christ Jesus was not dying as an example. He was dying as a substitute. He was dying in place of the believers.

BARABBAS

There is a physical, material illustration of the substitutionary death of Christ that is found in all four of the Gospels, and that shows this truth in a simple, yet profound manner. It is rare to find any given event mentioned in all four of the Gospels, for the Lord is not writing mere history in these accounts but is setting forth four portraits of Christ in different phases of His life and ministry. In the recital of the events that took place at the trial of Jesus, there is mention of one Barabbas. In one of the Gospels he is said to have been a robber, in another that he had been mixed up in an act of sedition in the city, and that he had committed murder. He was, we read, a notable prisoner. Now it was the custom at that time to free some one prisoner at the occasion of the high Jewish festival, and Pilate thought that he might get out of his predicament by releasing Jesus Christ, since the evidence showed that there was no fault in Him. But the crowd cried out that they wished Barabbas released and that they wished Jesus Christ to be crucified (Matt. 27:15-26; Mark 15:6-15; Luke 23:13-25; John 18:38-40). If we count carefully we discover no less than thirty-eight verses used in the four Gospels to tell that simple story. Anyone who is really familiar with Scripture knows that

God does not give lengthy emphasis to a subject through mere whim, but that this is a part of "all Scripture," given by inspiration of God, and profitable for instruction (II Tim. 3-16). Even the balance, the length given to the story of Barabbas is important, and the story is given half a dozen verses more than the entire account of the betrayal of Christ by Judas. Let us look a little more closely at this man Barabbas.

In the first place, the name Barabbas is pure Hebrew, *Bar* means "son" and *abba* means "father." Barabbas, then, means son of the father. It can readily be seen that he is a representative type of all the sons of all the fathers who have ever begotten children in this world. We are all of Adam's race. We have been bound over for our sedition against God. We are robbers of His glory. We are murderers of our souls and the souls of others. We find ourselves bound in the darksome prison house of sin. We feel in our hearts that we merit the sentence that has been announced to us and we wait in trembling for the time of judgment. Every man loves freedom. To be put in a cell is a horrible curtailment of human liberty, and the necessity of such confinement shows what society thinks of the terrible outbreaks that endanger the smooth flow of what men call civilization.

The Roman soldiery had stopped the riot and had taken Barabbas. His blood-guiltiness was established. He was flung in his cell, there to wait the moment of his death. I have read several stories of the thoughts of prisoners before their death. A man who is to be hanged has difficulty in keeping his hand away from his throat where the rope is soon to choke him. I have been told by a chaplain in a prison where men are executed in a gas chamber that the condemned practice long breathing, and sometimes will hold their breath until it seems that their eyes will pop from their sockets. They know that they are going to be put into a gas chamber and that they will hear a little hissing sound of incoming death, and that the breath they are now forcing into their lungs will be the last that they shall ever know. They will hold on and on, straining at the thongs that tie them to their chair, until they are forced by the inexhorable law of breathing to exhale the last breath that contained pure oxygen and take in the death that floats around them.

Barabbas must have looked at the palms of his hands and wondered how it would feel to have the nails ripping through the flesh. He must have remembered scenes of crucifixion death, and the slow agony of the victims who suffered at times for a day or two before merciful death came to release them. He must have awakened with a start if he heard any hammering in the jail, and his mind must have anticipated the sound of the clanging hammers that would bring death near to him. And then, in his prison, he heard the vague murmuring of the crowd that roared outside like the murmur of a troubled sea. He thinks he hears his own name. He can tell that there are angry cries, and fear rises in his heart. Then he hears the sound of a key in the lock, and a jailer comes to him and releases him from the chain that is wound around him, for the Bible tells that he was bound. He must have thought that his time had come, but the jailer takes him to the door and tells him that he is free.

In his stupefaction he moves toward the crowd. There is little welcome for him, and he senses the deep preoccupation of the people. If he meets one of his old companions in the crowd, he is greeted with but a moment's word, and then he hears the surging roar, "Crucify Him! crucify Him!" In modern language he would say to his companion, "What is the pitch? Give me the low down?" And he would be briefly answered that the roar is against Jesus, and that He is to be crucified, and that the crowd had cried out for the release of Barabbas.

THE CRUCIFIXION

Stunned, he walks nearer to the center of the scene and sees the Man who is to die in his place. Finally the procession begins toward Golgotha. He follows and sees Jesus fall under the weight of the cross. He sees Simon of Cyrene pressed by the soldiers to fall in line and carry the cross, and finally they arrive at Calvary. What must have been his thoughts? He hears the echoing blows of the hammer striking the nails, and looks down at his own hands. He had thought that this would be his day. He had thought that the nails would tear his flesh. And here he is breathing the air of springtime and looking at the dark cloud that is gathering in the sky. Does he say, "Those hammer blows were meant for me, but He is dying in my place"? He could have said it in literal truth that day.

The cross is lifted up and he sees the silhouette against the sky. The sun grows dark and he hears voices that come to him like thunder. "Father, forgive them, for they know not what they do." The centurion passes near Him, and seeing the look upon His face, says, "Truly this was the Son of God." And Barabbas, more than before, looks with wonder and amazement at the man who is dying for him. There comes a cry, "It is finished," and a little while later he sees the soldiers take down the body and put it in its temporary grave. He goes on back to the city, and all the little things that he had expected to see no more come before his eyes with freshness of new creation. He took my place. Jesus took my place. They released me, Barabbas, who deserved to die, and they crucified Jesus instead of me. He took my place. He died instead of me.

Now Barabbas was the only man in the world who could say that Jesus Christ took his physical place. But I can say that Jesus Christ took my spiritual place. For it was I who deserved to die. It was I who deserved that the wrath of God should be poured upon me. I deserved the eternal punishment of the lake of fire. He was delivered up for my offenses. He was handed over to judgment because of my sins. This is why we speak of the substitutionary atonement. Christ was my substitute. He was satisfying the debt of divine justice and holiness. That is why I say that Christianity can be expressed in the three phases: I deserved Hell; Jesus took my Hell; there is nothing left for me but His Heaven.

THE RESURRECTION

And because He purchased Heaven for me when He suffered on the cross, God raised Him from the dead as a sign that the account was settled in full. Note well that it was not His resurrection that produced our justification, but our justification that produced His resurrection. It was our merited condemnation that caused His death, and it was our accomplished justification that caused His resurrection. The Swiss commentator, Godet, has a beautiful paragraph on this point. He writes, "Our sin had killed

Him; our justification raised Him again. How so? The expiation of our trespasses once accomplished by His death, and the right of God's justice proved in earnest God could pronounce the collective acquittal of future believers, and He did so . . . So long as the security is in prison the debt is not paid; the immediate effect of payment would be his liberation. Similarly, if Jesus were not raised, we should be more than ignorant whether our debt were paid; we might be certain that it was not. His resurrection is the proof of our justification, only because it is the necessary effect of it."

Every one of us at some time or other has walked into some office to pay a bill, perhaps for telephone service, for electricity, or some other obligation which we had incurred. We handed the money to the teller who was appointed to act for the company to whom we were indebted. The teller counted our money, took the bill that was against us, and taking a rubber stamp, pressed it upon the ink pad and then stamped our bill and handed us the receipt. The company could never collect that bill from us again. If they tried to do so, we could produce the receipt and they would know that the matter had been cleared, and that we were free from the obligation forever. The Lord Jesus Christ walked up to Calvary, which was God's desk for the payment of the bill of our sins. The account was heavy against us, and the Lord Jesus Christ could settle the account only by shedding His blood in dying for us. There was no other way in which the account could be settled. He offered up His life, and God the Father took that life, handed it over to His justice for execution, while His holiness turned away from the scene, leaving the Saviour alone to cry out, "My God! My God! Why hast thou forsaken me?" (Matt. 27:46). When the three hours of daylight and the three hours of darkness were ended, the payment had been made in full. Those hours were eternal as far as God is concerned. It is He who does not reckon time as we count it, but for whom a day is as a thousand years and a thousand years as but a day. For God the Father and God the Son, those six hours were as all the days and all the nights of all the years of all eternity. Christ paid the eternal punishment of every one of those who were chosen in Christ before the foundation of the world.

NO MORE DEBT

They took that body and reverently cared for it, putting it in the tomb, wrapping it in linen with the myrrh that was the symbol of death. But it was not possible that the Lord Jesus Christ should be holden of death at this point. He had paid the complete debt, and the Lord God Almighty reached out, as a cashier might stamp a bill paid in full, and raised His Son Jesus Christ from the dead, as the sign that there was nothing more to pay.·

Jesus paid it all . . .

We sing that with joy—Jesus paid it all—and it is the truth about the death of Christ upon the cross. He paid it all, and the resurrection is receipt for the bill.

The last chapter of Romans tells us that Paul wrote this epistle while he was a guest of a Corinthian Christian, Gaius. Sitting in the house of Gaius, Paul dictated this epistle, and said that Christ was delivered up and that He was raised up. When? About twenty-five years before he wrote this. Where? On Calvary's hill outside of Jerusalem. Bishop Moule says, "There were at that moment about five hundred known living people, at least (I Cor. 15:6), who had seen the Risen One with open eyes, and heard Him with conscious ears. From one point of view, all was eternal, spiritual, invisible. From another point of view our salvation was as concrete, as historical, as much a thing of place and date, as the battle of Actium, or the death of Socrates. And what was done, remains done."

He was delivered up because of my offences, my sins, my transgressions. And because God justified me, and counted the bill as paid in full, forever, the Lord Jesus Christ was raised from the dead.

ΩΙ Η ΔΟΞΑ ΕΙΣ ΤΟΥΣ
ΑΙΩΝΑΕ ΤΩΝ ΑΙΩΝΩΝ
ΑΜΗΝ

INDEX

Aaron, 16
Abel and Cain, 292-3
Abraham, atheist describes, 135; biography, 258, 264, 277; circumcision, 258; covenant, 304, 315; Devil worshiper, 262; faith, 194-204, 268-76, 317; father of many, 310-18; friend of God, 341; in Galatians, 277, 281, 314; good works of, 196-7; Israel's claim, 195-6; justification, 196-7; law, 258, 277; name, 316; righteous, 21, 207; seed, 181-2, 195-6, 268-76, 279, 281
Accountability, 54, 61
Adam, federal head, 45, 78, 88, 133; fig leaves, skins, 119; tomb, 127
Adamic nature, of unsaved, 45, 56; of saved, 45-6, 55, 59, 274, 324
Alford, Henry, 27
Alps, 1
Angels, orders of, 118-20; recording, 205
Animals, no immortality, 180
Anti-Semitism, 259, 305
Apocalypse, see Revelation
Arch of Triumph (France), 74
Archaeology, 102
Ark of Covenant, 37, 114-20
Assurance, see Eternal Security
Atheist, defined, 248; pamphlet on Abraham, Moses, Jacob, and David, 135-6
Atonement, Hodge on, 252; meaning, 138; opponents of, 190; Quaker position, 189; vicarious, 18, 188-9, 211, 375; see Death of Christ
Augean Stables, 28
Augustine, Saint, 111

Babylon, 181
Balaam, curse, 148-51; doctrine of, 151
Balak, 148-51
Baptism, by rain, 35; regeneration, 261; salvation, 260; water, 3, 289
Barabbas, 375-8
Barnes, Harry Elmer, 219

Believing, cannot, 58-9; salvation a reward for, 96
Beza, Theodore, 87
Bible, only arbiter, 64; contradictions, 50, 143-4; defending, 15; doctrinal plot, 75; faith, 330, 366, 368; inspiration, 207, 334; interpretation, 60-1, 237, 334; rules for entering Heaven, 75; summary, 6, 11, 55; system of marking, 5-6; studying, 133, 366; what is not written, 128
Binney, 88
Blood, chemistry of, 128; of Christ, 122-32; "Feast of Holy Blood," 127; pagan religions, 125-27
Bombs, hydrogen and atom, 326
Bookkeeping, God's, 205-7, 210; in Heaven, 45, 54
Bradbury, Thomas, 212
Bready, Wesley, 220
British Law, 47
Bunyan, John, 328-9

Cain and Abel, 292-3
Caleb and Joshua, 342
Calvin, John, 87
Camel and the Needle, see Needle
Cantor, Eddie, 313
Chalmers, Thomas, 12
Character, salvation by, 8, 12, 76, 100, 215
Cherubs, 118-20
Children, of Abraham, 181-2; of the Devil, 183; of God, 179, 182-3
Christ Jesus, analogies, 16, 114, 224; blood of, 124, 128; eligible to save, 18, 58; errors about, 8, 14; God's name vindicated by, 133-43; how manifested, 5, 10; intercessor, 192; justifier, 54, 99, 279, 379; Lamb, 15-6, 188-9, 327; law, 188-9; Messiah, 107; names, 107; "only God good," 158; peace of world, 25; Pharisees, 155; resurrection, 52; righteousness, 10; true vicar, 61; see Atonement